“God whispers to us in our
megaphone to

The Spiritual Awakening of America

How God uses Pain to Prepare us for Revival

Tom Quick

This book is dedicated to you, a believer who hears God's call for revival, and is willing to "pray" the price for revival.

"If I shut up heaven that there be no rain, or if I command the locusts to devour the land, or if I send pestilence among my people; if my people, who are called by my name, shall humble themselves, and pray, and seek my face, and turn from their wicked ways; then will I hear from heaven, and will forgive their sin, and will heal their land." *~ 2 Chronicles 7:13-14 KJV*

All Scripture references are from the World English Bible (WEB), unless noted otherwise. The WEB is a free, public domain, modern-English translation of the entire Old and New Testament.

ISBN-13:979-8638267537

1. Nonfiction. 2. Religion. 3. Faith. 4. Spiritual Renewal
   I. Title.

Table of Contents

~§~

“For whatever things were written before were written *for our learning*, that through perseverance and through encouragement of the Scriptures we might have hope.”
~ Romans 15:4

~§~ ~§~

“Righteousness exalts a nation, but sin is a disgrace to any people.” *~ Proverbs 14:34*

~§~ ~§~ ~§~

“Surely at the commandment of Yahweh this came on Judah, to remove them out of his sight, for the sins of Manasseh, according to all that he did, and also for the innocent blood that he shed; for he filled Jerusalem with innocent blood, and Yahweh would not pardon.”
~ 2 Kings 24:3-4

~§~ ~§~

“Now all these things happened to them [*the nation of Israel*] by way of example, and they were written [*in the Old Testament*] for our admonition [*warning*], on whom the ends of the ages have come.” *~ 1 Corinthians 10:11*

~§~

Introduction:

Hello, fellow citizen. My name is Tom Quick, "Brother Quick" to many of my friends. I want to thank you for meeting with me over the next week or so, and I pray our time together will be fruitful and glorifying to the Most High God. I'll share more about myself as we go along, but for now, let's get down to business.

Paul Harvey was a friendly and familiar radio voice to millions of Americans. "*The Rest of the Story*" is his famous segment that began as part of a newscast during World War II. It premiered on ABC Radio in 1976 and continued until his death in 2009. Like many of us today, Paul Harvey was concerned about the state of affairs in our nation. In 1964, Mr. Harvey printed and shared with his radio audience an essay entitled "If I Were the Devil." It's an interesting, almost prophetic piece that outlines the devil's plan to seize control of the United States. Over the years, Paul revised the essay to reflect the times. Below is a version he shared on the air over twenty-five years ago.

If I Were the Devil

If I were the Prince of Darkness, I'd want to engulf the whole world in darkness, and I'd have a third of its real estate and four-fifths of its population, but I would not be happy until I had seized the ripest apple on the tree – thee.

So, I'd set about however necessary to take over the **United States**. *I'd subvert the churches first.* I'd begin with a campaign of whispers. With the wisdom of a serpent, I would whisper to you as I whispered to Eve: "Do as you please."

To the young, I would whisper that the Bible is a myth. I would convince them that man created God instead of the other way around. I would confide that what's bad is good and what's good is square. And the old, I would teach to pray after me, "Our Father, which art in Washington…"

And then I'd get organized. I'd educate authors in how to make lurid literature exciting so that anything else would appear dull and uninteresting. I'd threaten TV with dirtier movies and vice versa.

I'd peddle narcotics to whom I could. I would sell alcohol to ladies and gentlemen of distinction. I'd tranquilize the rest with pills.

If I were the devil, I'd soon have families at war with themselves, churches at war with themselves, and nations at war with themselves until each, in its turn, was consumed. And with promises of higher ratings, I'd have mesmerizing media fanning the flames.

If I were the devil, I would encourage schools to refine young intellects but neglect to discipline emotions – just let those run wild. Until before you knew it, you'd have to have drug-sniffing dogs and metal detectors at every schoolhouse door.

Within a decade, I'd have prisons overflowing. I'd have judges promoting pornography. Soon, I could evict God from the courthouse, and then from the schoolhouse, and then from the houses of Congress. And in his own churches, I would substitute psychology for religion and deify science. I would lure priests and pastors into misusing boys and girls and church money.

If I were the devil, I'd make the symbol of Easter an egg and the symbol of Christmas a bottle.

If I were the devil, I'd take from those who have and give to those who wanted until I had killed the incentive of the ambitious. And what'll you bet I couldn't get whole states to promote gambling as the way to get rich?

I would caution against extremes in hard work, in patriotism, in moral conduct. I would convince the young that marriage is old-fashioned, that swinging is more fun, that what you see on TV is the way to be. And thus, I could undress you in public, and I could lure you into bed with diseases for which there is no cure.

In other words, if I were the devil, I'd just keep right on doing what he's doing.

Paul Harvey, Good Day!

Chapter One:

As the Church goes, so goes America

"Jealousy arouses the fury of the husband." Have you ever heard that statement before? It's as true a statement as I've ever heard. I call it a universal truth. It's true in America. It's true in Timbuktu. It's true everywhere! The declaration is from the Old Testament book of Proverbs, chapter six, verse 34.

My mother was a very pretty lady, God rest her soul. My father was a very jealous husband, God rest his soul. Many of my earliest memories as a kid are those of my dad going into a rage because of his jealous spirit. My parents loved each other and stayed together their entire lives, but my father sure was a jealous man. I'll be the first to confess that I have that same spirit. I am my father's son.

You'll find in 1 Corinthians 12:13, that believers are "all baptized into one body, whether Jews or Greeks, whether bond or free." According to the teachings of the New Testament, all believers are members of ONE spiritual body. It makes no difference if you're black or white, male or female, rich or poor, Jew or Greek. When a person exercises their faith to trust in the Lord Jesus, they're baptized into the universal body of believers. It's truly an amazing concept. "For the body is *not* one member, but many" (v.14). A variety of believers or "members" of all races and nationalities make up the ONE spiritual body.

In Ephesians 5, this body is described as a bride, with Christ as her "head" or husband. Jesus Christ is her husband, and Jesus has the spirit of his Father. Now hold on to your seat. Let's take a quick look at the spirit of the Father. Listen to what God says to his people regarding his nature and his name. Exodus 34:10-14,

> He said, "Behold, I make a covenant: before all your people I will do marvels, such as have not been worked in all the earth, nor in any nation; and all the people among whom you are shall see the work of Yahweh; for it is an awesome thing that I do with you. Observe that which I command you today. Behold, I will drive out before you the Amorite, the Canaanite, the Hittite, the Perizzite, the Hivite, and the Jebusite. *Be careful,* lest you make a covenant

> with the inhabitants of the land where you are going, lest it be for a snare among you; but you shall break down their altars, and dash in pieces their pillars, and you shall cut down their Asherah poles; for you shall worship no other god; for Yahweh, whose name is Jealous, is a jealous God."

God tells the newly liberated children of Israel that he has even more mind-blowing things in store for them. "I will do marvels." If they thought what Yahweh did in Egypt was incredible, God says, and I paraphrase: "You ain't seen nothing yet!" The LORD said he's making a "covenant" with them, meaning he is entering into a relationship with them. He says they'll encounter many other nations in their travels, and those nations will have their own false deities.

The Most High God warns them to be careful, lest they make a "covenant" with someone else. He declares that he is "a jealous God." Bible teacher Matthew Henry said jealousy "is God's holy and just displeasure. They cannot worship God alright, who do not worship him alone." The LORD will not tolerate rivals or unfaithfulness, and he will not share his honor with another. And then he states something that's absolutely fascinating. God says his name is Jealous! Wow, I didn't see that coming.

I thought I had a pretty good handle on the names of God, having graduated from Columbia Bible College many moons ago. His names reveal his character, and his names are many. God's name is Jehovah, and JAH, and El Roi. God's name is Holy, and Yahweh, and YAH. God's name is El Elyon, and Elohim, and El Shaddai. But who knew that one of the names of God is Jealous, El Kanna? In the *Complete Jewish Bible*, verse 14 reads, "Because you are not to bow down to any other god; since ADONAI - *whose very name is Jealous* - is a jealous God"!

Our Lord Jesus told the children of Israel, "I and the Father are one" (John 10:30). What's the spirit of the Father? Here's a hint - the Father's name is Jealous. Do you think it's too much of a stretch to say that the bride of Christ has a jealous husband? I think not.

So what's the point? The world is going to think and behave like the world. The "Amorite, the Canaanite, the Hittite, the Perizzite, the Hivite, and the Jebusite" will do what they do. But when God's own people begin to think and behave like the world, that's a problem. When the bride of Christ starts playing kissy kissy with the world, that's a big problem!

The Bible warns believers: You adulterers and adulteresses, don't you know that friendship with the world is hostility toward God? Whoever therefore wants to be a friend of the world makes himself an enemy of God. *Or do you think that the Scripture says in vain, "The Spirit who lives in us yearns jealously"*? (James 4:4, 5).

Let's take a closer look at that last verse, verse five, in several translations of the Bible to help us gain a better understanding of its meaning.

The **Bible in Basic English** reads like so: *Or does it seem to you that it is for nothing that the holy Writings say, The spirit which God put into our hearts has a strong desire for us?*

The **Common English Bible** reads: *Or do you suppose that scripture is meaningless? Doesn't God long for our faithfulness in the life he has given to us?*

The **New Century Version** translates it: *Do you think the Scripture means nothing that says, "The Spirit that God made to live in us wants us for himself alone?"*

And finally, **The Message Bible** gives us a rather dramatic rendering when it states: *And do you suppose God doesn't care? The proverb has it that "he's a fiercely jealous lover."*

All true believers are not only "baptized" into the body of the bride, all true believers also possess the Spirit of Christ. It could be said the Spirit of our spouse resides within us. "Christ lives in me" (Galatians 2:20). Think about that. The Spirit of our spouse lives within each of us, and that Spirit longs "for our faithfulness." The Spirit of Christ "has a strong desire for us." "The Spirit who lives in us yearns jealously" and "wants us for himself alone." For, "he's a fiercely jealous lover."

~§~

As the Church goes, so goes America. Today, America is at a crossroads because the bride is at a crossroads. The bride of Christ is conflicted. The "god of this world" stands on one path, and our husband stands on the other. Christ our Lord beckons us to be true to him and love only him. Our spouse longs for our faithfulness. But the "god of this world" is trying his best to steal our hearts and minds through the appeal of the flesh, the appeal of the eyes, and the pride of life (1 John 2:16). Taking the right path should be a simple decision, but Satan is a smooth operator and a master seducer.

> "For I am jealous over you with a **godly jealousy**. For I married you to one husband, that I might present you as a pure virgin to Christ. But I am afraid that somehow, as the serpent deceived Eve in his craftiness, so your minds might be corrupted from the simplicity that is in Christ." ~ *2 Corinthians 11:2-3*

And so the bride, and thus the country, is at the crossroads. One path leads to us experiencing the favor of the Most High. The other path leads to us experiencing his fury.

Like the unfaithful spouse in the book of Hosea, if the bride desires the things of this world, she can run after the god of this world (Hosea 2:5). However, he is nothing like her true husband. The god of this world is slick, a fast talker, and the father of lies. He promises a good time and pays with sorrow and regret; he promises profit and pays with loss; he promises life and pays with sickness, disease and death.

"Good understanding wins favor, but the way of the unfaithful is hard" (Proverbs 13:15). Good understanding is manifested by fearing the LORD and obeying his word, which wins his favor (Psalm 111:10; 5:12). **But why is the way of the unfaithful hard?** It's hard because the unfaithful have turned away from God, so God has turned away from them. "Whoever therefore wants to be a friend of the world makes himself an enemy of God"! The way is hard because the unfaithful have placed themselves in opposition to the LORD, and in so doing, they have removed themselves from his covering and his protection (Hosea 4:16,17).

Left in the world without the covering of God is not a good thing for the bride. Without the holy protection of the Most High, we become easy pickings for the evil one, who only comes to steal, kill and destroy (John 10:10). *"Unless Yahweh builds the house, they who build it labor in vain. Unless Yahweh watches over the city, the watchman guards it in vain"* (Psalm 127:1). Make no mistake about it - Satan desires the downfall of America! What are his chances of success if the Most High God is not our spiritual ally and protective covering? If the citizens of America are equipped with only human resources, how can we expect to be victorious when we're attacked by spiritual forces of wickedness?

Later in this chapter, and in subsequent chapters, we'll take a unique look at the handiwork of the devil in the USA from August 8, 2018 through August 13, 2018. I think you'll be shocked and appalled at the level of violence and bloodshed that occurred during this typical week in America. It was bad. And since that time, things have gone from bad to worse! So, it raises a few questions: *"Is the LORD removing his protective covering from the United States? Is God using pain to call attention to our sins? Has the spiritual decline in America made us more vulnerable to attacks from our enemies, foreign and domestic?"* In our nation today, we're experiencing social and racial unrest, childish political gridlock, and a dreadful pandemic. Yet, in spite of these woes, man's inhumanity to man is on full display every single day.

As "One Nation under God," we simply can't afford to be naive about our gradual downward spiral. The Bible tells us in Proverbs 28:13, *"He who conceals his sins doesn't prosper, but whoever confesses and renounces them finds mercy."* Escalating violence is a strong indicator that things are not right in this country. In her darkest days just before her fall, the Scriptures tell us Jerusalem was filled from one end to the other with innocent blood (2 Kings 21:16; 24:4). The violence was an overflow of her corruption from within. As we shall see later, the citizens of Jerusalem attempted to conceal their sins, which only facilitated the devil's handiwork.

Before we look at Satan's misdeeds in the entire United States on August 8, 2018, let's first consider his devilry in Washington, D.C. during the summer of 1881.

James Abram Garfield was a brilliant man of humble beginnings. He was actually born in a log cabin in Orange Township (now called Morland Hills), Ohio on November 19, 1831. His father passed away when he was only two years old and James grew up poor. He was raised by a strong-willed mother who enjoyed telling her youngest child about their Welsh ancestry. According to his mother, one of their ancestors served as a knight at the Caerphilly Castle in South Wales.

Garfield was mocked by other boys for being poor. He would later say, "I lament that I was born to poverty, and in this chaos of childhood, seventeen years passed before I caught any inspiration." When his "inspiration" finally hit, Garfield determined to make up for lost time.

On March 3, 1850, James was at a religious camp meeting when he experienced a spiritual awakening. The next day he was baptized in the icy waters of the Chagrin River. He wrote in his journal, "Today I was buried with Christ in baptism and arose to walk in newness of life." He studied theology and was ordained as a minister in the Disciples of Christ denomination, also known as the Christian Church. Garfield preached his first sermon in 1853. The congregation sat attentive as he compared the life of Napoleon Bonaparte to the life of Jesus Christ. He held revival meetings in Northeast Ohio. During one of those meetings, Garfield preached 19 times and 34 people responded to the call to accept Christ.

He attended Western Reserve Eclectic Institute (now Hiram College) and worked his way through school as a janitor, a carpenter, and later as a teacher. In 1857, when he was 26 years old, he was appointed as a professor of ancient languages at Hiram College, and was elevated to president of the school that same year. Even then, James continued to expand his horizons. He studied jurisprudence, and in 1861, he was admitted to the bar.

When the Civil War started, Garfield received a commission as a Colonel in the 42nd Ohio Infantry Regiment. Like many Union soldiers of that period, he regarded the war as a holy crusade against the Slave Power. Following a successful military campaign in Kentucky, when he was only 30 years old, James Garfield was promoted to Brigadier General. In October of 1862, General Garfield entered the world of politics when he was elected for a seat in the 38th United States Congress.

Mr. Garfield was ambidextrous. Some say he could write, at the same time, Greek with one hand and Latin with the other. In 1876, Garfield developed a trapezoid proof of Pythagoras' theorem, which displayed his mastery of advance mathematics. By all accounts, he was an extraordinarily gifted person.

During the National Convention in 1880, two warring factions of the Republican Party were fighting it out in New York, the "Half-Breeds" and the "Stalwarts." The "Half-Breeds" were a moderate group in favor of civil service reform and establishing a merit system for government jobs. Their two leading candidates were James G. Blaine, a senator from Maine and John Sherman, a senator from Ohio and the brother of General Sherman. The "Stalwarts," led by Roscoe Conkling of New York, favored political machines. Their leading candidate was General Ulysses S. Grant.

The Stalwarts supported the spoils patronage system, which is the practice of the winning party doling out civil service jobs to their friends and relatives, regardless of merit. The spoils system served as both a reward for helping the party and an incentive to continue helping the party.

Garfield gave the nomination speech for John Sherman at the opening of the Republican Convention. After 35 ballots, the Stalwarts and the Half-Breeds were still at odds regarding the nomination. But on the 36th ballot, in an unusual turn of events, both Sherman supporters and Blaine supporters shifted their votes to a "dark horse" candidate, James Garfield. In what was a complete surprise to everyone involved, the Half-Breeds managed to win the nomination by selecting Garfield as their last-minute candidate. As a compromise, Chester A. Arthur of the Stalwart faction was nominated for vice-president.

In his campaign against Democrat Winfield Scott Hancock, Garfield often spoke in two languages, English and German. He was the epitome of America's self-made man, and he wisely highlighted his lowly beginnings to make the most of his rags-to-riches background. Former President Rutherford Hayes would say of Garfield, "No man ever started so low that accomplished so much, in all our history."

After all the ballots were counted, Garfield was elected President by a very narrow margin in the popular vote. On March 4, 1881, just 16 years after the end of the War Between the States, our newly appointed leader, James A. Garfield, delivered his Inaugural Address.

In order to gain some perspective, it should be noted that this was one of the most contentious, dynamic and volatile episodes in American history. This period is called the Gilded Age. The Republic was recovering from the ravages of war and beginning her arduous advance toward the promise of liberty and justice for all. For the first time in the history of our country, gigantic factories employed thousands of people and created massive stores of wealth for their owners. Unfortunately, the common worker was viewed as expendable and was often found struggling to support his family. Crooked machine politicians cut backroom deals to hoard the spoils of crooked campaigns. The rich were getting richer, while farmers and laborers got the short end of the stick. To the many who felt the American dream was leaving them behind, President Garfield offered hope.

Excerpts from the Inaugural Address on March 4, 1881

"There can be no permanent disfranchised peasantry in the United States. Freedom can never yield its fullness of blessings so long as the law or its administration places the smallest obstacle in the pathway of any virtuous citizen."

"It is the high privilege and sacred duty of those now living to educate their successors and fit them, *by intelligence and virtue,* for the inheritance which awaits them."

"The census has already sounded the alarm in the appalling figures which mark how dangerously high the tide of illiteracy has risen among our voters and their children."

"The voters...who make and unmake constitutions, and upon whose will hang the destinies of our governments, can transmit their supreme authority to no successors save the coming generation of voters, who are the sole heirs of sovereign power. If that generation comes to its inheritance *blinded by ignorance and corrupted by vice,* the fall of the Republic will be certain and remediless."

President Garfield was a skilled orator, a man of conviction, and a battle-tested leader. It goes without saying that he wasn't a perfect man, but he was uniquely gifted for such a time to be our Commander-in-Chief, and the President of the United States of America.

~§~

"If a man is not rising upwards to be an angel, depend upon it, he is sinking downwards to be a devil." ~ *Samuel Taylor Coleridge*

On May 13, 1881, Charles Guiteau is banned from visiting the White House. During Garfield's campaign for the Oval Office, Guiteau wrote and distributed hundreds of copies of a speech called "Garfield vs. Hancock" in support of the then-candidate. After Garfield's narrow win, Guiteau listened to whispers that told him it was his efforts that seized the victory for the new president. Charles convinced himself that he deserved a position in the new administration. But from another point of view, he was just one of hundreds who stood in line at the White House every day hoping to cash in on the spoils patronage system.

About two months earlier, Charles Guiteau had a face-to-face meeting with the president on March 8, 1881. For his assistance in helping Garfield win the election, Guiteau asked for a diplomatic role in the administration, the Paris consulship. He displayed a copy of his speech as proof of his contribution to the victory. After visiting the president, Guiteau hounded and pestered various cabinet members to help him win the favor of Garfield. Finally, due to Charles Guiteau's constant badgering, his tattered appearance and his erratic behavior, James Blaine, the new Secretary of State told him, "Never speak to me again of the Paris consulship as long as you live."

In the summer of 1881, Guiteau is not in a good place. He's alone and destitute. He's unable to pay for his basic needs of food and shelter. He skips out on boarding house after boarding house. He drifts from one hotel lobby to the next, reading old newspapers, and sulking over being denied the consulship. About five years earlier, his father back in Illinois feared his son was possessed by the evil one. Charles was judged insane and his family agreed to have him committed, but he somehow managed to avoid confinement.

Now years later, Guiteau is walking the streets of Washington. Voices whisper to him. The whispers slowly grow stronger and louder. "Re-mov-al, RE-MOV-AL." Many of the D.C. newspapers in June of 1881 reported on the fierce infighting happening within the Republican Party. President Garfield was being blamed for all the troubles and some were calling for his removal. They felt he betrayed the Stalwarts and was destroying the party. In a show of protest, Stalwart leader Roscoe Conkling resigned from the Senate.

As Guiteau is reading these political stories in the daily papers, he imagines that since it was his efforts which placed the president in office, he is now being called to remove him. He convinces a relative to loan him $15 and he buys a British Bulldog revolver. Since he never handled a gun before, he goes outside the city and puts in some shooting practice. Charles Guiteau then moves about the city, walking the streets alone, except for the voices.

Washington, D.C. experienced an unusually hot summer in 1881. Families that could afford to do so took their leave of the heat. Local newspapers reported the president would be departing on July 2nd for a vacation in New England. Early in the morning on July 2nd, Charles Guiteau gets a shoe shine at the Baltimore and Potomac Railroad Station. Cabinet member Robert Todd Lincoln, son of the late President Lincoln, is at the station to wish the first family a good trip.

James Garfield entered the station with his family and with Secretary of State James Blaine. That's when Guiteau stepped out of the shadows. The delusional office seeker sneaks up behind the party, takes out the revolver, and fires two shots. One bullet grazed Mr. Garfield's shoulder, but the other bullet entered deep into his back. Garfield cries out, "My God, what is that?" and collapses. As the president is bleeding on the floor of the train station, Guiteau, with the revolver still in his pocket, is apprehended by D.C. policeman Patrick Kearney. Charles Guiteau gives the officer a letter addressed to General Sherman, and states, "I'm a Stalwart, and Arthur is now President." Several witnesses assist in taking Guiteau into custody.

At the station, people panic as confusion and anger win the day. Alas, Robert Todd Lincoln is forced to relive another national tragedy. Every doctor near the station is summoned to help. They decide to roll Garfield on his side and prod the wound for the bullet. He is later taken back to the White House where his condition shifts back and forth.

For the next two and a half months, the life of Mr. Garfield is in the balance. Leading physicians are called in to find and remove the bullet. None are successful. Every news outlet is covering the situation daily. People all over the world hear the story that another American president has been shot. The whole nation is on edge.

Alexander Graham Bell moved to D.C. and invents the world's first metal detector in order to locate the bullet. He too was unsuccessful. The Navy invents the first air conditioner to make it more comfortable for the president in the White House. Because of the gunshot wound, Garfield is not able to properly digest food. He's reduced from 210 pounds down to 130 pounds. Prayer meetings are held all over the nation.

Like many other leaders around the country, the governor of Massachusetts called for special prayer for our commander-in-chief. He requested that all factories and other businesses suspend normal activity on September 8th from 10 a.m. to 12 p.m. so that citizens could offer their prayers for the recovery of Mr. Garfield.

The entire country prayed, but James Abram Garfield, the 20th president of the United States, passed away on September 19, 1881. It was one of the saddest days in the history of our young nation.

~§~

I want you to do an activity. It will not be an easy one. We're going to take a peek at the devil's handiwork in America over a 24-hour period. Why so? First, to step back and gain a broad view of what's happening in our nation. Secondly, to take a hard and sympathetic look at the real suffering our fellow citizens endure on a daily basis. Thirdly, to see how the devil is actively carrying out his mission to kill, steal and destroy. And finally, to examine a small sampling of what happens if we remove ourselves from the covering and holy protection of our God.

I'm going to show some actual news stories from every corner of the nation. I respectfully ask that you don't flinch, and don't pretend it's not happening. If we ignore what's taking place on a national level, and only pay attention to local or regional events, we'll miss the big picture. The trees can distort our view of the forest. *You may decide to not read every single entry, yet they happened, and similar transgressions happen every day*. Throughout this work, we will look at only six days. At the end of each of the first five days, we'll be led in prayer by one of our presidents. On the sixth day, we'll be led in prayer by "America's Pastor," the late Evangelist Billy Graham.

We've seen the devil's dirty work on July 2, 1881. A wimp of a man sneaks up behind our president and shoots him in the back. I ask now that we review his attacks on August 8, 2018. These are the wicked manifestations of our enemy, and they happened all across our beloved country in one day. Behold his handiwork...

Wednesday, August 8, 2018 United States of America

Washington, D.C. police responded to a shooting and were later dispatched to an area hospital where a 44-yr old gunshot victim was seeking treatment. He later died. This is the District's 96th homicide of 2018, a 40% increase from this time last year.

South Philadelphia police report six people were shot when a gunman in a minivan fired at a crowd of people. Two of the victims, a 34-yr old female and a 32-yr old male, later died at Temple University Hospital.

Louisiana authorities report two 24-yr old men were found fatally shot in a car in the Natchitoches Parish. When officers arrived at the scene, the car was in a ditch and had struck a tree.

Hagerstown, Maryland police officer, who was accused of stealing pain medication from a paralyzed woman, commits suicide days before he was scheduled to be in court.

North Houston police are looking for four men after a 36-yr old father was shot and killed in his home. The four suspects were seen driving away in the victim's truck.

New Orleans police arrested a 72-yr old woman for a fatal hit-and-run crash. The 25-yr old father of two was transported to University Medical Center, where he later died.

New York police report a 71-yr old man, upset by his 70-yr old wife's illness, shot her to death in her hospital bed in Valhalla, NY and then killed himself.

Nevada authorities identified a 39-yr old male victim who was shot and killed following an altercation inside a home in the Elko Indian Colony.

Chicago police report a driver crashed after being shot in West Garfield Park, leaving two dead from gunshot wounds. The 21-yr old male and the 22-yr old female were pronounced dead at Mount Sinai Hospital.

Kentucky authorities report a 34-yr old man was shot while attempting to break into an apartment in Lexington. He later died at the UK Medical Center.

Florida law enforcement say a 52-yr old man was shot to death in Hollywood when he set his own house on fire, exited his home and confronted officers with a gun.

Chicago investigators say two painters were shot while standing on the sidewalk in Washington Heights. One of them, a 37-yr old male was pronounced dead at Christ Medical Center.

Alabama police arrested a 20-yr old man for shooting and killing a 29-yr old man in the Northport community in Tuscaloosa, following an argument over an alleged illegal transaction.

Kentucky State police are investigating the death of a 38-yr old man who was found shot to death in a pickup truck on Elm Shoal Branch in the Combs community of Perry County.

Florida detectives found a 33-yr old man with a fatal gunshot wound along an empty stretch of road in Rubonia, in Manatee County. Police believe he was killed elsewhere.

Texas police report a 15-yr old aspiring rapper was shot and killed during a home invasion in East Fort Worth. He was living with his older brother who was wounded in the attack.

Alabama officials arrested a 23-yr old man after he shot and killed a 22-year old woman and injured a 30-yr old man in a home in Attalla, in Etowah County.

Fort Wayne, Indiana road rage ends with the death of a 60-yr old man who was punched several times by a 27-yr old male who then fled the scene.

San Diego police used a taser, and then shot and killed a suspect who had earlier attacked someone with a machete. He refused to drop a metal chain when officers attempted to arrest him.

Virginia State troopers found the bodies of a 57-yr old man and a 50-yr old woman in their car after it crashed on I-264 in Virginia Beach, victims of an apparent murder-suicide.

Mississippi deputies in Lamar County responded to a call about a shooting and found a 42-yr old man who was shot in the chest. He died later at Forrest General Hospital.

Texas police responded to a report of multiple gunshots in Houston and found a 35-yr old man fatally wounded inside the doorway of a residence in Independence Heights.

Maryland police report a 24-yr old man was shot and killed in Capital Heights, Seat Pleasant. He was an aspiring athlete and father of an 11-month old child.

Georgia Bureau of Investigation agents arrested two suspects in connection with the death of an 18-yr old man who was shot and killed in the North Georgia city of Toccoa.

Wisconsin police say a 23-yr old Milwaukee woman was shot and killed while seating in her car on the city's north side. One child was found unharmed in the vehicle. This is the 8th murder in 8 days in the city.

Maryland police say four men were killed in recent violence in Baltimore. Ten people have been killed in the city in the first eight days of the month.

Nashville police report a 23-yr old man was found unresponsive lying in the street from a fatal gunshot wound. The victim was wanted for attempted murder and carjacking. 2017 marked a 20-year high in the number of murders in Nashville.

Missouri officials report a 33-yr old man was shot and killed in the JeffVanderLou neighborhood of St. Louis. Investigation is ongoing.

North Carolina authorities say a 12-yr old boy handed a gun to his 15-yr old sister, who then shot and killed a 46-yr old man as he was strangling their mother in Forest City.

St. Louis police were requested after a 29-yr old man was found shot to death in a grassy area near Halls Ferry Circle in the Baden neighborhood.

Louisiana police report a 29-yr old Shreveport man and a woman struggled for control of a gun, when it discharged and shot the man. He died at University Health Hospital.

South Carolina law enforcement responded to a shots fired call in North Charleston to find a 38-yr old man on the ground with fatal gunshot wounds.

Virginia police say a 19-yr old woman was shot and killed at a Fredericksburg restaurant. A short time later, the 22-yr old suspect was found in a wooded area with a fatal self-inflicted gunshot wound.

Nebraska authorities report a 54-yr old man stabbed three women at a homeless shelter in Omaha before he was shot and killed by police after he refused to put down the knife.

Tennessee officers responded to a report of a suspicious vehicle parked at the Smith County Hospital in Carthage. The 25-yr old driver was shot to death when he attempted to hit an officer with the vehicle.

North Carolina police shot and killed a Durham man hours after his wife took out a domestic violence protective order. He had threatened to kill her and himself.

Los Angeles police report an 18-yr old man was shot and killed in Boyle Heights. The victim's grandparents say he was in a program that helps reorient former gang members.

Chicago police arrest a 34-yr old man after they witness him and others kicking a 64-yr old man in the West Englewood neighborhood. The victim later died at UC Medical Center.

Tulsa, Oklahoma police respond to a hit and run call, and discover a 37-yr old man fatally shot. A 17-yr old male is in custody. The victim had allegedly abused the mother of the teenage gunman.

Nevada police say a 30-yr old man was attacking his wife with a knife outside an apartment complex in Las Vegas before he was shot and killed by police.

Arkansas deputies say an argument between two neighbors led to the fatal shooting of a 30-yr old man in the town of Combs, in Madison County. The suspect was arrested.

Baltimore police officers were called to Cedonia Avenue for a shooting incident. They find a male victim of a gunshot wound to his upper body. He was pronounced dead at the scene.

Chicago authorities say a 31-yr old female was fatally shot in the head as she drove away from what she thought was a robbery. She later died at UC Medical Center.

Los Angeles County coroner records indicate a 58-yr old man died after being shot in Encino, and in a separate incident a 27-yr old man died after being stabbed.

Illinois police say a 29-yr old Chicago man is accused of fatally shooting a 32-yr old man in Fuller Park after he tracked his wife's phone and found her in a car with the victim.

Tennessee police in LaFollette say a 9-yr old girl was accidentally shot in the head and killed by her 10-yr old brother while sitting in a car outside a pizza restaurant.

Los Angeles County deputies are searching for suspects after a 33-yr old female passenger of a vehicle was fatally shot in the head by a stray bullet from a nearby shooting in East L.A.

~§~

President George Washington's Prayer for the Nation

Almighty GOD, we make our earnest prayer that Thou wilt keep the United States in *Thy holy protection*, that Thou wilt incline the hearts of the citizens to cultivate a spirit of subordination and obedience to government; and entertain a brotherly affection and love for one another and for their fellow citizens of the United States of America at large.

And finally that Thou wilt most graciously be pleased to dispose us all to do justice, to love mercy and to demean ourselves with that charity, humility and pacific temper of mind which were the characteristics of the Divine Author of our blessed religion, and without whose example in these things we can never hope to be a happy nation. Grant our supplication, we beseech Thee, through Jesus Christ our Lord. Amen.

Chapter Two:

"If My People, Who are Called by My Name,"

The trial of Charles Guiteau for the assassination of President Garfield started in our nation's capital on November 14, 1881. Eighty days passed between the time Garfield was shot and the time he died. The story gained momentum day by day. It was an international disgrace. Another American president gunned down. Charles Guiteau becomes the most notorious man in the land. Before, during and after the trial, he was a media sensation.

The stenographer of the legal proceeding, H.H. Alexander, wrote a detailed account of the entire ordeal in his book, *The Life of Guiteau.* The quotes in this chapter are taken directly from his work. The jury selection was tough because most people were thoroughly convinced of his guilt. One panel member said, echoing the sentiment of many, "He ought to be hung or burnt." Over 170 potential jurors were questioned. Guiteau objected to being tried by "nigger jurors," but his opinion didn't carry much weight. After three days, twelve men were selected to serve on the jury, including one African American.

The presiding judge was Walter S. Cox. The D.C. district attorney, George Corkhill, was part of a five-lawyer-team for the prosecution. Charles Guiteau insisted on representing himself in the case, but Judge Cox appointed George Scoville, Esq., to defend him. Scoville was married to Guiteau's sister, and took the case out of family obligations. Some eighteen years earlier, George Scoville helped Guiteau gain admission to the bar in Chicago. Charles conducted his bill-collecting work out of his brother-in-law's office.

In his opening statement, District Attorney Corkhill stated:

> "This trial is a remarkable illustration of the genius and spirit of our Government. Although our chief ruler was murdered, although the effects of that death were felt in every station of life, in every avenue of business, in every department of society, yet the prisoner, his murderer, stands before you to-day entitled to the same rights, to the same privileges, panoplied by the same guarantees of the

> constitution, as if he had killed the lowliest member of this community."

While the District Attorney delivered his initial comments, Guiteau appeared completely indifferent as he devoted himself to the morning papers. But when his sister started lamenting during the opening argument, Guiteau responded by shaking his head in approval or disapproval of Corkhill's statements.

The courtroom was filled daily with high society ladies who packed their lunches and showed up early to get a good seat inside. Guiteau smiled for his spectators and waved at the newspaper reporters. He argued that since the "Deity" had taken over his free will when he fired the gun, he was not responsible for his actions. At times, he openly opposed his own lawyer's line of questioning.

> "What is the use of going into that, Scoville? You are a consummate jackass. I would rather have a ten-year-old boy to try this case than you. You have got no brains, no conception. You cannot see a foot ahead of you. Get off the case, and I will do the business myself!"

Charles Guiteau claimed he was not medically insane, but should be acquitted on the grounds that he was "legally insane" when he attempted to remove the president. He revels in the spotlight. He reads of himself in all the newspapers. The trial of Charles Guiteau for the assassination of President Garfield is the hottest ticket in town. Everyone in the country knows his name. Foreigners who were in Washington at the time visit the courtroom or the jailhouse. From the very start, Guiteau is quite the performer. He's rude to Judge Cox. He insults Attorney Corkhill constantly.

> "Do you believe in a God, Corkhill? I have been digging up your record, and it stinks worse than a mackerel."

> "I generally paid for my board, too. I always did when I had the money. That is more than Corkhill does when he has the money. He does not pay anybody."

During the entire trial, Charles Guiteau refused to admit that he murdered or assassinated the president. He felt others in the community should also assume responsibility.

> "I want the newspapers and doctors who actually killed the President to share with me the odium of his death."

At one point in the hearing when the D.A. mentioned "the murder of the President," Guiteau replied, *"The doctors did that, I simply shot at him."* He claimed he prayed for two weeks after he first felt the "divine pressure" to remove President Garfield. And when the pressure failed to leave, he took that as a sign the Deity wanted him to do it.

The D.A. presented the state's position point by point. It was an obvious open and shut case, but he left no stone unturned. Corkhill delineated how Charles Guiteau slithered from one stage of his devilish plan to the next.

> "On the 8th day of June he borrowed from an acquaintance in this city fifteen dollars, representing that he was out of money and desired the amount to pay his board-bill. After procuring his loan he at once visited the store of Mr. O'Meara, on the corner of Fifteenth and F streets, for the purpose of purchasing a weapon. In this, as in all other acts connected with the commission of this crime, he displayed the malignity of his determination and the wickedness of his motives. He asked for a pistol of the largest calibre, and one that would do the most effective work, and was shown and purchased the pistol which he finally used – a weapon terrible to behold, carrying a bullet of the largest size – a weapon that was self-cocking, in order that there might be no delay in its use when an emergency occurred."

Guiteau played the innocent until the very end. He entertained his audience and stuck to the script. "The Deity was responsible" – "The doctors were responsible" – "I did the country a great service by removing the President, thus preventing another civil war." After weeks of his courtroom shenanigans, it was apparent to all that Charles Guiteau was crazy as a loon and guilty as sin.

On January 16, 1882, Scoville offered his final appeal to the jury. It lasts for five full days. On January 25th, after the delivery of the Judge's charge, the jury retired at 4:40 p.m. to decide on a verdict. When Guiteau was asked what he thought the jury would do, he replied, "I think they will acquit me or disagree, don't you?" Less than one hour later,

> "The musty, antique room is devoid of gas and the score or more of candles which had been placed upon the desks of the Judge, counsel and reporters imparted a weird and fancifully unnatural aspect to the grim old place. The shadows thrown upon the dark background of the walls seemed like flitting spectres to usher in the sombre procession of those who held in their hands the destiny of a human life.
>
> "First came the prisoner, with quick, nervous step, and as he seated himself in the dock, perhaps for the last time, the light of a solitary candle fell full upon his face and disclosed its more than usual pallor. Not a tremor of the limbs or a movement of the muscles of the face was observable as he threw back his head and fixed his gaze upon the door through which the jury were to enter. Judge Cox soon afterward took his seat, the crier called "Order" and the jury, at 5.35, filed slowly into their seats. Every sound was hushed save the voice of the Clerk as he propounded to the foreman the usual inquiry. Clear and distinct came the reply: "We have."
>
> "What is your verdict, guilty or not guilty?"
>
> With equal distinctness came the reply: "GUILTY AS INDICTED."
>
> Then the pent-up feelings of the crowd found expression in uproarious demonstrations of applause and approval. "Order! Order!" shouted the bailiffs.
>
> Mr. Scoville, still upon his feet, demanded a poll of the jury, which was granted, and each juror was called by name and each, in a firm voice, promptly responded, "Guilty." As the last name was called the prisoner shrieked: "My blood will be upon the heads of that jury. Don't you forget it."

Charles Guiteau fully expected President Arthur and his other Stalwarts to view his action as that of a loyalist, not that of a murderer. "I would have staked my life that they would defend me." Instead, they denounced him as an insane office-seeker. Was he insane? Consider his expectations. On the day he shot Garfield, he expected General Sherman to deliver him from the jail in D.C. He expected the Republican Party to see him as a hero. He expected to have a successful book tour after his acquittal. He expected the country to eventually view him as a patriot and elect him as our national leader.

On Friday, June 30, 1882, Charles Guiteau would meet his Maker. A large tub of water is carried into his cell early in the morning. "He splashed and squirmed in it, like a lobster in a pot, with evident relish." After a big breakfast and lunch, he exits his cell, and walks fearlessly to the scaffold outside the jail. His hands are tied behind his back, as he calls down curses upon the President and the country. He breaks down and sobs pitifully as he reads a poem written that morning called, "I am going to the Lordy."

The hangman adjusted the noose around Guiteau's neck, and the black cap is pulled over his face. Guiteau shouts in a loud, clear voice: "Glory! Ready! Go!" The drop door of the scaffold falls open and poor Charles is dispatched to the world beyond. A mighty shout erupts when the prisoners hear the noise of his fall, and a thousand spectators cheer outside the jail and join in the celebration.

While he was a prisoner, hundreds of people visited Guiteau and asked for his autograph. Hundreds more approached him in the courtroom to do the same. In the age before radio, television and the internet, he was an international media sensation. On the day of his death, scores of eager souvenir seekers paid for small slices of the hangman's rope. And to this day, sections of Charles Guiteau's brain are kept at the Mütter Medical Museum in Philadelphia.

What do we make of his position, "Yes, I shot him, but his doctors killed him"? Was the crazy man actually stating the truth? There's a saying back home in South Carolina that even a blind pig can find an acorn every now and then. A broken clock is right twice a day. Did the insane man actually state a fact?

On the day Guiteau shot President Garfield in the back, doctors prodded the bullet wound with unwashed fingers. All throughout his 80-day ordeal, physicians used unsterilized instruments to search for the bullet. To make matters worse, it was discovered after the autopsy that doctors were probing the wrong side of the wound, thus creating further damage. In the last days before his passing, Garfield's body was infected with pus-filled abscesses. His dirty, painful death was the result of blood poisoning and infection, due partly to doctors contaminating the wound with unwashed hands and unsterilized instruments.

In the 1880s, the American medical community was still skeptical regarding the germ theory of disease. It's really surprising if you think about it. Humans have lived on this globe for millenniums, but we just discovered about 150 years ago that we share the planet with life-threatening germs! Think of all the lives that have been lost throughout human history because we were ignorant of germs and viruses which cause deadly infections. But why did it take us thousands of years to figure out in order to stop the spread of infection, we should wash our hands and cough into our sleeve?

I pondered the question for a moment until I ran across a line in a *Big Picture* article entitled "The History of Germ Theory." It states, "In the 19th century, improvements in microscope technology enabled a generation of microbiologists to investigate further the world of previously unseen disease-causing organisms." That's it! There's the answer. For the majority of our time on planet Earth, we've been interacting with a "world of *previously unseen* disease-causing organisms."

Before the invention of the modern microscope, we had no insight into this biosphere of harmful creatures residing just beyond our physical senses. Humans were totally ignorant of germs for thousands of years because we couldn't see them. Ignorance = bondage. Deadly diseases, caused by germs and viruses, have inflicted pain and suffering on the human race for ages, yet we knew nothing about them until we *looked through the lens* of a microscope. The unaided human eye cannot see a whole world of potentially lethal creatures that live all around us.

The article closes with, "By 1900 the discoveries of [Louis] Pasteur and [Robert] Koch, and the work of their fellow scientists, had led to the identification of 21 disease-causing microorganisms in just over two decades. As Koch himself said, 'As soon as the right method was found, discoveries came as easily as ripe apples from a tree.' "

Aided by the microscope, scientist saw things humans had never seen in the entire history of mankind. That's a big deal, because once we were able to identify the source of the problem, then we were able to isolate the problem. And when any problem is identified and isolated, the remedy to that problem is likely to follow shortly thereafter.

What a stupendous difference the microscope made, and is still making, in the area of health and disease research. Untold millions of lives have been spared by this instrument which allows us to see into a world of the "previously unseen."

But think about this. When a man or woman looks *through* their microscope, they see worlds beyond. But what do they see if they look *at* their microscope? Let's say the microscope is inside a lab on a table, and our researcher is sitting at the table looking at her microscope. What does she see? She sees the instrument, right? It's a rather unique looking instrument no doubt, but that's not the purpose of the thing. The microscope is an apparatus to be looked through to see the world beyond.

Now, I want to introduce you to another scope. It's also an astounding, life-saving tool. Let's call it the "Biblescope." This instrument empowers us to see a spiritual world that we cannot see with the naked eye. When we view the world, *through the lens of Scripture*, we see things we could never see on our own. But what happens if we only look *at* the Biblescope? One possible outcome is we'll just see a book of old letters. It's a rather unique collection of old letters no doubt, but that's not the purpose of the thing. The Biblescope is another apparatus to be looked *through* to see the world beyond our physical senses.

There's an intriguing incident in Scripture that illustrates the point. The nation of Syria is at war with Israel. Whenever the king of Syria communicated his plan of attack against Israel, somehow that plan would leak and Israel would avoid an ambush. Unbeknownst to the king of Syria, Elisha is a prophet of Israel, and God relays to his prophet whatever the king whispers in secret. But my focus of the story is on the servant of Elisha. Yahweh has something really special in store for him. Let's say a quick prayer together as we go to 2 Kings 6:8-17,

~ Lord, give us spiritual insight as we look into Your Word. ~

Now the king of Syria was at war against Israel; and he took counsel with his servants, saying, "My camp [ambush] will be in such and such a place." The man of God sent to the king of Israel, saying, "Beware that you not pass this place; for the Syrians are coming down there." The king of Israel sent to the place which the man of God told him and warned him of; and he saved himself there, not once nor twice.

The king of Syria's heart was very troubled about this. He called his servants, and said to them, "Won't you show me which of us is for the king of Israel?" One of his servants said, "No, my lord, O king; but Elisha, the prophet who is in Israel, tells the king of Israel the words that you speak in your bedroom." He said, "Go and see where he is, that I may send and get him." He was told, "Behold, he is in Dothan."

Therefore he sent horses, chariots, and a great army there. They came by night, and surrounded the city. When the servant of the man of God had risen early, and gone out, behold, an army with horses and chariots was around the city. His servant said to him, "Alas, my master! What shall we do?" He answered, *"Don't be afraid; for those who are with us are more than those who are with them."* Elisha prayed, and said, "Yahweh, please open his eyes, that he may see." **Yahweh opened the young man's eyes; and he saw:** and behold, the mountain was full of horses and chariots of fire around Elisha."

~§~

For a brief moment in space and time, God blessed Elisha's servant in a way that undoubtedly changed his life forever. *His eyes were empowered to look into the world of the spirit*. And what did he see? He saw the innumerable, invisible heavenly host! "The chariots of God are tens of thousands and thousands of thousands" (Psalm 68:17). The Scripture proclaims, "Yahweh's angel encamps around those who fear him, and delivers them" (Psalm 34:7). Elisha's servant saw into the spirit world that resides just beyond our physical senses.

With the aid of the Biblescope, believers gain insight into that world. It's one of "serving spirits, sent out to do service for the sake of those who will inherit salvation" (Hebrews 1:14). And it's a world of "seducing spirits" and "spiritual forces of wickedness" and "rulers of the darkness"

(1 Timothy 4:1; Ephesians 6:12). *When you pull back the curtain of our physical world and peer into the world of the spirit, you see that it's a world at war.* There are intangible forces at work, good and ill, that seek to interplay with the affairs of men. It behooves us all to be intently aware of this war in the spirit world, for in a very real sense, we're smack dab in the middle of it.

BibleScope Assignment

Do you remember in science lab when your assignment was to examine various slides under the microscope? Well, scattered throughout this book are a few "BibleScope Assignments." During these assignments we start with a hypothesis or a supposition, such as: *"Salvation is not a reward that we earn by good works; salvation is a gift of God that we accept by faith."* Is that hypothesis true or false? How can we test it? We test the hypothesis by looking at various slides (verses) through the lens of our BibleScope. Slide #1. Slide #2. Etc. Some slides are simple and short. Others are more complex. All the slides in the assignment are from the *World English Bible,* unless otherwise noted. After we examine the slides, we then draw a conclusion. Please feel free to cross-check the verses with the "BibleScope" version of your choice. Sound doctrine is not dependent upon a particular version of the Bible. If the teaching is true, it will be supported by reliable translations.

Are you ready for your first BibleScope Assignment? Here we go!

Hypothesis: *"God refers to Israelites or Jews as a people called by his name. However, non-Jewish believers are also a people called by his name."* Is that true or false?

Slide #1: Exodus 19:4-6 » (Addressed to the people of Israel.) "You have seen what I did to the Egyptians, and how I bore you on eagles' wings, and brought you to myself. Now therefore, *if* you will indeed obey my voice and keep my covenant, *then* you shall be my own possession from among all peoples; for all the earth is mine; and you shall be to me a kingdom of priests and a holy nation."

Slide #2: 1 Peter 2:9 » (Addressed to believers in Christ.) "But you are a chosen race, a royal priesthood, a holy nation, a people for God's own possession, that you may proclaim the excellence of him who called you out of darkness into his marvelous light."

Slide #3: Acts 15:12-17 » (This is at the Jerusalem council, where it was determined that Gentiles are not bound to Judaism.) "All the multitude kept silence, and they listened to Barnabas and Paul reporting what signs and wonders God had done among the *Gentiles* through them. After they were silent, James answered, 'Brothers, listen to me. Simeon has reported how God first visited the nations [not just Israel] to take out of them a people *for his name*. This agrees with the words of the prophets. As it is written, 'After these things I will return. I will again build the tabernacle of David, which has fallen. I will again build its ruins. I will set it up that the rest of men may seek after the Lord; all the *Gentiles who are called by my name,* says the Lord, who does all these things.' "

Slide #4: Romans 9:24-25 NKJV » (Addressed to Jewish and Gentile believers in Rome, beloved of God, called *to be* saints.) "...even us whom He called, not of the Jews only, but also of the Gentiles? As He says also in Hosea: *'I will call them My people, who were not My people,...'* "

Slide #5: John 10:14-16 NJKV » (Addressed to Jews.) "I am the good shepherd; and I know My *sheep*, and am known by My own. As the Father knows Me, even so I know the Father; and I lay down My life for the sheep. And other sheep I have *which are not of this fold*; them also I must bring, and they will hear My voice; and there will be one flock *and* one shepherd."

Hypothesis: *"God refers to Israelites or Jews as a people called by his name. However, non-Jewish believers are also a people called by his name."*

Conclusion: Gentile believers are a part of the "one flock" God is gathering under one chief shepherd, the Lord Jesus Christ. Jews and Gentiles alike make up this universal flock of believers (Romans 15:7-12; 1 Corinthians 12:13-27). Various ethnic groups of all nations make up the one flock of God. Here's a key point:

We may not be of the same fold, but all believers are of the same flock. Many Folds, One Flock, One LORD!

Jesus said there's only one flock of God. God's one flock is composed of people who are being called out from all the nations of the world. Whenever a person exercises saving faith in the gospel of Christ, he or she is spiritually adopted into that ONE flock of God, baptized into that ONE spiritual body. Rich folk and poor folk, young and old, males and females in one flock with the same shepherd. For believers in the USA, from sea to shining sea, we're many folds in the same flock under the same LORD. We're Hispanics, Asians, Caucasians, African Americans, Native Americans all under the same FLAG, in the same FLOCK, worshipping the same Chief Shepherd who gave his life as a ransom for all.

A Nation within a Nation

Believers may not be of the same fold, but all believers are members of the same flock that's guided by the selfsame Leader. This is what makes believers a special group of people. The flock of God is "a nation within a nation." *All true believers have dual citizenship*. I'm a citizen of the United States of America. God bless America! I'm also a citizen of the Kingdom (Philippians 3:17-21). All glory and honor to Christ Jesus our Lord! I pledge allegiance to the United States of America. My highest allegiance is to the King of Kings and Lord of Lords!

As a believer in the Lord Jesus Christ, I'm also a fellow-citizen with other believers of various nationalities. A female believer in Spain is my sister in the LORD, and a fellow-citizen of the Kingdom. A male believer in Australia is my brother in the LORD, and a fellow-citizen of the Kingdom. It's an amazing, supernatural unity that binds together brothers and sisters of all races into what could be called a bustling international household of faith (Ephesians 2:11-19)!

When the apostle Paul writes to the Gentile believers in Ephesus, he wants them to recognize their seven-fold spiritual unity, and he urges them to be "eager to keep" that unity.

> "I therefore, the prisoner in the Lord, beg you to walk worthily of the calling with which you were called, with all lowliness and humility, with patience, bearing with one another in love, being eager to keep the unity of the Spirit in the bond of peace. [What's the basis of our unity?] There is **one** body and **one** Spirit, even as you also were called in **one** hope of your calling, **one** Lord, **one** faith, **one** baptism, **one** God and Father of all, who is over all, and through all, and in us all." ~ *Ephesians 4:1-6*

In light of what all believers have in common, we're called to be eager to keep the unity of the SPIRIT. It's not a unity that needs to be created and manufactured by us. *It's an automatic, supernatural, seven-*

fold unity all believers have in Christ! When the apostle sends his letter to the Gentile believers in the assemblies of Galatia, his message is the same. In Christ, people from all social and economic levels are *fellow members* of the ONE universal flock of God.

> "For you are all sons of God, through faith in Christ Jesus. For as many of you as were baptized into Christ have put on Christ. There is neither Jew nor Greek, there is neither slave nor free man, there is neither male nor female; for you are all one in Christ Jesus." ~ *Galatians 3:26-28*

Why am I emphasizing the point that Gentile believers are also included in the "one body" that's called by his name? Because some have argued that the Old Testament (OT) passage, 2 Chronicles 7:14, applies only to the nation of Israel. They would contend Christians in America are taking this verse out of context. They assert it's wrong for the New Testament (NT) church today to lay claim on the passage, "If my people, *who are called by my name,* shall humble themselves..." But as we've seen in the "slides," Gentile believers are also a people called by his name. Of course, the context in 2 Chronicles 7 shows us Yahweh is speaking directly to King Solomon about the people of Israel. It's clear God is speaking about healing *their* land. Subsequently, for the people of the "fold" of Israel, this is obviously a direct and specific promise to them. On the other hand, for the people of the greater "flock" of God, this isn't a direct promise as much as it is a precept or principle. This distinction is important, I'm not just splitting hairs. All of the Bible is written *for* us (2 Tim. 3:16,17), but not every verse of Scripture is addressed *to* us. We must not presume upon the LORD (Psa. 19:13). Correctly interpretating the Word is vital as we humble ourselves to lay hold of both the promises *and* precepts of God.

I maintain 2 Chronicles 7:14 is a promise to Israel and a principle to the NT church because we also find other passages which highlight the fact that **God responds when his people, any people, humble themselves before him** (Jonah 3:5-10; Acts 8:4-8; Jas. 4:8-10; 1 Pet. 5:5-7). Aren't Christians exhorted in the NT to repeat the actions God called the Jews to do in 2 Chronicles 7:14? Yes, we are. *But do Christians go to a temple and seek God's mercy by making animal sacrifices?* Isn't that something God called his chosen people to do in the OT? Yes, it is. Then why don't Christians do it? Because the NT teaches us otherwise (Heb. 10:1-10). Therefore, seeking atonement by offering animal sacrifices is not an OT practice that crosses over into the NT. But we are definitely commanded in the NT to pray and turn from our sinful ways and seek first God's Kingdom, *and afterwards,* to humbly expect the LORD to move on our behalf. That is a principle which spans the Old and New Testament. So, while this compelling verse may not be a specific promise to the NT church, Christians down through the ages have gravitated toward this passage because it captures in a single, easy-to-understand verse the key ingredients of revival. The fact that it's not a direct promise to Gentile believers is irrelevant. It's a precept woven throughout the OT and NT!

Christians look at 2 Chronicles 7:14 and see how God expects his people to respond when he chastens them for their sin. We see OT examples of God delivering his people from distress whenever they follow the pattern set forth in this one awesome verse. When the people of Ammon and Moab attacked Israel, King Jehoshaphat and the citizens of Jerusalem followed the teaching of 2 Chronicles 7:14. *And how did God respond when his people humbled themselves before him?* He rewards Judah with a victory so great that "they took plunder [spoils] for three days, it was so much" (2 Chronicles 20:1-25)!

Believers are told the very reason we have the record of how God dealt with the Israelites is so that we can learn from their example: the good, the bad and the ugly example of Jeshurun. We find in 1 Corinthians chapter 10, the Spirit of God is teaching believers about the wilderness experience of the Jews.

> "*Now these things were our examples*, to the intent we should not lust after evil things, as they also lusted. Neither be idolaters, as some of them were. As it is written, "The people sat down to eat and drink, and rose up to play." Neither let us commit sexual immorality, as some of them committed, and in one day twenty-three thousand fell. Neither let us test the Lord, as some of them tested, and perished by the serpents. Neither grumble, as some of them also grumbled, and perished by the destroyer. *Now all these things happened to them by way of example, and they were written for our admonition [warning], on whom the ends of the ages have come.* Therefore let him who thinks he stands be careful that he doesn't fall." ~ 1 Corinthians 10:6-12

Scripture states plainly we're to consider what happened to God's chosen people in the OT as an example and a warning. That's a major focus of this book. We'll examine how God used pain to prepare the nation of

Israel for revival. But they refused to turn from their wicked ways; ergo, instead of experiencing revival in the land, they provoked manifestations of divine anger. And now, America must avoid making the same disastrous mistake. A jealous God used a foreign superpower as his "rod of correction" to discipline the unfaithful nation of Israel. Does a similar fate await the citizens of America?

Our sacred text provides us with invaluable insights, warnings, and principles we can apply in our daily walk. Think of the episode in 2 Kings 6, where the servant of the man of God was allowed to see into the spirit world. The LORD can save by many or by few (1 Sam.14:6), but isn't it empowering to know *"those who are with us are more than those who are with them"!* According to Romans 15:4, this is one of the reasons why God gave us the "BibleScope" in the first place: "For whatever things were written before were written for our learning, that through perseverance and through encouragement of the Scriptures we might have hope."

The Bible shows us time and again that God is unquestionably and completely reliable. Therefore, we have hope through the encouragement of the Scriptures. Do you see how that works? By reading and believing the Bible, we encounter a miraculous God who is totally keen on fulfilling his word. The LORD told his prophet, "**I watch over my word to perform it**" (Jeremiah 1:12). God wants his truth to be our source of inspiration, so that during the many trials of life we can have hope, because we *know* his word and we *trust* his word.

God expects us to learn from the precepts and principles in his book (see Psalm 119:27,93,100). He's given us 2 Chronicles 7:13-14 as a recipe for spiritual restoration and renewal. Whenever natural and supernatural disasters strike a nation (droughts, shortages, military conflicts, a plague of insects and other vermin, an outbreak or epidemic), when the populace is gripped by distress and anxiety, or when it seems like Satan is winning the day, this passage gives us an action plan and a reason to keep looking up. *If* we submit to his word, *if* we humble ourselves and pray and seek his face and turn from our wicked ways, *then* we can trust God to "perform" according to his word.

One of the fundamental truths of Scripture is that God is no respecter of persons. Yet anyone can see there are myriads of promises that JAH made to the people of Israel, specific promises to a specific people to be fulfilled at a specific time. And "Scripture cannot be broken"

(Jn 10:35). But it doesn't change the fact that the principles and truths found throughout the Bible apply equally to Jews and non-Jews alike.

For example, in the book of Proverbs, it speaks primarily of the righteous person and the unrighteous person, not of the Jew and the non-Jew. The truth we encounter in Proverbs is universal truth, not just Jewish truth. Proverbs 15:29 states, "Yahweh is far from the wicked, but he hears the prayer of the righteous." Is that truth just for Jews? Or, is Proverbs 15:29 a universal truth? God says repeatedly that he is no respecter of persons or people groups. *Which implies any person who willingly submits to the righteous ways of the LORD can confidently expect him to hear their prayers.* This truth is echoed in 1 Peter 3:8-12.

A faithful Welsh brother in Cardiff, Wales has the ear of Heaven just like a faithful Israeli sister in Haifa. A prayer group of righteous Hispanic believers in Houston has access to the same throne of grace as a prayer group of righteous Jewish believers in Tel Aviv.

In this same book of 2 Chronicles in chapter 16, we find a passage that puts to rest this whole question of whether or not Christians today should look to 2 Chronicles 7:14 as a principle for revival. The context is during the Civil War of Israel. Yes, Israel too experienced civil war. A split occurred which resulted in a "Northern Kingdom" of ten tribes, with Samaria as their capital. The "Southern Kingdom," made up of the tribes of Benjamin and Judah, retained Jerusalem as their capital. During this time in the Bible, the northern kingdom is commonly called "Israel" and the southern kingdom is commonly called "Judah."

Hanani the seer, or prophet, has a strong word from the Lord for Asa, the king of Judah. When Asa was confronted in battle with the much larger northern kingdom of Israel, he decided to increase his chances of success by making a treaty with Syria. In the eyes of the LORD, this showed a lack of faith on Asa's part. Faithfulness is a big thing with Yahweh, and he frowned upon Asa's lack of it. A jealous God sent Hanani to proclaim:

> "Because you have relied on the king of Syria, and have not relied on Yahweh your God, therefore the army of the king of Syria has escaped out of your hand. Weren't the Ethiopians and the Lubim a huge army, with chariots and exceedingly many horsemen? *Yet, because you relied on Yahweh, he delivered them into your hand.* For Yahweh's eyes run back and forth throughout the whole earth,

> to show himself strong in the behalf of them whose heart is perfect toward him. You have done foolishly in this; for from now on you will have wars."
>
> "Then Asa was angry with the seer, and put him in the prison; for he was in a rage with him because of this thing. Asa oppressed some of the people at the same time" (vv. 7-10).

This is an incredible passage of Scripture and a fine example of how we can benefit by studying the entire Bible. The prophet Hanani is God's microphone for the moment and he's been charged to speak truth to power. I dare say, that's no small feat, especially if the word Hanani is delivering is a rebuke instead of a word of praise. It's easy to pass along a positive word, but rebuking the king of Judah is a whole different matter. Even so, the anointed are called to "preach the word; be urgent in season and out of season; reprove, rebuke, and exhort, with all patience and teaching" (2 Timothy 4:2).

Hanani was put in prison for speaking truth to power, but he was faithful to deliver a word we desperately need to hear today:

> **For Yahweh's eyes run back and forth throughout the whole earth, to show himself strong in the behalf of them whose heart is perfect toward him.**

This is a foundational truth we must understand. Not just understand in our head, but we must understand this truth in our heart and deep in our soul! God is no respecter of persons or races. Scripture affirms this repeatedly (Acts 10:34,35; Jas. 2:8,9; 1 Pet. 1:17). The Most High God is the creator of **all people**, and he's eager to show up STRONG for **any people** who love him. The eyes of the LORD run back and forth throughout the whole earth looking for co-workers, i.e., believers that he can work on, and work for, and work through to advance his agenda.

Our God rides the heavens to help those who are willing to "pray" the price for revival. When our numbers reach critical mass, the Almighty will show himself strong. The problem is not that God is too weak to send down revival fires on the United States of America. The issue is he's still searching for that group of worshippers who are all-out for the Kingdom. His eyes are scanning our nation even now for a courageous, humble band of believers he can use to get the fires of revival started.

Let's not be deceived into believing non-Jewish people can't stand on 2 Chronicles 7:14, when 2 Chronicles 16:9 states the eyes of the LORD survey the whole earth so that he can show up for any people who are faithful to him. Fellow believers in America, let's not be robbed of our blessing because we're ignorant of the Scriptures. When speaking to a group of religious leaders about the resurrection, Jesus said their understanding on the topic was incorrect. He states two reasons for their error: 1) they didn't know the Scriptures, and 2) they didn't know the power of God (Mark 12:24). Many of our errors today, in both doctrine and conduct, can be traced back to these same two reasons.

In Hosea 4:6, God said, *"My people are destroyed for lack of knowledge. Because you have rejected knowledge, I will also reject you..."* Many believers today are deprived of blessing after blessing in their homes, and on their jobs, and within their community - because they're not hungry for the knowledge of the Holy. And so it follows, they don't know the Scriptures and they don't know the power of God. But as we draw near to the Lord, he draws near to us.

Jesus said, "If you remain in my word, then you are truly my disciples. You will know the truth, and the truth will make you free" (John 8:31,32). Many of us emphasize the last part of that verse, "The truth will make you free." But as I learned years ago at Bible college, in our quest for proper biblical interpretation - context is king. Scripture interprets Scripture. We're called to be diligent students, rightly dividing the word of truth (Ezra 7:10; Nehemiah 8:1-3,8; 2 Timothy 2:15; 2 Peter 1:20,21). Three questions are helpful. First, what does the text *say*? Next, what does the text *mean* by what it says? And third, how do we *apply* the text?

The truth WILL make you free - IF you know it! It's not the "truth" floating around out there that makes you free. It's the *knowing of it*, and the *believing in it*, and the *applying of it* – that makes you free. Jesus said true disciples will remain in his word. Why do they do that? Because the word of God is truth, and we must know the truth in order for it to "make" us free. **Truth = freedom; ignorance = bondage!**

Listen up, Jews and Gentiles. According to 1 Peter 2:9, believers in Christ Jesus are also "a chosen race." We too are "a holy nation." We too are "a royal priesthood." And we too are "a people for God's own possession." "Then I will say to *those who were* not My people, 'You *are* My people!' And they shall say, '*You are* my God!' " (Hosea 2:23 NKJV).

For centuries, Christians the world over have humbly claimed the responsibilities and benefits of 2 Chronicles 7:14 with great success. God's people in all nations have appropriated this one magnificent verse as a principle of revival, a pattern for restoration, a catalyst for change, and a spark to ignite the flames of renewal.

The eyes of the LORD run back and forth from Maine to Florida, from Virginia to California, looking for an assembly of people who love him. God is willing and able to show up STRONG on our behalf! He is no respecter of persons. What our wonderful Deliverer has done for his prayerful people in the past, he's eager to do again, and more! By the grace of God, we can yield to the Most High and allow him to work on us, and for us, and through us to heal our land.

The next chapter will reveal more painful episodes of man's inhumanity to man that occur every day in America. It's a sad and tragic thing to witness. Fellow citizens are being victimized by the evil one in ever increasing numbers. Isn't it high time we *stir up ourselves* to take hold of the Lord? If we are truly one nation under God, now is the time to show it!

> "Give us help against the enemy, for the help of man is vain. Through God, we will do valiantly. For it is he who will tread down our enemies." ~ *Psalm 108:12-13*

> "Through you [God], we will push down our adversaries. Through your name, we will tread down those who rise up against us. **For I will not trust in my bow, neither will my sword save me**. But you have saved us from our adversaries." ~ *Psalm 44:5-7*

Against the true enemy of the people, the help of man is vain. "[Only] through God, will we do valiantly"! Our adversary is fierce, highly skilled and experienced, and he's closing in. As a nation, we have two possible outcomes: In the power of the LORD, we "will tread down our enemies," trusting in his word which declares in Romans 8:31,

"If God be for us, who can be against us?"

However, if we're not one nation under God and only pretending to be, then time will tell, and the Most High will oppose us. If that ever happens, then woe to America! Because...

If God be against us, who can be for us?

Chapter Three:

God's Conditional Promises

Let's start this chapter by taking a look at the devil's handiwork on August 9, 2018. Please keep in mind this all happened in one day across our land. A few incidents make it to the national news level. Most do not, but they happen just the same. Satan is a murderer from the beginning (John 8:44). He is America's #1 threat, the true enemy of the people.

Allow me to be blunt. If Satan had his way, he would kill you. Our adversary would prefer to first use you to kill and destroy others. After he's done using you, he'll then dispose of you like yesterday's trash. It is his malicious spirit that energizes so many acts of deadly violence. And it's only by God's grace that we stand.

As we look again at headlines from across our great nation, it's helpful to be reminded of the words from the late church planter and spiritual warrior John Wimber. He states,

> "We're in a declared war, but unless we're clear about who the enemy is, *we'll waste our time fighting enemies that aren't enemies at all.* There's only one enemy and no matter what people do, say or react - people are never the enemy. The enemy is our only enemy."

I would add that believers also war against the world (1 John 2:15,16; 2 Timothy 4:10) and our own dumb flesh (Romans 7:18), but I understand Brother Wimber's point. Fellow citizen and fellow believer in Christ Jesus, our adversary is the devil, it is not people. People can become tools of the enemy, but if we wish to cut off the head of the snake, we must realize that the real enemy of our souls is Satan. He is Public Enemy #1, the activating force of all the evil we see spreading across our land.

The enemy of our nation is not the person of a different race or gender or political persuasion or sexual orientation. The Bible clearly states that our chief adversary is the devil (1 Peter 5:8). Also, according to Scripture, we're not to be ignorant of his tactics and wiles. In other words, don't turn a blind eye to what the opposition is doing. Behold his handiwork, the deceiver of the nations...

Thursday, August 9, 2018 United States of America

Maine police report a 34-yr old Massachusetts man shot and killed himself after being pulled over at a traffic stop in Gardiner. Police then find his murdered 28-yr old girlfriend in the trunk of the car.

Miami-Dade police report a 64-yr old woman shot and killed herself. When her 49-yr old boyfriend found her, he called 911, and then shot and killed himself.

Utah authorities report a 64-yr old man arranged an appointment with a West Valley City code enforcement officer. When the 52-yr old officer arrived at the residence, he shot her to death.

Wisconsin authorities say a 60-yr old man died after he swallowed heroin during a federal drug bust at a home on Milwaukee's north side.

South Carolina police report a 56-yr old woman was beat to death in Columbia. She was found by her roommate, who told police the door of their home was left open.

Baltimore police officers responded to a report of a cutting incident in the Northwest District. When the officers get to the scene, they find a 43-yr old male with fatal stab wounds to his upper body.

Tennessee authorities have charged a 31-yr old Nashville woman with vehicular homicide by intoxication in connection with a wreck that killed her male passenger.

New Jersey police say a 37-yr old football coach was shot and killed in a middle school parking lot in Millville. It's reported many children were in the area at the time.

North Carolina law enforcement report a 66-yr old woman was killed by two pit bulls while on a walk at Lake Tillery in Stanly County.

Texas authorities report a 45-yr old man is dead, and a 31-yr old man arrested in a deadly motorcycle racing accident in Amarillo.

Louisiana police say a 41-yr old man from Gretna is charged with murder after he stabbed his 25-yr old girlfriend over 20 times in front of her one-yr old son.

West Virginia State police arrested a Green Valley couple after a two-yr old boy died from alleged abuse after being taken to a Charleston hospital.

San Antonio police respond to a call to discover a 26-yr old male gunshot victim dead, apparently hidden between air conditioning units at an East Side Apartment complex.

Phoenix police responded to a shooting call and found a 26-yr old male victim with fatal gunshot wounds at the barber shop where he worked. A 32-yr old suspect was arrested.

Chicago detectives report three men approached a 28-yr old man in the Oakland area and opened fire. He was pronounced dead at the scene.

Atlantic City, NJ police say a 17-yr old was shot and killed by a 21-yr old in broad daylight. The Atlantic County Prosecutor said in a statement, "A 21-year old killing a 17-year old has cost society two lives."

Maryland police say a 38-yr old man in Waldorf shot and wounded the mother of his child. He was later found in the stairwell dead from a self-inflicted gunshot.

Chicago police say four people entered a Longwood Manor home, and shoot a 43-yr old man in the chest and back. The victim was pronounced dead at Christ Medical Center.

North Carolina investigators in Alexander County arrested a 51-yr old man for the murder of a 77-yr old man. The suspect was wearing an ankle monitor at the time of the murder.

Tulsa, Oklahoma police say a 34-yr old man was shot and killed inside a motel room. This marks the 29th homicide in Tulsa this year.

Pennsylvania police report a 48-yr old man was shot and killed after he ran from and then fired his gun at two officers in South Philadelphia.

Georgia Bureau of Investigation report a 60-yr old man was found with a fatal gunshot wound in the yard of his home in Cairo. The case is being investigated as a homicide.

Florida investigators discover that a 21-yr old man inside a crashed SUV is also a gunshot victim. He later died at the Orlando Regional Medical Center.

Pittsburgh police charged a 32-yr old man with the shooting death of a 24-yr old man after they got into a tussle in the Knoxville neighborhood.

Texas investigators say three masked robbers killed a 25-yr old man and held his girlfriend at gunpoint during a home invasion in Houston.

California sheriff deputies say a 24-yr old man was sitting in a parked car in Castro Valley when another man walked up and shot him. He died at the scene.

Texas police report a 32-yr old convenience store owner in Houston was shot and killed as he was leaving the store with bank deposits.

California police respond to a shooting call at a home in northeast Modesto and find "a distraught male who apparently committed suicide."

Ohio authorities report a 19-yr old Canton man was playing around with a stolen gun, when it discharged and killed a 16-yr old boy in a house in Barberton.

Newark, New Jersey police respond to a shooting call to find a 58-yr old man on the ground with a fatal gunshot wound to his head. Investigation is ongoing.

Maryland police were investigating a report of drug dealing in Landover when the 40-yr old suspect fled carrying a gun. Suspect was tackled and then shot to death by police.

Kansas police report a 21-yr old man of Junction City was found shot to death in a parking lot. Three suspects, ages 17, 18, and 24, have been arrested and charged with murder.

Hampton, Virginia dispatchers received calls about a crime scene. When officers arrived, they find a 33-yr old man from Newport News shot to death. Investigation is ongoing.

Minneapolis police arrested a 33-yr old man in connection with the fatal shooting of a 28-yr old man in the Near North neighborhood. This is the city's 20th slaying of the year.

South Carolina deputies say three suspects broke through the door of a Blacksburg home looking for drugs. One of the suspects shot and killed a 26-yr old man and wounded a 19-yr old female.

Richmond, Virginia police were called to the scene of a shooting and located a 19-yr old man down from a gunshot wound. He was later pronounced dead at the scene.

Baltimore officers were patrolling when they heard gunshots near Hollins Street. They find a 29-yr old man with gunshot wounds to his body. He later died at an area hospital.

Chicago investigators say two men approached a 29-yr old woman and shot her in the Cragin neighborhood on the Northwest Side. She later died at Masonic Medical Center.

New Jersey authorities say a 19-yr old man was arrested and charged for the shooting death of a 20-yr old man from Keyport.

Seattle, Washington police have charged a 16-yr old suspect with the shooting death of a 37-yr old man at a High Point bus stop.

Arizona authorities arrested a man after he shot and killed three men from one family at a home in Wittmann.

California law enforcement report an estranged husband was arrested after police find two female bodies just three miles apart in Escondido. The two women were sisters.

Denver police are investigating a homicide scene where three homeless adults were found dead. All three were killed by gunshot. A 38-yr old suspect was later arrested.

California authorities report a 16-yr old male was stabbed to death in a Eureka cemetery. A 38-yr old woman and her 16-yr son have been charged with homicide.

Ohio police say a 59-yr old doctor was found dead from multiple gunshot wounds inside his home in Beachwood, near Cleveland. Police have identified his two sons as persons of interest.

North Carolina authorities report a 61-yr old High Point woman was shot and killed while she stood near a car that was mistaken as gang-related. Two 18-yr old men are charged.

~§~

"Man's inhumanity to man makes countless thousands mourn!" ~ Robert Burns, *Man Was Made to Mourn: A Dirge*

President Thomas Jefferson's Prayer for the Nation

Almighty God, Who has given us this good land for our heritage; we humbly beseech Thee that we may always prove ourselves a people mindful of Thy favor and glad to do Thy will. Bless our land with honorable ministry, sound learning, and pure manners. *Save us from violence, discord, and confusion, from pride and arrogance, and from every evil way.*

Defend our liberties, and fashion into one united people, *the multitude brought hither out of many kindreds and tongues.* Endow with Thy spirit of wisdom those whom in Thy name we entrust the authority of government, that there may be justice and peace at home, and that through obedience to Thy law, we may show forth Thy praise among the nations of the earth.

In time of prosperity fill our hearts with thankfulness, and in the day of trouble, suffer not our trust in Thee to fail; all of which we ask through Jesus Christ our Lord. Amen.

~§~

South African pastor Andrew Murray begins his twenty-first lesson of ***With Christ in the School of Prayer*** with these inspiring lines: "In all God's intercourse with us, the promise and its conditions are inseparable. *If we fulfill the conditions, He fulfills the promise.* What He is to be to us depends upon what we are willing to be to Him." I urge you to "enroll" in this school of prayer ASAP.

BibleScope Assignment

It's time for another assignment. Biblescopes in the ready. Let's go.

Hypothesis: *"God uses pain to get our attention."* Is this true or not?

Slide #1: Psalm 119:67 » "Before I was afflicted, I went astray; but now I observe your word."

Slide #2: Psalm 119:75 » "Yahweh, I know that your judgments are righteous, that in faithfulness you have afflicted me."

Slide #3: Psalm 119:71 » "It is good for me that I have been afflicted, that I may learn your statutes."

Slide #4: Hebrews 12:5-6 » "My son, don't take lightly the chastening of the Lord, nor faint when you are reproved by him; for whom the Lord loves, he chastens, and scourges every son whom he receives."

Slide #5: Lamentations 3:31-33 » "For the Lord will not cast off forever. For though he causes grief, yet he will have compassion according to the multitude of his loving kindnesses. For he does not afflict willingly, nor grieve the children of men [willingly]."

Slide #6: 2 Chronicles 7:12-14 » Then Yahweh appeared to Solomon by night, and said to him, "I have heard your prayer, and have chosen this place to myself for a house of sacrifice. If I shut up the sky so that there is no rain, or if I command the locust to devour the land, or if I send pestilence among my people, *if* my people, who are called by my name, will humble themselves, pray, seek my face, and turn from their wicked ways, *then* will I hear from heaven, will forgive their sin, and will heal their land."

Hypothesis: *"God uses pain to get our attention."*

Conclusion: "We can ignore even pleasure. But pain insists upon being attended to. God whispers to us in our pleasures, speaks to our conscience, but shouts in our pains: it is His megaphone to rouse a dead world." *~ C.S. Lewis*

The Almighty declares he may use a pandemic, a plague of vermin, and other painful means to get our attention. How should we respond if we witness these things taking place in America today? *What should we start or stop doing? What attitudes should we cultivate or terminate?*

In the last slide, Yahweh said he's chosen the new temple in Jerusalem for himself as a house of sacrifice. Earlier in 2 Chronicles 7:1-3, when the people of Israel dedicated this house to God, the glory of the LORD filled the temple. In this instance, "the glory of the LORD" refers to the visible manifestation of the invisible God. Some call it the Shekinah Glory, which is nothing less than God's abiding presence, the protective covering of the Most High. When the glory of the LORD filled the temple, this was the visible sign of his presence and his protection. But will his glory reign over Jerusalem if the people rebel against his word? No way! *If* those who are called by his name run after the gods of this world, Yahweh said, "*then* I will pluck them up by the roots out of the land...and this house, which I have made holy for my name, I will cast out of my sight, and I will make it a proverb and a byword among all peoples" (2 Chr.7:20).

The nation of Israel is to serve as an example for believers today (Romans 15:4; 1 Corinthians 10:11). This is a truth we often discount. As a result, we tend to miss the spiritual connections between ancient Israel and the body of Christ. If we desire to grow into mature soldiers of the cross, it's imperative that we take in, and teach to others, the whole counsel of God (Acts 20:25-27). Without an understanding of the nation of Israel, as it is conveyed in the Bible, we'll have major gaps in our understanding of how the LORD deals with his people today.

In this work, we'll consider several lengthy passages that will provide key insight into the nation. We'll see her rise, her rebellion, and her removal from the land. We'll witness what happens to a people when they turn their backs on God (Jeremiah 32:33). Please stay engaged as you read these passages from Scripture. I trust you'll discover that the dramatic episodes in the Bible makes for some of the best reading you'll find anywhere! Shakespeare has nothing on the author of Scripture. Plus, I've found that studying the Bible is a much better use of my time than watching another ball game or reality show. I pray that our heavenly Father, who knows all and sees all, will bless you for your diligence.

I'm a big fan of both the King James Version of the Bible as well as the New King James Version. One reason I decided to use the World English Bible (WEB) is because it's a free, public domain, very reliable, modern-English translation of the Scriptures. This allows me to include as many verses as I need to tell a full story. Sometimes, I'll insert a word or two within brackets [like so], in order to amplify a passage. I also emphasize words or sections by using underline, **bold** and *italic*.

We now move into the captivating history of Israel. The best person to provide a review of the rise of the nation is her famous deliverer, Moses. Deuteronomy, the last of the five books of Moses, is especially helpful when studying Yahweh's interaction with Israel. Let's drop in at chapter ten. This is forty years after the exodus from Egyptian bondage, and just before the children of Abraham venture into the land of milk and honey promised to their fathers.

As you read the following passage, please take note of a few things. *First*, notice how many times they are told to love God. Loving the Lord is not just a NT concept. "You shall love Yahweh your God with all your heart, with all your soul, and with all your might" (Deut. 6:5). *Secondly*, notice how Yahweh wants his word to be an integral part of their day-to-day life. Their religion was not to be just a "Temple on the Sabbath Day" kind of thing. It was to be an everywhere, everyday thing. They were commanded to focus on God's word from sunup to sundown (Deut. 11:19). *Finally*, notice the "If-Then" scenario. The Bible is teeming with them. As it so happens, 2 Chronicles 7:14 is a perfect example. God says, "**If** you do this, **then** I will do that." These are his conditional promises based upon their response to his word. Basically, the Most High is saying, "How you interact with my word, determines how I'll interact with you."

~ Lord, give us spiritual insight as we look into Your Word. ~

Moses said:

"Now, Israel, what does Yahweh your God require of you, but to fear Yahweh your God, to walk in all his ways, to love him, and to serve Yahweh your God with all your heart and with all your soul, to keep Yahweh's commandments and statutes, which I command you today for your good? Behold, to Yahweh your God belongs heaven, the heaven of heavens, and the earth, with all that is therein. *Only Yahweh had a delight in your fathers to love them, and he chose their offspring after them, even you above all peoples, as it is today.*

"Circumcise therefore the foreskin of your heart, and be no more stiff-necked. For Yahweh your God, he is God of gods and Lord of lords, the great God, the mighty, and the awesome, *who doesn't respect persons* or take bribes. He executes justice for the fatherless and widow and loves the foreigner in giving him food and clothing. Therefore love the foreigner, for you were foreigners in the land of Egypt. You shall fear Yahweh your

God. You shall serve him. You shall cling to him, and you shall swear by his name. He is your praise, and he is your God, who has done for you these great and awesome things which your eyes have seen. Your fathers went down into Egypt with seventy persons; and now Yahweh your God has made you as the stars of the sky for multitude. Therefore you shall love Yahweh your God, and keep his instructions, his statutes, his ordinances, and his commandments, always.

"Know this day – for I don't speak with your children who have not known, and who have not seen the **chastisement of Yahweh** your God, his greatness, his mighty hand, his outstretched arm, his signs and his works, which he did in the middle of Egypt to Pharaoh the king of Egypt, and to all his land; and what he did to the army of Egypt, to their horses, and to their chariots; how he made the water of the Red Sea to overflow them as they pursued you, and how Yahweh has destroyed them to this day; and what he did to you in the wilderness until you came to this place; and what he did to Dathan and Abiram, the sons of Eliab, the son of Reuben – how the earth opened its mouth and swallowed them up, with their households, their tents, and every living thing that followed them, in the middle of all Israel; but your eyes have seen all of Yahweh's great work which he did. Therefore you shall keep the entire commandment which I command you today, *that you may be strong,* and go in and possess the land that you go over to possess; and that you may prolong your days in the land which Yahweh swore to your fathers to give to them and to their offspring, a land flowing with milk and honey.

"For the land, where you go in to possess isn't like the land of Egypt that you came out of, where you sowed your seed and watered it with your foot, as a garden of herbs; but the land that you go over to possess is a land of hills and valleys which drinks water from the rain of the sky, a land which Yahweh your God cares for. Yahweh your God's eyes are always on it, from the beginning of the year even to the end of the year.

"It shall happen, **if** you shall listen diligently to my commandments which I command you today, to love Yahweh your God, and to serve him with all your heart and with all your soul, that [**then**] I will give the rain for your land in its season, the early rain and the latter rain, that you may gather in your grain, your new wine, and your oil. I will give grass in your fields for your livestock, and you shall eat and be full. *Be careful, lest your heart be deceived,* and you turn away to serve other gods and worship them; and Yahweh's anger be kindled against you, and he shut up the sky so that there is no rain, and the land doesn't yield its fruit; and you perish quickly from off the good land which Yahweh gives you.

"Therefore you shall lay up these words of mine in your heart and in your soul. You shall bind them for a sign on your hand, and they shall be for frontlets between your eyes. You shall teach them to your children, talking of them when you sit in your house, when you walk by the way, when you lie down, and when you rise up. You shall write them on the door posts of your house and on your gates; that your days and your children's days may be multiplied in the land which Yahweh swore to your fathers to give them, as the days of the heavens above the earth.

"For **if** you shall diligently keep all these commandments which I command you – to do them, to love Yahweh your God, to walk in all his ways, and to cling to him – **then** Yahweh will drive out all these nations from before you, and you shall dispossess nations greater and mightier than yourselves. Every place on which the sole of your foot treads shall be yours: from the wilderness and Lebanon, from the river, the river Euphrates, even to the western sea shall be your border. No man will be able to stand before you. Yahweh your God will lay the fear of you and the dread of you on all the land that you tread on, as he has spoken to you.

"Behold, I set before you today a **blessing** and a **curse**: the blessing, *if* you listen to the commandments of Yahweh your God, which I command you today; and the curse, *if* you do not listen to the commandments of Yahweh your God, but turn away out of the way which I command you today, to go after other gods which you have not known."

~ Deuteronomy 10:12-11:28

Four quick takeaways:

1. God is fulfilling his promise to the fathers. "Now Yahweh said to Abram, 'Leave your country, and your relatives, and your father's house, and go to the land that I will show you. I will make of you a great nation. I will bless you and make your name great. You will be a blessing. I will bless those who bless you, and I will curse him who treats you with contempt. All the families of the earth will be blessed through you.' " *~ Genesis 12:1-3*

Abraham is the physical father of the nation of Israel and the spiritual father of all believers in Christ (Galatians 3:26-29). The Abrahamic covenant, which the LORD announced in Genesis 12 and confirmed in Genesis 15, contains three distinct promises:

A) **The Promise of a Great Savior**. Pending! On this special day for Israel, the promise that "all the families of the earth will be blessed through you" is waiting for "the fullness of the time" when God will send the Savior "Jesus Christ, the son of David, the son of Abraham" (Galatians 3:7-9; 4:4; Matthew 1:1).

B) **The Promise of a Great Land**. Fulfilled! This is the day Israel will go in and possess it. "The land which Yahweh swore to your fathers to give to them and to their offspring, a land flowing with milk and honey" (Deuteronomy 11:9).

C) **The Promise of a Great Nation**. Fulfilled! "Your fathers went down into Egypt with seventy persons; and now Yahweh your God has made you as the stars of the sky for multitude" (Deuteronomy 10:22). *"Only Yahweh had a delight in your fathers to love them."* And now, God is making good on the great promises he made to them.

2. Moses reminds the children of Abraham that they are eye witnesses to the awesomeness of their God (Exodus 14:30,31). They are not being asked to trust in a God they don't know. These folks have seen Yahweh show up STRONG on their behalf time and time again.

3. Moses points out that Yahweh longs for their love, not just their obedience. God doesn't want his people to just "go through the motions" of a formal, cold, ritualistic religion. He wants a passionate relationship; he wants their heart, their whole heart.

4. God's name is Jealous, El Kanna. So Moses forewarns Israel that the road into the promise land will soon split into two paths, figuratively speaking. The god of this world walks along one path. Jealous walks along the other. One path will lead to blessings; the other will lead to curses. The message of the LORD is crystal. No gray area. No fuzziness. No ambiguity. Two distinct options: "Behold, I set before you today a blessing and a curse."

Chapter Four:

"Shall humble themselves,"

On August 31, 1986, during the peak summer vacation period, the SS *Admiral Nakhimov*, a Russian passenger liner, is sailing in the Black Sea en route to Sochi. The ship carries 1,234 souls on board.

At 11:00 p.m., many of the passengers are enjoying the night-life, listening to music and dancing on the deck of the ship. But at 11:12 p.m., from out of the darkness roars a massive Russian carrier ship. This bulk carrier, the *Pyotr Vasev*, is hauling a full cargo of oats and barley from Canada. It slams into the starboard side of the passenger liner, and rips a 900 square foot hole in the hull.

Three minutes after the collision, electrical power on the liner is completely lost, leaving passengers scrambling in the dark. The crash caused the ship to lean hard on her side, and since the windows in the cabins were open, she rapidly took on water. Four minutes after losing electricity, the SS *Admiral Nakhimov* sank to the bottom of the Black Sea, taking her trapped passengers with her. The liner went down so fast there was no time to launch the lifeboats. Hundreds of desperate men, women and children dove into the Black Sea, clinging to anything that floated.

By the grace of God, rescue ships began arriving just 10 minutes after the vessel went down. The *Pyotr Vasev* was also able to assist in the rescue. Some people were so slick with fuel oil, it was impossible to pull them from the sea. Instead, rescuers had to jump into the water and push them to safety. Over 800 souls were saved from a watery grave, but 423 people lost their lives.

News of the disaster was made even worse after the Soviet government launched an inquiry into the disaster. They discovered that the cause of the collision was not due to a technical issue like the radio not working, or a radar malfunction, or even thick fog. It was discovered the cause of the collision was human error. More specifically, it was human stubbornness. Each captain was aware of the other ship's presence nearby. The two shipmasters actually communicated to each other via radio. The inquiry showed both captains knew they were on a collision course, but neither one slowed down. Neither captain altered his course. Either one of them could have steered clear of the other. Either one of them could have responded in a way that would have saved the lives of 423 passengers. But sadly, such was not the case. Both captains were so committed to their own course, they refused to be the first one to yield. By the time a change in direction was absolutely imperative, it was too late. Based upon the evidence revealed during the inquiry, both captains were found guilty of criminal negligence and sentenced to 15 years in prison.

In his autobiography, Benjamin Franklin writes, "There is perhaps not one of our natural passions so hard to subdue as pride. Beat it down, stifle it, mortify it as much as one pleases, it is still alive. Even if I could conceive that I had completely overcome it, I should probably be proud of my humility."

Evangelist D. L. Moody of Chicago warns us, "**Be humble or you'll stumble**." It's not easy for humans to be humble. Americans, in particular, are not generally known as humble people. We are a proud and self-governing people. We're proud of our history, our accomplishments, and especially our independence. Which begs the question: *Are we so independent that we no longer sense our need for the Lord? Has our pride put us on a collision course with God?*

Dr. Billy Graham said, "Self-centered indulgence, pride and lack of shame over sin are now emblems of the American lifestyle. My heart aches for America and its deceived people."

When the country was torn apart by civil war, our leaders knew only the Prince of Peace could restore prosperity and peace. So guess what they did? They called for a national day of fasting, humiliation and prayer. We need more of these, i.e., entire days set aside for the nation to fall on our face before the King of heaven to repent and pray for revival. Our country is entangled in many debilitating issues today, but this Gordian knot is no match for the sword of the LORD! *We know the remedy.* The question now is, will we accept God's remedy or seek another?

The following is the actual text of the *Proclamation for a National Day of Fasting, Humiliation and Prayer* issued by President Lincoln, declaring April 30, 1863 as a national day of fasting. Read it slowly and prayerfully. This is how the timeless principle of 2 Chronicles 7:14 is activated for those who have understanding of the times, to know what the nation should do.

A Proclamation by the President of the United States

Whereas, the Senate of the United States, devoutly recognizing the supreme authority and just government of Almighty God, in all the affairs of *men* and *nations*, has, by a resolution, requested the President to designate and set apart a day for National prayer and humiliation;

And whereas, it is the duty of *nations*, as well as of *men*, to own their dependence upon the overruling power of God, to confess their sins and transgressions, in humble sorrow, yet with assured hope that genuine repentance will lead to mercy and pardon, and to recognize the sublime truths announced in the Holy Scriptures, and proven by all history, that those nations only are blessed whose God is the Lord;

And, inasmuch as we know that, by his divine law, *nations, like individuals,* are subjected to **punishments** and **chastisements** in this world, may we not justly fear that the awful calamity of civil war which now desolates the land, may be but a punishment inflicted upon us for our presumptuous sins, to the needful end of our national reformation as a whole people? We have been the recipients of the choicest bounties of Heaven. We have been preserved, these many years, in peace and prosperity. We have grown in numbers, wealth and power, as no other nation has ever grown. But we have forgotten God, we have forgotten the gracious hand which preserved us in peace, and multiplied and enriched and strengthened us; and we have vainly imagined, in the *deceitfulness of our hearts,* that all these blessings were produced by some superior wisdom and virtue of our own. Intoxicated with unbroken success, we have become too self-sufficient to feel the necessity of redeeming and preserving grace, too proud to pray to the God that made us!

It behooves us, then, to humble ourselves before the Offended Power, to confess our national sins, and to pray for clemency and forgiveness. Now, therefore, in compliance with the request, and fully concurring in the views of the Senate, I do by this proclamation designate and set apart Thursday, the 30th day of April, 1863, as a day of national humiliation, fasting and prayer. And I do hereby request all people to abstain from their ordinary secular pursuits, and to unite, at their several places of worship and their respective homes, in keeping the day holy to the Lord, and devoted to the humble discharge of the religious duties proper to that solemn occasion.

All this being done in sincerity and truth, let us then rest humbly in the hope, authorized by the Divine teachings, *that the united cry of the Nation will be heard on high* and answered with blessings, no less than the pardon of our national sins, and the restoration of our now divided and suffering country to its former happy condition of unity and peace.

In witness whereof, I have hereunto set my hand and caused the seal of the United States to be affixed. Done at the City of Washington, this thirtieth day of March, in the year of our Lord one thousand eight hundred and sixty-three, and of the independence of the United States the eighty-seventh.

~ Abraham Lincoln

~§~

I trust you'll agree that a similar proclamation is just what America needs today. *"It behooves us, then, to humble ourselves before the Offended Power, to confess our national sins, and to pray for clemency and forgiveness."* This decree is full of timeless, biblical principles we must apply today.

The very first step on the pathway to revival is to humble ourselves before the Most High. The Lord's indictment against the last ruler of Judah, King Zedekiah, is this: *"He didn't humble himself before Jeremiah the prophet speaking from Yahweh's mouth"* (2 Chronicles 36:12). God used the prophet to warn the king of impending judgment. But Zedekiah refused to give heed, and we'll see how that turned out later in the book.

Let's direct our attention now to another king and another kingdom. The king is Nebuchadnezzar. The kingdom is Babylon, one of the world's first superpowers. The Hanging Gardens of Babylon was one of the Seven Wonders of the Ancient World. The famous gardens were constructed alongside a grand palace by Nebuchadnezzar for his queen. She was from the land of Medes, and apparently the queen longed for the valleys and green hills of her region. To make her feel more at home, the king built the spectacular hanging gardens.

Babylon was the ruling military power of her day. There came a time when God used this nation to discipline the people of many other nations. Howbeit, when the king of Babylon got too big for his britches, Yahweh had to step in and put him in his place. The following account from the Old Testament book of Daniel will tell us all about it. And remember, we're not reading just to take in a great Bible story. "For whatever things were written before were written *for our learning,* that through perseverance and through encouragement of the Scriptures we might have hope." ~ *Romans 15:4*

~ Lord, give us spiritual insight as we look into Your Word. ~

Daniel 4

Nebuchadnezzar the king, to all the peoples, nations, and languages, who dwell in all the earth: Peace be multiplied to you. It has seemed good to me to show the signs and wonders that the Most High God has worked toward me. How great are his signs! And how mighty are his wonders! His kingdom is an everlasting kingdom, and his dominion is from generation to generation.

I, Nebuchadnezzar, was at rest in my house, and flourishing in my palace. I saw a dream which made me afraid; and the thoughts on my bed and the visions of my head troubled me. Therefore I made a decree to bring in all the wise men of Babylon before me, that they might make known to me the interpretation of the dream. Then the magicians, the enchanters, the Chaldeans, and the soothsayers came in; and I told the dream before them; but they did not make known to me the interpretation of it.

But at the last Daniel came in before me, whose name was Belteshazzar, according to the name of my god, and in whom is the spirit of the holy gods. I told the dream before him, saying, "Belteshazzar, master of the magicians, because I know that the spirit of the holy gods is in you, and no secret troubles you, tell me the visions of my dream that I have seen, and its interpretation.

These were the visions of my head on my bed: I saw, and, behold, a tree in the midst of the earth; and its height was great. The tree grew, and was strong, and the height of it reached to the sky, and its sight to the end of all the earth. Its leaves were beautiful, and it had much fruit, and in it was food for all. The animals of the field had shade under it, and the birds of the sky lived in its branches, and all flesh was fed from it.

I saw in the visions of my head on my bed, and, behold, a *watcher* and a *holy one* came down from the sky. He cried aloud, and said this, 'Cut down the tree, and cut off its branches! Shake off its leaves and scatter its fruit! Let the animals get away from under it, and the fowls from its branches. Nevertheless leave the stump of its roots in the earth, even with a band of iron and brass, in the tender grass of the field; and let it be wet with the dew of the sky. Let his portion be with the animals in the grass of the earth. Let his heart be changed from man's, and let an animal's heart be given to him. Then let seven times pass over him.

The sentence is by the decree of the watchers, and the demand by the word of the holy ones; to the intent that the living may know that the Most High rules in the kingdom of men, and gives it to whomever he will, and sets up over it the lowest of men.

This dream I, king Nebuchadnezzar, have seen; and you, Belteshazzar, declare the interpretation, because all the wise men of my kingdom are not able to make known to me the interpretation; but you are able; for the spirit of the holy gods is in you."

Then Daniel, whose name was Belteshazzar, was stricken mute for a while, and his thoughts troubled him. The king answered, "Belteshazzar, don't let the dream, or the interpretation, trouble you."

Belteshazzar answered, "My lord, may the dream be for those who hate you, and its interpretation to your adversaries. The tree that you saw, which grew, and was strong, whose height reached to the sky, and its sight to all the earth; whose leaves were beautiful, and its fruit plentiful, and in it was food for all; under which the animals of the field lived, and on whose branches the birds of the sky had their habitation: **it is you, O king**, that have grown and become strong; for your greatness has grown, and reaches to the sky, and your dominion to the end of the earth.

Whereas the king saw a *watcher* and a *holy one* coming down from the sky, and saying, "Cut down the tree, and destroy it; nevertheless leave the stump of its roots in the earth, even with a band of iron and brass, in the tender grass of the field, and let it be wet with the dew of the sky. Let his portion be with the animals of the field, until seven times pass over him."

"This is the interpretation, O king, and it is *the decree of the Most High*, which is come on my lord the king: that you shall be driven from men, and your dwelling shall be with the animals of the field. You shall be made to eat grass as oxen, and shall be wet with the dew of the sky, and seven times shall pass over you; until you know that the Most High rules in the kingdom of men, and gives it to whomever he will. Whereas they commanded to leave the stump of the roots of the tree; your kingdom shall be sure to you, after that you will have known that **the heavens do rule**. Therefore, O king, let my counsel be acceptable to you, and break off your sins by righteousness, and your iniquities by showing mercy to the poor. Perhaps there may be a lengthening of your tranquility."

All this came on the king Nebuchadnezzar. At the end of twelve months he was walking in the royal palace of Babylon. The king spoke and said, "*Is not this great Babylon, which I have built for the royal dwelling place, by the might of my power and for the glory of my majesty?*"

While the word was in the king's mouth, a voice came from the sky, saying, "O king Nebuchadnezzar, to you it is spoken: The kingdom has departed from you. You shall be driven from men; and your dwelling shall be with the animals of the field. You shall be made to eat grass as oxen. Seven times shall pass over you, until you know that the Most High rules in the kingdom of men, and gives it to whomever he will."

This was fulfilled the same hour on Nebuchadnezzar. He was driven from men, and ate grass as oxen, and his body was wet with the dew of the sky, until his hair was grown like eagles' feathers, and his nails like birds' claws.

At the end of the day I, Nebuchadnezzar, lifted up my eyes to heaven and my understanding returned to me, and I blessed the Most High, and I praised and honored him who lives forever; for his dominion is an everlasting dominion, and his kingdom from generation to generation. All the inhabitants of the earth are reputed as nothing; and he does according to his will in the army of heaven, and among the inhabitants of the earth; and no one can stop his hand, or ask him, "What are you doing?"

At the same time my understanding returned to me; and for the glory of my kingdom, my majesty and brightness returned to me. My counselors and my lords sought me; and I was established in my kingdom, and excellent greatness was added to me. Now I, Nebuchadnezzar, praise and extol and honor the King of heaven; **for all his works are truth, and his ways justice; and those who walk in pride he is able to abase.**

~§~

Yahweh humbled a grand heathen leader, the king of Babylon, in order to show him who's boss. An awesome God who reigns from heaven above is ruler over all the earth (Psalm 103:19-22). And now this humbled and grateful king wants all nations of the world to know the same. The Most High is Lord of all, "and those who walk in pride he is able to abase."

Our God hates it when we're arrogant and puffed up. Far too many Christians today seem to forget that Jesus Christ was a humble person (Matt. 11:29). Jesus Christ, meek and lowly in heart, is our ultimate role model (1 Cor. 11:1; Eph. 4:1-3; 5:1,2). Did you notice what Nebuchadnezzar was doing at the exact moment when he was judged? *What was he saying just before he lost his mind?* He was boasting. And "while the word was in the king's mouth, there fell a voice from the sky..."

The counsel from Proverbs or "Lady Wisdom" says, "Pride goes before destruction, and an arrogant spirit before a fall" (Proverbs 16:18). Sinners in need of grace have no reason to be prideful. According to Proverbs 6:16-17, the Lord **hates** arrogant eyes. He also **hates** a lying tongue, and a false witness who utters lies, and a person who sows discord among brothers. These acts are abominations to him.

We run across the word "abomination" a lot in the Bible. But what does it mean? **An abomination is a thing or action that causes disgust or hatred.** For example, "Lying lips are an abomination to Yahweh" (Proverbs 12:22). Lying lips are an abomination to the Lord, which means lying lips disgust God and arouses his hatred. Then we have, "A righteous man **hates** lies" (Proverbs 13:5). Why does a righteous person hate lies? The righteous man hates lies because God hates lies, and the righteous hate whatever God hates. The righteous man or woman loves whatever God loves, and hates whatever God hates. *Isn't that sort of what it means to be righteous?* So, when we see the word "abomination" in Scripture, that's a definite red flag.

Before the children of Abraham moved forward into the land promised to their fathers, Moses did his best to get them spiritually ready for what was ahead of them. He warned them of the many abominations they were to avoid. Moses warns Israel to not copy the behavior and the religion of the people groups they are about to displace. Because if they do, there'll be another displacement!

As we'll soon see, El Kanna will not tolerate his people playing kissy kissy with the gods of the world. Jealousy arouses the fury of a husband. God is so serious about this, that if someone attempted to cause a Jewish person to go after another god, that person was to be put to death. Even if a family member, or a best friend, or a so-called prophet enticed one to worship another god, that person was to be put to death. That's serious business! Yahweh says they may even be tested to see if they truly love their God. To observe how the preparation is going, let's pick up the account in Deuteronomy 12:28 – 13:11,

~ Lord, give us spiritual insight as we look into Your Word. ~

"Observe and hear all these words which I command you, that it may go well with you and with your children after you forever, when you do that which is good and right in Yahweh your God's eyes. When Yahweh your God cuts off the nations from before you where you go in to dispossess them, and you dispossess them and dwell in their land, *be careful* that you are not ensnared to follow them after they are destroyed from before you, and that you not inquire after their gods, saying, 'How do these nations serve their gods? I will do likewise.' You shall not do so to Yahweh your God; for every abomination to Yahweh, **which he hates**, they have done to their gods; for they even burn their sons and their daughters in the fire to their gods. Whatever thing I command you, that you shall observe to do. You shall not add to it, nor take away from it.

"If a prophet or a dreamer of dreams arises among you, and he gives you a sign or a wonder, and the sign or the wonder comes to pass, of which he spoke to you, saying, 'Let's go after other gods' (which you have not known) 'and let's serve them,' you shall not listen to the words of that prophet, or to that dreamer of dreams; *for Yahweh your God is testing you,* to know whether you love Yahweh your God with all your heart and with all your soul. You shall walk after Yahweh your God, fear him, keep his commandments, and obey his voice. You shall serve him, and cling to him. That prophet, or that dreamer of dreams, shall be put to death, because he has spoken rebellion against Yahweh your God, who brought you out of the land of Egypt and redeemed you out of the house of bondage, to draw you aside out of the way which Yahweh your God commanded you to walk in. So you shall remove the evil from among you.

"If your brother, the son of your mother, or your son, or your daughter, or the wife of your bosom, or your friend who is as your own soul, entices you secretly, saying, 'Let's go and serve other gods' – which you have not known, you, nor your fathers; of the gods of the peoples who are around you, near to you, or far off from you, from the one end of the earth even to the other end of the earth – you shall not consent to him nor listen to him; neither shall your eye pity him, neither shall you spare, neither shall you conceal him; but you shall surely kill him. Your hand shall be first on him to put him to death, and afterwards the hands of all the people. You shall stone him to death with stones, because he has sought to draw you away from Yahweh your God, who brought you out of the land of Egypt, out of the house of bondage. All Israel shall hear, and fear, and shall not do any more wickedness like this among you."

Moses continues to instruct them in Deuteronomy 18:9-14,

"When you have come into the land which Yahweh your God gives you, you shall not learn to imitate the abominations of those nations. There shall not be found with you anyone who makes his son or his daughter to pass through the fire, one who uses divination, one who tells fortunes, or an enchanter, or a sorcerer, or a charmer, or someone who consults with a familiar spirit, or a wizard, or a necromancer. For whoever does these things is an abomination to Yahweh. **Because of these abominations**, Yahweh your God drives them out from before you. You shall be blameless with Yahweh your God. For these nations that you shall dispossess listen to those who practice sorcery and to diviners; but as for you, Yahweh your God has not allowed you so to do."

Here we see the Almighty God warn his people to not "imitate the abominations of those nations." The false gods or deceiving spirits of that land had people committing all kinds of abominations to appease the deity. We're talking sacrificing their children in fire kind of stuff! How wicked is that! The devil works through false religions. But by means of religion or not, his objective is always the same. "The thief *only* comes to steal, kill, and destroy" (John 10:10).

God is saying to Israel, "Be careful, lest your heart be deceived. It is because of these abominations that I am now dispossessing these wayward people; so don't be like them, or you too will be dispossessed!" *The LORD God of the universe is no respecter of persons.* In his sight, we are all dust. Every race, every tribe. And every abominable act offends Yahweh. It arouses his hatred, and it makes no difference who commits it.

It was not their military might that would cause Jacob to possess the land. It was the God of Jacob who was leading the way (Psalm 44:1-3). Israel's role was to humbly follow their fearsome God. That was their role then. That's still their role, and our role, today. "He has shown you, O man, what is good. **What does Yahweh require of you**, but to act justly, to love mercy, and to walk humbly with your God?" (Micah 6:8).

If I asked you to define a paradox, what would you say? You might say something along these lines. "A paradox is a statement that seems to contradict itself, but when investigated, may prove to be true." Did you know the Bible is full of paradoxical ideas?

We lead by serving others, we become wise by being fools for Christ's sake, we find rest under his yoke, we see the unseen, we receive by giving, we conquer by yielding, and we live by dying.

It's no wonder the world doesn't understand us (Acts 26:22-25; 1 Cor. 1:18,19; 2:14)! Listen to the words of our Lord Jesus Christ.

> "He who loves his life will lose it, and he who hates his life in this world will keep it for eternal life." ~ *John 12:25 NKJV*
>
> "Assuredly, I say to you, unless you are converted and become as little children, you will by no means enter the kingdom of heaven. Therefore whoever humbles himself as this little child is the greatest in the kingdom of heaven." ~ *Matthew 18:3-4 NKJV*
>
> "And whoever exalts himself will be humbled, and he who humbles himself will be exalted." ~ *Matthew 23:12 NKJV*

We are exalted when we humble ourselves. Or, as Lady Wisdom put it, "Before honor is humility" (Proverbs 15:33). And conversely, we are humbled when we exalt ourselves. Or, as Lady Wisdom put it, "When pride comes, then comes shame" (Proverbs 11:2). Or, as the apostle Paul put it,

"Therefore let him who thinks he stands take heed lest he fall." ~ *1 Corinthians 10:12 NKJV*

General John Sedgwick was an 1837 graduate of the U.S. Military Academy at West Point. His grandfather was also a general who served with President Washington. After Sedgwick's commission, he assisted in the relocation of the Cherokee Nation from Georgia in 1838 to 1839. In the early 1840s, he engaged in warfare against the Seminoles in Florida. And he saw action in the Mexican-American War from 1846 to 1848. When our own Civil War broke out, he was stationed on the western frontier. He returned to Washington, assumed the role of inspector general of the city for a brief period, but was soon back in the thick of things.

General Sedgwick believed in leading from the front. At the battle of Antietam, he was carried unconscious from the field, but not before being wounded twice and having his horse shot from under him. The men loved General Sedgwick and often referred to him as "Uncle John." One of his most notable feats was leading the exhausted troops of the 6th Army Corps on a forced march in order to join the fight at Gettysburg. Yet, letters to his sister indicate he'd grown war-weary by the spring of 1864. Lots of American soldiers had fallen by that time. After nearly three decades of soldiering, Sedgwick witnessed his fair share of suffering.

On May 9, 1864, at the beginning of the Battle of Spotsylvania Court House, General Sedgwick was inspecting his troops and personally directing artillery placements. The Confederate line was set up about 1,000 yards away. "Uncle John" was talking with his staff and artillerymen when a bullet from the enemy line whizzed past them. They all ducked for cover, all except the general. He questioned them, "What? Men dodging this way for single bullets? What will you do when they open fire along the whole line?" Then another bullet whizzed by and they all flinch again. "Why are you dodging like this?" the general said, "They couldn't hit an elephant at this distance." Shortly after he spoke those words, a bullet struck the general under his left eye and he fell down mortally wounded. Talk about famous last words! When General Grant received notice back in Washington, he couldn't believe it. He kept asking, "Is he really dead?"

General Sedgwick was the highest-ranking Union officer killed in the entire war. His statue stands today at West Point. Maybe it's a reminder to our future leaders that whoever exalts himself will be humbled, and he who humbles himself will be exalted. I reckon that word "whoever" takes in just about everybody. No matter who you are, if you exalt yourself, you will be humbled. It makes no difference if you're the king of Babylon, or a military general, or a shoeshine specialist at LaGuardia Airport. If you exalt yourself, God says you will be humbled. Please note that the flip side of the paradox is backed by the same authority. "Humble yourselves therefore under the mighty hand of God, that he may exalt you in due time" (1 Peter 5:6).

Brothers and sisters of America, the Lord is keen on fulfilling his word, and he looks kindly on humble sons and daughters of Adam who tremble at his word (Isaiah 66:2). But those who forget the lesson of King Nebuchadnezzar in Babylon will be forced to go through remedial training. A wise nation learns from the experience of other nations. Some nations learn from their own experience. A foolish nation won't learn from anyone's experience.

"Be not proud of race, face, place, or grace." ~ C.H. Spurgeon

"For the high and lofty One who inhabits eternity, whose name is Holy, says: 'I dwell in the high and holy place, [I dwell] with him also who is of a contrite and humble spirit, to revive the spirit of the humble, and to revive the heart of the contrite.' " ~ *Isaiah 57:15*

"The LORD is near to those who have a broken heart, and saves such as have a contrite spirit." ~ *Psalm 34:18 NKJV*

"Like a father has compassion on his children, so Yahweh has compassion on those who fear him. For he knows how we are made. He remembers that we are dust." ~ *Psalm 103:13-14*

Chapter Five:

Why Satan Hates America

In this chapter, we'll spy the devil's work on August 10, 2018. It was another graphic display of man's inhumanity to man - which is energized by the evil one. But why does Satan hate us? Three motivations stand out in my mind. You may have never given much thought to these reasons before, but I hope you'll see where I'm coming from.

Three Reasons why Satan Hates the USA

First of all, if you have some cash handy, take it out and hold it in front of you. Look on the back side of the bill. What words do you see in the center? Do you see the words "In God We Trust"? Imagine that! A proclamation of faith in God printed on our money! How many other nations make such a statement of faith on their money? Hardly any. I believe this is one of the reasons why the devil has it in for America. **Words matter**. Satan hates us because we have the words, *"In God We Trust"* on our money. Think about the many ways those four simple words can inspire our citizens. What message does it send to other countries?

The term "In God We Trust" was adopted as our nation's official motto in 1956. It's been printed on our money for the last sixty-five years. Every time anyone in the world handles our paper money of any amount, they're handling official currency of the United States of America. And printed on our currency, for all the world to see, are the words: IN GOD WE TRUST. Does Russia or China have such a statement on their money? How about Germany or Japan or Canada or North Korea? No, they do not. The United States of America is one of the only nations on earth that prints on its money such a strong, bold affirmation of faith in God. It's a powerful message, especially in these later times (1 Timothy 4:1,2).

The dollar bill's message to her citizens is plain and simple, "Don't trust in me – Trust in God. Use me for good, but don't put your trust in me." The lesson is: Even though I'm holding this money in my hand, my faith is not in the money. Be it a $1 bill, or a $5 bill, or a $100,000 bill! It doesn't matter the amount; I will not trust in it. In God We Trust. The Bible says, "**He who trusts in his riches will fall**, but the righteous shall flourish as the green leaf" (Proverbs 11:28). First Timothy 6:17 has a word about money: "Charge those who are rich in this present world that they not be arrogant, nor have their hope set on the uncertainty of riches, *but on the living God...*" James 1:9-11 charges the rich to rejoice in being brought low, i.e., to the place where they trust in God instead of in riches.

In Psalm 121, King David of Israel asks the question, "Where does my help come from?" He then answers his own question. "My help comes from Yahweh, who made heaven and earth. He will not allow your foot to be moved. He who keeps you will not slumber. Behold, he who keeps Israel will neither slumber nor sleep. Yahweh is your keeper."

Since God is no respecter of persons, he who keeps America will neither slumber nor sleep. He who shields New Jersey, and covers the Carolinas, and shelters Colorado will not slumber. He who protects Pennsylvania, and defends Delaware, and watches over Small Town, USA, will not sleep. The God who supports the Golden Gate Bridge, and sits atop the Gateway Arch, and stands alongside the Statue of Liberty will neither slumber nor sleep!

The nations that submit to the Most High can rest assured that God is their keeper. Our faith is not in our troops, tanks, ships, subs, and planes. In God We Trust! Why? Because, *"There is no king saved by the multitude of an army. A mighty man is not delivered by great strength. A horse is a vain thing for safety, neither does he deliver any by his great power"* (Psalm 33:16,17). **God alone is our supreme protector**.

On July 30, 2006, during the anniversary of the 1956 bill to adopt "In God We Trust" as our national motto, our President stated, "As we commemorate the 50th anniversary of our national motto and remember with thanksgiving God's mercies throughout our history, we recognize a divine plan that stands above all human plans and continue to seek His will."

Fellow citizen, is Satan happy about our proclamation to trust in the Lord? Is the devil pleased that we tell all the other nations on the planet - "In God We Trust"? Does Lucifer want the world to know that Americans recognize a divine plan that stands above all human plans? Does Beelzebub want our nation exalted like a shining city on a hill as we proclaim our faith in Almighty God? Is our adversary delighted to see the US dollar travel around the globe carrying our bold affirmation of faith? I think not. Will the devil work for us or against us?

Satan, the father of lies and deceiver of nations, is not thrilled that we proclaim to trust in God. His desire is that we trust in his lies. Jesus Christ said Satan is a murderer and the father of lies. *Lies and death are running buddies.* Nations have fallen because her people trusted in lies. Herr Hitler proclaimed to the Germans that they were a superior race of people, and that "might makes right." He promised the German nation if they trusted in him, he would subdue the lower races of people, and usher in a kingdom that would last 1,000 years. Italy's leader, Mussolini, foolishly threw in his lot with Hitler. Japan also embraced the tall tale that they were a superior race blessed with a divine leader. *It was the lies of racial supremacy, and eugenics, and Darwinism that fostered the hyper-nationalism which steered the eager masses into World War I and II.* But how did the lies work out for the Germans and Italians by the spring of 1945? How did it work out for Japan by August of 1945?

Who won WWI and WWII? We say the Allies "won" the war, but on another level, Satan won. He brought death and destruction to between 105 and 115 million people! These were the deadliest military conflicts in the long history of the human race, and they were fueled by his lies. A nation is blessed when her people trust in God (Psalm 33:12). Recent history shows us lies serve as a faulty foundation for any country. We've witnessed nations reduced to rubble because her people put their trust in falsehoods, conspiracies, and half-truths. Hitler lied and Germans died!

Satan hates America because we proclaim on our money, for all the nations of the world to see, "In God We Trust." We know it's not wise to trust in man. The LORD is our strong tower. "He <u>alone</u> is my rock and my salvation, my fortress. I will not be shaken" (Psalm 62:6). In Psalm 146:3 KJV, we find this admonition: "Put not your trust in princes, nor in the son of man, in whom is no help." The sweet psalmist knew the right one to ask for protection: "Give us help against the enemy, **for the help of man is vain**" (Psalm 108:12).

Another reason the devil hates America is because we have Bibles in our homes. Did you know the Bible is kryptonite to the devil? Indeed, it is! God wrote a book, one of the earliest and most potent forms of technology known to man. And in that book the light of God shines forth. But that's a problem if you're trying to keep people in spiritual darkness. Did you know there are entire nations where the Bible is outlawed? The Voice of the Martyrs, an organization founded by a minister who was imprisoned for 14 years because of his faith, has compiled a long list of countries, such as Iran and North Korea, where sharing the gospel message and giving someone a Bible could land you in jail for a long time. Is that God's will? Why is there such animosity towards the Holy Bible? At least part of the answer can be found in the NT book of 2 Cor. 4:3-4 KJV,

> "But if our gospel be hid, it is hid to them that are lost: In whom the god of this world hath *blinded the minds of them which believe not,* lest the light of the glorious gospel of Christ, who is the image of God, should shine unto them."

Satan, the god of this world, blinds the minds of unbelievers. How so? One way is by keeping the lost as far away from the Bible as he can! The Bible carries the gospel and the gospel carries the light. If your mission is to keep people in darkness, then you get rid of the light.

As citizens of America, we can take heart in knowing that owning the Holy Bible is a part of our Constitutional Rights. Freedom of Religion is safeguarded in the First Amendment. But riddle me this: *What's the difference between a lady in North Korea who can't read the Bible and a lady in North Carolina who won't read the Bible?*

If the devil had his way, there would be Bible-burning parties on every block in this country until the last Bible is burnt to ashes. When Satan had Germany by the throat, the Nazis publicly burned the Hebrew Scriptures. Later in the book, we'll see his other attempts to destroy the word of God.

The devil hates the Bible. If Satan hates the Bible, how should we feel about it? The righteous person loves whatever God loves, and hates what God hates. The righteous person will also hate whatever Satan "loves," and love what Satan hates. Satan hates the word of God. Correspondingly, "How **I love your law**! It is my meditation all day." "I hate double-minded men, but **I love your law**." "I hate and abhor falsehood. **I love your law**." "Those who **love your law** have great peace. Nothing causes them to stumble." ~ *Psalm 119: 97, 113, 163, 165*

I love the LORD and I love his Word! Why? Because the Bible reveals Satan's past defeats and his ultimate demise. The Holy Bible also teaches us how to live a Spirit-filled, victorious life. And virtually everyone in this country either owns a Bible or has access to one. No wonder the devil hates America.

Do you want to take a guess at the very first book published in North America? That would be the Book of Psalms from the Old Testament. Back in 1640, Stephen Daye published the first book in what would later become the United States of America at Harvard College in Cambridge, Massachusetts. It is entitled – *The Whole Booke of Psalmes, Faithfully Translated into English Metre*.

It's better known as the *Bay Psalm Book*. The work was meant to be a faithful translation into English of the original Hebrew Psalms. Some 1,700 copies were printed, a remarkable achievement just 20 years following the Pilgrims' landing at Plymouth. One of the eleven last known surviving copies of the first edition of the *Bay Psalm Book* sold at auction in November 2013 for $14.2 million. From her infancy, America has been a nation of the Word.

But why does Satan hate the Bible again? He hates the Word because it carries the light of the glorious gospel of Christ. It's the light of the gospel that shines the way out for those who are trapped in the den of sin. He also hates the Bible because it exposes him. Satan is the great deceiver. **His greatest deception is convincing humans there is no Satan.** The prince of darkness likes to operate in ... darkness. This is where the Bible comes in, because it shines the light of God on everything, including the deceiver of the nations.

Evangelist Billy Graham would say, "On the cover of your Bible and my Bible appear the words *'Holy Bible.'* Do you know why the Bible is called holy? Why should it be called holy when so much lust and hate and greed and war are found in it? I can tell you why. It is because the Bible tells the truth. It tells the truth about God, about man, and about the devil."

Indeed! Satan hates the Bible because it tells the truth about him and it exposes him. The Bible reveals to us the tricks and schemes and wiles of the evil one. And most importantly, the Bible shows us how to fight back and win.

There's a moment in the classic movie, *Wizard of Oz*, when Toto pulls back the curtain in the court, and Dorothy discovers that the so-called "Great Oz" isn't a wizard at all, he's just a showman. When the Oz fears he's exposed, he franticly works his contraption and thunders, *"Pay no attention to that man behind the curtain!"* But it's too late. By looking at the world through the lens of Scripture, the curtain to the spirit world is pulled back. Those who read and believe the Bible understand the truth about Satan.

In John 8:44, he is a murderer, and branded "a liar" and "the father of lies" by our Lord Jesus. In 2 Corinthians 2:11, he takes advantage of believers who are ignorant of his schemes. In Genesis 3:1-15, he is disguised as the serpent in the garden. In Isaiah 14:12-15, he is Lucifer, son of the morning, before his fall. In Ezekiel 28:12-19, he is the anointed cherub that covers, before his fall. In 1 Chronicles 21:1-8, he stood up against Israel and energized David to sin. In Job 1:7-2:7, he accused and afflicted Job, a man who was blameless and upright. In Matthew 4:1-11 and Luke 4:1-13, he is the brash tempter of our Lord Jesus. In Acts 10:38 and Matthew 12:22, he oppresses those under his power.

In Ephesians 2:2, he is the prince of the powers of the air. In Matthew 4:6, he perverts the Word of God. In Zechariah 3:1, he is Satan, the adversary who opposes Joshua the high priest. In John 13:2, 27, he caused Judas to betray Christ. In Mark 8:32, he spoke through Peter to hinder God's plan of redemption. In Acts 5:3, he caused Ananias to lie. In 2 Corinthians 4:4, he is the god of this world who blinds the minds of unbelievers. In 1 Peter 5:8, he is our adversary, the devil who walks around seeking his next victim. In Ephesians 2:2, he is the spirit who now works in the children of disobedience. In John 8:44, he is the father of the unredeemed. In Ephesians 6:12, he heads a celestial hierarchy of principalities, powers, and spiritual forces of wickedness. In 2 Thessalonians 2:9, he works through the "son of destruction" with all power and signs and lying wonders. In John 12:31 and 14:30, Jesus calls him the prince of this/the world. In Luke 13:16, he bound a daughter of Abraham for eighteen years.

In Matthew 13:19, he snatches away the Word from the hearts of those who don't understand. In Revelation 12:10, he is the accuser of our brothers, who accuses them before our God day and night. In Matthew 13:38-39, he is the enemy, the evil one who sows his children (weeds) among God's children (wheat). In Revelation 20:1-3, he is called the dragon, the old serpent, the devil and Satan.

In 1 Thessalonians 2:18, he hinders the will of believers. In Revelation 12:9, he is the great dragon and the deceiver of the whole world. In Luke 22:31, the Lord Jesus said Satan asked for Simon, that he might sift him as wheat. In Revelation 2:9-10, he has a synagogue of legalists who oppress and imprison the faithful. In Acts 13:10, he fills Elymas the sorcerer with all deceit, making him the enemy of all righteousness. In Hebrews 2:14, he holds the power of death. And in 2 Corinthians 11:14, the deceiver Satan masquerades as an angel of light!

Now the good part! In Luke 10:18, Jesus said He saw Satan having fallen like lightning from heaven. In Ephesians 6:16, we can take up our shield of faith to quench all of his fiery darts. In 1 Peter 5:9, we can resist him by living steadfast in the faith. In Ephesians 6:11, we can put on the whole armor of God in order to stand against his wiles. In Matthew 4:1-11 and Luke 4:1-13, our Lord showed us how to wield the sword of the Spirit against his lies. In James 4:7, when we submit to God and resist the devil, he will flee from us. In Matthew 25:41, the Most High has prepared a terrible end for him and his team. In Revelation 20:10, he is the deceiver who will be thrown into the lake of fire. And in Romans 16:20, the God of Peace will soon crush him under our feet!

Is it any wonder Satan can't stand the Holy Scriptures? He hates America because we have our affirmation of faith in God on our money, we have the Word of God in our homes, and thirdly, he hates America because we're still the top missionary-sending nation in the world. After my time in the military, I was fortunate to attend and graduate from Columbia Bible College, now called Columbia International University in Columbia, SC. Our school motto is *"To Know Him and to Make Him Known."* About 25% of the students from that university and seminary serve in foreign mission fields after they graduate.

Moody Bible Institute, Columbia Bible College, Dallas Theological Seminary, and various denominational and interdenominational schools of like faith all across America are training camps for spiritual warriors who spread the glorious gospel of Jesus Christ around the globe. Nationwide, over 100,000 devoted Christians travel abroad to do mission work each year. No other nation sends out more missionaries with the good news, and that's bad news for Satan.

The apostle Paul was arguably the finest missionary in the history of the church. As you probably know, Paul did not start out as a missionary and apostle for Jesus Christ. There was a time when Paul's name was Saul, and he was a fierce opponent of Jesus. He actually oversaw the arrest and death of Christians! Saul was a Jew. Not just a Jew, but a devout Pharisee, which was the strictest sect of their religion (Acts 26:5). Therefore, he was an enemy of the gospel (Romans 11:28a). He hated the faith and the faithful. But God saw fit to grant him grace and call him to a special work with the Gentiles. Listen as he shares his extraordinary testimony to King Agrippa.

> "I myself most certainly thought that I ought to do many things contrary to the name of Jesus of Nazareth. I also did this in Jerusalem. I both shut up many of the saints in prisons, having received authority from the chief priests, and when they were put to death I gave my vote against them. Punishing them often in all the synagogues, I tried to make them blaspheme. *Being exceedingly enraged against them,* I persecuted them even to foreign cites. Whereupon as I traveled to Damascus with the authority and commission from the chief priests, at noon, O king, I saw on the way a light from the sky, brighter than the sun, shining around me and those who traveled with me. When we had all fallen to the earth, I heard a voice saying to me in the Hebrew language, 'Saul, Saul, why are you persecuting me? It is hard for you to kick against the goads.'
>
> "I said, 'Who are you, Lord?'
>
> "He said, 'I am Jesus, whom you are persecuting. But arise, and stand on your feet, for I have appeared to you for this purpose: to appoint you a servant and a witness both of the things which you have seen, and of the things *which I will reveal to you* [see Eph. 3:1-6]; delivering you from the people, and from the Gentiles, to whom I send you, **to open their eyes, that they may turn from darkness to light and from the power of Satan to God,** that they may receive remission of sins and an inheritance among those who are sanctified by faith in me.' " ~ *Acts 26:9-18*

Saul was already under conviction before his encounter with Christ on the road to Damascus, "It is hard for you to kick against the goads." Jesus Christ himself appeared to Saul and commissioned him to be a witness to the Gentiles. Jesus Christ himself makes an important statement regarding salvation. He says that the "remission of sins and an inheritance among those who are sanctified" comes about how? *"By faith in me."* And Jesus Christ himself said Paul was being sent to the Gentiles to do what? "To open their eyes, that they may turn from darkness to light and from the power of Satan to God."

In Paul's day, as well as in our day, when a co-worker of the Lord bears witness to the gospel of Jesus Christ, God is able to open the eyes of the unbeliever in order "that they may turn from darkness to light and from the power of Satan to God." Now that's a remarkable statement from our Lord Jesus Christ! Is he a liar? People can actually turn from darkness to light, from the power of Satan to God? Wow. Isn't that an interesting concept. In Colossians 1:12-14, we find this treasure:

> "Giving thanks to the Father, who made us fit to be partakers of the inheritance of the saints in light, who **delivered us out** of the power of darkness, and **translated us into** the Kingdom of the Son of his love, in whom we have our redemption, the forgiveness of our sins."

The Bible is clear. Children of Adam can actually be forgiven of their sins, delivered out of the power of darkness, and translated into the Kingdom of God. Which implies unbelievers are lost in their sins, trapped in the power of darkness, and blinded by the god of this world. But when the Spirit-filled missioner comes to town and shares the good news, unbelievers become believers, and the captives are set free from the powers that be. Isn't that exactly what our Master was anointed to do? Isn't that what our Master calls and equips us to do?

> "The Spirit of the Lord is on me, because he has anointed me to preach good news to the poor. He has sent me to heal the broken hearted, to proclaim release to the captives, recovering of sight to the blind, to deliver those who are crushed, and to proclaim the acceptable year of the Lord." *~ Luke 4:18-19*

You may recall hearing the story of a missionary in China who was contacted by an international oil company. She worked in a small village deep in the interior of the country. The executives at the oil firm figured this experienced missionary would be a valuable asset to them since she was well-versed in the culture, the language, and the lay of the land. The company offered her a handsome salary to work for them, but the missionary turned it down. A week later, the firm doubled the proposition. She turned it down again. A few days later, they made her a third, very generous offer. But again, she declined. Finally, the company representative said, "Ma'am, what do you want? We can't offer more money than that." The missionary replied, "You don't understand. The money doesn't have anything to do with it. The job is too small."

For many believers, there's no job in the world more important than obeying the great commission to reach the unredeemed for Christ. "For the Son of Man came to seek and to save that which was lost" (Luke 19:10). "As the Father has sent me, even so I send you" (John 20:21).

The Spirit teaches us in Daniel 12:2-3, "Many of those who sleep in the dust of the earth will awake, some to everlasting life, and some to shame and everlasting contempt. Those who are **wise** will shine as the brightness of the expanse. *Those who turn many to righteousness* will shine as the stars forever and ever." Lady Wisdom declares, "The fruit of the righteous is a tree of life. He who is **wise** wins souls" (Proverbs 11:30).

Aside from the plain command to do so, why do the wise set out to win souls? Is it because wise people live life focused on both time *and* eternity, on both their present life *and* their future life? The foolish focus only on the here and now. The wise know JAH inhabits eternity (Isaiah 57:15). Therefore, their focus is on the here *and* the hereafter. They're very conscious of the fact that "those who sleep in the dust of the earth" will one day awake and face the Judge of Eternity. And since the Lord Jesus Christ told us there's joy up yonder when one sinner repents (Luke 15:10), the wise invest their resources to create joy and happiness in heaven.

Believers who obey the command to reach the lost for Christ will be greatly rewarded in the world to come. They'll shine as the stars forever. But the foolish ones who live only for themselves, and waste their short time on earth (James 4:14), will awake to shame and everlasting contempt. Soul-winning is the bane of Satan, and the blessed work of every believer. In that great getting up morning, will you be counted among the wise?

"Now, little children, remain in him, that when he appears, we may have boldness and not be ashamed before him at his coming" (1 John 2:28). Jesus Christ commands us to lay up treasures in heaven (Matthew 6:20), but how can we do that? When our Lord appears, how can we have confidence and not be ashamed before him?

The apostle gives us a clue when he writes to a group of believers that he and Silas recently won to the Lord. He states in 1 Thessalonians 2:19-20, "For what is our hope, or joy, or crown of rejoicing? **Isn't it even you**, before our Lord Jesus at his coming? For you are our glory and our joy." In Acts 17:1-4, we see Paul and Silas winning souls for Christ. Later on, in his letter to these same believers, Paul says on the day of the Lord's return these converts will be, for himself and Silas, a crown of rejoicing, "our glory and our joy." Satan hindered Paul from visiting his children in Christ (1 Thess. 2:18), but nothing can stop the return of our Lord Jesus! And on that wonderful day, the souls led to Jesus Christ by Paul and his co-workers will be like a winner's wreath, a victor's crown of rejoicing. Therefore, if we desire to have boldness and not be ashamed when Jesus returns, we must remain in him and lay up heavenly treasures now.

- *When I enter that beautiful city,*
- *And the saints in glory draw near,*
- *I want someone to greet me and tell me,*
- *"It was you who invited me here!"*

~§~

Satan hates America because we proclaim "In God We Trust" on our money, we have Bibles in our homes, and we support our foreign ambassadors of Christ. He seeks to destroy us from within and without.

Friday, August 10, 2018 United States of America

North Carolina Sheriff's Office report a 14-yr old male was shot in the town of Robbins. He was taken to FirstHealth Moore Regional Hospital in Pinehurst where he was pronounced dead.

Florida investigators say a 32-yr old woman was in a drive-thru line in Jacksonville when she was shot and killed by a man who then fled the scene.

Arizona authorities say that when a 24-yr old Phoenix man discovered his 22-yr old husband wanted a divorce, he beat him to death with a hammer.

California Highway Patrol report a 74-yr old mother and her 56-yr old daughter were killed after a DUI driver caused a wrong way crash on the 91 Freeway in Riverside.

Kansas police report a 26-yr old mother from Columbia, Missouri intentionally drove an SUV into the Kansas River, killing her five-yr old daughter and injuring her one-yr old son.

Georgia police report a 44-yr old man was shot and killed in the living room of his house in Columbus. Investigation is ongoing.

Chicago authorities say a 28-yr old woman was shot in the back and killed by a man that she was getting an order of protection against. A 15-yr old boy was wounded.

Detroit police believe a 19-yr old man was dancing and playing with a handgun, when it discharged and killed him.

North Carolina couple in Marion is facing manslaughter charges after their son's friend accidentally shot and killed himself with one of the weapons in their house.

Tennessee police say a 33-yr old man is dead and another in critical condition after their argument escalated into a barrage of bullets in the Orange Mound section of Memphis.

Baton Rouge police report a 20-yr old man was arrested after he fired into a car, injuring a 35-yr old Port Allen man, who later died in an area hospital.

Phoenix police arrested a 26-yr old man on suspicion of fatally shooting his 19-yr old cousin after they struggled over a gun.

California Highway Patrol arrested a 24-yr old Boulder Creek woman on suspicion of DUI after a pedestrian was struck and killed on California Highway 9.

Florida authorities arrested a man from Stanford for murder and kidnapping after police find his 82-yr old wife tied to a bed at home and fatally wounded from multiple stabs.

Louisiana police report finding the body of an unidentified male on the roadside near Denham Springs. Livingston Parish Sheriff's Office is regarding the case as a homicide.

Florida investigators say they discovered the body of a 44-yr old man in a freshly dug hole in the backyard of a home in Orlando. A 31-yr old man was arrested.

Georgia law enforcement responding to a shooting in southwest Atlanta find a woman with a fatal gunshot wound to the chest. Investigation is ongoing.

California police report a 25-yr old man shot two people at a family gathering in Carlsbad. A female victim was wounded. A male victim died from his wounds.

Indiana police say a 37-yr old female passenger in a stolen car died when the driver lost control and crashed into a tree on the south side of Indianapolis.

Texas police in Henderson County say a 76-yr old male shot and killed a 50-yr old woman at a convenience store in Frankston, then went home and killed himself.

Shreveport police find a 36-yr old man shot to death in the passenger seat of a stolen SUV in Caddo Parish. Authorities later find the 35-yr old driver of the stolen vehicle, who was also fatally wounded.

Wisconsin authorities say three people were shot at a Milwaukee gas station, including a 41-yr old man who died. The gunfire was the result of an on-going dispute.

Texas law enforcement found a 36-yr old man shot to death inside a wrecked car in southeast Dallas. Witnesses say an SUV was seen driving from the scene.

Virginia police report a 56-yr old man pushed aside his 84-yr old stepfather as he attacked and killed a 54-yr old female with a blunt object inside a Manassas home.

Georgia authorities say a 38-yr old woman was found stabbed to death at a hotel in Norcross after a domestic dispute. A 37-yr old man was taken into custody.

Illinois police report a 24-yr old man was stabbed to death in Decatur when he refused to share a $150 poker machine jackpot. A 48-yr old man has been charged with murder.

Detroit law enforcement report a 24-yr old man was shot multiple times and killed while driving on the city's west side. Police say two men fled the scene.

Arkansas police say a couple was having an argument when the husband shot and killed his wife in their home in Paragould.

Los Angeles police report a woman who had been reported missing was found shot to death along with a dead man in a possible murder-suicide in the Westlake District.

Alabama police responded to a call about a subject down in Montgomery, and found a 29-yr old victim of a fatal gunshot wound. Five suspects have been arrested.

Ohio authorities report a woman told dispatchers that she and a 57-yr old man were outside in Dayton, when someone shot him. He later died at Miami Valley Hospital.

California authorities say a 78-yr old man was crossing the street in downtown Los Angeles when he was fatally struck by an SUV that fled the scene.

Chicago police report an 18-yr old man was found with a fatal gunshot wound to the head in an alley in the Brighton Park neighborhood. The previous weekend, 74 people were shot and 12 people killed in Chicago.

Louisiana State police report officers responded to a domestic disturbance call in Denham Springs to find an armed man, who was later shot and killed.

Richmond, Virginia police discovered a 21-yr woman of Louisa County shot to death in the driver's seat of an SUV. Police also find two children unharmed in the back seat.

North Carolina authorities say a 47-yr old man was shot and killed in front of his home in Harnett County by a 39-yr old man. Three other people were charged with accessory.

Pennsylvania authorities say a pizza delivery man in Beaver Falls shot and killed a 29-yr old man who stabbed him and attempted to rob him. The driver was not charged.

Massachusetts police report a 24-yr old man was shot multiple times after he attempted to rob a cab driver in New Bedford. The victim was pronounced dead at St. Luke's Hospital.

Louisiana authorities say a 31-yr old New Orleans man faces charges after he beat to death another man who attempted to steal his wallet.

Nevada police report a 38-yr old man faces murder charges after an alleged fight left his 38-yr old male roommate dead inside their downtown Las Vegas apartment.

California police report a 30-yr old man from Pinole was shot and killed and two others were wounded in a gang-related feud between North Richmond and Central Richmond.

Florida police report a Miami Beach man, who was charged days before for violating fishing regulations, is charged in the beating death of his girlfriend's three-yr old daughter.

Michigan authorities report a 27-yr old Detroit mother, accused of driving under the influence, caused a wrong-way crash on 7 Mile Road that killed her three-yr old son.

Texas officials say a 55-yr old man from Ingleside was found dead inside the living room of his home from apparent gunshot wounds. The victim's 30-yr old son was charged with murder.

~§~

President Ronald Reagan's Prayer for the Nation

It is time to realize that we need God more than He needs us. The time has come to turn to God and reassert our trust in Him for the healing of America. We also have His promise that we can take to heart with regard to our country, that *"If my people, which are called by my name, shall humble themselves, and pray, and seek my face, and turn from their wicked ways; then I will hear from heaven and will forgive their sin, and will heal their land."* Our country is in need of, and ready for, a spiritual renewal. Today, we utter no prayer more fervently than the ancient prayer for peace on Earth. It is that one we're so familiar with: "The Lord bless you and keep you; the Lord make His face to shine upon you and be gracious unto you; the Lord lift up His countenance upon you and give you peace. Amen."

I wonder how American believers would respond if we were given the option of receiving the blessings of God because of our obedience, or receiving the curses of God because of our disobedience? The choice may seem obvious, but reality and the biblical record show some things are easier said than done. As we are about to see, Israel was called out to be the special and peculiar people of God. In Deuteronomy 26:16-19, Moses is quick to inform the witness nation that privilege comes with well-defined expectations. In other words, to whom much has been given, much will be required.

> "Today Yahweh your God commands you to do these statutes and ordinances. You shall therefore keep and do them with all your heart and with all your soul. You have declared today that Yahweh is your God, and that you would walk in his ways, keep his statutes, his commandments, and his ordinances, and listen to his voice. **Yahweh has declared today that you are a people for his own possession**, as he has promised you, and that you should keep all his commandments. He will make you high above all nations that he has made, in praise, in name, and in honor; and that you may be a holy people to Yahweh your God, as he has spoken."

This was truly an exceptional, red-letter day for Israel. According to Deuteronomy 1:3, this happened "in the fortieth year, in the eleventh month, on the first day of the month." As you may recall from Sabbath school or Bible study, the Lord condemned Israel to 40 years of wandering around in the wilderness of Sinai as judgment for their rebellion at Kadesh-Barnea (Numbers 14:33-35). Well, this is the fortieth year! The children of Abraham served their time of punishment and it's a new day for them. On this day they "avouched" or affirmed their commitment to Yahweh. Look at Deuteronomy 26:17 in several translations.

Complete Jewish Bible: "You are agreeing today that ADONAI is your God and that you will follow his ways."

New King James Version: "Today you have proclaimed the LORD to be your God, and that you will walk in His ways."

King James Version: "Thou hast avouched the LORD this day to be thy God, and to walk in his ways."

Not only did the nation of Israel affirm their commitment to God on this day, but God also affirmed his commitment to them. Brother James tells us, “Draw near to God, and he will draw near to you.” Consider Yahweh’s response in Deuteronomy 26:18.

Complete Jewish Bible: “In turn ADONAI is agreeing today that you are his own unique treasure, as he promised you...”

New King James Version: “Also today the LORD has proclaimed you to be His special people, just as He promised you...”

King James Version: “And the LORD hath avouched thee this day to be his peculiar people, as he hath promised thee...”

So on this day, after serving their 40-year sentence, Israel stands on the brink of the promise land. They proclaim to the Lord that he is their God, and God proclaims to Israel that they are his own possession. This must have been a great day. “The Lord is our God, and we are His people!” Folks, it doesn’t get much better than that. My dream is for this to become our rallying cry, our shout of praise, the battle-cry of America: **“The LORD is our God, and we are His people!”** Why do I say that? Because Satan hates America and he conspires against us every hour of every day! But if *God* be for us, who can be against us? For poor, undeserving sinners in need of grace, that’s the greatest privilege imaginable. But if *God* be against us, who can be for us?

Israel is to be God’s witness nation, set high above all other nations in praise, in name, and in honor. For this reason, Yahweh sets before them a long list of possible blessings, and a longer list of possible curses. As his witness to the world, Israel is to live up to certain expectations. Meeting those expectations will result in blessings galore. Failing to meet them will result in curses galore. Deuteronomy 28 or D28 is one of the most astonishing chapters in the entire Bible. I don’t want to oversell it, but if this is your first time reading D28, prepare to be blown away. If you’ve read it before, I ask that you put yourself in a state of mind as if this is your first time hearing about these blessings and curses. Read it carefully and prayerfully (Psalm 119:18). Take your time. For “these are the words of the covenant which Yahweh commanded Moses to make with the children of Israel.”

~ Lord, give us spiritual insight as we look into Your Word. ~

Deuteronomy 28

"It shall happen, **if** you shall listen diligently to Yahweh your God's voice, to observe to do all his commandments which I command you today, that [**then**] Yahweh your God will set you high above all the nations of the earth. All these blessings will come upon you, and *overtake you,* **if** you listen to Yahweh your God's voice. You shall be blessed in the city, and you shall be blessed in the field. You shall be blessed in the fruit of your body, the fruit of your ground, the fruit of your animals, the increase of your livestock, and the young of your flock. Your basket and your kneading trough shall be blessed. You shall be blessed when you come in, and you shall be blessed when you go out. Yahweh will cause your enemies who rise up against you to be struck before you. They will come out against you one way, and will flee before you seven ways. Yahweh will command the blessing on you in your barns, and in all that you put your hand to. He will bless you in the land which Yahweh your God gives you.

"Yahweh will establish you for a holy people to himself, as he has sworn to you, **if** you shall keep the commandments of Yahweh your God, and walk in his ways. All the peoples of the earth shall see that you are called by Yahweh's name [witness nation], and they will be afraid of you. Yahweh will grant you abundant prosperity in the fruit of your body, in the fruit of your livestock, and in the fruit of your ground, in the land which Yahweh swore to your fathers to give you. Yahweh will open to you his good treasure in the sky, to give the rain of your land in its season, and to bless all the work of your hand. You will lend to many nations, and you will not borrow. Yahweh will make you the head, and not the tail. You will be above only, and you will not be beneath, **if** you listen to the commandments of Yahweh your God which I command you today, to observe and to do, and shall not turn away from any of the words which I command you today, to the right hand or to the left, to go after other gods to serve them.

"But it shall come to pass, **if** you will not listen to Yahweh your God's voice, to observe to do all his commandments and his statutes which I command you today, that [**then**] all these curses will come on you and *overtake you.* You will be cursed in the city, and you will be cursed in the field. Your basket and your kneading trough will be cursed. The fruit of your body, the fruit of your ground, the increase of your livestock, and the young of your flock will be cursed. You will be cursed when you come in, and you will be cursed when you go out. Yahweh will send on you cursing, confusion, and rebuke in all that you put your hand to do, until you are destroyed and until you perish quickly, because of the evil of your doings, by which you have forsaken me. Yahweh will make the pestilence cling to you, until he has consumed you from off the land where you go in to possess it. Yahweh will strike you with consumption, with fever, with inflammation, with fiery heat, with the sword, with blight, and with mildew. They will pursue you until you perish.

"Your sky that is over your head will be bronze, and the earth that is under you will be iron. Yahweh will make the rain of your land powder and dust. It will come down on you from the sky, until you are destroyed. Yahweh will cause you to be struck before your enemies. You will go out one way against them, and will flee seven ways before them. You will be tossed back and forth among all the kingdoms of the earth. Your dead bodies will be food to all birds of the sky, and to the animals of the earth; and there will be no one to frighten them away. Yahweh will strike you with the boils of Egypt, with the tumors, with the scurvy, and with the itch, of which you can not be healed. Yahweh will strike you with madness, with blindness, and with astonishment of heart. You will grope at noonday, as the blind gropes in darkness, and *you shall not prosper in your ways*. You will only be oppressed and robbed always, and there will be no one to save you.

"You will betroth a wife, and another man shall lie with her. You will build a house, and you won't dwell in it. You will plant a vineyard, and not use its fruit. Your ox will be slain before your eyes, and you will not eat any of it. Your donkey will be violently taken away, from before your face, and will not be restored to you. Your sheep will be given to your enemies, and you will have no one to save you. Your sons and your daughters will be given to another people. Your eyes will look, and fail with longing for them all day long. *There will be no power in your hand*. A nation which you don't know will eat the fruit of your ground and all of your work. You will only be oppressed and crushed always, so that the sights that you see with your eyes will drive you mad. Yahweh will strike you in the knees and in the legs with a sore boil, of which you cannot be healed, from the sole of your foot to the crown of your head.

"Yahweh will bring you, and your king whom you will set over yourselves, to a nation that you have not known, you nor your fathers.

There you will serve other gods of wood and stone. You will become an astonishment, a proverb, and a byword among all the peoples where Yahweh will lead you away. You will carry much seed out into the field, and will gather little in, for the locust will consume it. You will plant vineyards and dress them, but you will neither drink of the wine, nor harvest, because worms will eat them. You will have olive trees throughout all your borders, but you won't anoint yourself with the oil, for your olives will drop off. You will father sons and daughters, but they will not be yours, for they will go into captivity. Locusts will consume all of your trees and the fruit of your ground. The foreigner who is among you will mount up above you higher and higher, and you will come down lower and lower. He will lend to you, and you won't lend to him. He will be the head, and you will be the tail.

"All these curses will come on you, and will pursue you and *overtake you,* until you are destroyed, because you didn't listen to Yahweh your God's voice, to keep his commandments and his statutes which he commanded you. They will be for a sign and for a wonder to you and to your offspring forever. *Because you didn't serve Yahweh your God with joyfulness and with gladness of heart, by reason of the abundance of all things; therefore you will serve your enemies whom Yahweh sends against you, in hunger, in thirst, in nakedness, and in lack of all things. He will put an iron yoke on your neck until he has destroyed you.* Yahweh will bring a nation against you from far, from the end of the earth, as the eagle flies: a nation whose language you will not understand, a nation of fierce facial expressions, that doesn't respect the elderly, nor show favor to the young. They will eat the fruit of your livestock and the fruit of your ground, until you are destroyed. They also won't leave you grain, new wine, oil, the increase of your livestock, or the young of your flock, until they have caused you to perish.

"They will besiege you in all your gates until your high and fortified walls *in which you trusted* come down throughout all your land. They will besiege you in all your gates throughout all your land which Yahweh your God has given you. You will eat the fruit of your own body, the flesh of your sons and of your daughters, whom Yahweh your God has given you, in the siege and in the distress with which your enemies will distress you. The man who is tender among you, and very delicate, his eye will be evil toward his brother, toward the wife whom he loves, and toward the remnant of his children whom he has remaining, so that he will not give to any of them of the flesh of his children whom he will eat, because he has nothing left to him, in the siege and in the distress with which your enemy will distress you in all your gates.

"The tender and delicate woman among you, who would not venture to set the sole of her foot on the ground for delicateness and tenderness, her eye will be evil toward the husband that she loves, toward her son, toward her daughter, toward her young one who comes out from between her feet, and toward her children whom she bears; for she will eat them secretly for lack of all things in the siege and in the distress with which your enemy will distress you in your gates.

"**If** you will not observe to do all the words of this law that are written in this book, that you may fear this glorious and fearful name, YAHWEH your God, **then** Yahweh will make your plagues and the plagues of your offspring fearful, even great plagues, and of long duration, and severe sicknesses, and of long duration. He will bring on you again all the diseases of Egypt, which you were afraid of; and they will cling to you. Also every sickness and every plague which is not written in the book of this law, Yahweh will bring them on you until you are destroyed. You will be left few in number, even though you were as the stars of the sky for multitude, because you didn't listen to Yahweh your God's voice.

"It will happen that as Yahweh rejoiced over you to do you good, and to multiply you, so Yahweh will rejoice over you to cause you to perish and to destroy you. *You will be plucked from the land that you are going in to possess. Yahweh will scatter you among all peoples, from one end of the earth to the other end of the earth.* There you will serve other gods which you have not known, you nor your fathers, even wood and stone. Among these nations you will find no ease, and there will be no rest for the sole of your foot; but Yahweh will give you there a trembling heart, failing of eyes, and pining of soul. Your life will hang in doubt before you. You will be afraid night and day, and will have no assurance of your life. In the morning you will say, "I wish it were evening!" and at evening you will say, "I wish it were morning!" for the fear of your heart which you will fear, and for the sights which your eyes will see. Yahweh will bring you into Egypt again with ships, by the way of which I told to you that you would never see it again. There you will offer yourselves to your enemies for male and female slaves, and nobody will buy you.

"These are the words of the covenant which Yahweh commanded Moses to make with the children of Israel." ~ *Deuteronomy 28:1-29:1*

This remarkable covenant with Israel is essentially a very detailed conditional promise! *If* the people of God follow hard after his righteous ways, *then* they can expect to be overtaken by blessing after blessing, according to verses two thru 13. However, *if* the people of God forsake his righteous ways, *then* they can expect to be overtaken by curse after curse; even great plagues, an oppressive military occupation, and severe sicknesses, according to verses 15 thru 68. Twelve wonderful verses of potential blessings (D28A), followed by fifty-four dreadful verses of potential curses (D28B).

I often compare this chapter to two roads in life. One road is called Blessings Boulevard, the other is called Curses Curve. Israel was very familiar with these roads. When she murmured and rebelled at Kadesh-Barnea in Numbers 14, the LORD declared, "Your children shall be wanderers in the wilderness forty years, and shall bear your prostitution, until your dead bodies are consumed in the wilderness" (v.33).

Disbelief in the Word of God is tantamount to disrespect for the God of the Word! The people of Israel were sentenced to travel along Curses Curve in the Sinai Peninsula for 40 years because of their stubbornness and disbelief! Everyone over 20 years old was consumed in the wilderness, "except Caleb the son of Jephunneh, and Joshua the son of Nun" (Numbers 14:30). And now, after enduring the "prostitution" of their parents for four decades, a new generation of Israelites stand ready to possess the land promised to their fathers.

Figuratively speaking, high above the road at the entrance to the land of milk and honey hangs a large sign that reads: Highway D28. As the children of Yahweh move underneath the first sign, the next two signs indicate there's a fork in the road, two options to travel. One sign points to **D28A**. It's a slight merge to the right that takes you unto Blessings Boulevard. The other option is **D28B**. It's a slight merge to the left that takes you unto Curses Curve. It's decision time. The young nation is now at the fork on Highway D28. The two paths are clearly marked, but will that be enough for Israel? For believers today, does knowing the way mean we'll always go the way? What might cause us to stray?

"The heart is deceitful above all things, and desperately wicked: who can know it?"

~ Jeremiah 17:9 KJV

Chapter Six:

"And Pray,"

"Now I lay me down to sleep. I pray the Lord my soul to keep. If I should die before I wake, I pray to God my soul to take. If I should live for other days, I pray the Lord to guide my ways. Amen."

Many of us can still recall this bedtime prayer from back in the day. It's an old classic. But how many of us recall this one?

"Almighty God, we acknowledge our dependence upon Thee, and we beg Thy blessings upon us, our parents, our teachers, and our country. Amen"

What do you think of that prayer? Is it a "good" prayer? Are you familiar with it? You probably don't recall this one because it was this prayer that got prayer "outlawed" in our public schools. Can you imagine the blessings we missed because our children were not allowed to offer this simple prayer to Almighty God at the start of their school day? Can you imagine how saying this prayer could shape a person's character?

The 6-to-1 Supreme Court Decision in Engel v. Vitale (1962) sparked outrage among religious Americans. Many will claim today that this decision to "kick God out of the public schools" paved the way for a sharp decline in the quality of public education, and a dramatic rise in delinquency and immorality.

That may be true, but let's not miss the forest for the trees. The high court of the land didn't outlaw prayer altogether. Americans can still pray. Engel v. Vitale is not a barrier to prayer; it should be a call to prayer. Thank God we can still gather our little ones and pray before they leave home for school every day, if that is our desire. We can pray with them when they get home from school. We can pray before we eat, or before we sleep. The Supreme Court did not outlaw prayer. We can pray till the cows come home. The problem is: *that's not really our desire*. Besides, who has time to do any serious praying when there're so many other pressing matters to address, so many ball games and shows to watch, so many people to talk to, so many new spots in town to check out?

Let's be honest with ourselves, brothers and sisters of light, God knows our heart (1 Samuel 16:7). The United States Supreme Court did indeed rule against prayer in our public schools in 1962. They ruled again in 1963 against Bible reading in public schools. But the truth of the matter is, as citizens of the United States of America, we can still pray and read our Bible and worship our God pretty much as we desire.

Consider this. No human being or human law can prevent a believer from communicating to the One who "searches all hearts, and understands all the imaginations of the thoughts" (1 Chronicles 28:9). Prayer need not be some formal, "religious," outward act for all the world to see. Some of our best praying is done "in secret." Jesus taught us to "pray to your Father *who is in secret*; and your Father *who sees in secret* will reward you openly" (Matthew 6:6).

No one can stop you from praying. The laws of man may allow you to be jailed and thrown to the lions for praying, but no law of man can *stop* you from praying. This is one of the most appealing aspects about prayer and fellowship with the Most High. It can happen in that secret place where only you and God abide. If we want to do so, we can always pray. The question now is, do we submit to God or seek another remedy?

"If my people, who are called by my name, will humble themselves, and pray..." Humility is the first step toward revival. Prayer is the second step. Bible teacher Matthew Henry states, "Whenever God intends great blessings for His people, He first sets them to praying." Evangelist J. Edwin Orr said, "Every revival begins in a prayer meeting."

How should we pray? Brother Henry teaches, "To pray, is by faith to take hold of the promises and the declarations God has made of his good-will to us, and to plead them with him." During Israel's darkest days of sin, the prophet Isaiah proclaimed, "There is none who calls on your name, who **stirs up himself** to take hold of you..." (Isa. 64:7). No one rises to God without effort. We must rouse or stir up ourselves to pray and lay hold of God. Do we truly want revival? Are we willing to "pray" the price for revival? Per James 4:2 » *We have not because we ask not!* We're not experiencing God's outpouring because we're not praying for it as intently as we should. We can work hard for revival, and we should work for revival, but we must never forget that without prayer, our work is not enough. It's prayer that incites God to infuse his power and vitality into the machinery of human effort. Without the fuel of prayer, the machine shuts down.

On January 25, 1990, Avianca Flight 52 from Bogotá, Colombia is completing her long journey of 2,500 miles to New York's Kennedy International Airport. The weather is bad as the plane approaches NYC. A member of the flight crew communicates to air traffic control to request a "priority" landing. It's a busy day at JFK, lots of air traffic, and the weather didn't help. Since the flight crew member did not request an "emergency" landing, the plane from Bogotá is put on a holding pattern. After flying 2,500 miles and circling the New York skies to complete their first holding pattern, air traffic control places Avianca Flight 52 on a second holding pattern. And then a third!

Realizing they're now dangerously low on fuel, the pilots of AF-52 attempt to land at JFK. But they have to abort their attempt due to scanty communication with the tower and poor visibility. Before they can make a second attempt to land, the plane dropped out of the sky. It crashed into a Long Island hillside about 15 miles from the airport, narrowly missing several million-dollar homes. Seventy-three passengers were killed. The reason for the crash? The plane simply ran out of fuel and couldn't maintain flight. That's almost unbelievable in this day and age, but it actually happened. Without jet fuel, Avianca Flight 52 had no power to overcome the force of gravity and stay in the air. Likewise, unless we're fueled by mighty prevailing prayer, we have no chance in overcoming the prince of the powers of the air.

The key to revival is prayer. Although the wickedness of our world and the lukewarm spirit of some believers can be discouraging, this is really an incentive to pray. "It is time for thee, LORD, to work: for they have made void thy law" (Psalm 119:126 KJV). Many saints have recognized the need to pray, *"O God, it is time for You to work!"*

Shortly after the LORD led the children of Israel through the sea and destroyed the host of the Egyptians, they find themselves being attacked again. This time, the Amalekites oppose the people of Yahweh. But what Amalek meant for evil, God turned into good. Because in this flashback episode of Scripture, God gives us a cogent example of the vital role prayer plays in our "good fight of faith." Let's pick up the account in Exodus 17:8-16,

> Then Amalek came and fought with Israel in Rephidim. Moses said to Joshua, "Choose men for us, and go out, fight with Amalek. Tomorrow I will stand on the top of the hill with God's rod in my

hand. So Joshua did as Moses had told him, and fought with Amalek; and Moses, Aaron, and Hur went up to the top of the hill. It happened, when Moses held up his hand, that Israel prevailed; and when he let down his hand, Amalek prevailed. But Moses' hands were heavy; and they took a stone, and put it under him, and he sat on it. Aaron and Hur held up his hands, the one on the one side, and the other on the other side. His hands were steady until sunset. Joshua defeated Amalek and his people with the edge of the sword. Yahweh said to Moses, "**Write this for a memorial in a book**, and rehearse it in the ears of Joshua: That I will utterly blot out the memory of Amalek from under the sky." Moses built an altar, and called the name of it Yahweh our Banner [Jehovah-Nissi]. He said, "Yah has sworn: 'Yahweh will have war with Amalek from generation to generation.' "

~§~

In the heat of battle, Moses lifts God's rod to the sky, which signifies asking Yah for help. When his hands were raised to heaven, the children of Israel prevailed over their enemy. When Moses lowered his hands, the forces of Amalek prevailed.

Prayer, which represents our humble reliance on God, is the key to victory. Prayer is lifting our hands to heaven, the way a child would raise their hands to say, "Pick me up." Prayer is simply acknowledging our dependence on our heavenly Father. "**I desire therefore that the men in every place pray, lifting up holy hands, without anger and doubting**" (1 Timothy 2:8). We lift holy hands. Without anger towards any. Without doubt that God hears.

But mighty prevailing prayer is hard work, and Moses' hands grew heavy. As he let down his hands, the Israelites experienced defeat. So what does Moses do? He recruits Aaron and Hur to join in the intercession. They each take one of the hands of Moses and they hold it up steady for the duration of the battle. The outcome: "Joshua defeated Amalek and his people with the edge of the sword."

What could be clearer than that? The Bible tells us, "The insistent prayer of a righteous person is powerfully effective." In simple terms, the prayers of a single righteous person can incite the Lord to move heaven and earth on their behalf. "Elijah was a man with a nature like ours, and he prayed earnestly that it might not rain, and it didn't rain on the earth for three years and six months. He prayed again, and the sky gave rain, and the earth produced its fruit" (James 5:16-18). But what happens if we combine the insistent prayer of a righteous man or woman with the insistent prayer of another righteous man or woman? Do we double the effectiveness of their prayers? There's a lot to be said regarding the power of united intercession (Matthew 18:19,20).

William Wilberforce was a great Christian philanthropist and vigorous opponent of the slave trade in England during the early 1800s. His life was transformed when he received the living Savior in 1784 at the age of twenty-five. The partying and loose living he once enjoyed was no longer becoming. The condition of the poor now disturbed him. The young lawyer soon led the legal battle in Great Britain to put a stop to the inhumane marketing of slaves. In 1823, he became a founder of the Anti-Slavery Society. As he surveyed the moral and spiritual climate of his day, he did not lose hope and his faith was not shaken. He wrote,

> "My own solid hopes for the well-being of my country depend, not so much on her navies or armies, nor on the wisdom of her rulers, nor on the spirit of her people, as on the persuasion that she still contains many who love and obey the gospel of Christ. *I believe that their prayers may yet prevail."*

Brother Wilberforce died in 1833. One month following his death, the Emancipation Bill abolishing slavery in England became law. What power fueled the political machinery to pass the bill? Wilberforce did his due diligence in the court of law, and he had the backing of "many who love and obey the gospel of Christ." The spiritual warriors and intercessors in William's circle *stirred up themselves* to pray and plead the promises of God for three hours a day. They asked God to crown the statesman's industry with success. Within a few years, the country he loved experienced a nation-wide revival, known as the Second Great Awakening. This international revival swept thousands of souls into the Kingdom of Light and ushered in widespread social reforms. Whenever God intends great blessings for His people, He first sets them to praying (Phil. 2:13).

Three generations earlier and across the Atlantic, in Enfield, Connecticut, the Christian theologian Jonathan Edwards delivered one of the most famous sermons ever preached in North America. It's entitled, *Sinners in the Hands of an Angry God.* This sermon, and others like it, preached by Spirit-filled messengers in the 1740s, sparked a spiritual revival that went across our thirteen colonies. This first recorded "nation-wide" revival has been called the First Great Awakening. It caught fire from the fervent and insistent prayers of God's people.

Jonathan Edwards was well aware, from biblical and historical accounts, that united prayer is the way to sustain the spiritual awakening that was spreading throughout the colonies. He called for Christians on both sides of the Atlantic to keep on praying. In 1746, Jonathan Edwards published a book on the topic of united prayer. The title of the book alone tells the story: *"A Humble Attempt to Promote explicit Agreement and Visible Union of God's People in extraordinary Prayer, for the Revival of the Church and the advancement of Christ's Kingdom on Earth."*

Brother Edwards knew if the children of God hoped to overcome the attacks of the enemy and keep the flames of revival burning bright, they must pray. It must be "extraordinary prayer," like that of Moses on the hill at Rephidim with his hands stretched out to the Lord for hours while the battle raged below. There must be "explicit agreement and visible union" in prayer, like that of Aaron and Hur on the hilltop also, holding steady the hands of their brother-in-arms.

Do you recall Romans 15:4? "For whatever things were written before were written for our learning, that through perseverance and through encouragement of the Scriptures we might have hope."

This episode in Exodus 17 is a great example of that. All this is "written for our learning." *That being the case, what have we learned?* When the people of God were attacked, Yahweh's leader assigned some people to fight the battle on the physical plain, and he partnered with other people to fight the battle on the spiritual plain. In the case with Brother Wilberforce, the counselor battled in the *court of England,* while his prayer partners battled in the *court of Heaven*. For Moses and the children of Israel, the physical battle was victorious because the spiritual battle was victorious. Had they failed in heaven, they would have failed on earth. They won on earth because they won in heaven.

This is how "through encouragement of the Scriptures we might have hope." By reading about Moses lifting his hands to heaven and the Lord granting Israel the victory over Amalek, it gives us hope. How so? *Because God is no respecter of persons.* If we pray to him and recruit others to pray, we too can win the day! Moses was God's man, and we see how Yahweh responded to his prayers. Well, God has many sincere followers in my town, in your town also. As we walk in the light and unite in the battle, the same LORD said he'll respond to our prayers. Yahweh told Moses to write these faith-building examples in a book. Why? So that when we read about how an omnipotent God showed up STRONG for his people in the past, "we might have hope" he'll do the same for us today.

Allow me to ask you two personal questions. Do you know that you are a child of God? Do you know that God hears your prayers? If you have any doubt, please consider carefully the following Scripture from 1 John 5:10-15,

> "He who doesn't believe God has made him a liar, because he has not believed in the testimony that God has given concerning his Son. The testimony is this, **that God gave to us eternal life, and this life is in his Son.** He who has the Son has the life. He who doesn't have God's Son doesn't have the life. These things I have written to you who believe in the name of the Son of God, that you may <u>know that you have eternal life</u>, and that you may continue to believe in the name of the Son of God. This is the boldness which we have toward him, that, if we ask anything according to his will, he listens to us. And if we know that he listens to us whatever we ask, we <u>know that we have the petitions</u> which we have asked of him."

Words matter, and this word from God is quick and powerful. According to this inspired passage of Scripture, there are two things I can know for sure. First of all, I can know that I have eternal life. The Bible teaches us eternal life is not in a religion, it's in a PERSON! *"He who has the Son has the life."* It doesn't read, "He who joins a religious group has life." It doesn't read, "He who performs a religious ritual or sacrament has life." You can do all that and still not have life.

The life is in his Son. If we don't believe this testimony that GOD gave concerning his Son, we make GOD a liar! Eternal life is not in a religion or denomination, it's in a person. If you have your religion without having the person, you don't have life, see John 5:36-40. The Scriptures are explicit concerning salvation. Therefore, based upon God's word, I can know now, at this very moment in time, that I have eternal life. How can I know? Because I have the Son, and I believe the testimony of the Lord!

I have vivid recall of my life as an undisciplined, confused soul when I didn't have the Son. And then, there came a Sunday, while stationed at Fort Ord, California, when I received the "Wonderful Counselor" in Sixth Avenue Chapel (Psalm 34:6; Isaiah 9:6). A few days later, I paid $40 for a study Bible from Monterey Bible Bookstore. My first reading through Genesis was amazing. I wanted more. As I consumed God's word (1 Peter 2:2), the Spirit confirmed the truth to my spirit, and I've had the blessed assurance of being God's child ever since (Romans 8:12-16)! Faith concludes what JAH declares.

Check this out. "As many as received him [Jesus], to them he gave the right to become God's children, to those who believe in his name" (John 1:12). The "right" (or "power" in the KJV), to become God's children is given to those who receive God's son. Thus, "*He who has the Son has the life.*" It's not complicated. The Lord isn't being evasive or shifty. The Spirit teaches in 1 Corinthians 14:33 that God is not the author of confusion. The enemy of God is busy complicating and deceiving, but God is very forthright regarding the matter of salvation. Which means we can trust his word, and be very plainspoken as well. Per 2 Corinthians 11:3, there is a "simplicity that is in Christ" which the serpent forever seeks to corrupt. Jesus said, "unless you are converted and become as little children, you will by no means enter the kingdom of heaven" (Matthew 18:3 NKJV).

I know I have the life because I know I have the Son. It's as simple, and as profound, as that! But it doesn't stop there. I can also know that God hears me when I call on him. "This is the **boldness** [confidence] which we have toward him, that, if we ask anything according to his will, he listens to us." These words are clear as a bell. If we ask God for ANYTHING that's in accordance to his will, we KNOW he hears us. That's the first part. We know he listens when we ask in the power of his will. And the rest of the passage seals the deal: "And if [since] we know that he listens to us whatever we ask, *we know that we have the petitions* which we have asked of him." Since we know he listens, we know we have! When we pray in the power of his will, we know he hears us and *"we know that we have the petitions"* we are praying for.

Let me ask you, "Is the revival of the saints in America according to the will of God?" Is that something the Most High would desire? Did not the Spirit of Yahweh move the sweet psalmist to cry out: "Won't you revive us again, that your people may rejoice in you?" (Psalm 85:6). I firmly believe it is God's will to revive us again (Isaiah 57:15).

Second question. Is the salvation of the lost according to the will of God? Did not the Spirit of Yahweh move the apostle to write: "The Lord is...not willing that any should perish, but that all should come to repentance" (2 Peter 3:9 KJV)? See also Acts 17:29-30. Later in the book, we'll examine two nation-wide revivals that broke out first in Wales, and then in America. In both cases, two things happened. We should expect two manifestations to accompany every true revival:

1. The saints are revived.
2. The lost are won to Christ.

Both these things happen when God pours out a fresh anointing on his people. Believers are strengthened in the faith and non-believers become believers. Since both are manifestations of true revival, and since both are in accordance with the declared will/word of God, *should we have any doubt that God will answer us if we pray for true revival?* Of course not! It's not like we're asking for a mink coat or a supercar. I might be challenged to scripturally justify the mink and the ride, but I can easily justify scripturally the reviving of the saints and the salvation of the lost. I just did. So, my fellow recipients of grace, it's with this boldness and simplicity of faith that we come before the throne of grace to plead the promises and declarations of God.

What's the Foundation of our Faith?

Life is not as complicated as we often make it out to be. It's not so hard to exercise faith. You do it every time you obey the green light, hoping others will obey the red light. You don't know the other drivers will stop on red as you zoom through the intersection, but you have faith that they will. As a matter of fact, you risk your life that they will obey the red light.

But riddle me this, Speed Racer: *As you drive toward the intersection, what's the basis for your faith?* Is it your feelings? No! Is it the feelings of other drivers? I hope not! The basis for your faith is a written law. Or one might say, the reason you're willing to drive through an intersection in busy noonday traffic is because at some point in the past someone said, **"It is written, green means go, and red means stop."**

We actually risk life and limb on that law every time we get in a car. We exercise "saving faith" in that law every time we drive, but notice it's not blind faith. Our faith has a resting place or a foundation. As believers, we're not commanded to have faith "in faith." What then is the foundation on which we rest our faith?

As we saw earlier, the military leader Joshua assisted Moses during the exodus. And when Moses passed away, it was Joshua who took over the top leadership position. But now we come to the day when Joshua himself will pass away. What will he say to the people of God on his last day in the land of the living? He states,

> "Take good heed therefore to yourselves, *that you love Yahweh your God.* ...Behold, today I am going the way of all the earth. **You know in all your hearts and in all your souls that not one thing has failed of all the good things which Yahweh your God spoke concerning you. All have happened to you. Not one thing has failed of it.** It shall happen that as all the good things have come on you of which Yahweh your God spoke to you, so Yahweh will bring on you all the evil things, until he has destroyed you from off this good land which Yahweh your God has given you, when you disobey the covenant of Yahweh your God, which he commanded you, and go and serve other gods, and bow down yourselves to them. Then Yahweh's anger will be kindled against you, and you will perish quickly from off the good land which he has given to you."
>
> "Joshua said to the people, 'You can't serve Yahweh, for he is a holy God. *He is a jealous God.* He will not forgive your disobedience nor your sins. If you forsake Yahweh, and serve foreign gods, then he will turn and do you evil, and consume you, after he has done you good.'
>
> "The people said to Joshua, 'No, but we will serve Yahweh.' Joshua said to the people, 'You are witnesses against yourselves that you have chosen Yahweh yourselves, to serve him.'
>
> They said, 'We are witnesses.' So Joshua made a covenant with the people that day, and...**wrote these words in the book of the law of God. ...Israel served Yahweh all the days of Joshua, and all the days of the elders who outlived Joshua**, and had known all the work of Yahweh, that he worked for Israel."
> *~ Joshua 23:11, 14-16; 24:19-22, 25-26, 31*

Joshua was a key player in the rise of Israel. He didn't live to witness her fall. But he knew exactly what would happen if his country rebelled against the One whose very name is Jealous. How did Joshua know? **He knew because God said it!** From his own experience, Joshua knew if God said it - that settles it (Psalm 119:89). As far as Joshua was concerned, Yahweh bats a thousand every season. God's scorecard is perfect! So he reminds the people that because they stayed on Highway D28A, *"not one thing has failed of all the good things which Yahweh your God spoke concerning you."*

That's pretty darn impressive! *Every single thing happened just like God said it would happen.* Followers of the Way, our prayer of faith and our walk of faith is not blind. Faith looks to what God says and believes it! Faith is not blindly stepping into the dark; faith is walking confidently in the light of his word. Faith refuses to put a question mark where God has put a period. The sure foundation of our faith is Yahweh's perfect record, his infallible word! I don't have faith "in faith." My faith is in an unrivaled God, and what he said in his phenomenal book.

Joshua tells the leaders to look back and see for themselves how God has kept his word. God told them earlier, if they prove faithful to him, he would fight for them. And as they looked back, they saw for themselves that their God did not let them down. They knew, *from their own experience with him,* that God can be counted on to fulfill his word. And they stood in that faith for the rest of their lives!

Believers who are walking in the light can be bold at the throne of grace (Heb. 4:14-16). Mighty prevailing prayer is the key to victory. Fierce attacks may come, storm clouds may block the Son, and our enemy may win momentarily. I say look steadfast to God's eternal word. "This is the victory that has overcome the world: your faith" (1 John 5:4)!

What a tremendous way to go through life! Walking humbly before the LORD, with complete assurance of our salvation, coupled with complete assurance that God will grant our petitions as we pray in the power of his will. Boldly praying to the Almighty, full of faith and confidence that he will grant our request. How can it possibly get any better than that? That's awesome, my friend, and you better know it! As it is written, it will be done. My faith in God is *unshakable* (Psalm 62:2) because God's word is *unbreakable* (John 10:35)!

Public Fasting and Extraordinary Prayer

"In general we must hold that whenever any religious controversy arises, ... whenever a minister is to be chosen; whenever, in short any matter of difficulty and great importance is under consideration: on the other hand, *when manifestations of the divine anger appear*, as pestilence, war, and famine, the sacred and salutary custom of all ages has been for pastors to exhort the people to public fasting and extraordinary prayer." ~ John Calvin, *Institutes*, IV, Chapter 12, Section 14.

The Holy Bible points out that "we are God's fellow workers" (1 Corinthians 3:9). In the *Complete Jewish Bible* it reads, "we are God's co-workers." Christians are to work with the Most High to advance his Kingdom. As fellow workers with God, we *can't* do his part and he *won't* do our part. We must do our part first, while exercising faith that he'll do his part. Before our Lord performed the supernatural work of resurrecting his friend Lazarus in the cave, he commanded humans to "take away the stone" (John 11:39). We do the natural part; JAH does the supernatural.

The wisdom of Proverbs 21:31 tells us, "**The horse is prepared for the day of battle; but victory is with Yahweh**." We shouldn't expect God to leave the throne of heaven and prepare our horse for battle, that's our job. Yet we must not place our faith for the victory in the horse (Psalm 33:17). There's no substitute for a prepared horse (doing our part), but our ultimate faith is not in the horse. Our trust is in the Creator God who made heaven and earth! We don't trust in the horse; we trust in the One who made the horse. Victory is with our co-worker, Yahweh.

Many believers are familiar with E.M. Bounds. He has written extensively on the subject of prayer. In *Preacher and Prayer*, he states, "The pulpit of this day is weak in praying. The pride of learning is against the dependent humility of prayer. Prayer is not to the modern pulpit the mighty force it was in Paul's life or ministry. Every preacher who does not make prayer a mighty factor in his own life and ministry is weak as a factor in God's work and is powerless to project God's cause in this world."

A prayerless believer is a powerless believer. But why do we resist praying? Is it because "the pride of learning is against the dependent humility of prayer"? I'm afraid so. The pride of learning and knowing and doing for oneself is against the dependent humility of prayer. We Americans have a "can do" attitude. Whenever there's a problem or a challenge, we're quick to roll up our sleeves and get to work. Go to the moon and back? No problem! Take this lung from him and put it in her? No problem! Who needs prayer to move mountains when good ol' American ingenuity and a team of bulldozers can do the job just as well? Dependent humility is not a part of our DNA.

Our dumb flesh (Rom. 7:18) is the enemy of dependent humility. The same flesh that recoils against walking humbly with God is the same flesh that recoils against humbly praying to God. Which is why "they that are in the flesh cannot please God" (Rom. 8:8). And why we must overrule the flesh (1 Cor. 9:27), and *stir up ourselves* to pray and take hold of God.

Human pride is against dependent humility, but dependent humility is exactly what God expects from us. He's delighted when we pray to him and listen for his voice and trust in him alone. Did you know the Bible says that **JAH rides the heavens to help us**? See Psalm 68:4 KJV and Deuteronomy 33:26 KJV. I love the imagery of the Most High riding on the clouds to help those who hope in his mercy. The eyes of the LORD run back and forth throughout all of America in search of faithful servants. Isn't it encouraging to know that God Almighty is on the hunt for those who are willing to "pray" the price for revival? He's eager to work his wonders on our behalf, and He'll most definitely respond when we, without anger or doubt, lift up holy hands in prayer. *When our numbers reach critical mass, the Almighty will show himself strong.*

In this next episode from the history of Israel, King David provides an excellent example of dependent humility. It's a short passage, but it contains sweet truth from on high. It's from 1 Chronicles 14:8-17. I call this section:

God strategizes for Israel

> When the Philistines heard that David was anointed king over all Israel, all the Philistines went up to seek David; and David heard of it, and went out against them. Now the Philistines had come and made a raid in the valley of Rephaim. **David inquired of God**, saying, "Shall I go up against the Philistines? Will you deliver them into my hand?"
>
> Yahweh said to him, "Go up; for I will deliver them into your hand."

> So they came up to Baal Perazim, and David defeated them there. David said, God has broken my enemies by my hand, like waters breaking out. [Co-workers: *God* did it - by *my* hand.] Therefore they called the name of that place Baal Perazim. They left their gods there; and David gave a command, and they were burned with fire.
>
> The Philistines made another raid in the valley. **David inquired again of God**; and God said to him, "You shall not go up after them. Turn away from them, and come on them opposite the mulberry trees. When you hear the sound of marching in the tops of the mulberry trees, then go out to battle; for God has gone out before you to strike the army of the Philistines."
>
> David did as God commanded him; and they attacked the army of the Philistines from Gibeon even to Gezer. The fame of David went out into all lands; and Yahweh brought the fear of him on all nations.

I love the LORD and I love his Word! "Yahweh is a man of war" (Exodus 15:3). "He makes the clouds his chariot. He walks on the wings of the wind" (Psalm 104:3). This account of how God answered the prayers of King David should thrill all those who trust in the Most High. At this point in the history of Israel, the twelve tribes of Jacob have consolidated into one nation, under one human king, who is under God. David is her second king. Israel's first selection for a king was Saul.

King Saul was tall, dark and handsome. He was easy on the eyes, but his heart was not right toward the Lord. One of his major errors was consulting with a familiar spirit when "the Philistines gathered their armies together for warfare, to fight with Israel" (1 Samuel 28:1). As you recall, just before Israel entered the land promised to their fathers, Yahweh said, "For these nations that you shall dispossess listen to those who practice sorcery and to diviners; but as for you, Yahweh your God has not allowed you so to do" (Deuteronomy 18:14).

Israel is Yahweh's witness nation. She is not to chase after the gods of the world. ADONAI is in covenant with Israel. They are a holy nation, meaning they are separated unto the LORD. The nations of the world may consult with those who practice sorcery and with diviners, but the people of the true and living God must not copy them. "For whoever does these things is an **abomination** to Yahweh" (Deuteronomy 18:12). Consequently, we read in 1 Chronicles 10:13-14,

> "So Saul died for his trespass which he committed against Yahweh, because of Yahweh's word, which he didn't keep; and also because he asked counsel of one who had a familiar spirit, to inquire, and didn't inquire of Yahweh. Therefore he killed him, and turned the kingdom over to David the son of Jesse."

Saul's replacement is David, the sweet psalmist of Israel. Not a perfect man, but one after God's own heart. In 1 Chronicles 14, when the Philistines came up against David, what did he do? King Saul inquired of one who had a familiar (demon) spirit, but David inquired of God. And what did God say to him? "Go up; for I will deliver them into your hand."

And so it happened just as the LORD said. David broke through his foe like the overwhelming force of waters breaking out. The enemy of the newly appointed king was thoroughly routed. They didn't even have time to gather up their false gods or idols; they left them on the field of battle. But why did King David command these idols be burned?

> "You shall burn the engraved images of their gods with fire. You shall not covet the silver or the gold that is on them, nor take it for yourself, lest you be snared in it; for it is an **abomination** to Yahweh your God." ~ *Deuteronomy 7:25*

Just before the nation entered the land of promise, Moses instructed them to have nothing to do with the gods of the people who currently occupy that space. God said to burn the images and idols of the false gods. He said to also burn the gold and silver that is on them, "lest you be snared in it." David was very much aware of what happened to the last king who disobeyed God's law. He wasn't about to make that mistake. In accordance to the law, David commanded his men to burn the idols.

Apparently, the Philistines got the impression that David's victory over them was beginner's luck. So they go up against the new king a second time. Notice how David responds to this later attack. He doesn't make the assumption that since Yahweh gave the green light before, he need not pray about it anymore. *He goes to the Lord again to ensure he's moving in line with the Divine.* And this time, God has a different plan of attack. Situations may appear outwardly identical to us, but there are forces at work that reside beyond our senses. Did something change in the heavenlies that "caused" Yahweh to employ a different strategy? Is there some sort of ebb and flow in spiritual warfare? Daniel fasted and prayed, but the dark prince of Persia detained God's messenger for 21 days (Dan. 10:12,13). In 1 Thessalonians 2:18, Paul said Satan hindered him from visiting his children in Christ. Things change. The battle shifts. The devil is busy. I won't go into "the sound of marching in the tops" of trees and those other details. The main takeaway for now is David didn't presume upon the Lord and move hastily into this second conflict without checking in first. "David inquired *again* of God." And God gave him a different strategy for the second battle. The new king wisely followed the new plan. And how did God respond? He went out before David's army and showed up STRONG for his people again! *"The fame of David went out into all lands; and Yahweh brought the fear of him on all nations."*

King David

D28A: Yahweh will cause your enemies who rise up against you to be struck before you. ~ *Deuteronomy 28:7*

All the peoples of the earth shall see that you are called by Yahweh's name, and they will be afraid of you. ~ *Deuteronomy 28:10*

King Saul

D28B: Yahweh will cause you to be struck before your enemies. ~ *Deuteronomy 28:25*

All these curses will come on you, and will pursue you and overtake you, until you are destroyed, because you didn't listen to Yahweh. ~ *Deuteronomy 28:45*

Let's continue to trace the amazing history of Israel. Our next episode occurs after the reign of King David and King Solomon. At this point in time, because of the sins of the nation, Israel has split into two warring kingdoms. Ten of the twelve tribes revolt against Solomon's son, Rehoboam. They then establish the Northern Kingdom and set up **Jeroboam**, from the tribe of Ephraim, as their first king. Following in the bloodline of David and Solomon is **Abijah**, ruler of the Southern Kingdom. The Southern Kingdom is now called Judah. It's made up of the tribes of Benjamin and Judah, with Jerusalem as their worship center.

The larger northern kingdom of ten tribes is referred to as Israel. Sometimes it's called Ephraim because Jeroboam is from that large tribe. They will set up idolatrous worship centers north of Jerusalem.

Israel's Civil War

In this scene, the North and the South are at war. The larger northern kingdom takes the field of battle with 800,000 soldiers. Judah has half that number. When studying this section of Scripture, I'm reminded of Proverbs 28:1, which states, **"The righteous are as bold as a lion."** You will soon see why. Consider *2 Chronicles 13:1-21,*

"In the eighteenth year of king Jeroboam, Abijah began to reign over Judah. He reigned three years in Jerusalem. His mother's name was Micaiah the daughter of Uriel of Gibeah. *There was war between Abijah and Jeroboam.* Abijah joined battle with an army of valiant men of war, even four hundred thousand chosen men; and Jeroboam set the battle in array against him with eight hundred thousand chosen men, who were mighty men of valor.

"Abijah stood up on Mount Zemaraim, which is in the hill country of Ephraim, and said, "Hear me, Jeroboam and all Israel: Ought you not to know that Yahweh, the God of Israel, gave the kingdom over Israel to David forever, even to him and to his sons by a covenant of salt? Yet Jeroboam the son of Nebat, the servant of Solomon the son of David, rose up, and rebelled against his lord. *Worthless men were gathered to him*, wicked fellows who strengthened themselves against Rehoboam the son of Solomon, when Rehoboam was young and tender hearted, and could not withstand them.

"Now you intend to withstand the kingdom of Yahweh in the hand of the sons of David. You are a great multitude, and the golden calves which Jeroboam made you for gods are with you. Haven't you driven out the priests of Yahweh, the sons of Aaron, and the Levites, and made priests for yourselves according to the ways of the peoples of other lands? Whoever comes to consecrate himself with a young bull and seven rams may be a priest of those who are no gods [1 Kings 12:26-31].

"But as for us, Yahweh is our God, and we have not forsaken him. We have priests serving Yahweh, the sons of Aaron, and the Levites in their work; and they burn to Yahweh every morning and every evening burnt

offerings and sweet incense. They also set the show bread in order on the pure table; and the lamp stand of gold with its lamps, to burn every evening; *for we keep the instruction of Yahweh our God, but you have forsaken him*. Behold, **God is with us at our head**, and his priests with the trumpets of alarm to sound an alarm against you. Children of Israel, don't fight against Yahweh, the God of your fathers; for you will not prosper."

[The righteous are as bold as a lion! King Abijah is not cocky or arrogant, but bold before God and man because he knows he and his people are walking in the light of the law! He warns his rebellious brothers to stand down. But how will Jeroboam react?]

"But Jeroboam caused an ambush to come behind them; so they were before Judah, and the ambush was behind them. When Judah looked back, behold, the battle was before them and behind them; *and they cried to Yahweh,* and the priests sounded with the trumpets.

"Then the men of Judah gave a shout. As the men of Judah shouted, God struck Jeroboam and all Israel before Abijah and Judah. The children of Israel fled before Judah, and God delivered them into their hand. Abijah and his people killed them with a great slaughter, so five hundred thousand chosen men of Israel fell down slain.

"Thus the children of Israel were brought under at that time, and the **children of Judah prevailed, because they relied on Yahweh**, the God of their fathers. Abijah pursued Jeroboam, and took cities from him, Bethel with its villages, Jeshanah with its villages, and Ephron with its villages. Jeroboam didn't recover strength again in the days of Abijah. Yahweh struck him, and he died [D28B]. But Abijah grew mighty" [D28A].

By the time the Civil War ended in America in 1865, it would take the lives of over 600,000 men. In this one battle alone between the Southern Kingdom of Judah and the Northern Kingdom of Israel, 500,000 chosen men of Israel fell down slain. What a tragic loss of life, and a graphic example of the faithfulness of the Lord. The larger forces of Israel were brought under, while the smaller forces of *"Judah prevailed, because they relied on Yahweh"!* May God grant us the wisdom and grace to rely on Him, first and foremost (Psalm 33:16,17; 44:4-8; 62:2).

"Whatever gets you too busy for prayer time, whatever distracts you from holy prevailing, whatever robs you of hunger for God, for souls, and for time for prayer warfare is a hindrance to God and His kingdom. You cannot afford it. The great and godly people of the church have always been those who know how to prevail in prayer. There is nothing higher or holier in Christian living and service. In prevailing prayer you rise to your full potential as created in the image of God and as exalted to the heavenlies to share with Christ His intercessory throne (Eph. 1:20,21; 2:6).

"Think of it: The very God who raised up Jesus to heaven after His death and resurrection, placing Jesus at His right hand on the throne of the universe, has also "raised us up with Christ and seated us with him in the heavenly realms" (Eph.2:6). You sit potentially where Jesus sits – on the throne, to share His rule! When? Now! How? By intercession! You have no greater ministry or no leadership more influential than intercession. There is no higher role, honor, or authority than this. You have been saved to reign through prayer. You have been Spirit-filled to qualify you to reign by prayer. You reign as you prevail in prayer."

~ *Wesley L. Duewel,* "Mighty Prevailing Prayer" - Read this book!

~§~

"Each time, before you intercede, be quiet first, and worship God in His glory. Think of what He can do, and how He delights to hear the prayers of His redeemed people. Think of your place and privilege in Christ, and expect great things!" ~ *Andrew Murray*

~§~

Dr. J. Edwin Orr was a leading authority on international revivals. Over twenty-five years ago, I saw one of his video presentations entitled ***The Role of Prayer in Spiritual Awakening***. I never forgot it! Please go online and check it out. It's somewhat dated and blurry, but it will definitely quicken your spirit and expand your faith. After viewing it, you'll want to encourage others to watch it as well. It's a 27-minute investment that could transform our nation! Set a reminder on your phone to watch it or write yourself a note. Let's close this chapter by praying together...

O Lord, stir up Yourself to our cause (Psalm 35:23), as we stir up ourselves to pray and take hold of You (Isaiah 64:7)!

Chapter Seven:

Awaken a Sleeping Giant

Before we consider our enemy's evil work on August 11, 2018, let's first go back to December 6, 1941. It's an ordinary Saturday in the USA. What do Americans enjoy doing on a weekend in December? Many folks all over the country attend college football games. Olivia de Havilland and Errol Flynn are playing at the movies, so is Joan Fontaine and Cary Grant. Some people head out to do Christmas shopping. By any measure, it's an ordinary day in America. But all that is about to change.

"Yesterday, December 7, 1941, a date which will live in infamy...."

Those words, spoken by President Franklin D. Roosevelt in the famous Pearl Harbor Speech to the US Congress, launched us into World War II. Actually, it wasn't the words of the Pearl Harbor speech that pushed us into battle, it was what President Roosevelt called "the unprovoked and dastardly attack by Japan" that galvanized our nation for war.

You might find it interesting that the mastermind behind the attack on Pearl Harbor was a Japanese military leader who was personally against the war. His name was Isoroku Yamamoto. He opposed war against the United States partly because he lived here for many years. Yamamoto spoke fluent English. He studied at Harvard University in Cambridge, Massachusetts between 1919 and 1921. He was also posted in Washington, D.C., as a naval military expert.

When Yamamoto lived in America, he didn't confine himself to D.C. and Boston. He travelled all over this country. With the sharp observation of a foreign agent, he took note of our factories, our places of worship, our business practices, our customs and our values. He saw us at the ball park on Saturday, and he saw us go to church on Sunday. Some even went to church on Saturday and Wednesday night.

While many of Japan's political and military leaders wanted war with America, Yamamoto didn't think it was wise. He had serious reservations as he wrote to a colleague:

> "Should hostilities once break out between Japan and the United States, it would not be enough that we take Guam and the Philippines, nor even Hawaii and San Francisco. To make victory certain, we would have to march into Washington and dictate the terms of peace in the White House. I wonder if our politicians, who speak so lightly of a Japanese-American war, have confidence as to the final outcome and are prepared to make the necessary sacrifices."

It's apparent from this quote, especially in the last sentence, that Mr. Yamamoto was no warmonger. But the hyper-nationalist who received the note spread it far and wide – *and he purposefully omitted the last sentence*. If you read the statement without that sentence, it appears Yamamoto is hoping to conquer America from coast to coast. And that's exactly how it was interpreted in America.

Words matter. The truth matters. Here's a clear example of how a lie or a half-truth can cause irreparable damage to a nation. The admiral was not for military aggression against America, but someone distorts his message to make it appear he actually wants war. His country will suffer greatly because of it.

In Japanese mythology, the emperor and his family are said to be direct descendants of the sun-goddess Amaterasu. Therefore, a loyal military officer would never disobey the wish of his "divine" superiors. If the emperor called for war, Yamamoto would do his duty. He devised a battle plan that would give his nation the best chance for victory.

The mastermind behind the assault on Pearl Harbor never planned it as a "sneak attack." When Japan officially declared war against America, Yamamoto hoped that by quickly crippling our naval powers with a preemptive strike at Pearl Harbor, Guam and the Philippines, Japan could then force America to negotiate for peace. It wasn't a bad plan on paper, but things don't always go as planned. As it turned out, Japan sent their declaration of war to its embassy in Washington, but due to numerous delays in translation, the Japanese ambassador did not deliver it to the U.S. Secretary of State until *after* the attack had begun. This was a major breach in the international rules of war.

When Yamamoto heard Japan's declaration of war was not delivered until after their assault started, he realized Americans would see it as a low-down "sneak attack." After that, he knew the citizens of the United States would never negotiate for peace. Instead, we rallied to avenge the death of our 2,403 fellow Americans.

From a purely military point of view, the attack was effective. But on another level, it was a disaster for Japan. American passions boiled over for revenge due to it being an unprovoked attack. Where's the honor in killing sailors who are still in their bunks on a Sunday morning in an undeclared war? To most US residents, the sneak attack was despicable.

As the Japanese military leaders bragged about handing the lazy Americans a crushing defeat at Pearl Harbor, it is reputed Admiral Yamamoto replied,

"I fear all we have done is to awaken a sleeping giant and fill him with a terrible resolve."

Yamamoto was so right. He lived here for years and he knew how the citizens of the United States would react. No one picks a fight with the USA and not pay the price. The small segment of our population that opposed going to war changed their mind overnight after so many Americans were killed at Pearl Harbor. The sleeping giant was fully awake, obsessed with a terrible resolve, and ready for battle.

On April 14, 1943, our intelligence division intercepted and decrypted a message that detailed Yamamoto's flight itinerary. President Roosevelt ordered our forces to take him down. On the morning of April 18th, a squadron of Lockheed P-38 fighter planes attacked and shot down the aircraft that was carrying Admiral Yamamoto. He didn't survive the encounter.

In the second week of August 1945, the United States military dropped the first two atomic bombs ever used in the world on Hiroshima and Nagasaki. On August 15th, Japanese Emperor Hirohito announced their unconditional surrender in a radio address, citing the devastating power of "a new and most cruel bomb."

Saturday, August 11, 2018 United States of America

Virginia authorities in Fairfax say the second daughter has died six days after the 33-yr old mother shot both her daughters. Her first child died at the scene.

Indiana authorities say a 24-yr old woman admitted to throwing a 19-month-old boy to the floor when he wouldn't stop crying. He died in an area hospital of a skull fracture.

Ohio police report that after a 12-hour standoff with SWAT, two sons of a murdered doctor are dead from self-inflicted gunshot wounds near Cleveland.

Louisiana police arrest three suspects, ages 13, 15, and 16, after a 32-yr old man was fatally wounded in the parking lot of a Baton Rouge restaurant.

New Jersey police say a teenager is charged with murder after he shot a 32-yr old man in the head in Woodbury. The 19-yr old suspect was awaiting trial on an earlier gun charge.

Michigan police say a 34-yr old man from Lansing has been arrested and charged with murder after he shot a 51-yr old man inside a rental cabin at Trout Lake.

Missouri authorities in Jasper County report an 18-yr old male was found dead on the back porch of his home in Joplin from a self-inflicted gunshot wound.

Las Vegas Metropolitan police report a 38-yr old was shot and killed while he was outside near his car during a work-break in East Las Vegas. Investigation is ongoing.

New Orleans police say a couple's argument ended when he left their home in his car and she followed him in another car. Shortly afterwards, she lost control of the car, crashed into a tree and later died.

Michigan police say a pregnant mother of four was killed when an SUV ran a stop sign in Grand Rapids and crashed into her minivan. She was thrown from the vehicle. Her baby survived the crash.

South Carolina authorities report an argument over a car purchase results in a 34-yr old man being shot and killed by a 38-yr old man at an auto shop in Sumter.

Texas police are investigating after a man was found shot to death on the sidewalk outside a home in West El Paso.

Detroit police charge a 20-yr old man with murder in connection with the beating death of his 23-yr old girlfriend of Clearwater, Florida.

Texas authorities report a woman was killed at a home in Southeast Houston. When police arrive, a man holding a knife was tased and taken into custody.

Houston police report one man is dead, one man arrested after their cars race on the I-10 East Freeway and cause a deadly crash. The surviving driver was intoxicated.

South Carolina Highway Patrol report a 42-yr old man was found dead off the shoulder of a road in Simpsonville. Police ruled the incident a hit and run.

Texas law enforcement in Ector County discovered the body of a 30-yr old gunshot victim south of Odessa. A 30-yr old suspect is in custody at the county detention center.

Denver police report four people were shot and a female bartender killed in what law enforcement called a large disturbance with weapons at a Thornton sports bar.

San Antonio police say a 75-yr old homeowner approached a suspicious vehicle outside his house when he was shot in the chest. He died on the way to the hospital.

Georgia officials report a homicide investigation is ongoing after a 30-yr old man was found shot and killed on Dahlia Drive in Augusta.

Florida deputies in Marion County were on their way to investigate a "verbal altercation" when a 42-yr old man was shot to death inside a home in McIntosh.

South Carolina law enforcement arrested and charged a 22-yr old man in Pageland for the shooting death of a 19-yr old man. The victim is from Cheraw.

Chicago police charged a 23-yr old woman with accidentally shooting and killing her cousin who was celebrating her 22nd birthday in a Skokie hotel.

Florida Highway Patrol report a 23-yr old man was killed when a 43-yr old drunk driver crashed into the back of his car that was stopped at a traffic light on US-41.

Ohio deputies in Fayette County found a 35-yr old man shot outside a mobile home park in Union Township in southern Ohio. He was pronounced dead at an area hospital.

Georgia authorities report a 45-yr old man was found shot and killed in the backyard of a home in Albany. Two suspects are at large.

Indiana authorities report two customers opened fire and killed a person who was trying to rob a convenience store in northeast Indianapolis.

Des Moines police say a 32-yr old man violated a court protection order and assaulted a man before being shot once in the abdomen. He later died at Iowa Methodist Hospital.

Louisiana authorities report a suspect drove a vehicle down Red Bud Lane in Shreveport and started shooting into a house. A man was wounded, an unidentified woman was killed.

New Mexico police respond to reports of gunfire outside a motel in Albuquerque and find a man on the ground with a gunshot wound. He later died at a local hospital.

New York State police report two drivers were charged with DUI and vehicular manslaughter after a three car crash leaves one person dead on I-90 near East Greenbush.

Ohio police have charged a 40-yr old man with murder, after the 41-yr old man he physically assaulted in Hamilton later died at an area hospital.

Mississippi authorities report a 23-yr old is charged after a 59-yr old man is dead and two others are injured following a shooting at a residence in Hattiesburg.

New Mexico police discover a girl, between 6 and 7 years old, dead in her home in Rio Rancho. They are investigating the death as a homicide.

Missouri authorities report a 22-yr old man was fleeing Kansas City police when he crashed into another driver and killed him. He is charged with involuntary manslaughter.

North Carolina deputies in Wayne County respond to reports of gunfire and find a 17-yr old male shot to death in his home in Seven Springs. Three suspects have been charged.

Alabama police say a 49-yr old male is confirmed dead at a home in Huntsville in what police are saying was possible domestic violence.

New York deputies arrest a 48-yr old woman for DUI after she nearly crashed her car into a Genesee County patrol vehicle. Unbeknownst to police, 30 minutes earlier she struck an 18-yr old in a hit and run. His body was discovered the following morning.

Texas law enforcement say a 29-yr old man shot a 56-yr old man outside a northwest Dallas convenience store. The victim later died at Parkland Memorial Hospital.

Houston officers report a 27-yr old man was shot and killed inside a music studio when someone from outside fired multiple shots into the building.

Idaho authorities say a 34-yr old man was shot and killed by a security guard at a Credit Union in Coeur d'Alene. The victim was a former employee of the credit union.

Phoenix investigators report a 29-yr old woman admitted to police she had strangled an 18-yr old runaway. She then led officers to the plastic-wrapped body in a dumpster.

Houston law enforcement respond to a shooting call and discover a 25-yr old woman was shot in the head while driving her vehicle. She later died at an area hospital.

New Jersey officials report a 44-yr old woman was shot in the head while she and others were on the porch of her house in Bridgeton. She died at Cooper University Hospital.

San Francisco police are looking for five suspects in connection with a shooting in the Crocker-Amazon neighborhood that left a 19-yr old man dead and four others wounded.

Philadelphia police report they are looking for two gunmen who ambushed a man, then shot him to death in Feltonville.

New Jersey police report a 46-yr old mother of five was shot as she sat in a car at a busy intersection in Camden. She was later pronounced dead at Cooper University Hospital.

North Carolina police report a 15-yr old boy is charged with murder for shooting and killing a 25-yr old man after the two argued at an apartment complex in Raeford.

Galveston, Texas investigators say an argument turned violent when a 58-yr old man shot at two women inside a home in Bacliff. One of the victims died from her wounds.

Kentucky State police discovered the 19-yr old male victim of a fatal gunshot wound in a home near Corbin. Pipe bombs were also found inside the home.

California police responded to a possible gang-related shooting in Tulare to discover three gunshot victims – ages 16, 17 and 18. The 17-yr old died from his wounds.

Illinois police respond to a shooting at the Joliet Housing Project and find a 24-yr old man bleeding from gunshot wounds. He was pronounced dead at Silver Cross Hospital.

California police say a man was killed in a shooting incident in East Oakland. One of the bullets missed the intended target and hit the 40-yr old father of four.

Mississippi police arrested and charged a 29-yr old man with murder in the shooting death of a man in Leland.

Pittsburgh law enforcement found a 34-yr old man with multiple gunshot wounds outside his car at a bar in Fairmount. He was pronounced dead at Hahnemann University Hospital.

Cleveland, Ohio investigators say an argument resulted in a 28-yr old man shot outside a convenience store on Euclid Ave. He later died at University Hospitals.

California police respond to sounds of gunfire and discover a 37-yr old woman with several gunshot wounds in a crashed car in Richmond. She later died at a local hospital.

South Carolina deputies find the body of a 51-yr old woman in a vehicle at a Greenville cemetery. Investigation is ongoing.

Pennsylvania police were sent to an apartment in Sharon and found a 21-yr old man shot. He later died at the Regional Medical Center. An 18-yr old man has been charged.

Kentucky State police say a 30-yr old man shot and killed a woman in his Bardwell home. He was arrested for possession of methamphetamine and other charges.

Indiana police say a 32-yr old mother of two was fatally shot during a drive-by in Indianapolis. Her two children lost their father eight months earlier.

Nashville police report an 18-yr old man shot and attempted to rob a 24-yr old man at an apartment in Antioch. The victim later died at Vanderbilt University Medical Center.

Baltimore Central District police were called to a shooting scene on Madison Avenue. When they arrive, they find a male with gunshot wounds who later died in an area hospital.

Alabama authorities report a 38-yr old man was killed in a hit-and-run on Green Springs Highway in Birmingham. A witness saw the victim struck by a car that left the scene.

Ohio authorities say a 49-yr old man fatally shot his wife earlier in the day, and was later shot and killed in an officer-involved shooting with Akron police.

Arkansas police say a 51-yr old man shot and killed a 41-yr old man outside the home he shared with his girlfriend in Forrest City. Detectives blame a love triangle for the tragedy.

Missouri authorities report a 10-week old girl died after being left inside a hot vehicle at a trailer park in Cape Girardeau. Investigation is ongoing.

Florida police say two groups started shooting at each other in a mall parking lot in Jacksonville, and a seven-year old girl was shot and killed in the crossfire. Five suspects arrested.

~§~

President Roosevelt's Prayer on D-Day, 1944

Almighty God: Our sons, pride of our nation, this day have set upon a mighty endeavor, a struggle to preserve our Republic, our religion and our civilization, and to set free a suffering humanity. Lead them straight and true; give strength to their arms, stoutness to their hearts, steadfastness in their faith. They will need Thy blessings. Their road will be long and hard. For the enemy is strong. He may hurl back our forces. Success may not come with rushing speed, but we shall return again and again; and we know by Thy grace, and by the righteousness of our cause, our sons will triumph.

They will be sore tried, by night and by day, without rest – until the victory is won. The darkness will be rent by noise and flame. Men's souls will be shaken with the violences of war. Some will never return. Embrace these, Father, and receive them, Thy heroic servants, into Thy kingdom.

With Thy blessing, we shall prevail over the unholy forces of our enemy. *Help us to conquer the apostles of greed and racial arrogances*. Lead us to the saving of our country, and with our sister nations into a world unity that will spell a sure peace – a peace invulnerable to the scheming of unworthy men. And a peace that will let all men live in freedom, reaping the just rewards of their honest toil. Thy will be done. Amen.

Manasseh: Israel's Most Evil Ruler!

Rome had Nero. The Soviet Union had Stalin. Germany had Hitler. Uganda had Idi Amin. Belgium had Leopold II. Italy had Mussolini. Haiti had Papa Doc. No country has a monopoly on evil. The prince of the powers of the air is not hindered by national borders or walls. Most people know about the above-mentioned dictators. Their evil deeds are almost common knowledge. But how many people today know about Israel's most evil ruler, King Manasseh? He reigned longer than any other king in Israel, and was the worst of them all. Go figure! This leader of the nation was so wicked, and he caused so much evil in Israel, that Yahweh was compelled to cast off his people. The LORD is good and merciful, but he isn't playing games with those who are called by his name.

> "Manasseh was twelve years old when he began to reign, and he reigned fifty-five years in Jerusalem. He did that which was evil in Yahweh's sight, after the abominations of the nations whom Yahweh cast out before the children of Israel. For he built again the high places which Hezekiah his father had broken down; and he raised up altars for the Baals, made Asheroth, and worshiped all the army of the sky, and *served them.*
>
> "He built altars in Yahweh's house, of which Yahweh said, 'My name shall be in Jerusalem forever.' He built altars for all the army of the sky in the two courts of Yahweh's house. He also made his children to pass through the fire in the valley of the son of Hinnom. He practiced sorcery, divination, and witchcraft, and dealt with those who had familiar spirits and wizards. **He did much evil in Yahweh's sight, to provoke him to anger.**
>
> "He set the engraved image of the idol, which he had made, in God's house, of which God said to David and to Solomon his son, 'In this house, and in Jerusalem, which I have chosen out of all the tribes of Israel, I will put my name forever. I will not any more remove the foot of Israel from off the land which I have appointed for your fathers, *if only* they will observe to do all that I have commanded them, even all the law, the statutes, and the ordinances given by Moses.' Manasseh *seduced* Judah and the inhabitants of Jerusalem, so that they did *more evil* than did the

> nations whom Yahweh destroyed before the children of Israel. Yahweh spoke to Manasseh, and to his people; but they didn't listen." ~ *2 Chronicles 33:1-10*

~§~

> "Moreover Manasseh shed innocent blood very much, until he had filled Jerusalem from one end to another; in addition to his sin which he made Judah to sin, in doing that which was evil in Yahweh's sight." ~ *2 Kings 21:16*

"They didn't destroy the peoples, as Yahweh commanded them, but mixed themselves with the nations, and learned their works. They served their idols, which became a snare to them. Yes, they sacrificed their sons and their daughters to demons. They shed innocent blood, even the blood of their sons and of their daughters, whom they sacrificed to the idols of Canaan. The land was polluted with blood. Thus they were defiled with their works, and prostituted themselves in their deeds. **Therefore Yahweh burned with anger against his people.** He abhorred his inheritance." ~ *Psalm 106:34-40*

I say again fellow citizen, the reason why God put this in his book is for the stated purpose of giving us examples to follow and examples to avoid. What are we learning from the example of Israel? How does this apply to our walk of faith today? A. W. Tozer said, "Danger approaches the Christian life from three directions: The world through which we journey, the god of this world, and our unmortified flesh. That's why we need a rock, a fortress, a Deliverer, a buckler, a high tower to run to."

Is God the rock of our nation? Are we standing firm on the faith of our fathers? Are we attentive to the three danger zones of the believer: our flesh, the devil, and the world? King Manasseh seduced a nation into engaging in deep sin. What role do ordinary citizens play in maintaining the holiness and righteousness of a nation? Are you crying out to the Lord to ignite the fires of revival in your community? How can you assist in forming a critical mass of intercessors within your sphere of influence? What are you doing to *rouse yourself* to pray and take hold of God?

Chapter Eight:

"And Seek my face,"

No human authority can stop a believer from praying. That's inspiring. If you're conscious, you can pray and no one can stop you. How is this possible? It's due to the fact that prayer can happen in a secret place where only you and God abide. *"Pray to your Father who is in secret; and your Father who sees in secret will reward you openly."* This teaching of Jesus in Matthew 6:6 is an empowering word and a sharp two-edged sword. For the same God who allows us to meet with him in secret is the same God who knows our hearts, and reads our thoughts, and discerns our intentions. Nothing is hidden from the Most High. "But all things are naked and laid open before the eyes of him to whom we must give an account" (Hebrews 4:13).

The Bible teaches us that our hearts and deepest thoughts are on open display before the One who sits high and looks low. King David instructs his son in 1 Chronicles 28:9,

> "You, Solomon my son, know you the God of your father, and serve him with a perfect heart and with a willing mind; *for Yahweh searches all hearts, and understands all the imaginations of the thoughts:* If you seek him, he will be found of you; but if you forsake him, he will cast you off forever."

If we seek the LORD with deceitful hearts and cunning imaginations, he will not be fooled. He "searches" our hearts, and "understands all the imaginations" of our thoughts! He's "able to discern the thoughts and intentions of the heart" (Hebrews 4:12)! The LORD knows if we're seeking him because we love him and truly repent of our sins, and he knows if we are seeking him for selfish reasons. God is not mocked. If we seek him with ill motives, he will know it and he'll withdraw himself from us.

Let's listen in as the prophet Hosea condemns both the house of Israel and the house of Judah concerning their wicked ways. In this passage, the large tribe of Ephraim is seen as the representative of the Northern Kingdom of Israel. Their first king was from the tribe of Ephraim. Judah is seen as the representative of the Southern Kingdom.

By this time in their history, the relationship between God and his chosen people has degraded so bad, and Israel's spiritual perception is so dull, that Yahweh will use his prophet as a living object lesson. God tells Hosea, "Go, take for yourself a wife of prostitution and children of unfaithfulness; for the land commits great adultery, forsaking Yahweh" (Hosea 1:2).

That's pretty drastic, but desperate times call for desperate measures. The prophet obeys and takes for his wife a prostitute by the name of Gomer. God is making it plain to see how he feels about their unfaithfulness to him. El Kanna is married to a harlot!

Back in Deuteronomy, God and Israel entered into a covenant and avouched themselves to one another. And in Joshua's day, the people reaffirmed their covenant with the LORD. But once the ten tribes broke away from Benjamin and Judah to establish a Northern Kingdom, they left Jerusalem behind. Since they didn't have access to their old worship center, alternative worship sites with unqualified leaders were set up in Bethel and Dan, which became a snare to them (see 1 Kings 12:26-31). The obstinate people of the Northern Kingdom quickly fell into idolatry.

> "I know Ephraim, and Israel is not hidden from me; [Is anything hidden from the LORD?] for now, Ephraim, you have played the prostitute. Israel is defiled. Their deeds won't allow them to turn to their God; for the spirit of prostitution is within them, and they don't know Yahweh.
>
> "The pride of Israel testifies to his face. Therefore Israel and Ephraim will stumble in their iniquity. Judah also will stumble with them. They will go with their flocks and with their herds to seek Yahweh; but they won't find him. He has withdrawn himself from them. *They are unfaithful to Yahweh;* for they have borne illegitimate children.
>
> "Now the new moon will devour them with their fields. The princes of Judah are like those who remove a landmark. **I will pour out my wrath on them like water**. Ephraim is oppressed, he is crushed in judgment, because he is intent in his pursuit of idols. Therefore I am to Ephraim like a moth, and to the house of Judah like rottenness. For I will be to Ephraim like a lion, and like a young lion to the house of Judah. I myself will tear in pieces and go away. I will carry off, and there will be no one to

deliver. I will go and return to my place, *until* they acknowledge their offense, and seek my face. In their affliction they will seek me earnestly." ~ *Hosea 5: 3-7, 10-12, 14-15*

Allow me to make a few observations. First, our sins stop us from turning to the LORD. Verse 4 says, *"Their deeds won't allow them to turn to their God."* Sin has a way of transmuting from a cool playmate into an evil dictator. If you give the devil an inch, he'll become your ruler. **Sin will take you farther than you want to go, keep you longer than you want to stay, and cost you more than you want to pay!**

Secondly, our sins cause the LORD to turn from us. Verse 6 is one of those sad situations where God has had enough. *"He has withdrawn himself from them."* What could be more dreadful than God turning his back on America because of our wicked ways? "I will go and return to my place, until they acknowledge their offense."

> *"They have turned their backs to me, and not their faces.* Although I taught them, rising up early and teaching them, yet they have not listened to receive instruction." ~ *Jeremiah 32:33*

> "I will scatter them as with an east wind before the enemy. *I will show them the back, and not the face,* in the day of their calamity." ~ *Jeremiah 18:17*

Yahweh is saying their sins have caused him to turn his back on them, and even if they seek him now, they will not find him *until* they acknowledge their sin. His back is turned to them and it will stay that way until they say/acknowledge about their ways what he says about their ways. Isn't that the essence of confession?

For example, God says stealing is wrong and a sin. But I contend stealing is cool, especially since I only steal from those who can afford it. God has his "opinion" and I have my "opinion." Our opinions don't agree. How can two walk together except they agree (Amos 3:3)? They can't. I've turned my back; God turns his back. And God will stay turned from me until I say (acknowledge) about stealing what he has said about stealing. Sin is not some casual plaything. Sin is an affront to God. He is not interested in hearing our "opinion" of sin. His interest lies in whether or not we feel about sin the way he feels about sin. To be nonchalant regarding iniquity is the way of a fool (Proverbs 10:23).

Our sins provoke God to do an about-face. Our misdeeds cause us to forfeit his blessings. JAH said to Israel, "your sins have withheld good from you" (Jeremiah 5:25). Our iniquities make God shun us, which in turn, robs us of many good things he wants to share. Therefore, Americans should be alarmed and indignant over the sins of our nation (Psalm 119:53). We mustn't ignore the pain and loss caused by our evil ways.

Psalm 97:10 declares, "**You who love Yahweh, hate evil!**" We can't love the LORD and quietly assume a neutral, dispassionate stance regarding evil. Those who love the King of heaven are commanded to take a stand and hate sin. Charles H. Spurgeon put it this way:

> "If I had a brother who had been murdered, what would you think of me if I daily consorted with the assassin who drove the dagger into my brother's heart; surely I too must be an accomplice in the crime. Sin murdered Christ; will you be a friend to it? Sin pierced the heart of the Incarnate God; can you love it?"

"**The fear of Yahweh is to hate evil!**" (Proverbs 8:13). Those who claim to fear the LORD must love whatever God loves, and hate whatever he hates. God hates sin. Therefore, I can't hold on to sin and walk with God at the same time. Jealous will not allow that. If I elect to walk with sin, by default, I am electing to walk away from God.

> "Behold, Yahweh's hand is not shortened, that it can't save; nor his ear dull, that it can't hear. *But your iniquities have separated you and your God,* and your sins have hidden his face from you, so that he will not hear. For your hands are defiled with blood, and your fingers with iniquity. Your lips have spoken lies. Your tongue mutters wickedness." ~ *Isaiah 59:1-3*

Third, God is counting on affliction to do its special work. *"In their affliction they will seek me earnestly."* God uses affliction and hardship and pain to focus our attention, see 2 Chronicles 6:36-39. Once he has our attention, hopefully we'll come to our senses, confess our sins, turn from our dusty ways, and submit to his will.

> "Furthermore, we had the fathers of our flesh chasten us, and we paid them respect. Shall we not much rather be in subjection to the Father of spirits, and live? For they indeed, for a few days, punished us as seemed good to them; but he for our profit, that we

may be partakers of his holiness. All chastening seems for the present to be not joyous but grievous; *yet afterward* it yields the peaceful fruit of righteousness to those who have been trained by it." ~ *Hebrews 12:9-11*

We saw in a BibleScope assignment that God uses pain to get our attention. The LORD takes no pleasure in chastening us, but he knows by sparing the rod, he'll spoil the child. Lady Wisdom says in Proverbs 29:15 NKJV: "**The rod and rebuke give wisdom**, but a child left to himself brings shame to his mother." Sometimes, a rebuke alone is not enough to impart wisdom. Sometimes, the rod needs to be added to the mix. "Foolishness is bound in the heart of a child; but the **rod of correction** shall drive it far from him" (Proverbs 22:15 KJV). Our heavenly Father says he may use a famine, a locust plague or a pandemic to get our attention (2 Chronicles 7:13)! When the hand of the Lord is heavy on us, the purpose behind the pain is to prompt us to humble ourselves, and pray, and seek his face, and get off Curses Curve, and get back on Blessings Boulevard. Pain prepares us for revival. *"In their affliction they will..."*

How to Seek His Face

We know what it means to humble ourselves. But what does it mean to seek his face? One day Will Rogers was entertaining at the Milton H. Berry Institute in Los Angeles. It was a health center that specialized in rehabilitating polio victims and people with broken backs and other extreme physical handicaps. Of course, Rogers had everybody laughing, even the patients in really bad condition.

But then he suddenly stopped his comedy routine, left the platform and made his way into the washroom. Milton Berry, wondering why the sudden pause in the show, followed Will to see if anything was wrong. When Mr. Berry opened the door, he saw Will Rogers leaning against the wall. As he got closer and looked him in the face, he saw Will Rogers was sobbing like a child. Milton Berry quietly walked out. A few minutes later, Rogers appeared back on the platform, as jovial and entertaining as before. Will Rogers was known for creating laughter, but the sight of those patients broke his heart. He also knew how to weep.

If you want to gain a better understanding of a person, just ask three questions: What makes them angry? What makes them cry? And what makes them laugh? *Is this our key to seeking God's face?* I believe so. It simply means to focus on him. Let's not overthink it. To seek his face means to get a better understanding of his person, of who he is, and what makes him tick. How do we do that? By asking a few questions.

BibleScope Assignment

Let's cover this section as our third and final assignment. Biblescopes in the ready!

Hypothesis: *We can seek God's face by asking three questions. What incites our Lord to display an angry face? What makes our Lord cry? And what causes our Lord to laugh?* Is this true or not?

Question 1. What incites our Lord to display an angry face? Scripture tells us to be angry, but do not sin, nor give place to the devil (Ephesians 4:26,27). How did Jesus strike that balance?

Slide #1: John 2:14-16 NKJV » "And He found in the temple those who sold oxen and sheep and doves, and the moneychangers doing business. When He made a whip of cords, He drove them all out of the temple, with the sheep and the oxen, and poured out the changers' money and overturned the tables. And he said to those who sold doves, "Take these things away! Do not make My Father's house a house of merchandise!"

Nothing is more telling of Jesus' outward expression of anger than when he entered his Father's house and drove out the money changers. Whenever we use the house of worship as a vehicle for economic activity instead of a place to foster spiritual vitality, it reveals a worldly heart that idolizes money and material stuff. *Our hearts and deepest thoughts are on open display to Jesus (1 Samuel 16:7).* He saw they weren't in the temple to encounter God. These people were only there to profit from those coming to make an offering to God. Let's be careful, sisters and brothers, lest we lust for filthy lucre and incite his anger.

Slide #2: Mark 3:1-6 » "He entered again into the synagogue, and there was a man there who had his hand withered. They watched him, whether he would heal him on the Sabbath day, *that they might accuse him*. He said to the man who had his hand withered, "Stand up." He said to them, "Is it lawful on the Sabbath day to do good or to do harm? To save a life or to kill?" But they were silent. When he had looked around at them with anger, *being grieved at the hardening of their hearts*, he said to the man, "Stretch out your hand." He stretched it out, and his hand was restored as healthy as the other. The Pharisees went out, and immediately conspired with the Herodians against him, how they might destroy him."

This episode makes me angry! These religious folk upset Jesus because they missed the point altogether. They were more interested in hiding behind the letter of the law than they were in understanding the true meaning of the law. Instead of focusing on the power of God, they saw an opportunity to misuse the law to condemn Jesus. Talk about lopsided thinking! It's easy to see why our Lord was angry with these people.

We have many Pharisees and Herodians in our midst today. Hard-hearted folk who love their religion more than they love God. People who are prone to miss the point and the power because they're too busy looking for a reason to condemn others (John 5:16-18; 7:23,24; 9:16). May JAH help us to not judge according to appearance.

Slide #3: John 11:5, 32-33 KJV » "Now Jesus loved Martha, and her sister, and Lazarus. ...Then when Mary was come where Jesus was, and saw him, she fell down at his feet, saying unto him, Lord, if thou hadst been here, my brother had not died. When Jesus therefore saw her weeping, and the Jews also weeping which came with her, he **groaned** in the spirit, and was **troubled**."

The Greek (Gr) verb used here for "groaned" is *embrimaomai.* In classical Greek, it literally means "to snort" as a horse does in anger or alarm. It means to be moved with indignation, to be very angry. The Greek word "troubled" is *tarasso,* which means to stir or agitate. But what's causing our Lord to react this way?

Let me ask you, in this current age who has the power of death? If we look at Hebrews 2:14-15 NKJV, we're told why the Son of God left heaven and became human. "Inasmuch then as the children have partaken of flesh and blood, He Himself likewise shared in the same, that through death He might destroy him who had the power of death, that is, the devil, and release those who through fear of death were all their lifetime subject to bondage."

Since "flesh and blood" sinned against the Most High, our Savior "shared in the same" in order to take our place. The just for the unjust. The righteous one taking the place and the punishment for the unrighteous one. Some religious groups and cults make the claim that Jesus was only an angel, or a spirit being. But what good would it do if an angel "died" for a man? An angel's "death" could possibly be a ransom for another angel, but it can't mediate for the sins of a human. A man had to die for man. Life for life, blood for blood. It was the *man* Christ Jesus who sacrificed his life for you and me. "For there is one God, and one mediator between God and men, the *man* Christ Jesus, who gave himself as a ransom for all" (1 Timothy 2:5,6). It was the *man* Christ Jesus who arose victorious over death, and in so doing, he delivered other *men* from the "bondage" of the fear of death. Believers no longer fear death. Why not? Because the "man Christ Jesus" conquered death, and praise God, he didn't stop there! He also destroyed (Gr *katargeō* – to render ineffective, but not annihilate) the one "who had the power of death, that is, the devil."

Jesus said it is the evil one who comes to steal, kill and destroy. Satan tempts people to sin and come under the penalty of sin, which is death. In 1 Corinthians 15:16, Paul tells us "the last enemy that shall be destroyed is death." But until we get to that day, the prince of this world still holds "the power of death." *He's defeated, but not annihilated.*

Jesus' friend is a victim of the devil's handiwork. The Christ is rightfully upset. Satan's relentless assaults on the human race troubled the Anointed One in his spirit. Satan ushered in sin and sin ushered in death. And now, his dear friend Lazarus is trapped in the grip of death. Mary is weeping, Martha is weeping, others are there crying at the gravesite. It moves Jesus with indignation. He's stirred. He's troubled! What does he do? After asking humans to remove the stone entrance to the cave, "He cried with a loud voice, **Lazarus, come forth.** And he that was dead came forth" (John 11:43,44 KJV).

BAM! Lazarus lives! Satan has the power of death, but our Lord has the power of LIFE and death. In raising Lazarus from the dead, Jesus shows us a small glimpse of his supreme authority and our ultimate victory over the last enemy – death itself. But until that day comes, death is an enemy. It's the handiwork of Satan, and it makes our Lord angry.

I'm tempted to add Revelation 3:14-22 NKJV to the list of slides that show Jesus angry. What do you think? Jesus is calling the people within the church of Laodicea to repent. Laodicea was a boom town, one of the wealthiest centers in the region. It was known for three industries: banking, clothing and medicine. Our Lord will mention all three in his warning to this lukewarm church.

> "And to the angel of the church of the Laodiceans write, 'These things says the Amen, the Faithful and True Witness, the Beginning of the creation of God: "I know your works, that you are neither cold nor hot. I could wish you were cold or hot. So then, because you are lukewarm, and neither cold nor hot, I will vomit you out of My mouth. Because you say, 'I am rich, have become wealthy, and have need of nothing' – and do not know that you are wretched, miserable, poor, blind, and naked – I counsel you to buy from Me gold refined in the fire, that you may be rich; and white garments, that you may be clothed, that the shame of your nakedness may not be revealed; and anoint your eyes with eye salve, that you may see. **As many as I love, I rebuke and chasten. Therefore be zealous and repent**. Behold, I stand at the door and knock. If anyone hears My voice and opens the door, I will come in to him and dine with him, and he with Me. *To him who overcomes I will grant to sit with Me on My throne, as I also overcame and sat down with My Father on His throne*. "He who has an ear, let him hear what the Spirit says to the churches."

Those who are loved by God can expect to be disciplined by God. These church folk were sinfully satisfied in their lukewarm ways. They thought they were rich, wealthy, in need of nothing. In the eyes of the Lord, they were wretched, miserable, poor, blind, naked, and ready to be taken to the woodshed! Jesus is not moving in this church; he's outside, knocking, waiting to enter. The self-satisfied people at the church of Laodicea don't anger Jesus as much as they disgust him. Their blasé attitude about the things of the Kingdom is repulsive to our Lord.

Question 2. What makes Jesus cry? What's the shortest verse in the Bible? **Slide #4:** John 11:35 » "Jesus wept." Jesus cried at the graveside of Lazarus. Funerals can be sad. Jesus loved his friend, and now Lazarus is dead. Mary is weeping, "the Jews also weeping which came with her." And Jesus wept. People around him are hurting and he feels their pain. The Bible exhorts us to, "Rejoice with those who rejoice. Weep with those who weep" (Romans 12:15). Depending on the occasion, we join in the celebration with others, or we join in the pain with others. This is a marvelous display of our Lord's humanity and his empathy.

Slide #5: Luke 19:28, 41, 43-44 NKJV » "When He had said this, He went on ahead, going up to Jerusalem." "Now as He drew near, He saw the city and wept over it." [Why is Jesus crying for Jerusalem?] "For days will come upon you when your enemies will build an embankment around you, surround you and close you in on every side, and level you, and your children within you, to the ground; and they will not leave in you one stone upon another, because you did not know the time of your visitation."

How can God allow such a tragedy to happen in the beloved city? Part of the answer is found in Matthew 27. When our Lord was sent to be condemned by Pilate, the governor knew Jesus was innocent and attempted to release him. Levi, the former tax collector, tells us, "the **chief priests** and the **elders** persuaded the multitudes to ask for Barabbas and destroy Jesus. But the governor answered them, "Which of the two do you want me to release to you?" They said, "Barabbas!" Pilate said to them, "What then shall I do to Jesus who is called Christ?" They all said to him, "Let him be crucified!" But the governor said, "Why? What evil has he done?" But they cried out exceedingly, saying, "**Let him be crucified!**" All the people answered, "May his blood be on us and on our children!" Then he released Barabbas to them, but Jesus he flogged and delivered to be crucified" (Matthew 27:20-23, 25,26).

How sad is that! Pilate knew Jesus was not worthy of death, but the mob ruled that day. Jesus cried for the fate of the people in Jerusalem. Like the prophet Jeremiah, he cried for the city because he knew they would reject him. They rejected and killed so many prophets before *and* after him (Acts 7:51-60). Jesus would be treated like all the others, and it broke his heart. The Jews received a "visitation" from their Messiah. But they didn't expect a suffering Savior. They expected a conquering King. How did they respond to the meek and lowly Jesus? They shouted, "Let him be crucified!" and "May his blood be on us and on our children!" They didn't have to wait long before Titus of Rome came a knocking in 70 A.D.

I think it's worth pointing out that Jesus cried for the masses as well as for an individual. He loves the masses and the individuals who make up the masses. Let us go and do likewise. Jesus cried at the gravesite of his friend Lazarus. This displays his humanity, as he shows us how to weep with those who weep. Jesus also cried over the city of Jerusalem, the blessed city of God, the city that murdered the prophets of Yahweh. He knows our fate when we reject him and it breaks his heart. We now come to the third question.

Question 3. What causes our Lord to laugh? We've seen what makes Jesus angry. We've seen what makes Jesus cry. You may be surprised to know we don't have a single example in the Bible of our Lord laughing. For reasons we still don't know, that part of his life here on earth is veiled to us (Isaiah 53:3,4). I would like to believe that Jesus appreciated a comedic scene just like everyone else, but the author of Scripture didn't leave us any examples. Some claim the camel trying to squeeze through the eye of a needle is pretty comical (Matthew 19:24), but I'm not sure it was meant to be funny. Jesus says there is joy in heaven when one sinner repents (Luke 15:10). He would know. But joy is not the same as laughter.

The Bible does tell us that the Father laughs. Psalm Two is regarded as messianic, which means even though the passage sits within the context of the Old Testament, on another level, it's making reference to the future reign of the Messiah.

> "Why do the nations rage, and the peoples plot a vain thing? The kings of the earth take a stand, and the rulers take counsel together, against Yahweh, and against his Anointed, saying, "Let's break their bonds apart, and cast away their cords from us." **He who sits in the heavens will laugh**. The Lord will have them in derision. Then he will speak to them in his anger, and terrify them in his wrath: "Yet I have set my king on my holy hill of Zion."
> ~ *Psalm 2:1-6*

In the devotional, *Our Daily Bread*, Dennis DeHaan comments:

> "I was washing my car one evening as the sun was preparing to kiss the earth goodnight. Glancing up, I impulsively pointed the hose at it as if to extinguish its flames. The absurdity of my action hit me, and I laughed. Then I thought of God's laughter in Psalm Two. Wicked nations were plotting to overthrow God's Anointed, thus ultimately opposing the Almighty Himself. But He sits in the heavens, calm and unthreatened. Man's boldest efforts to oppose such awesome power is ludicrous. The Almighty doesn't even rise from His throne; He just laughs in derision. But is this a heartless or cruel laughter? No! His same infinite greatness that mocks man's defiance also marks His sympathy for man in his lost condition. *He's the same God who takes no pleasure in the death of the wicked* (Ezekiel 33:11). God's laughter gives us the assurance that Christ will ultimately triumph over evil. Any defiance of Him and His will is futile. Instead of opposing the Son, we should submit to the Lord Jesus and take refuge in Him."

Amen! The Bible tells us Lady Wisdom laughs also. What Brother DeHaan says of the Son can also be said of her. Instead of opposing Lady Wisdom, we should submit to her and take refuge in her. If we snub her call, she will laugh in our day of trouble.

> "Because I have called, and you refused; I have stretched out my hand, and no one has paid attention; but you have ignored all my counsel, and wanted none of my reproof; *I also will laugh at your disaster*. I will mock when calamity overtakes you, when calamity overtakes you like a storm [sounds like D28B!], when your disaster comes on like a whirlwind, when distress and anguish come on you. Then they will call on me, but I will not answer. They will seek me diligently, but they will not find me, because **they hated knowledge, and didn't choose the fear of Yahweh**."
> ~ *Proverbs 1:24-29*

"He who sins against me wrongs his own soul. All those who hate me love death" (Proverbs 8:36). It's not wise to reject Lady Wisdom!

What made Jesus laugh? I can't say. But we do know that his Father laughs at the idea of feeble men attempting to thwart his plans. And we know that Lady Wisdom laughs at those who "hated knowledge" but suddenly find themselves in a bind. She laughs at those who are overcome by the storms of life (Matthew 7:26,27). Why? Because they didn't choose the fear of the LORD when they had the chance! God is not mocked. Our "Wonderful Counselor" cannot be conned. The Most High is the only God who "searches all hearts, and understands all the imaginations of the thoughts" (1 Chronicles 28:9). "And shall not he render to every man according to his work?" (Proverbs 24:12 KJV). Yes, he will!

We seek the face of God by asking ourselves key questions, and then we examine the Bible for answers. It tells us what makes Jesus angry. Religious pretenders, who hold to an outward form of godliness but deny its power, anger our Lord. The misery and pain caused by sin and death angers our Lord. The Scriptures also show us what makes Jesus cry. May we have a heart like his that cried for the deceived masses and the individuals who make up the masses. Furthermore, the Word reveals to us what makes the Father laugh - the ridiculous attempts of man to block the plans of the Most High. We also got a chance to see what causes Lady Wisdom to laugh - silly people looking for a "get out of jail free" card. And finally, our sacred text tells us how Jesus feels when we grow tepid, self-satisfied and indifferent to the things of the Kingdom. It makes him sick!

Hypothesis: *We can seek God's face by asking three questions. What incites our Lord to display an angry face? What makes our Lord cry? And what causes our Lord to laugh?* Is this true or not?

Conclusion: It's abundantly true! For Scripture reveals to us the mind, the heart, and the face of God. "Glory in his holy name. Let the heart of those who seek Yahweh rejoice. Seek Yahweh and his strength. Seek his face forever more." ~ *Psalm 105:4-5*

"The counsel of the LORD standeth for ever, the *thoughts of his heart* to all generations." ~ *Psalm 33:11 KJV*

"Oh, taste and see that the LORD is good; blessed is the man who trusts in Him! Oh, fear the LORD, you His saints! There is no want to those who fear Him. The young lions lack and suffer hunger; but those who seek the LORD shall not lack any good thing." ~ *Psalm 34:7-10 NKJV*

"Without faith it is impossible to be well pleasing to him, for he who comes to God must believe that he exists, and that he is a *rewarder* of those who seek him." ~ *Hebrews 11:6*

"Seek Yahweh while he may be found. Call on him while he is near. Let the wicked forsake his way, and the unrighteous man his thoughts. Let him return to Yahweh, and he will have mercy on him, to our God, for he will freely pardon." ~ *Isaiah 55:6-7*

I was weeping in the most bitter contrition of my heart, when I heard the voice of children from a neighboring house chanting, "Take up and read; take up and read." I could not remember ever having heard the like, so checking the torrent of my tears, I arose, interpreting it to be no other than a command from God to open the book and read the first chapter I should find. Eagerly then I returned to the place where I had laid the volume of the apostle. I seized, opened, and in silence read that section of which my eyes first fell: *"Not in revelry and drunkenness, not in licentiousness and lewdness, not in strife and envy; but put on the Lord Jesus Christ, and make no provision for the flesh, to fulfill its lusts" [Romans 13:13,14].* No further would I read, nor did I need to. For instantly at the end of this sentence, it seemed as if a light of serenity infused into my heart and all the darkness of doubt vanished away. ~ *St. Augustine of Hippo*

Chapter Nine:

The Weeping Prophet

God uses pain to get our attention. For whom the LORD loves, he disciplines (Hebrews 12:5,6). But he doesn't afflict us willingly. Like any caring parent today, the Father of spirits takes no pleasure in punishing his stubborn children. Before he afflicts us, he warns us. Yahweh used prophets and seers to warn his hardheaded people. One well-known prophet he used to call the nation of Israel to repentance and faith was Jeremiah. His ministry was to a people on the brink of divine judgment.

Jeremiah cared deeply for his country. As a matter of fact, he's called the "weeping prophet" due to his many tears over the state of his nation. He also wrote the Old Testament book of Lamentations, which are his "loud cries" over the horrid fate of Jerusalem. Please make time to read all 52 chapters of the book of Jeremiah. We can glean many insights from his message to Israel and their response to his message. In a word, we would be wise to consider how God has dealt with the Jewish nation. The Scripture states, "However with most to them, God was not well pleased, for they were overthrown in the wilderness. Now these things were our examples, to the intent we should not lust after evil things, as they also lusted." ~ *1 Corinthians 10:5-6*

Someone has well said, "A wise man learns by the experience of others. An ordinary man learns by his own experience. A fool learns by nobody's experience." What can be said of the man can also be said of a nation. "A wise nation learns by the experience of other nations. An ordinary nation learns by its own experience. A foolish nation learns by nobody's experience." Throughout this book, the nation of Israel has served as an example to us, a cautionary tale, so to speak. When you read God's message to Israel through the prophet Jeremiah, you'll notice that many of the sinful actions and boastful attitudes that Yahweh condemned in the Holy Land over 2,600 years ago are rampant in America today. Will we learn from their mistakes? The Jewish nation refused to heed the warnings of God. Instead, they rushed headlong into their sin and rebellion. Eventually, the LORD of hosts was compelled to punish Israel for her willfulness. And since God is no respecter of persons, unless America changes her ways, we too will be judged. May God grant us the grace to hear his word and heed his word (James 1:22).

Jealousy arouses the fury of the husband, and Yahweh is not happy. In chapter three of the book of Jeremiah, the prophet has a harsh message from the LORD for the unfaithful people of Judah:

They say, "If a man puts away his wife, and she goes from him, and becomes another man's, should he return to her again? Wouldn't that land be greatly polluted? But you have played the prostitute with many lovers; yet return again to me," says Yahweh. *v.1*

Moreover, Yahweh said to me in the days of Josiah the king, "Have you seen that which backsliding Israel has done? She has gone up on every high mountain and under every green tree, and has played the prostitute there. I said after she had done all these things, 'She will return to me;' but she didn't return, and her treacherous sister Judah saw it. I saw when, for this very cause, that backsliding Israel had committed adultery, I had put her away and given her a certificate of divorce, yet treacherous Judah, her sister, *had no fear;* but she also went and played the prostitute. Because she took her prostitution lightly, the land was polluted, and she committed adultery with stones and with wood. Yet for all this her treacherous sister, Judah, has not returned to me with her *whole heart,* but only in pretense," says Yahweh.

[*Our hearts and deepest thoughts are on open display to the LORD. He knows if we're whole-hearted, half-hearted, or quarter-hearted!*]

Yahweh said to me, "Backsliding Israel has shown herself more righteous than treacherous Judah. Go, and proclaim these words toward the north, and say, 'Return, you backsliding Israel,' says Yahweh; 'I will not look in anger on you; for I am merciful,' says Yahweh. 'I will not keep anger forever. **Only acknowledge your iniquity**, that you have transgressed against Yahweh your God, and have scattered your ways to the strangers under every green tree, and you have not obeyed my voice,' says Yahweh." "Return, backsliding children," says Yahweh; "for I am a husband to you." *vv. 6-14a*

"Surely as a wife treacherously departs from her husband, so you have dealt treacherously with me, house of Israel," says Yahweh. A voice is heard on the bare heights, the weeping and the petitions of the children of Israel; because they have perverted their way, they have forgotten Yahweh their God. Return, you backsliding children, and I will heal your backsliding." *vv. 20-22*

Even after all their treachery and backsliding, the unruly house of Israel can still find healing and forgiveness if they will only acknowledge their iniquity. Be not deceived, dear elect of God, we serve a gracious and compassionate Redeemer. He is Jehovah-Jireh, the LORD who provides, our merciful and strong Deliverer. So, if we ever find ourselves riding hard on D28B, may JAH give us the grace to quickly come to our senses and find our way home.

> "For the Lord will not cast off forever. For though he causes grief, *yet he will have compassion* according to the multitude of his loving kindnesses. For he does not afflict willingly, nor grieve the children of men [willingly]." ~ *Lamentations 3:31-33*

~§~

God is a master communicator. If we are without understanding, it certainly isn't his fault. Remember how he told the prophet Hosea to marry a prostitute in order to visualize the message for his unfaithful people? Yahweh uses Jeremiah in a similar fashion by having the prophet shoulder a yoke of wood, and later buy a field in the land of Benjamin. God uses all of our senses to reach us. Our ears, our eyes, our sense of touch and smell and taste, and our dreams. Even during NT times, the Almighty had prophets use "object lessons" to dramatize his message.

> "As we stayed there some days, a certain prophet named Agabus came down from Judea. Coming to us and taking Paul's belt, he bound his own feet and hands, and said, 'The Holy Spirit says: So the Jews at Jerusalem will bind the man who owns this belt, and will deliver him into the hands of the Gentiles.' " ~ *Acts 21:10-11*

I don't think Paul and company had any problem discerning the mind of God after meeting Brother Agabus! In chapter 13 of Jeremiah, we'll see the LORD use another belt to drive home his point.

~ *O God, give us spiritual insight as we look into Your Word.* ~

Yahweh said to me, "Go, and buy yourself a linen belt, and put it on your waist, and don't put it in water." So I bought a belt according to Yahweh's word, and put it on my waist.

Yahweh's word came to me a second time, saying, "Take the belt that you have bought, which is on your waist, and arise, go to the Euphrates, and hide it there in a cleft of the rock." So I went and hid it by the Euphrates, as Yahweh commanded me.

After many days, Yahweh said to me, "Arise, go to the Euphrates, and take the belt from there, which I commanded you to hide there." Then I went to the Euphrates, and dug, and took the belt from the place where I had hidden it; and behold, **the belt was ruined**. It was profitable for nothing.

Then Yahweh's words came to me, saying, "Yahweh says, 'In this way I, will ruin the pride of Judah, and the great pride of Jerusalem. *This evil people, who refuse to hear my words, who walk in the stubbornness of their heart, and have gone after other gods to serve them, and to worship them, will even be as this belt, which is profitable for nothing*. For as the belt clings to the waist of a man, so I have caused the whole house of Israel and the whole house of Judah to cling to me,' says Yahweh; 'that they may be to me for a people, for a name, for praise, and for glory; but they would not hear.' "

Hear, and give ear. Don't be proud, for Yahweh has spoken. Give glory to Yahweh your God, before he causes darkness, and before your feet stumble on the dark mountains, and while you look for light, he turns it into the shadow of death, and makes it deep darkness. But if you will not hear it, my soul will weep in secret for your pride. My eye will weep bitterly, and run down with tears, because Yahweh's flock has been taken captive. Say to the king and to the queen mother, "Humble yourselves. Sit down, for your crowns have come down, even the crown of your glory."

If you say in your heart, "Why have these things come on me?" Your skirts are uncovered because of the greatness of your iniquity, and your heels suffer violence. Can the Ethiopian change his skin, or the leopard his spots? Then may you also do good, who are accustomed to do evil.

"Therefore I will scatter them, as the stubble that passes away, by the wind of the wilderness. This is your lot, the portion measured to you from me," says Yahweh, "**because you have forgotten me, and trusted in falsehood [lies]**."

"Therefore I will also uncover your skirts on your face, and your shame will appear. I have seen your abominations, even your adulteries, and your neighing, the lewdness of your prostitution, on the hills in the field. Woe to you, Jerusalem!" ~ *Jeremiah 13:1-11, 15-18, 22-27*

That's awful news! Woe to you, Jerusalem! An Ethiopian can't change his skin, nor can a leopard change his spots. Can those who are accustomed to doing evil, change their sin nature and do good? Never! Not by their own power. But with God, all things are possible.

~§~

Satan desires the downfall of America. What are his chances of success if the LORD is not our rock, our buckler, our fortress, and our deliverer? If not God Almighty, who else can we rely on as our rock, fortress, and shield? See Isaiah 45:22, and King David's song of deliverance in 2 Samuel 22:1-11.

Sunday, August 12, 2018 United States of America

Boston police say someone broke down the front door of a 55-yr old city employee, and shot him to death on his birthday. His widow said, "it's just wickedness."

North Carolina authorities report a 31-yr old Fayetteville man who was found covered in blood has been charged in the fatal stabbing of his 72-yr old grandfather.

Detroit police say a 43-yr old man was helping to break up a fight outside a bar on the city's west side when he was shot and killed. The victim's brother calls it "another senseless Detroit crime."

Wisconsin authorities say a caller told dispatchers a man was intoxicated in a home in the Village of Hawkins. After an altercation with police, the subject was shot and killed.

Texas deputies say a woman created a standoff with police when she refused to put down a gun in Flint. After hours of unsuccessful negotiating, she shot and killed herself.

Arizona police report two men got into an argument at a Mesa apartment when one man shot and killed the other. The suspect is in custody.

South Carolina law enforcement responded to a call at an apartment in Rock Hill, and found a 32-yr old man with a fatal gunshot wound. A suspect was later captured in Charlotte.

Georgia Bureau of Investigation report a 29-yr old man was found shot to death in an alleyway in Quitman. A 27-yr old man and a 30-yr old man have been arrested.

Washington police report a 15-yr old boy was fatally wounded in a shooting in Toppenish. This was the third shooting on the Indian Reservation in two days.

Missouri authorities report officers responded to a home in Versailles to find a 29-yr man dead of a gunshot wound. His 30-yr old girlfriend was arrested on a gun charge.

North Carolina police in Concord responded to a shooting at a party that left a man dead and two others wounded. The 31-yr old victim died at Carolina Healthcare NE Medical.

California police was dispatched regarding an altercation and shooting in Long Beach. After a search, they find a 39-yr old male victim in the yard of a home with a fatal gunshot wound.

Illinois authorities report that hours after residents called Chicago police about shots fired, a 22-yr old male victim was found fatally shot next to a home in Harvey.

California police report a 27-yr old man, suspected of driving under the influence, died when he jumped off a bridge to escape police in Redding.

Milwaukee police respond to reports of gunfire and find a man unconscious in a yard near 76th and Melvina. Nine murders were committed in the first nine days of the month of August in Milwaukee.

Michigan deputies in Grattan Township are investigating after finding two victims of gunshot wounds. A 44-yr old man was transported to the hospital but later died.

Arkansas police say a 48-yr old man who was speeding through North Little Rock was killed when he wrecked just moments after police called off their pursuit.

Michigan authorities arrest a driver in Lincoln Township after a woman dies when the pontoon boat she was in fell off the trailer when the driver cornered too fast.

Minnesota police in St. Paul say a 21-yr old man died after being shot in the chest in the Eastview neighborhood. A 19-yr-old man is charged with robbery and murder.

North Carolina police responded to a call in North Charlotte and discovered a 23-yr old man was shot and killed inside a home. Police are searching for a suspect.

Omaha law enforcement report a 27-yr old man was pumping gas when two men shot him and stole his vehicle. The victim later died at Nebraska Medical Center.

Nevada police report a 30-yr old Las Vegas woman was killed in a car crash when a suspected DUI driver failed to stop for a red light.

Durham, North Carolina police say a 39-yr old woman was crossing the street when she was struck and killed by an SUV that fled the scene.

South Dakota police report a 24-yr old man shot and killed a 25-yr old man after they argued over disrespecting a young woman at a barbecue in Sioux Falls.

Birmingham, Alabama officials say a 28-yr old man forced his way into an apartment in Ensley, shot to death a 55-yr old woman, then carjacked a vehicle from another woman.

Tennessee deputies responded to a report of a shooting in Soddy-Daisy to find a 69-yr old man dead from a gunshot wound. A 46-yr old man is charged with murder and robbery.

North Carolina law enforcement report a 23-yr old father and a 22-yr old mother have been charged with murder in the death of their two-month old son in Rocky Mount.

Tennessee authorities say a man was shot at a West Memphis area gas station. He later died at Regional Medical Center. A suspect was spotted running from the scene.

Minnesota law enforcement report a 35-yr old male suspect is a person of interest in the stabbing death of a 27-yr old woman at a residence in Shakopee, a Minneapolis suburb.

Milwaukee police report multiple gunshots were fired at a group of people on the city's northside. A 28-yr old man was pronounced dead at the scene, while two boys, ages 4 and 14, were taken to Froedtert Hospital for treatment.

Arizona police say a 17-yr old unlicensed driver was traveling at a high rate of speed in Phoenix when he hit and killed a 52-yr old man who was crossing the street.

Texas authorities report a 21-yr old man was shot and killed, and another 21-yr old man was wounded in a shooting at a parking garage in the Houston Medical Center.

California Highway Patrol report an 18-yr old female faces DUI and manslaughter charges after two teenage male passengers died and two females were injured in a Walnut Creek car crash.

North Carolina law enforcement say a peaceful gathering at a house in Greensboro turned deadly when gunfire broke out, leaving a 20-yr old man dead and a 19-yr old man wounded.

California Highway Patrol report two deaths in a road rage incident near Sacramento. One man beat and killed another with a bat. As the murderer walked from the scene, he was struck by a car and killed.

Las Vegas police report a 44-yr old man was found shot in the doorway of an apartment used by squatters. He died at the scene from a gunshot to the chest.

Dallas police are investigating a shooting at an apartment complex that left a 25-yr old man dead in the parking lot. It is being looked at as a homicide.

Houston police are investigating the fatal shooting of a 35-yr old male outside a nightclub. A second 35-yr old man was wounded. An SUV was seen leaving the area.

Michigan police report an intoxicated man drove his vehicle onto his neighbor's yard in Grattan Township and threaten him. The homeowner armed himself and when the trespasser charged at him, the homeowner shot and killed him in self-defense.

Pittsburgh investigators are looking for suspects after finding a 63-yr old woman shot to death inside a parked SUV in Lincoln-Lemington.

Georgia police report a 23-yr old Brunswick man is dead and a 19-yr old woman is in custody after a shooting incident less than a mile from the College of Coastal Georgia.

Arizona police report two people shot at each other at a west Phoenix convenience store. One wounded victim crashed his car in a parking lot and later died in the hospital.

South Carolina deputies report a 23-yr old man was shot and killed just outside of Eutawville. A 23-yr old suspect was later captured in Stratford, Connecticut.

Modesto, California police report a 30-yr old man was shot in the parking lot of a gas station. He later died in an area hospital. A 20-yr old man was arrested.

Kansas City law enforcement say a 30-yr old man was dropped off at a local hospital with a fatal gunshot wound. Police determined the shooting occurred in Tracy.

Indiana authorities report a triple homicide. A 19-yr old, a 21-yr old, and a 24-yr old were shot and killed just blocks away from a jazz festival in Indianapolis.

California deputies approached a 22-yr old robbery suspect in East L.A. When he ran and pulled a gun from his waistband, two officers shot him. Suspect died at the scene.

South Carolina deputies report a 33-yr old mother of two died in Columbia when a bullet pierced the wall of her apartment and hit her. Two suspects, ages 24 and 26, are in custody.

California police were called to the train platform at Pomona Station to discover two homeless men shot to death, ages 31 and 37. A former railroad employee is in custody.

Maryland authorities report a 59-yr old man of Mitchellville killed his 55-yr old ex-girlfriend, before taking his own life in a murder-suicide in Upper Marlboro.

Georgia police report a man is accused of fatally shooting his ex-girlfriend in the face while she was retrieving her belongings from an apartment they shared in College Park.

Arkansas officials with the Helena-West Helena police report a man told 911 he had killed his pregnant girlfriend and planned to kill himself. They later find the couple dead inside a car in the Mississippi River.

Virginia police report a 40-yr old man from Waynesboro was shot dead by police while fleeing a crime scene where he had earlier shot and killed a 29-yr old woman in Afton.

Georgia deputies in Liberty County arrest a 16-yr old boy who shot and killed his father in their home just outside of Midway. The teen is being charged as an adult.

California authorities say a 39-yr old man, who had been arrested twice this year, shot and killed three of his children, then killed himself in Clearlake.

~§~

President Lincoln's National Call to Prayer

"Intoxicated with unbroken success, we have become too self-sufficient to feel the necessity of redeeming and preserving grace, too proud to pray to the God that made us! **It behooves us, then, to humble ourselves before the Offended Power, to confess our national sins, and to pray for clemency and forgiveness**. All this being done in sincerity and truth, let us then rest humbly in the hope, authorized by the Divine teachings, that the united cry of the Nation will be heard on high and answered with blessings, no less than the pardon of our national sins, and restoration of our now divided and suffering country to its former happy condition of unity and peace."

Keeping the Sabbath day holy unto the LORD was a key commandment for the children of Abraham. It's one of the "Big Ten." Breaking the Sabbath ranked right up there with adultery, stealing and lying. Unlike the nations around them, Israel was called to rest on the Sabbath day. God instituted the day of rest so that his people would recall and reflect, for an entire day every week, that Yahweh is their God. "It is he who gives you power to get wealth" (Deuteronomy 8:18). God wants them to remember he is the source of all good things. The power to get wealth flows from JAH, who is good and merciful. **But our God is also a consuming fire** (Hebrews 12:29). And there's a high price to pay for willful disobedience. So, in Jeremiah 17:19-27, the weeping prophet continues his work. I call this section:

Respect the gates, or there'll be no gates!

> Yahweh said this to me: "Go and stand in the gate of the children of the people, through which the kings of Judah come in and by which they go out, and in all the gates of Jerusalem. Tell them, 'Hear Yahweh's word, you kings of Judah, all Judah, and all the inhabitants of Jerusalem, that enter in by these gates: Yahweh says, "*Be careful,* and bear no burden on the Sabbath day, nor bring it in by the gates of Jerusalem. Don't carry a burden out of your houses on the Sabbath day. Don't do any work, but make the Sabbath day holy, as I commanded your fathers. *But they didn't listen. They didn't turn their ear, but made their neck stiff, that they might not hear, and might not receive instruction.*
>
> "It will happen, **if** you diligently listen to me," says Yahweh, "to bring in no burden through the gates of this city on the Sabbath day, but to make the Sabbath day holy, to do no work therein; **then** there will enter in by the gates of this city kings and princes sitting on David's throne, riding in chariots and on horses, they, and their princes, the men of Judah, and the inhabitants of Jerusalem; and this city will remain forever. They will come from the cities of Judah, and from the places around Jerusalem, from the land of Benjamin, from the lowland, from the hill country, and from the South, bringing burnt offerings, sacrifices, meal offerings, and frankincense, and bringing sacrifices of thanksgiving, to Yahweh's house.

> "But **if** you will not listen to me to make the Sabbath day holy, and not to bear a burden and enter in at the gates of Jerusalem on the Sabbath day, **then** I will kindle a fire in its gates, and it will devour the palaces of Jerusalem. It will not be quenched."

The people of Jerusalem were fully aware of God's restriction on working during the Sabbath. But for some, other priorities came before keeping the law. So now, Yahweh has some competition. Another suitor wants to win the heart of his beloved. Instead of his people resting on the holy day and loving on their Lord, many had other plans. *"There're places to go, things to do, people to see!"* A merciful God gives his willful spouse fair warning: If you continue to cross me by carrying your burden through these gates on the Sabbath, soon there'll be no gates!

"For jealousy arouses the fury of the husband." ~ *Proverbs 6:34*

~§~

An "If-Then" Scenario for the Nations

The word which came to Jeremiah from Yahweh, saying, "Arise, and go down to the potter's house, and there I will cause you to hear my words." Then I went down to the potter's house, and behold, he was making something on the wheels. When the vessel that he made of the clay was marred in the hand of the potter, he made it again another vessel, as seemed good to the potter to make it.

Then Yahweh's word came to me, saying, "House of Israel, can't I do with you as this potter?" says Yahweh. "Behold, as the clay in the potter's hand, so are you in my hand, house of Israel. At the instant I speak concerning a nation, and concerning a kingdom, to pluck up and to break down and to destroy it; **if** *that nation, concerning which I have spoken, turns from their evil,* [**then**] I will repent of the evil that I thought to do to them. At the instant I speak concerning a nation, and concerning a kingdom, to build and to plant it; **if** *they do that which is evil in my sight, that they not obey my voice,* **then** I will repent of the good with which I said I would benefit them.

Now therefore, speak to the men of Judah, and to the inhabitants of Jerusalem, saying, "Yahweh says: 'Behold, I frame evil against you, and devise a plan against you. Everyone return from his evil way now, and amend your ways and your doings.' "

Then they said, "Come! Let's devise plans against Jeremiah...Come, and let's strike him with the tongue, and let's not give heed to any of his words." *~ Jeremiah 18:1-11, 18*

~§~

Instead of submitting to the message, the people of Jerusalem attack the messenger! Sadly, Yahweh has to apply more pressure to get their attention. Remember Nebuchadnezzar, the king of Babylon? He was the one the Most High God cut low to teach a lesson in humility. Well, Nebuchadnezzar is back on the scene, and now Yahweh is calling him, "my servant." *The humbled one is now an exalted one.* The Lord of Lords has appointed the king of Babylon to subdue all surrounding nations, including the nation of Israel. In this episode from Jeremiah 27:2-15, we're introduced to the last ruler of Judah, King Zedekiah. I call this segment:

Lying Prophets and the Yoke of Babylon

> Yahweh says to me: "Make bonds and bars, and **put them on your neck**. Then send them to the king of Edom, to the king of Moab, to the king of the children of Ammon, to the king of Tyre, and to the king of Sidon, by the hand of the messengers who come to Jerusalem to **Zedekiah king of Judah**. Give them a command to their masters, saying 'Yahweh of Armies, the God of Israel says, "You shall tell your masters: 'I have made the earth, the men, and the animals that are on the surface of the earth by my great power and by my outstretched arm. I give it to whom it seems right to me. Now I have given all these lands into the hand of Nebuchadnezzar the king of Babylon, *my servant.* I have also given the animals of the field to him to serve him. All the nations will serve him, his son, and his son's son, until the time of his own land comes. Then many nations and great kings will make him their bondservant.
>
> "It will happen that I will punish the nation and the kingdom which will not serve the same Nebuchadnezzar king of Babylon, and that will not put their neck under the yoke of the king of Babylon,' says Yahweh, 'with the sword, with famine, and with pestilence, until I have consumed them by his hand. But as for you, don't listen to your prophets, to your diviners, to your dreams, to your soothsayers, or to your sorcerers, who speak to you, saying,

'You shall not serve the king of Babylon;' **for they prophesy a lie to you**, to remove you far from your land."

I spoke to Zedekiah king of Judah according to all these words, saying, "Bring your necks under the yoke of the king of Babylon, and serve him and his people, and live. Why will you die, you and your people, by the sword, by the famine, and by the pestilence, as Yahweh has spoken concerning the nation that will not serve the king of Babylon? Don't listen to the words of the prophets who speak to you, saying, 'You shall not serve the king of Babylon;' **for they prophesy a lie to you**. For I have not sent them," says Yahweh, "but they prophesy falsely in my name."

Lying prophets abound today, just like they did in Jeremiah's time. A fierce army will soon besiege Jerusalem. No supplies will enter the city. God's "evil arrows of famine" will cause great distress for the sinful citizens of Zion. Tragically, their spiritually dull leaders don't have a clue as to what the LORD of hosts is doing! A foreign superpower, the great Babylonian Empire, has been appointed by Yahweh to be his "rod of correction" to discipline the rebellious, unfaithful nation of Israel. God is setting the stage to pour out the curses of D28B on his people if they refuse to repent. The false prophets of Judah may say otherwise, but the sins of the land have reached a point where divine justice has to be served.

When Yahweh humbled Nebuchadnezzar, we were told, *"The sentence is by the decree of the watchers, and the demand by the word of the holy ones."* Apparently, these "watchers" and "holy ones" are observers of human conduct, and they had some say in how the king of Babylon was sentenced. According to Revelation 4:8, there are heavenly beings that "are full of eyes around and within. They have no rest day and night, saying, 'Holy, holy, holy is the Lord God the Almighty.' "

Are these angelic beings from Revelation chapter four, the same "watchers" and "holy ones" from Daniel chapter four? I'm inclined to say so. Hebrews 12:1 states we are surrounded by a great cloud of witnesses. Evidently, secret sins on earth are open scandals in heaven. The point I'm trying to make is - God is watching the people of America, *and the host of heaven is watching also*. Not only is the Judge of Eternity observing us, but the celestial jurors are surveying us too! How do they react when they look down on our self-satisfied, sin-soaked, sexualized, shameless society? What sentence will they pass? What demand will they decree?

These "watchers" and "holy ones" echo the mind of God that sin and unrighteousness must be punished (Daniel 4:17,24,25). Once their collective judgment is passed, no one can change it. Which is what we see in Jeremiah 15:1-6,

> Then Yahweh said to me, "Though Moses and Samuel stood before me, *yet my mind would not turn toward this people.* Cast them out of my sight, and let them go out! It will happen, when they ask you, 'Where shall we go out?' then you shall tell them, "Yahweh says: 'Such as are for death, [shall go] to death; such as are for the sword, to the sword; such as are for the famine, to the famine; and such as are for captivity, to captivity.' "
>
> "I will appoint over them four kinds," says Yahweh: "the sword to kill, the dogs to tear, the birds of the sky, and the animals of the earth, to devour and to destroy. I will cause them to be tossed back and forth among all the kingdoms of the earth, because of Manasseh, the son of Hezekiah, king of Judah, for that which he did in Jerusalem.
>
> "For who will have pity on you, Jerusalem? Who will mourn you? Who will come to ask for your welfare? You have rejected me," says Yahweh. "You have gone backward. Therefore I have stretched out my hand against you and destroyed you. *I am weary of showing compassion."*

Sometime earlier, El Kanna issued his prophet a serious challenge.

"Run to and fro through the streets of Jerusalem; see now and know; and seek in her open places if you can find a man, **if there is anyone who executes judgment, who seeks the truth, and I will pardon her**. ...When I had fed them to the full, then they committed adultery and assembled themselves by troops in the harlots' houses. ...Shall I not punish them for these things?" says the LORD. "Shall I not avenge Myself on such a nation as this? *An astonishing and horrible thing has been committed in the land:* The prophets prophesy falsely, and the priests rule by their own power; and My people love to have it so. But what will you do in the end?" ~ *Jeremiah 5:1, 7, 29-31 NKJV*

"There is none who calls on your name, who stirs up himself to take hold of you..." ~ *Isaiah 64:7*

Chapter 10:

"And Turn from their wicked ways;"

"The trouble with most of us is that we would rather be ruined by praise than saved by criticism." I fear Dr. Norman Vincent Peale makes a valid point. Oftentimes, when we're criticized or rebuked for some error, we recoil and push back. Instead of realizing a merciful God is using a willing servant to pass along his word or his warning (Leviticus 19:17,18), we attack the messenger.

Needless to say, the prophet Jeremiah wasn't growing in popularity as he went about Jerusalem declaring impending doom and destruction. Some leaders thought his word (Yahweh's Word) was having a negative effect on the people, so they conspire against the servant of God. In this section we'll see again Judah's last king, Zedekiah. And we're introduced to a brave Ethiopian. His name is Ebedmelech, and he serves in the king's house. I call this episode:

The Princes plot against the Prophet

Then Zedekiah the king commanded, and they committed Jeremiah into the court [prison] of the guard. They gave him daily a loaf of bread out of the bakers' street, until all the bread in the city was gone [during the siege]. Shephatiah the son of Mattan, and Gedaliah the son of Pashhur, and Jucal the son of Shelemiah, and Pashhur the son of Malchijah, heard the words that Jeremiah spoke to all the people, saying, "Yahweh says, 'He who remains in this city will die by the sword, by the famine, and by the pestilence; but he who goes out to the Chaldeans will live, and he will escape with his life, and he will live.' Yahweh says, 'This city will surely be given into the hand of the army of the king of Babylon, and he will take it.' "

Then the princes said to the king, "**Please let this man be put to death**; because he weakens the hands of the men of war who remain in this city, and the hands of all the people, in speaking such words to them: for this man doesn't seek the welfare of this people, but harm."

Zedekiah the king said, "Behold, he is in your hand; for the king can't do anything to oppose you."

Then they took Jeremiah and threw him into the dungeon of Malchijah the king's son, that was in the court of the guard. They let down Jeremiah with cords. In the dungeon there was no water, but mire [mud]; and Jeremiah sank in the mire.

Now when Ebedmelech the Ethiopian, a eunuch, who was in the king's house, heard that they had put Jeremiah in the dungeon (the king was then sitting in Benjamin's gate), *Ebedmelech went out of the king's house, and spoke to the king,* saying, "My lord the king, these men have done evil in all that they have done to Jeremiah the prophet, whom they have cast into the dungeon. **He is likely to die in the place where he is**, because of the famine; for there is no more bread in the city."

Then the king commanded Ebedmelech the Ethiopian, saying, "Take from here thirty men with you, and take up Jeremiah the prophet out of the dungeon, before he dies."

So Ebedmelech took the men with him, and went into the house of the king under the treasury, and took from there rags and worn-out garments, and let them down by cords into the dungeon to Jeremiah. Ebedmelech the Ethiopian said to Jeremiah, "Now put these rags and worn-out garments under your armpits under the cords."

Jeremiah did so. So they lifted Jeremiah up with the cords, and took him up out of the dungeon; and Jeremiah remained in the court of the guard. *~ Jeremiah 37:21-38:13*

~§~

When Jeremiah was called into service, he was told:

> Now Yahweh's word came to me, saying, "Before I formed you in the womb, I knew you. Before you were born, I sanctified you. I have appointed you a prophet to the nations. ...For, behold, I have made you today a fortified city, an iron pillar, and bronze walls against the whole land, against the kings of Judah, against its princes, against its priests, and against the people of the land. **They will fight against you, but they will not prevail against you; for I am with you", says Yahweh, "to rescue you.**" *~ Jeremiah 1:4-5, 18-19*

Step back in time again with me to November 15, 1861. The President of the Confederate States, Jefferson Davis, has called for that day to be "Set Apart for Fasting, Humiliation and Prayer." The war is showing no signs of reprieve, and people throughout the land are rightfully concerned. It's a Friday. The Rev. Henry H. Tucker, professor at Mercer University, is delivering his sermon before the Legislature of Georgia in the Capitol at Milledgeville. The title of this sermon: *God in the War*. Since we happen to be in the area, let's step inside the chambers for a few minutes to hear what God's man has to say.

"Desolation! Desolation! Thousands of our young men have been murdered. Thousands of fathers and mothers among us have been bereaved of their sons. Thousands of widows are left disconsolate and heart-broken, to struggle through life alone. Thousands of brave men are at this moment lying on beds of languishing, some prostrated by the diseases incident of the army and camp, and some by cruel wounds. Every house within reach of the seat of war is a hospital, and every hospital is crowded.

"Huge warehouses emptied of their merchandize, and churches, and great barns, are filled with long rows of pallets beside each other, containing each a sufferer, pale, emaciated and ghastly. Some writhe with pain; some rage with delirium; some waste with fever; some speak of home, and drop bitter tears at the recollection of wives soon to be widows, and babes soon to be fatherless. The pious chaplain whispers of Jesus to the dying. The surgeon is in frightful practice, bloody though beneficent; and as his knife glides through the quivering flesh and his saw grates through the bone and tears through the marrow, the suppressed groan bears witness to the anguish.

"A father stands by perhaps, to see his son mutilated. Mother and wife and sisters at home witness the scene by a dreadful clairvoyance, and with them the operation lasts not for moments but for weeks. Every groan in the hospital or tent, or on the bloody field, wakes echoes at home. There is not a city, nor village, nor hamlet, nor neighborhood that has not its representatives in the army, and scarcely a heart in our whole Confederacy that is not either bruised by strokes already fallen, or pained by a solicitude scarcely less dreadful than the reality. Desolation! Desolation! Hearts desolate, homes desolate, the whole land desolate! And alas! the end is not yet. Another six months may more than double the desolation. Relentless winter may aid the enemy in his work of death.

"Lay what plans you will, and set what schemes you please in operation, and at the summing up of all things at the end of the world, it will be found that God ruled and overruled all things according to the working of his power; and that the great statesmen and great captains who figure so largely in history, were but the unwitting instruments of accomplishing his purposes. Let us then do justly, and love mercy and walk humbly before God, and by thus falling in with his plans, we shall be on his side and he will be on ours.

"I have said that the way to enlist this almightiness on our side is to make the law of God the law of every man's life. Perhaps these terms are too general to convey the idea with power. What then more particularly is to be done? What specific duties must we discharge? What special evils must we forsake? All, all! The whole head is sick, the whole heart is faint, the whole body is corrupt. How small a proportion of our population are disciples of Jesus!—Counting out avowed unbelievers and false professors, how few are left! Here is the place to begin. **A pure Gospel is our only hope—I repeat it, a pure Gospel is our only hope**. If the Kingdom of Christ be not set up in the hearts of the people no government can exist except by force. All you then who have no personal experience of the grace of the Gospel are so far, in the way of your country's prosperity.

"The first step for you to take is to believe in the Lord Jesus Christ, confessing your sins and giving him your heart. But aside from this, let us look at our public morals. Passing by profanity, for we are a nation of swearers; passing by drunkenness, for we are a nation of drunkards; passing by Sabbath-breaking, for our cars thunder along the track on the Sabbath as on any other day, and our convivial gatherings are too often on the day of the Lord; passing by covetousness and lying, for too many of our citizens alas! will for the sake of defrauding the public out of a few dollars make false oath in giving in their tax returns; passing by the neglect of our children, for too few of them receive that religious instruction and training which is their due; passing by injustice of servants, for while their physical wants are in some cases unsupplied their moral wants are too generally neglected; passing by all these things, and each of the sins of private life which ought to be exchanged for its opposite virtue; let me call especial attention to three things of more public nature, and which are fairer samples of the average of public morals.

"In the first place, *how is it that in the State of Georgia it is almost impossible to convict a culprit of crime?* The most atrocious murders and other outrages are committed with impunity, in the very face of our so-called Courts of Justice. Is the Bench prostituted? Is the Bar prostituted? Or is it the Jury box? In either case it is clear that public virtue is at fault; otherwise these evils would not be tolerated. So notoriously defective is the administration of justice, that in many cases fresh within the memory of us all, citizens have felt it necessary in self-defense to execute criminals without the forms of law. Is not this a step towards barbarism? The example of disregarding the law being set by reputable citizens, *will be followed by others not so reputable.* When this system is inaugurated where will it stop? Whose life will be safe? This reign of the mob, this lawless execution of men which is little short of murder, will become the rule and not the exception, unless a more healthy public opinion shall correct the evils in our Courts of Justice.

"The second evil is kindred to the first. *How is it that in all the history of this Legislative body pardon has been granted to every criminal, almost without exception who has ever applied for it?* Can it be that all who have been pardoned were innocent? If so there must have been horrid injustice in the Courts which convicted them. The bloodthirsty Jeffreys would scarcely have sent so many innocent men to the gallows. No; under the loose administration of justice already referred to, none but the most glaring cases (with possibly a rare exception) could ever be convicted. – How comes it then that our Legislators turn loose these culprits upon society? It is because they are more anxious to secure a re-election than to promote the good of the State. How comes it that a vote adverse to pardon would endanger their re-election? It is because public opinion is rotten. **The fault lies in the low standard of public morals.**

"But for the third item. Without meaning to indulge in wholesale denunciation of any class of my fellow citizens, it may yet be pertinent to inquire, *how is it that so few of our public men are good men?* Is it to be supposed that all the talent, and all the learning, and all the wisdom, have been vouchsafed to the bad rather than to the good? Does Satan claim a monopoly of all the intellectual power and administrative ability of the world? Perhaps it is not surprising that he should; for he once offered to give to their rightful owner "all the Kingdoms of this world and the glory of them" on condition of receiving his homage in return. But it is preposterous to suppose that there are no good men to be found capable of discharging the highest public trusts. Why then are they not oftener found in eminent position? It is because the public in estimating a man's fitness for office, throw his morals out of the account; and because popularity can be obtained by means which bad men freely resort to, but which good men eschew. How sad a comment on public virtue! Every voter who allows personal interests, or preferences, or prejudices, or party zeal or anything to influence his suffrage in favor of a bad man in preference to a good one, if the latter be capable, is doing what he can to banish virtue from our councils and God from our support. It might be a fair subject of inquiry, whether he or the outbreaking felon whose place is in the Penitentiary inflicts the greatest injury upon society.

"The three evils just specified are only *outward manifestations* of an internal distemper, the mere efflorescence of evil deep seated in the public heart. The disappearance of these would indicate a radical change. Suppose public justice to be rightly administered, suppose the influence of virtue in our councils to be predominant; and this is to suppose that thousands upon thousands of individual men have grown wiser and better, that myriads of private faults have been exchanged for corresponding virtues, that the whole complexion of society is changed, and its whole nature improved. Suppose that the Gospel of Christ, *which alone can work these changes*, should continue thus to elevate, refine, ennoble and sanctify, until every heart were brought under its sacred influence. How much like heaven our earth would be! Can anyone suppose that in such a state of society as this, the heavenly tranquility would ever be disturbed by the clangor of war! **Let our whole people at once renounce their evil works and ways with grief, and follow hard after God,** and I confidently declare that he would with a mighty hand and an outstretched arm deliver us from our enemies and restore peace and prosperity."

~§~

I thank God for people like Henry H. Tucker. Bold servants who don't shy away from speaking a hard word from the Lord, even to the members of the Legislature! The anointed are called to "proclaim the message; be persistent whether the time is favorable or unfavorable; convince, rebuke, and encourage, with the utmost patience in teaching" (2 Timothy 4:2 New Revised Standard). You can read the entire sermon online. The body was so impressed with his message that they asked Minister Tucker to provide them with additional copies, which is one likely reason why it is preserved until this day. "You shall not hate your brother in your heart. **You shall surely rebuke your neighbor**, and not bear sin because of him" (Leviticus 19:17 NKJV).

Allow me to follow in the steps of Brother Tucker and "call especial attention to three things of more public nature, and which are fairer samples of the average of public morals."

In the first place, *how is it that in the United States of America* ***skepticism*** *toward the Bible is on the rise?* The American Bible Society compiled the results from their annual *State of the Bible* survey from 2011 to 2016. In that six-year period, Americans who view the Bible as a book of uninspired teachings increased from 10% to 22%. During the same six-year period, the percentage of Americans who view the Bible as sacred literature dropped from 86% to 80%. *In simple words, fewer and fewer Americans are holding to the fundamental belief that the Bible is the inspired, infallible Word of God.* That's not an encouraging trend. Among non-Christian Millennials, 62% have never read the Bible, and 27% believe it's a dangerous book of religious dogma used for centuries to oppress people. According to the *2017 State of the Bible* survey, the section of households in America that own at least one Bible was 87%. But in the *2018 State of the Bible* survey, that number was down to 82%. More than one-third of adults (35%) report never using the Bible in 2019, that's a 10 percentage point increase since 2011 (25%).

Who's fueling this rise in skepticism? Do you recall Satan's very first words to a human being? You'll find them in Genesis, chapter three. In light of our current hike in skepticism, this is significant. Satan's very first communication to humans was a question designed to raise doubt about what God said.

English Standard Version, *"Did God actually say, ...?"*

Bible in Basic English, *"Has God truly said...?"*

Orthodox Jewish Bible, *"Really? Hath Elohim said, ...?"*

~§~

Down through the ages, believers have had to guard against the deceiver's assault on the Word of God. The Spirit revealed that Satan can take advantage of us if we're ignorant of his devices (2 Corinthians 2:11). One of those "devices" is to undermine the authority of Holy Scripture. The father of lies is using the same tactic against us today. "To the young, I would whisper that the Bible is a myth." ~ *Paul Harvey*

From my very first days of being a born-again believer, I've been aware of Satan's attack against the authority of Scripture. *But I didn't really comprehend the significance of his attacks until I gained a better understanding of a popular Bible verse from Proverbs 29:18.* I'm sure you've heard it before, "Where there is no vision, the people perish." For years, I've heard speakers quote this verse. Entrepreneurs use it to rally support for their projects. It's a familiar passage, which is the reason for my surprise when I discovered the verse meant something totally different from how it is commonly "used" today.

In his excellent book, *Revive Us Again*, Dr. Walter C. Kaiser of Gordon-Conwell Theological Seminary, shares a key insight that unlocks the true force of the verse, and the reason why Satan attacks the authority of Scripture. He writes,

> "Proverbs 14:34 is still true: Righteousness exalts a nation, but sin is a disgrace to any people." It is also exceedingly true that *"Where there is no revelation [i.e., preaching of the Word of God to God's people or to any nation], the people cast off restraint"* (Prov.29:18). What better explanation is there for the brazen effrontery of lawlessness and wickedness in our day than this verse supplies? When the pulpit fails to declare the whole counsel of God and turns, instead, to pop psychology, self-realization talks, and identity types of searches in sermonettes, be sure that the populace, both inside the church and outside it, will see all hell break loose just as Moses witnessed after a mere forty-day hiatus of his presence and preaching while he was on Mount Sinai receiving the Ten Commandments. **Proverbs 29:18 borrowed the very same word used in Exodus 32:25 when it observed that the people "were running wild" (or "had broken loose") in sacred prostitution to the golden calf.** What will happen after months and years of such poor pablum and poppycock substitutes for the Word of God? Has not our culture, both church and secular, torn down the fences and gone wild? And whom shall we blame for this state of affairs? Or better still, to whom shall we go in repentance and hunger for revival given such a desperate state of affairs, no matter how they have come about?"

Wow! Thanks, Brother Kaiser. After that vivid and Bible-based explanation, Proverbs 29:18 will never be the same verse again.

New International Reader's Version: *Where there is no message from God, the people don't control themselves. But blessed are those who obey the law.*

King James Version: *Where there is no vision, the people perish: but he that keepeth the law, happy is he.*

Complete Jewish Bible: *Without a prophetic vision, the people throw off restraint; but he who keeps Torah is happy.*

New Century Version: *Where there is no word from God, people are uncontrolled, but those who obey what they have been taught are happy.*

Orthodox Jewish Bible: *Where there is no chazon (prophetic vision), the people cast off restraint [i.e., perish ungovernable], but he that is shomer over the torah, happy is he.*

New King James Version: *Where there is no revelation, the people cast off restraint; but happy is he who keeps the law.*

Good News Translation: *A nation without God's guidance is a nation without order. Happy are those who keep God's law!*

New Living Translation: *When people do not accept divine guidance, they run wild. But whoever obeys the law is joyful.*

World English Bible: *Where there is no revelation, the people cast off restraint; but one who keeps the law is blessed.*

Holman Christian Standard Bible: *Without revelation people run wild, but one who keeps the law will be happy.*

Is Satan acquainted with Holy Scripture? Do you think the deceiver is aware of this verse that's tucked away in the middle of the Old Testament? Proverbs 29:18 is just one of 915 verses in this book. Maybe the devil missed it.

Does Lucifer know that God himself declares that a nation without divine guidance is a nation without order? Do you think the evil one is privy to the truth that without a prophetic vision, the people throw off restraint? Will the enemy of America take advantage of the fact that where there is no message from God, the people don't control themselves? Is it any wonder he whispers the Bible is a myth?

My fellow citizen, if our nation is without divine revelation, the people run wild after sin! How will Satan use this information? We must be aware of how the devil operates. We should be alert to his tactics, his machinations, his conspiracies and his bottomless bag of tricks. As we observed in the essay *"If I Were the Devil,"* one way to heighten your awareness of his wiles is to mentally trade places with him and see how you would go about conducting his dirty work.

During World War II, over 230,000 German and Italian troops were taken as prisoners of war in a series of battles called the Tunisian Campaign. How did the Allied forces secure the victory? General Patton would think like General Rommel in order to see things from the perspective of his enemy. Patton read Rommel's book on combat.

If you were the enemy of America, and wanted her citizens to run hard after sin and incur the wrath of God, what strategy would you employ? If it were up to me, I would attack on at least two fronts. My first attack would be centered on the visuals and messages that Americans encounter day in and day out.

Working off the principle of **GIGO** – **G**arbage **I**n, **G**arbage **O**ut: I would make sure the people of America heard and saw, by way of radio-TV-internet-billboards, the sometimes subtle, sometimes loud message of "Do as you please." » "He who dies with the most toys wins." » "You only live once, so eat, drink and be merry!" » "Look out for #1." » "Greed is good." » "Get all you can, can all you get, then sit on the can!" » "Don't worry about tomorrow, live for today." » "Sex, drugs and rock & roll!" » "Me, Me, Me." » "More, More, More!" As I'm establishing this message on a 24-hour loop, I would attack on the second front.

This second front would consist of a sometimes subtle and sometimes loud message that the Bible is a myth. With my twisted appreciation of *"Without revelation, people run wild,"* I would do whatever I could to turn every American away from the Holy Scriptures. I would say the Bible cannot be trusted, that it's full of errors and contradictions, that only a religious fanatic or a nutjob would take the Bible seriously. I would instruct my media outlets to always portray Biblical Christianity in a negative, unflattering, unappealing manner. I'd broadcast scenes of religious fanatics holding up Bibles as they're being hauled away to the funny farm. I would put extra pressure on ministers to sin, and thus cause unbelievers to blaspheme (2 Sam. 12:14).

Once I have the citizens of the United States freely embracing the ever popular "Me, Me, Me" message, and once I've cleverly eroded their confidence in the Word of God, I'll have the whole country exactly where I want them. My con will be complete, and I can congratulate myself on how I used my knowledge of Scripture to cause Americans to turn their backs on Scripture! I know the Word of God will hold true. *When people are tricked into discarding divine revelation and authority, they run hard after sin » The wages of sin is death » They die! » I win!*

Is this not what we're witnessing in our beloved country today? As skepticism toward the Bible increases, morality decreases. As our confidence in the authority of Scripture goes down, crime goes up. Murders continue to climb in city after city. Suicides are increasing at an alarming rate. But at the same time, according to research conducted by the *Center for the Study of Religion and American Culture*, only 9% of Americans profess to reading their Bible on a daily basis.

The first national sin of America we must acknowledge and renounce is skepticism. We're falling away from our faith and trust in the God of the Bible. "The second evil is kindred to the first." *How is it that in America today we're obsessed with owning more and more stuff?* One sin follows another. If I reject the unseen God, I will embrace the god of the seen. Our second national sin is **materialism**.

All created beings have been called to worship and praise the Creator (Psalm 148 - 150). But what happens when we doubt the God who created us? What happens when we lose faith in Holy Scripture? Or, what happens when we stop looking to the LORD our Maker (Psa. 95:6,7)? Nature abhors a vacuum. If our focus strays from the unseen God, we re-focus on the seen god, the god of things, the god of materialism.

Over twenty years before he was elected President of the United States, James Garfield was a minister of the gospel of Christ in Ohio. We're fortunate today to have a large store of his writings, including political speeches, some personal letters, and even his sermons. In one of his messages from 1857, entitled *"The Material to the Spiritual,"* Minister Garfield states:

> Men are tending to materialism. Houses, lands, and worldly goods attract their attention, and as a mirage lure them on to death. Christianity, on the other hand leads only the natural body to

> death, and for the spirit, it points out a house not build with hands, eternal in the heavens...Let me urge you to follow Him, not as the Nazarene, the Man of Galilee, the carpenter's son, but as the ever living spiritual person, full of love and compassion, who will stand by you in life and death and eternity.

If men and women were "tending to materialism" back in 1857, where do you think we are today? Studies conducted by groups like eMarketer and Flurry show American consumers spend over five hours a day on mobile devices. What are we doing on our devices? We're looking at stuff, and buying more stuff, and showing off our stuff!

According to an August 2018 article in *The Atlantic*, Alana Semuels writes, "Thanks to a perfect storm of factors, Americans are amassing a lot of stuff. Before the advent of the internet, we had to set aside time to go browse the aisles of a physical store, which was only open a certain number of hours a day. Now, we can shop from anywhere, anytime – while we're at work, or exercising, or even sleeping. We can tell Alexa we need new underwear, and in a few days, it will arrive on our doorstep."

The article goes on to state, "Shopping online also feels good. **Humans get a dopamine hit from buying stuff**, according to research by Ann-Christine Duhaime, a professor of neurosurgery at Harvard Medical School. 'As a general rule, your brain tweaks you to want more, more, more – indeed, more than those around you – both of stuff and of stimulation and novelty – because that helped you survive in the distant past of brain evolution,' Duhaime wrote in a *Harvard Business Review* essay last year. Online shopping allows us to get that dopamine hit, and then also experience delayed gratification when the order arrives a few days later, which may make it more physiologically rewarding than shopping in stores."

Alana shares some interesting numbers. "In 2017, Americans spent $240 billion – twice as much as they'd spent in 2002 – on goods like jewelry, watches, books, luggage, and telephones. Over that time, the population grew just 13 percent. Spending on personal care products also *doubled* over that time period. We spent, on average, $971.87 on clothes last year. The average American bought 7.4 pairs of shoes last year, up from 6.6 pairs in 2000."

We love to shop and we love a bargain. But as one person pointed out, “It’s not a bargain if you don’t need it!” Are those new shoes, that are supposedly marked down 75%, really a “bargain” if I already have a closet full of shoes? Benjamin Franklin observed, “It is the eyes of other people that ruin us. If all but myself were blind, I should want neither a fine house nor fine furniture.” Nor a closet full of shoes.

According to the North American Association of State and Provincial Lotteries, in 2014, Americans spent a total of $70 billion on lottery tickets. In 2017, we spent over $80 billion on lottery tickets and electronic lottery games. A recent survey commissioned by Bankrate revealed that lotto ticket consumers shell out about $1,038 annually in their pursuit of winning some dough so they can buy more stuff.

Materialism is a trap and a mirage. Jesus Christ himself said in Luke 12:15, “Beware! Keep yourselves from covetousness, for a man’s life doesn’t consist of the abundance of the things which he possesses.” Covetousness means to have an excessive, undue desire for wealth and possessions. Colossians 3:5 says covetousness is idolatry! Jesus is warning us to not be deceived into thinking life is about possessing an abundance of stuff and keeping up with the Joneses. Amassing more and more “idols” is not our highest duty. So, what is our highest duty?

“Teacher, which is the greatest commandment in the law?” Jesus said to him, “ **‘You shall love the Lord your God with all your heart, with all your soul, and with all your mind.’** This is the first and great commandment. A second likewise is this, **‘You shall love your neighbor as yourself.’** The whole law and the prophets depend on these two commandments.” (Matthew 22:36-40). There you have it. The entire duty of man and woman summed up in 27 words!

My highest ambition in life is loving my LORD, and loving my NEIGHBOR as myself. *Anything short of that is a lie and a snare.* It was the American activist Peace Pilgrim who shared the following about the trap of materialism. “Unnecessary possessions are unnecessary burdens. If you have them, you have to take care of them! There is great freedom in simplicity of living. It is those who have enough but not too much who are the happiest.” I agree. Simplicity and contentment is a beautiful thing!

Russian painter Wassily Kandinsky states, “The nightmare of materialism, which has turned the life of the universe into an evil, useless game, is not yet past; it holds the awakening soul still in its grip." American poet Bryant H. McGill said, "The folly of endless consumerism sends us on a wild goose-chase for happiness through materialism."

~§~

Leo Tolstoy gave us an insightful short story about a peasant farmer named Pahom. One day Pahom happens to overhear his wife and her elder sister debate town life versus country life. The elder sister prefers to live in the "elegance" and "manners" within town, but Pahom's wife is convinced living in the country keeps her husband from the temptations of "cards, wine, or women." Pahom agrees he has no time for such nonsense, but thinks to himself the "only trouble is that we haven't land enough. If I had plenty of land, I shouldn't fear the Devil himself!"

But the evil one was crouching behind the oven and was pleased the peasant's wife had led her husband into boasting: if he had plenty of land, he would not fear the Devil himself. "All right," thought the Devil. "We will have a tussle. I'll give you land enough; and by means of that land I will get you into my power."

There was a lady who lived near Pahom who owned about 300 acres of fine farming land. She decided to sell some of it, and Pahom managed to put together enough money to buy a 40-acre plot. "When he went out to plough his fields, or look at his growing corn, or at his grass meadows, his heart would fill with joy." Things went well for Pahom until his neighbors started trespassing on his property. One thing led to another and soon, "threats of burning his building began to be uttered."

Pahom was sitting at home when a peasant stopped in and spoke about a place called Volga. He said the land there was so good "that the rye sown on it grew as high as a horse." Shortly after that, Pahom sold his homestead and his entire family relocated to Volga.

In Volga, Pahom was "ten times better off than he had been," but *"when he got used to it he began to think that even here he had not enough land."* A passing tradesman stopped at Pahom's place one day to get feed for his horse, and he told Pahom about the land of the Bashkirs. It was far away, but the tradesman had just closed a deal to get 1,300 acres for only 1,000 rubles. He told Pahom of the vast fields in Bashkirs. He said the people there "are as simple as sheep, and land can be got almost for nothing." Pahom gathered up 1,000 rubles, took along his servant, and set out for Bashkirs.

The people of Bashkirs "were all stout and merry, and all the summer long they never thought of doing any work." When Pahom informed them he was interested in purchasing some land, the Chief of the Bashkirs made him an incredible offer. For 1,000 rubles, he could buy all the land he could walk around in a day. The catch in the deal was he had to be back at the starting point by sundown or his money is lost. Pahom knows he can cover a lot of ground in a day, so he agrees to the deal and plans to set out early the next morning.

That night Pahom is so anxious he can't sleep. When he finally dozed off just before dawn, he sees in a dream the Bashkirs' Chief laughing outside his tent. But when he approached the Chief it was no longer the Chief, but the passing tradesman who stopped by his house and told him about this land. And as Pahom asked him how long he had been there, he saw it was not the tradesman but the peasant from Volga so many years before. "Then he saw that it was not the peasant either, but the Devil himself." Pahom then sees himself lying dead on the ground, with the Devil standing over his dead body, laughing. "He awoke horror-struck" but brushed it off with, "What crazy things one does dream." No time to think about that, for this is his chance to possess as much land as he can walk around in a day.

The Bashkirs all meet Pahom at the starting point. The Chief puts his fox-fur cap on the ground and Pahom places his 1,000 rubles on the cap. He burns no time and sets out walking towards the rising sun. He moves at a fast step, and by midday he is already exhausted from the summer heat. But he knows full well this is the deal of a lifetime, so he keeps moving, covering more and more ground. He is thrilled to know that every step he takes gives him more land. So Pahom walks, and walks some more. He would think of turning back from time to time, but then, just before he changed his glance - there would be another lovely spot of land he simply couldn't pass up.

It was well into the afternoon before Pahom realized his greed had taken him far from the starting point. He turned about and headed back towards the waiting Bashkirs. As the burning sun began to sink lower and lower in the sky, he walked even faster. He could not bear the thought of losing his money because he didn't get back to the starting point by sundown. He forced himself to progress from a walk, to a jog, to a run. Even though Pahom was "seized with terror lest he should die of the strain," he could not stop running. "After having run all that way they will call me a fool if I stop now."

As the sun began to slowly descend below the horizon, he came within sight of the finish line and the cheering Bashkirs. "Their loud cries inflamed his heart still more." He saw the Chief's cap, his money, and the Chief standing above it laughing. Pahom gathered his last reserve of strength and ran on. His heart pounding, gasping for breath, he fell forward across the finish line just before the sun was gone. "Ah, what a fine fellow!" exclaimed the Chief. "He has gained much land!"

"Pahom's servant came running up and tried to raise him, but he saw that blood was flowing from his mouth. Pahom was dead!" Afterwards, his servant dug a grave and buried him in it. The grave was "six feet from his head to his heels." Which answered the question raised by the title of the story: *How Much Land Does a Man Need?*

~§~

I grew up next door to our family business, a funeral home, so you can see why that story appeals to me. I attended about 100 funeral services every year from the time I was big enough to wash and drive the hearse (13-yrs old), until I left home for college and the military. I helped my father prepare hundreds of bodies for burial. We laid to rest singles, couples, and twins. The young and the old, the rich and the poor. Both my parents are dearly departed. So I'm very familiar with death and dying, probably more than most. Therefore, I can say with absolute certainty that when we depart this land of the living, we don't carry any of our precious stuff from this world into the next. *You never see a u-haul behind a hearse!* God says, **"For we brought nothing into the world, and we certainly can't carry anything out"** (1 Timothy 6:7)! Nevertheless, we invest so much time and energy and pure affection into our STUFF. But the day will come when we'll leave behind the cars, the houses, the toys, the jewelry, the clothes, the shoes, the gadgets, the money, and all that other stuff. The day will come when we'll stand naked before the Judge of Eternity to give account of how much time and energy and pure affection we invested into his Kingdom. *"There is no creature that is hidden from his sight, but all things are naked and laid open before the eyes of him to whom we must give an account"* (Hebrews 4:13)!

But for the third item. *How is it that after nearly two hundred and fifty years as a free nation,* ***racism*** *is still America's greatest disease?* George Sweeting, past president of Moody Bible Institute in Chicago writes, "Respect of persons is inconsistent with God's grace. It is inconsistent with God's law. In fact, respect of persons is an act of sin. Racial discrimination and racism are an insult to God." Muhammad Ali said, "Hating people because of their color is wrong. And it doesn't matter which color does the hating. It's just plain wrong."

The following account was published by The Atlanta Journal-Constitution about an event that occurred one hundred years earlier in Brooks County and Lowndes County, Georgia, USA.

Hampton Smith was the 25-year old 'boss' of the Old Joyce Plantation. He bore a very poor reputation in the community because of ill treatment to his Negro employees. When Smith couldn't find enough workers, he would pay for convict labor. One of the workers Smith gained this way was Sidney Johnson, who had been convicted for playing dice. Hampton Smith would punish Johnson for any minor offense. He even beat Johnson for being too sick to work. Hampton Smith had a violent history with several other black workers on the Old Joyce Plantation. When 'boss' Smith beat a young black married woman named Mary Turner, Mary's husband, Hayes Turner threatened Smith. When Mr. Smith pressed charges against Hayes Turner, the black man was convicted by an all-white jury and sent to a chain gang.

In May of 1918, after enduring another whooping, Sidney Johnson shot and killed Smith. He then fled the scene and went into hiding. A white mob soon formed, and the manhunt was on for Sidney Johnson. He was the only suspect in the murder of Smith, but soon innocent Blacks were caught up in the rampage of mob violence. Eventually, Sidney Johnson died in a shootout with the police on May 22nd. But five days before that, the mob captured Will Head, Will Thompson and Julius Jones on May 17th. That night, Head was lynched near Troupville in Lowndes County, and Thompson and Jones were lynched near Barney in Brooks County.

On May 18th, the mob lynched Eugene Rice near the Old Camp Ground, although it was acknowledged that he was never associated with Hampton Smith's murder in any way. On that same day, they arrested Mary Turner's husband in Valdosta. Hayes Turner did time for threatening Smith, after Smith beat his wife. As deputies transported Turner from

Valdosta to Brooks County, a mob seized him and lynched him near the Little River. They left his mutilated body hanging from a tree over the weekend. Chime Riley was killed when he was thrown into the Little River with turpentine cups tied to his hands and legs to weigh him down. The bodies of three unidentified black men were also taken from the river.

Mary Turner's husband was lynched on May 18th. The next day she was taken by the mob. Mary was a mother of two, and eight months pregnant at the time. What was her crime? She had the audacity to complain about the lynching of her husband, arguing publicly that he was not involved in the murder of Smith. She threatened to report the names of the men who killed him. The mob seized her, for what the local newspapers called at the time, making "unwise remarks." They carried Mary to the Little River and took her past the body of her dead husband, still hanging from a tree.

The mob of several hundred bloodthirsty people then took Mary to the bank near Folsom Bridge. They hung Mary Turner upside down by her ankles across the sturdy limb of an oak tree. Then they doused her body with gasoline and motor oil, and set her on fire. We don't know whether she was still alive after the mob burned off her clothes, but that hardly mattered. As she hung upside down from the tree, someone took a knife, "such as one used in splitting hogs," and cut open her belly. Her child fell to the ground and gave forth two feeble cries. Then a member of the mob crushed the baby's head under the heel of his boot, and the crowd shot loads of bullets into Mary's body.

Later that night, Mary Turner was cut down and buried with her child near the tree, with a whiskey bottle marking the grave. Even though a complete report of these murders was given to Georgia governor Hugh Dorsey, no charges were ever brought against known or suspected participants in these barbaric crimes.

In 2012, the Georgia Historical Society, along with Valdosta State University, and The Mary Turner Project, erected a memorial marker just a few yards from where she died. Shortly after the marker was put in, someone shot holes into it. When a state official asked one of the relatives of Mary Turner whether he wanted to replace the damaged memorial, he stated, "I told them no. It has five bullet holes in it and those bullet holes were put there by someone who this sign doesn't matter to. Just like Mary Turner's life didn't matter."

A man charged with the 2018 burning death of a black man wrote a letter to a white supremacist group from jail, in which he admitted to setting the victim on fire and saying he did it for race-related reasons.

"To my brothers and sisters in Jesus Christ our savior and Lord, My name is --- and I believe the Bible is about white people and for white people. I am in --- County jail for burning a black man. I set him on fire with lighter fluid poured on his head" states the handwritten letter intercepted at the jail by the sheriff's office. It also asks people to send him a study Bible. This person was convicted of 2nd degree murder in 1999, and was charged with 2nd degree murder again in 2011, before pleading guilty to a lower charge.

The letter was addressed to a publisher of white supremacy propaganda. Some followers in these movements believe white Europeans are the true Israelites, that Jewish people are the spawn of Satan, and that non-whites are sub-human "mud people." This twisted, hell-inspired, belief system has been embraced by many supporters of racial supremacy. The devil is busy! Even some black groups have a parallel theology. I find it interesting that both white and black supremacy groups tend to embrace similar misinterpretations of Scripture (see 1 Tim. 4:1,2; 2 Pet. 3:14-16).

But truth be told, racism has been around since the dawn of civilization. It's a consequence of the fall of man. Satan's trickery in the garden had a devastating effect on all life, animals and plants included.

Two apples up in a tree were looking down on a war-torn world. The first apple said, "Just look at all those simple-minded people fighting and robbing and killing – no one seems willing to get along with his fellow man. Someday we apples will be the only ones left. Then we'll rule the world." This prompted the second apple to reply, "Which of us – the reds or the greens?" ~ *Anonymous*

~§~

"Racism isn't born, folks, it's taught. I have a two-year-old son. You know what he hates? Naps! End of list." ~ *Denis Leary*

"No one is born hating another person because of the color of his skin, or his background, or his religion. People must learn to hate, and if they can learn to hate, they can be taught to love, for love comes more naturally to the human heart than its opposite." ~ *Nelson Mandela*

I love Denis Leary and Nelson Mandela. But I beg to differ on this point. I believe one reason racism thrives is because we have misassigned the origin of racism to bad learning. We treat racism as if it's a matter of the head. But what if the true origin of racism is not bad learning but bad genes? If that's the case, then it changes the direction of our attention and our resources. What if the origin of racism is our fallen human nature? *I assert racism is not a matter of the head, but of the heart.* The enemy is not bad learning; the enemy is our flesh. The heart of the human problem is the problem of the human heart (Jeremiah 17:9). Our flesh is bad stuff.

~§~

You have heard people say unto you, "Racism isn't born, racism is taught." But I say unto you, "We need not teach children to be racist, but we must train them to be kind towards all. We need not teach children to be liars, but we must instruct them to be truthful. We need not teach children to be selfish, but we must inspire them to be generous. For as surely as blood flows through all bodies, racism and lying and selfishness streams through all souls."

Our flesh is dumb (Romans 7:18-25). Consider what the eternal Scriptures declare about every person's capacity to sin. Biblescopes up!

"But I say, walk by the Spirit, and you won't fulfill the lust of the flesh. For the flesh lusts against the Spirit, and the Spirit against the flesh; and these are contrary to one another, that you may not do the things that you desire...Now the deeds of the flesh are obvious, which are: adultery, sexual immorality, uncleanness, lustfulness, *idolatry, sorcery, hatred, strife, jealousies, outbursts of anger, rivalries, divisions, heresies,* envy, murders, drunkenness, orgies, and things like these; of which I forewarn you, even as I also forewarned you, that those who practice such things will not inherit God's Kingdom." ~ *Galatians 5:16-17,19-21*

That's not a pretty picture, but it's the inborn tendency of our flesh, our sin nature. We're programmed to desire "the deeds of the flesh," especially in the absence of divine revelation. Because of our fallen state, we all have a natural inclination to run wild and sin and live for pleasure. I'm inherently hateful and selfish and dusty, and guess what? So are you! No one had to *teach* Cain to hate his brother Abel. Cain didn't need to *learn* about envy or murder. Those evils are just a few of the vices we have lurking in our flesh. We naturally lean toward the dark side (John 3:19).

Did you spot racism on the list from Galatians? Let's take a closer look at Galatians 5:20. By comparing the verse in several translations, we get a raw and ugly picture of just how sinister our flesh can be. Focusing only on verse 20, the works of the flesh are:

New Century Version: "worshiping gods, doing witchcraft, hating, making trouble, being jealous, being angry, being selfish, making people angry with each other, causing divisions among people." Bingo!

Common English Bible: "idolatry, drug use and casting spells, hate, fighting, obsession, losing your temper, competitive opposition, conflict, selfishness, group rivalry."

King James Version: "Idolatry, witchcraft, hatred, variance, emulations, wrath, strife, seditions, heresies."

The Message Bible: "trinket gods; magic-show religion; paranoid loneliness; cutthroat competition; all-consuming-yet-never-satisfied wants; a brutal temper; an impotence to love or be loved; divided homes and divided lives; small-minded and lopsided pursuits."

Revised Standard Version: "idolatry, sorcery, enmity, strife, jealousy, anger, selfishness, dissension, party spirit."

New International Reader's Version: "It worships statues of gods. It also worships evil powers. It is full of hatred and fighting. It is full of jealousy and fits of anger. It is interested only in getting ahead. It stirs up trouble. It separates people into their own little groups."

~§~

In my opinion, Gal. 5:20 lays the foundation for RACISM: party spirit, hating, making people angry with each other, strife, group rivalry, enmity, jealousy, causing divisions among people. We're encoded with a desire to create conflict and competitive opposition. We instinctively want to separate people into little boxes to be labeled and categorized. Racism is a spin-off of our fallen human nature. We're all "preset" to commit these sinful deeds of the flesh. We're all dust. Every man, woman and child.

You don't need to be enlightened or uneducated to be racist, you just need to be human. Which may be the reason why the "wise old owl" of the US Senate, George D. Aiken, states candidly:

~§~

"If we were to wake up some morning and find that everyone was the same race, creed and color, we would find some other cause for prejudice by noon."

~§~

Racism is standard equipment on all models of the human race. It's just one of the many sinful impulses of our dumb flesh. All people of all nations are infected with the pandemic of racism because we're all made of the same bad stuff! Be that as it may, we can still praise God for the victory believers have in Christ Jesus. Unfortunately, unbelievers do not have the same spiritual resources that citizens of the Kingdom possess to combat racism. Which means for the majority of the deceived people in this country, the beat goes on.

How can believers overcome the scourge of racism? How can the "nation within the nation" live above it? The Holy Scriptures provide the answer. *"Walk by the Spirit, and you won't fulfill the lust of the flesh."* Praise God for his word! If I fail to walk by the Spirit, I will fall into the deeds of the flesh. The reverse is also true. If I walk and live by the Spirit, I will not fulfill the works of the flesh. The key is living by the Spirit. The key is being filled with the Spirit. So how do I do that?

Allow me to share something I learned that helped to demystify this idea of being filled with the Spirit. I believe God fills us with the Spirit of Christ when we fill ourselves with the word of Christ. Our walk of faith, our good fight of faith, our entire Christian journey involves coordinating our actions with those of our Lord, who works in us (Phil. 2:13; Col. 1:29). We do the natural part; JAH does the supernatural part (Mk. 4:26,27; 1 Cor. 3:6). For example, in his helpful little book, *How to Obtain Fullness of Power,* Dr. R.A. Torrey examines two passages from letters in the NT.

> And let the peace of God rule in your hearts, to which also you were called in one body, and be thankful. *Let the word of Christ dwell in you richly;* in all wisdom teaching and admonishing one another with psalms, hymns, and spiritual songs, singing with grace in your heart to the Lord. ~ *Colossians 3:15-16*

He compares that to a notably similar passage in a circular letter that was sent to a group of believers about 125 miles from Colossae.

> Don't be drunken with wine, in which is dissipation, but *be filled with the Spirit,* speaking to one another in psalms, hymns, and spiritual songs; singing and making melody in your heart to the Lord. ~ *Ephesians 5:18-19,*

~§~

"**Let the word of Christ dwell in you richly**; in all wisdom teaching and admonishing one another with psalms, hymns, and spiritual songs,"

"**Be filled with the Spirit**, speaking to one another in psalms, hymns, and spiritual songs,"

Now layer in what Jesus Christ said in John 6:63,

"The words that I speak to you are spirit, and are life."

To the believers at Ephesus, God tells them to "Be filled with the Spirit." Within the same context of another letter to the believers in nearby Colossae, God tells them to "Let the word of Christ dwell in you richly." Is there a correlation between being filled with God's Spirit and being filled with God's word? And then we hear Jesus saying, "The words that I speak to you are spirit..." Eureka! The key to being Spirit-filled is to be word-filled. To let the *word of Christ* dwell in me richly **is doing my part** in being filled with the *Spirit of Christ* because his word is...spirit!

> Dr. Torrey writes, "It is well to bear in mind that precisely the results which Paul in one place ascribes to being filled with the Spirit (Ephesians 5:18-22), he in another place ascribes to letting the word of Christ dwell in you richly (Colossians 3:16-18). Evidently Paul knew of no filling with the Holy Spirit divorced from deep and constant meditation upon the Word. To sum all up, anyone who wishes to obtain and maintain fullness of power in Christian life and service must feed constantly upon the Word of God."

Therefore, the key to not fulfilling the lust of the flesh, e.g., racism, hatred, selfishness, etc., is to saturate my heart and mind with the word of Christ. That's an offensive, proactive move I can make in my battle against the flesh. Ultimately, I know the victory is in the fullness of the Spirit. But who does that? Can I fill myself with God's Spirit? I think not. But I can *stir up myself* and *set my mind* to let the word of Christ dwell in me richly!

It's hard to overstate the crucial role the Word has in our victory over the world, the devil, and our flesh. It's the agent the Spirit uses to transform us into the image of Christ. "For this cause we also thank God without ceasing, that when you received from us the word of the message of God, you accepted it not as the word of men, but as it is in truth, the **word of God**, which also *works* in you who believe" (1 Thess. 2:13).

The believers in Thessalonica did not fall prey to skepticism. They accepted the word of the message of God, "not as the word of men, but as it is in truth, the word of God"! Holy Scripture is the living word of God. Holy Scripture is spirit and life. This living Word-Spirit *works* in those who believe. It supernaturally transforms us from weak sinners who are bullied by the flesh into saints of light who reflect the glory of Christ!

> "Don't be conformed to this world, but *be transformed by the renewing of your mind,* so that you may prove what is the good, well-pleasing, and perfect will of God." ~ *Romans 12:2*

D.L. Moody would point to his Bible and say, "This book will keep you from sin, or sin will keep you from this book!" By doing our part in memorizing and meditating on God's word (Psa. 1:1,2), and discussing divine truth (Pro. 27:17), we provide our co-worker, the Spirit of Christ, with a key resource to countermand the temptations of the flesh (Psa. 119:133). No wonder the thrice anointed King David said in Psa. 119:11, "I have *hidden your word in my heart*, that I might not sin against you."

The flesh lusts against the Spirit, and the Spirit against the flesh. They are contrary to one another. They're each at war with the other. They are pulling you in two very different directions. Do you feel it? Since Jesus said plainly that people loved darkness rather than light (John 3:19), how do we get the victory over the dark deeds of our flesh? The Word declares,

> "For the weapons of our warfare are not of the flesh, but mighty before God to the throwing down of strongholds, throwing down imaginations and every high thing that is exalted against the knowledge of God and **bringing every thought into captivity** to the obedience of Christ." ~ *2 Corinthians 10:4-5*

Whenever a desire or imagination runs contrary to the knowledge of God, we throw it down and bring "every thought into captivity to the obedience of Christ." For instance, when the deceiver whispers that my race descended from a "superior" god, and other races are poor sub-humans, the indwelling Spirit thwarts the lie of Satan with the *word of God that's hidden in my heart.* "The rich and the poor have this in common: Yahweh is the **maker of them all**" (Proverbs 22:2). "**He made from one blood** [one man] **every nation of men**..." (Acts 17:26). "Behold, I am the LORD, **the God of all flesh**" (Jeremiah 32:27). BAM! Get outta here, Satan! You can leave now and take your dirty lies with you! Later in the book, we'll observe our Master wield the sword of the Spirit to counter the fiery attacks of the evil one. It's an archetypal battle you don't want to miss between the prince of darkness and the LORD of Light!

"Death and life are in the power of the tongue" (Proverbs 18:21)). Our Spirit-filled words and thoughts are mighty weapons that cast down strongholds and wicked imaginations and every high thing that's exalted against the knowledge of God. But what happens if we have not *hidden his word in our hearts*, if we don't have the knowledge of God? Or, what happens if we have it - but don't believe it? Then there's no counter to the lies of the evil one. Without divine revelation, we have little to pull down the evil strongholds and imaginations and high things that are exalted against the truth of God. Which confirms why skepticism is so dangerous.

A nation without God's guidance is a nation without order = When people do not accept divine guidance, they run wild = Where there is no word from God, people are uncontrolled = Without a prophetic vision, the people throw off restraint = Where there is no message from God, the people don't control themselves = Proverbs 29:18!

~§~

He was sensitized to racism by the years of Nazi-inspired threats and harassment he suffered during his tenure at the University of Berlin. He was in the United States when the Nazis came to power in 1933. Fearful that a return to Germany would place him in mortal danger, he decided to stay, accepting a position at the Institute for Advanced Study in Princeton, NJ. He became an American citizen in 1940. But what he witnessed in America shocked him. He realized that Blacks in Princeton, NJ were being treated like the Jews in Nuremberg, Germany. Finally, he had to express himself.

"I do not intend to be quiet about it. The more I feel an American, the more this situation pains me. I can escape the feeling of complicity in it only by speaking out. Racism is America's greatest disease." *~Albert Einstein*

~§~

One of America's greatest novels offers a valuable bit of advice that may help cure America's greatest disease. In *To Kill A Mockingbird,* widowed lawyer Atticus Finch shares, "First of all, if you learn a simple trick Scout, you will get along a lot better with all kinds of folks. You never really understand a person until you **consider things from his point of view** – until you climb into his skin and walk around in it."

Are you willing to climb into the skin of another race and walk around in it? If you're not African American, in your mind's eye, consider for a moment being Black like me. It's a fact that Africans were brought here in chains, not to participate in the American Dream, but to work hard without pay, for their entire lives, in order to build that dream for others. A whole race of people brutally subjugated, assigned the permanent status as "inferior," illiterates by law! What effect would 250 years of state-sanctioned, negative mega-programming have on any group of people? Think about the two surviving children of Hayes and Mary Turner. Consider things from their point of view. Not a single person was held accountable for the savage murder of their parents and a baby sibling, even though hundreds of people participated in it. What effect did that have on their psychological well-being? Climb into their skin and walk around in it. What impact would that make in your life?

Dr. Martin Luther King, Jr. writes in *Where Do We Go From Here: Chaos or Community?* - "Being a Negro in America means trying to smile when you want to cry. It means trying to hold on to physical life amid psychological death. It means the pain of watching your children grow up with clouds of inferiority in their mental skies. It means having your legs cut off, and then being condemned for being a cripple. It means seeing your mother and father spiritually murdered by the slings and arrows of daily exploitation, and then being hated for being an orphan."

While keeping in mind the orphaned children of Hayes and Mary Turner, the comments from Dr. King, and the sage advice of Atticus Finch, read slowly and thoughtfully Philippians 2:2-11,

> "Make my joy full by being like-minded, have the same love, being of one accord, of one mind; doing nothing through rivalry or through conceit, but in humility, *each counting others better than himself;* each of you not just looking to his own things [interests], but each of you also to the things [interests] of others. Have this in your mind, which was also in Christ Jesus, who, existing in the form of God, didn't consider equality with God a thing to be grasped, but emptied himself, taking the form of a servant, being made in the likeness of men. And being found in human form, he humbled himself, becoming obedient to the point of death, yes, the death of the cross. Therefore God also highly exalted him, and gave to him the name which is above every name, that at the name of Jesus every knee should bow, of those in heaven, those on earth, and those under the earth, and that every tongue should confess that Jesus Christ is Lord, to the glory of God the Father."

~§~

Is the lie of racism stronger than the truth of Scripture? I think not. Is the work of the flesh mightier than the indwelling Spirit of Christ? I know not! Our key to victory is walking in the fullness of his anointed word, which works in us! Or, as Brother Torrey taught us, "Anyone who wishes to obtain and maintain fullness of power in Christian life and service must feed constantly upon the Word of God."

A missionary established a foothold among a tribe of natives in the hills of North Carolina. He was teaching, one-on-one, a recent convert named "Sight of Eagle." The lessons were on the keys to living a Spirit-filled life. Sight of Eagle was thrilled to discover the truth of Galatians 5:16-17, "But I say, walk by the Spirit, and you won't fulfill the lust of the flesh. For the flesh lusts *against* the Spirit, and the Spirit *against* the flesh; and these are contrary to one another."

Sight of Eagle wanted to share this mighty word with his peers, but his people knew nothing of letters. The problem was while he had been taught the language of the missionary, his peers had not. How can he convey the truth of the Word if they don't understand the letters? One day the new believer got an idea. After reading about Jesus in the gospels, Sight of Eagle thought he would tell his friends a story that would carry the truth of Galatians 5:16-17. He shared the story with the missionary first to make sure it hit home.

"When the Most High Spirit calls a person into his Kingdom, he plants inside that man or woman a new spirit. This new spirit is born from above and desires to please the One above. The old spirit is from my flesh and desires to please itself. Two spirits in one body. New spirit from above and old spirit from flesh." The missionary nods. "That's good, Sight of Eagle. Tell me more."

"The new spirit is like a strong gray dog; gray dog wants to please the One above. But the old spirit of the flesh is like a strong red dog. Red dog wants to please only the flesh. *In my heart, these two dogs fight day and night.* Gray dog wants me to do good, red dog wants me to do bad. Dogs fight all the time." The missionary nods again. "I like where you're going. Dogs fighting in your heart makes the point just fine. But what if your friends ask which dog wins the fight? What do you say to that?"

Sight of Eagle anticipated the question. He flashed a big smile and replied, "Dogs fight every day, but the dog that wins is the one I feed the most."

One of the most beneficial questions to ask yourself throughout the day is: *Am I feeding the old me or the new me?* Am I consuming the base, the vile, the worldly, and the unwholesome (Psalm 141:3,4)? Have I gobbled up the tasty fibs of skepticism, materialism and racism? Or, am I feasting on things that are true, honest, noble, just, pure and lovely (Philippians 4:8)? Am I starving to death the Spirit and feeding my flesh [old man]? Or, am I putting to death daily my flesh and feeding the Spirit [new man]? *The starved one will succumb; the fed one will overcome!*

~§~

"**Set your mind** on the things that are above, not on the things that are on the earth. ...**Put to death** therefore your members which are on the earth: sexual immorality, uncleanness, depraved passion, evil desire, and covetousness, which is idolatry. *For these things' sake the wrath of God comes on the children of disobedience.* You also once walked in those, when you lived in them; <u>but now you also put them all away</u>: anger, wrath, malice, slander, and shameful speaking out of your mouth. Don't lie to one another, seeing that you have **put off the old man** with his doings, and have **put on the new man**, who is being renewed in knowledge after the image of his Creator." ~ *Colossians 3:2, 5-10*

~§~ ~§~ ~§~

"There is truth, and there is falsehood. There is good, and there is evil. There is happiness, and there is misery. There is that which ennobles, and there is that which demeans. There is that which puts you in harmony with yourself, with others, with the universe, and with God, and there is that which alienates you from yourself, and from the world, and from God. These things are different and separate and totally distinguishable from one another."

~ Charles Habib Malik

~§~ ~§~ ~§~

"Woe to those who call evil good, and good evil; who put darkness for light, and light for darkness; who put bitter for sweet, and sweet for bitter! Woe to *those who are* wise in their own eyes, and prudent in their own sight!"

~ Isaiah 5:20,21 NKJV

Chapter Eleven:

The Glory of the LORD departed

Jeremiah wasn't the only faithful prophet that Yahweh used to admonish his unfaithful people. Many others like Isaiah, Hosea, Joel, Zephaniah, and Ezekiel also spoke against the sinful actions and attitudes of Jeshurun. Before we take our last look at the enemy's handiwork during a typical week in America, and before we examine the final fall of Israel, let's consider the words of two other prophets.

First, we'll hear a dreadful announcement from Ezekiel 5:5-16. Please keep in mind that the fall of Israel is a cautionary tale for us today. As you read, I want you to ask yourself: *What if this was God's judgment against the United States?* It's terrifying!

~§~

"The Lord Yahweh says: 'This is Jerusalem. I have set her in the middle of nations, and countries are around her. She has rebelled against my ordinances in doing wickedness more than the nations, and against my statutes more than the countries that are around her; for they have rejected my ordinances, and as for my statutes, they have not walked in them.'

"Therefore the Lord Yahweh says: 'Because you are more turbulent than the nations that are around you, and have not walked in my statutes, neither have kept my ordinances, neither have followed the ordinances of the nations that are around you; therefore the Lord Yahweh says: '**Behold, I, even I, am against you**; and I will execute judgments among you in the sight of the nations. I will do in you that which I have not done, and which I will not do anything like it any more, because of all your abominations.

"Therefore the fathers will eat the sons within you, and the sons will eat their fathers. I will execute judgments on you; and I will scatter the whole remnant of you to all the winds. Therefore as I live," says the Lord Yahweh, "surely, because you have defiled my sanctuary with all your detestable things, and with all your abominations, therefore I will also diminish you.

My eye won't spare, and I will have no pity. A third part of you will die with the pestilence, and they will be consumed with famine within you. A third part will fall by the sword around you. A third part I will scatter to all the winds, and will draw out a sword after them.

"Thus my anger will be accomplished, and I will cause my wrath toward them to rest, and I will be comforted. They will know that *I, Yahweh, have spoken in my zeal,* when I have accomplished my wrath on them.

"Moreover I will make you a desolation and a reproach among the nations that are around you, in the sight of all that pass by. So it will be a reproach and a taunt, *an instruction* and an astonishment, to the nations that are around you, when I execute judgments on you in anger and in wrath, and in wrathful rebukes – **I, Yahweh, have spoken it** – when I send on them the *evil arrows of famine* that are for destruction, which I will send to destroy you."

The LORD has spoken, and we know he's keen on fulfilling his word. Israel's sin and rebellion is at the point where God says, *"I will execute judgments on you"* and *"My eye won't spare, and I will have no pity."* Her fall and destruction is an awful "instruction" to us today. Yahweh is longsuffering, but his patience is not eternal. Fellow citizens of America, our arms are too short to box with God! Do we desire his favor or his fury? Are we hanging out on D28A or D28B?

Now we hear more chilling words from Zephaniah 1:4, 14-18.

"I will stretch out my hand against Judah, and against all the inhabitants of Jerusalem. ...The great day of Yahweh is near. It is near, and hurries greatly, the voice of the day of Yahweh. The mighty man cries there bitterly. That day is a day of wrath, a day of distress and anguish, a day of trouble and ruin, a day of darkness and gloom, a day of clouds and blackness, a day of the trumpet and alarm, against the fortified cities, and against the high battlements.

"I will bring distress on men, that they will walk like blind men, because they have sinned against Yahweh, and their blood will be poured out like dust, and their flesh like dung. Neither their silver nor their gold will be able to deliver them in the day of Yahweh's wrath, but the whole land will be devoured by the *fire of his jealousy;* for he will make an end, yes, a terrible end, of all those who dwell in the land."

Satan tempts us to run after sin, and thus incur the wrath of God. *His goal is the downfall of America.* I'll ask again - What are his chances of success if the LORD is not our spiritual ally and protective covering? For the last time, from coast to coast, behold the devil's handiwork...

Monday, August 13, 2018   United States of America

San Francisco police say a city employee for the Street Violence Prevention program was gunned down in broad daylight. The 43-yr old violence prevention worker later died at an area hospital. This marks the 31st homicide in San Francisco so far this year.

Florida law enforcement was called to a shooting in the Pine Forest area in Jacksonville and found a 43-yr old victim lying unresponsive in a driveway. Later in the day, police find a 37-yr old man dead on the floor of a house in the Moncrief Park community.

California police in Oxnard respond to a call in the Southwinds neighborhood and discover a man with a gunshot wound to the head. He later died in the hospital.

Dallas police responded to a shooting call and found a 55-yr old man with a gunshot wound in a vacant grassy lot next to the street. He was pronounced dead at the scene.

Chicago police say a 20-yr man was shot in the head and his 64-yr old grandmother was shot in the arm as they walked in the Albany Park neighborhood. He died at the scene.

Illinois deputies in Jefferson County discovered a 23-yr old man shot to death on the ground next to a vehicle that had been stolen earlier. The victim is from Centralia.

Milwaukee authorities report a 48-yr old man, wanted in a felony domestic abuse case, drew a gun during a traffic stop and was fatally shot by police.

Pennsylvania police report a 38-yr old man, upset because his former girlfriend was seeing a man in Lewisburg, shot to death the man and then took his own life.

Oklahoma City law enforcement say a man threaten to "shoot up" a convenience store when he was approached by officers. When he pointed a gun at the officers, he was shot to death.

Pittsburgh police on patrol saw a 40-yr old man shoot another man in the Hill District. Officers arrested the suspect after a brief chase. The gunshot victim later died.

Iowa authorities responded to a call about a 31-yr old man with a gun sitting in McKinley Park in Creston. When the police approached, the suspect charged at them, and was shot. The suspect later died.

Washington State Patrol report a driver ran a stop sign and created a four-car collision in Walla Walla. A 23-yr old woman was pronounced dead at the scene.

Connecticut police report a 25-yr old man was killed and a 36-yr old woman was injured when someone drove up and shot them as they sat in a parked car in Bridgeport.

San Diego deputies report a 33-yr old man was shot and killed after two groups of people were arguing in the Gaslamp Quarter. Investigation is ongoing.

Florida authorities report a man stole a deputy's jeep in St. Augustine. During his attempt to get away, the suspect crashed the vehicle. He was partially ejected and died at the scene.

Chicago police say a wounded man provided a description of the suspect who shot him. When police approached the suspect, he fired a gun. Officers returned fire and killed him.

Louisiana State police report a 29-yr old woman has been arrested in connection with a deadly hit and run that killed a 31-yr old male pedestrian in Prairieville.

Michigan State police report a 34-yr old man turned himself in and confessed to Novi police to killing his 38-yr old girlfriend at a mobile home neighborhood.

St. Louis police report a 28-yr old man has been charged with murder after he shot his accomplice in the head during a robbery attempt. The homeowner was critically injured.

Virginia officers were called to a home in Manassas and discovered a 60-yr woman fatally stabbed in her bed. Her 68-yr old roommate was charged with murder.

Florida law enforcement detectives report a 35-yr old man was found dead on public swale in Fort Lauderdale in an apparent homicide.

Aurora, Colorado police were called to an apartment complex and found an unresponsive male inside a home. He was pronounced dead at the scene.

Florida deputies conducting a welfare check in Sarasota discovered the bodies of a couple inside a home in what they suspect was a murder-suicide. Both were 67-yrs old.

Kansas law enforcement say a fight started inside and moved outside at a south Wichita sports bar that left a 24-yr old man shot to death. Two suspects have been arrested.

Louisville Metro police believe a 29-yr old woman was not the intended target when she was shot and killed outside a motorcycle club in the Chickasaw neighborhood.

Illinois authorities report a 72-yr old Chicago lawyer was shot and killed in his home in Northfield. A 66-yr old suspect was taken into custody after a standoff in Winnetka.

North Carolina officials say a 21-yr old man is accused of stabbing and killing a 20-yr old woman in Raleigh. Police say the suspect and the victim knew each other.

Indiana authorities report five people are in custody after a man's body was discovered in a wooded area in Anderson. A woman's body was found the next day. Both were shot.

North Carolina authorities report a 27-yr old man in Murphy shot and killed a 57-yr old woman, and after a long standoff with police, he shot and killed himself.

Pittsburgh area police responded to a call about a shooting inside a Duquesne bar. They found a 55-yr old man with a fatal gunshot wound. A 27-yr old suspect is in custody.

South Carolina deputies find the body of a 20-yr old man shot in the head near railroad tracks in Greenville. A murder suspect is in custody. The victim is from Dillon.

Philadelphia police say a 41-yr old man was sitting in a car in Feltonville when someone shot him several times. He was pronounced dead at Einstein Medical Center. Ninety minutes later, a 20-yr old man was shot in the head in Olney. He was pronounced dead at the scene.

Georgia Bureau of Investigation report a sanitation worker found the dismembered body of a female while dumping a container at a landfill in Cartersville.

New York police report a 66-yr old woman, wanting to "rid the house of evil," fatally stabbed a 60-yr British tourist she had just met hours earlier through a mutual friend.

Texas police report a 24-yr old man shot his brother in West El Paso during an argument. He also shot and killed his brother's friend who attempted to intervene.

South Carolina deputies in Hampton County are investigating a homicide after a 30-yr old woman was shot in Brunson. A 36-yr old man from Fairfax is in custody.

Alaska police say an argument broke out in a house in Fairview and a 47-yr old man shot and killed his 33-yr old brother. This is the 13th homicide in Anchorage this year.

Colorado law enforcement was dispatched to a shooting incident in Pueblo and found a 28-yr old man unresponsive with a fatal gunshot wound. An 18-yr old man was charged.

Ohio authorities report a 29-yr old woman shot and wounded her husband in Painesville. She was later found dead from a self-inflicted gunshot wound.

Virginia police respond to a call in Norfolk and find a 15-yr old boy shot. He later died at Sentara Norfolk General Hospital. Four suspects, between the ages of 19 and 20, have been arrested.

Georgia authorities report a Savannah police officer and his wife were stabbed to death on Wilmington Island. The wife's 16-yr old brother is charged with murder.

Philadelphia police arrested two teenagers, 15 and 16-yrs old. While attempting a house break-in, they shot and killed an 18-yr old college bound athlete who lived in the home.

Utah authorities say just hours after a man assaulted his wife, he crashes a small plane into his own house, knowing his wife and a boy were in the residence. He died in the crash. His wife and the boy were unharmed.

Colorado authorities say a 34-yr old pregnant woman and her two daughters are reported missing in Frederick. Her husband later confessed to strangling his wife to death. Their daughters were also killed.

Ohio Department of Health report fatal drug overdoses increased to a record 4,854 in Ohio in 2017, a 20% increase from 2016, and the eighth year in a row that drug deaths increased.

~§~

Dr. Billy Graham's Prayer for the Nation

Our Father and our God, we praise You for Your goodness to our nation, giving us blessings far beyond what we deserve. *Yet we know all is not right with America.* We deeply need a moral and spiritual renewal to help us meet the many problems we face. Convict us of sin. Help us to turn to You in repentance and faith. Set our feet on the path of righteousness and peace. We pray today for our nation's leaders. Give them the wisdom to know what is right, and the courage to do it. You have said, *"Blessed is the nation whose God is the Lord."* May this be a new era for America, as we humble ourselves and acknowledge You alone as our Savior and Lord. This we pray in Your holy name, Amen.

Tingling Ears and Itching Ears

"Because Manasseh king of Judah has done these abominations, and has done wickedly above all that the Amorites did, who were before him, and has also made Judah to sin with his idols; therefore Yahweh the God of Israel says, 'Behold, I bring such evil on Jerusalem and Judah that whoever hears of it, *both his ears will tingle.* I will stretch over Jerusalem the line of Samaria, and the plummet of Ahab's house; and I will wipe Jerusalem as a man wipes a dish, wiping it and turning it upside down. I will cast off the remnant of my inheritance, and deliver them into the hands of their enemies. They will become a prey and a plunder to all their enemies, because they have done that which is evil in my sight, and have provoked me to anger, since the day their fathers came out of Egypt, *even to this day.*' " ~ *2 Kings 21:11-15*

Jeremiah is called the "weeping prophet" because the word he was charged to deliver to his own people was not a positive, feel-good message. It was a hard message for hard times, and the prophet weeps because they would not listen (Psalm 119:136; Mark 6:4). The Babylonian siege created a severe famine in Jerusalem. God is using pain to get their attention. The purpose behind the pain is to prompt the people to repent and surrender to God. Will they humble themselves and plead the promise of 2 Chronicles 7:14, or will they harden their faces and provoke greater manifestations of divine anger (Jeremiah 5:3)? Some of the so-called prophets in Judah contradict Jeremiah. They feel the people need a positive message, so they proclaim there will be no famine or sword. These tearless false prophets said to the citizens of Jerusalem – which was on the brink of divine judgment - exactly what the people wanted to hear.

"Stop listening to that Bible-thumping Jeremiah. Everyone knows he's a crank. No need for alarm. Those crazy prophets come and go all the time! Trust me, we'll be just fine. We can weather this storm too."

All those who claim to speak for God will do well to heed the following.

> "I command you therefore before God and the Lord Jesus Christ, **who will judge the living and the dead at his appearing and his Kingdom:** preach the word; be urgent in season and out of season; reprove, rebuke, and exhort with all patience and

> teaching. For the time will come when they will not listen to the sound doctrine, but having *itching ears,* will heap up for themselves teachers after their own lusts, and will turn away their ears from the truth, and turn away to fables. But you be sober in all things, suffer hardship, do the work of an evangelist, and fulfill your ministry." ~ *2 Timothy 4:1-5*

False teachers and jelly back preachers know itching ears will always welcome a watered-down message. But faithful Jeremiah aimed to fulfill his ministry. This meant no compromise. It meant speaking for the LORD instead of speaking for himself.

> Then Yahweh said to me, "The prophets prophesy lies in my name. I didn't send them. I didn't command them. I didn't speak to them. They prophesy to you a lying vision, divination, and a thing of nothing, and *the deceit of their own heart.* Therefore Yahweh says concerning the prophets who prophesy in my name, but I didn't send them, yet they say, 'Sword and famine will not be in this land.' *Those prophets will be consumed by sword and famine.* The people to whom they prophesy will be cast out in the streets of Jerusalem because of the famine and the sword. They will have no one to bury them – them, their wives, their sons, or their daughters, for I will pour their wickedness on them." ~ *Jeremiah 14:14-16*

That's a stern word from the Lord. Woe to you, Judah and Israel! A plague on both your houses! The entire nation is corrupt. Her lewdness, her prostitution, her neighing, and her adulteries have reached a tipping point. And now God declares, "I will pour their wickedness on them." The prophet Zephaniah said, "the whole land will be devoured by the fire of his jealousy." *Be careful, fellow Americans!* For what's about to happen to unfaithful, unrepentant Israel can surely happen to our country also. God said to them: "**Behold, I, even I, am against you**." That's tragic! Because if the LORD be against you, who can be for you?

In 2 Chronicles 7:1, when Solomon dedicated the temple, the glory of the LORD appeared and sanctified the house. But the people of Judah defiled Yahweh's house, and the prophet Ezekiel sees in a vision the glory of the LORD leave the temple (Eze. 10:18,19; 11:22,23). Alas, the glory of God has departed from Israel. Ichabod! The protective covering of the Most High has been lifted. The day of reckoning has come.

Do you ever wonder if our God is true to his word? All you have to do is look at the nation of Israel. These are his people, a called out nation, that they might be for him a people, a name, a praise, and a glory! "But Jeshurun grew fat, and kicked...Then he abandoned God who made him, and rejected the Rock of his salvation" (Deuteronomy 32:15). The disloyal and stubborn residents of Jerusalem rejected Yahweh. And now in 2 Chronicles 36, the Holy One of Israel, whose very name is Jealous, "will make an end, yes, a terrible end, of all those who dwell in the land."

The Tragic and Final Fall of Israel

"Zedekiah was twenty-one years old when he began to reign, and he reigned eleven years in Jerusalem. He did that which was evil in Yahweh his God's sight. **He didn't humble himself before Jeremiah the prophet speaking from Yahweh's mouth**. He also rebelled against king Nebuchadnezzar, who had made him swear by God; but he stiffened his neck, and hardened his heart against turning to Yahweh, the God of Israel.

"Moreover all the chiefs of the priests, and the people, trespassed very greatly after all the abominations of the nations; *and they polluted Yahweh's house which he had made holy in Jerusalem.* Yahweh, the God of their fathers, sent to them by his messengers, rising up early and sending, because he had compassion on his people, and on his dwelling place; *but they mocked the messengers of God, and despised his words, and scoffed at his prophets,* until Yahweh's wrath arose against his people, until there was no remedy.

"Therefore he brought on them the king of the Chaldeans, who killed their young men with the sword in the house of their sanctuary, and had no compassion on young man or virgin, old man or gray-headed. He gave them all into his hand. All the vessels of God's house, great and small, and the treasures of Yahweh's house, and the treasures of the king, and of his princes, all these he brought to Babylon. They burned God's house, and broke down the wall of Jerusalem, and burned all its palaces with fire, and destroyed all of its valuable vessels. He carried those who had escaped from the sword away to Babylon, and they were servants to him and his sons..." ~ *2 Chronicles 36:11-20*

Before the invasion, JAH besieged Jerusalem for over two years, but they would not repent. Did treacherous Judah forget what happened earlier to her unfaithful sister Israel? Did she not witness how Yahweh rained down on her rebellious sibling the terrible curses of D28B?

> As the king of Israel was passing by on the wall, a woman cried to him, saying, "Help, my lord, O king!" He said, "If Yahweh doesn't help you, where could I get help for you? From of the threshing floor, or from the wine press?" The king said to her, "What is your problem?" She answered, "This woman said to me, 'Give your son, that we may eat him today, and we will eat my son tomorrow.' So we boiled my son, and ate him; and I said to her on the next day, 'Give your son, that we may eat him;' and she has hidden her son." When the king heard the words of the woman, he tore his clothes. *~ 2 Kings 6:26-30*

After the Assyrian invaders caused the terrible famine and downfall of the northern kingdom of Israel, one would think her sister Judah would straighten up and fly right. It doesn't get much worse than mothers boiling and eating their babies. But in spite of that, Judah still continued her affair with other gods. Does she dare to provoke the LORD? Did she forget the words of Lady Wisdom? "For jealousy arouses the fury of the husband. *He won't spare in the day of vengeance*" (Proverbs 6:34)!

The OT book of 2 Kings, chapter 25, provides additional details about the tragic siege of Jerusalem and what happened to the hard-hearted King Zedekiah. We'll also see how God dealt with "all the chiefs of the priests, and the people" who "trespassed very greatly after all the abominations of the nations." Psalm 62:12 declares a merciful God will render to every man, woman, boy and girl according to their works.

~§~

"Then Zedekiah rebelled against the king of Babylon. In the ninth year of his reign, in the tenth month, in the tenth day of the month, Nebuchadnezzar king of Babylon came, he and all his army, against Jerusalem, and encamped against it; and **they built forts against it around it.**

"So the city was besieged until the eleventh year of king Zedekiah. On the ninth day of the fourth month [two and a half years later], the famine was severe in the city, so that there was no bread for the people of the land. Then a breach was made in the city, and all the men of war fled by night by the way of the gate between the two walls, which was by the king's garden (now the Chaldeans were against the city around it); and the king went by the way of the Arabah.

"But the Chaldean army pursued the king, and *overtook him* in the plains of Jericho; and all his army was scattered from him. Then they captured the king, and carried him up to the king of Babylon to Riblah; and they passed judgment on him. **They killed Zedekiah's sons before his eyes, then put out Zedekiah's eyes, bound him in fetters, and carried him to Babylon.**

"They took away the pots, the shovels, the snuffers, the spoons, and all the vessels of bronze with which they ministered. The captain of the guard took away the fire pans, the basins, that which was of gold, in gold, and that which was of silver, in silver.

"The captain of the guard took Seraiah the chief priest [of Judah], Zephaniah the second priest, and the three keepers of the threshold; and out of the city he took an officer who was set over the men of war; and five men of those who saw the king's face, who were found in the city; and the scribe, the captain of the army, who mustered the people of the land; and sixty men of the people of the land, who were found in the city. Nebuzaradan the captain of the guard took them, and brought them to the king of Babylon at Riblah. The king of Babylon attacked them, and put them to death at Riblah in the land of Hamath. So Judah was carried away captive out of his land." ~ *2 Kings 24:20-25:7, 14-15, 18-21*

~§~

Without a doubt, this is one of the saddest episodes in the long history of Israel. The Shekinah Glory, God's abiding presence, departs the temple. Jerusalem, the beloved and holy city of God, besieged and utterly destroyed. The house of the LORD burned to the ground. The king of Judah, Zedekiah, who *"didn't humble himself before Jeremiah the prophet speaking from Yahweh's mouth,"* is captured by the invading army. The poor man is forced to watch the execution of his sons. And then the Chaldeans put out his eyes. Which means one of the last images etched in King Zedekiah's mind is the extermination of his lineage. That's awful! The blind and broken king is then chained and taken to Babylon, where he's put in prison till the day of his death (Jeremiah 52:11).

The friends of Zedekiah, who shared in his sin and his material prosperity, were all gathered up and brought before the king of Babylon, who "attacked them, and put them to death at Riblah." I don't know if the king himself killed all 73 of them. Maybe it was more like what happened when Joshua led the nation back in their days of glory, when they were in the blessed zone of D28A. Since Jacob is now in the cursed zone of D28B, the sinful leaders of Judah may have been on the receiving end of what the faithful leaders of Israel once did to their foes.

Back in the book of Joshua, chapter ten, the warriors of Israel cornered five kings of the Amorites who sought to escape by hiding in a cave. But, "when they brought those kings out to Joshua, Joshua called for all the men of Israel, and said to the chiefs of the men of war who went with him, 'Come near. Put your feet on the necks of these kings.' They came near, and put their feet on their necks. Joshua said to them, 'Don't be afraid, nor be dismayed. Be strong and courageous, for Yahweh will do this to all your enemies against whom you fight.' Afterward Joshua struck them, put them to death, and hanged them on five trees."

I don't know if the Babylonian leaders humiliated them first by putting their feet on the necks of these 73 unfortunate citizens of Judah, or not. But at the end of the day, all of them were executed. The small remnant still alive after the famine and the sword was carried off to Babylon to serve as slaves in a foreign land.

Listen up, America! "**It is a fearful thing to fall into the hands of the living God**" (Hebrews 10:31)! He is not playing games with those who are called by his name, and he's keen on fulfilling his word. The Northern Kingdom of Israel was besieged and taken captive by the Assyrians around 722 B.C. After that event, the LORD declared in Jeremiah 3:8: "I saw when, for this very cause, that backsliding Israel had committed adultery, I had put her away and given her a certificate of divorce, yet treacherous Judah, her sister, *had no fear;* but she also went and played the prostitute." Instead of learning from what happened to her unfaithful sister to the north, the people of Jerusalem chose not to fear the LORD. A foolish nation won't learn from anyone's experience. They continued in their idiotic ways, even during a terrible siege that lasted for two and a half years! They sinned against El Kanna until the day their wickedness was poured on them. The Southern Kingdom of Judah and Jerusalem was taken captive by Babylonian invaders around 586 B.C. From this date on, until May 14, 1948 A.D., Israel as a nation would cease!

D28B

"Because you didn't serve Yahweh your God with joyfulness and with gladness of heart, by reason of the abundance of all things; therefore you will serve your enemies whom Yahweh sends against you, in hunger, in thirst, in nakedness, and in lack of all things. He will put an iron yoke on your neck until he has destroyed you." ~ Deut. 28:47-48

After the thoroughgoing destruction of Jerusalem, we read in Lamentations, "The LORD has done what He purposed; He has fulfilled His word which He commanded in days of old. He has thrown down and has not pitied, and He has caused an enemy to rejoice over you; He has exalted the horn of your adversaries." ~ *Lam. 2:17 NKJV*

Beware, America! "Do we provoke the Lord to jealousy? are we stronger than he?" (1 Cor. 10:22 KJV). There's a high price to pay for disobedience! Again, it was Dr. Billy Graham who said, "Self-centered indulgence, pride and lack of shame over sin are now emblems of the American lifestyle. My heart aches for America and its deceived people."

Sin will take us farther than we want to go, keep us longer than we want to stay, and cost us more than we want to pay!

"Righteousness exalts a nation, but sin is a disgrace to any people" (Proverbs 14:34). Why is sin a disgrace to the people of America? Because **if** we cast off restraint and run hard after sin, **then** we will surely reap the wages of sin, which is death and subjugation and disgrace. And why does righteousness exalt the people of America? Because **if** we *stir up ourselves* to take hold of the LORD and follow hard after His righteous ways, **then** we will be lifted up and shielded by the LORD. Therefore, righteousness exalts a nation!

Where will the Judgment of God begin?

"For the time has come for judgment to begin with the household of God. If it begins first with us, what will happen to those who don't obey the Good News of God? 'If it is hard for the righteous to be saved, what will happen to the ungodly and the sinner?' " ~ *1 Peter 4:17-18*

"Wrath is cruel, and anger is overwhelming; but who is able to stand before jealousy?" ~ *Proverbs 27:4*

~§~

Revival is that sovereign work of God in which He visits His own people, restoring and releasing them into the fullness of His blessing. *~ Robert Coleman*

Revival is an invasion from heaven that brings a conscious awareness of God. *~ Stephen Olford*

Revival cannot be organized, but we can set our sails to catch the wind from heaven when God chooses to blow upon His people once again. *~ G. Campbell Morgan*

Revival is the people of God living in the power of an ungrieved, unquenched Spirit. *~ James A. Stewart*

The kingdom of God is not going to advance by our churches becoming filled with men, but by men [and women] in our churches becoming filled with God. *~ Howard Spring*

A true revival means nothing less than a revolution, casting out the spirit of worldliness, making God's love triumph in the heart. *~ Andrew Murray*

In revival, the minds of people are concentrated upon things of eternity, and there is an awareness that nothing else really matters. *~ Brian Edwards*

Revival begins when you draw a circle around yourself and make sure everything in that circle is right with God. *~ Anne Graham Lotz*

Revival is the church falling in love with Jesus all over again. *~ Vance Havner*

~§~

Chapter Twelve:

"Then will I hear from heaven, and will forgive their sin, and will heal their land."

For this section of our journey together, we have four witnesses who will come before us. Each one has a very specific task. The first witness is Dr. C.S. Lovett. He will explain how Satan saps the power from the church. Our second witness is Dr. J. Edwin Orr. He will share how God sent a mighty revival to Wales and America in response to the fervent prayers of his people. The third witness is Georgia Anne Geyer. She will tell us why moral societies are the only ones that work. And our last witness is Dr. John R. Rice. His focus will be on our current and dire need for Holy Spirit power.

Spectator Christianity ~ Dr. C.S. Lovett

Gasoline gets stale. That powerful stuff which sends cars zipping down the freeway gets stale. And the same Christianity which can send a person zinging through life in the power of God also gets stale. Do you know what produces staleness in gasoline? The very same thing which brings monotony and dullness to Christianity – idleness.

You've driven past an oil refinery. Ever notice those huge storage tanks? At the bottom of those tanks is a valve. Every now and then the oil companies drain off the stale gas and sell it to the cut-rate gas stations at a reduced price. Gasoline loses its power when it is stored. In six weeks time it not only loses half its strength, it even clogs carburetors by forming gum deposits in the jets. As idleness drains the vitality of gasoline, so can it render a Christian powerless. Idleness does to Christians exactly what it does to gasoline – saps strength.

By idleness I mean disobedience to the Great Commission, not inactivity in church programs. A Christian can be furiously churchy, yet idle as far as God is concerned. The idleness of disobedience is robbing God's people of supernatural power today. It can be a shock for the average Christian to learn the Great Commission rests as fully on him as it does any pastor or evangelist. You're about to see why.

How Satan Saps the Saints

Suppose you were Satan. Dare we pretend such a thing for a moment? Let's go back in history 1700 years. Christianity has been gathering momentum for two centuries. The saints of God are on the move. Subjects are being scooped from your kingdom at an alarming rate. Your empire is evaporating. If anything is to be left, this sweep of the saints must be stopped.

But how? You've tried persecution. That only served to fan the fire of Christian fervor. Ten rose up to take the place of each who died a martyr. You can't put out a forest fire by kicking the glowing embers. If only you could find a way to IDLE those Christians. That would do it. Then the church would lose its power. With the power of the Spirit missing from her ranks, the church would no longer be able to prosecute the task of world evangelism. But how do you go about idling millions?

What kind of a stratagem do you suppose would cause the bulk of God's people to shun His command and fall into idleness? The suggestion would have to be subtle, yea even sound godly, if masses of Christians are to fall for it. It must be such that when they believe the notion, they immediately stop their marching and become idle. It would have to produce staleness to sap the saints of their spiritual power.

Let's see now, what kind of a scheme might inactivate the army of the Lord in such a fashion? While you're racking your brain, something startling happens in history. It answers your dilemma. Since history solves the problem, we don't need to pretend you are Satan any more. The devil can take it from here. He has just gotten a big break. The course of human events has played into his hands.

Satan's Big Break

In the year 312 A.D., a military commander named Constantine the Great is marching on Rome. He is going to give Satan just what he needs to stem the tide of Christianity. He doesn't mean to be Satan's man, but he ends up giving the devil precisely what it takes to drain the power of God from the Christian church.

As the emperor was leading his troops toward Rome, a cross suddenly appeared in the clouds. He interpreted it as a token of victory. That very day he ordered the cross of Christ to be placed on his soldiers' shields. That night the apparition returned to find its continuation in a dream. Constantine was soundly and decisively converted to Christianity. Rome fell into his hands on October 28, 312 A.D. From that day on, he made no secret of his new faith in Christ. Though wisely tolerating the pagan forces within his empire, he made Christianity the "official" religion of the realm.

Constantine's victory was also a victory for Satan. However, the devil's victory came as a by-product of the emperor's zeal for Christ. In the process of solidifying his empire under the Christian banner, the monarch granted sweeping powers to the church at Rome. As early as 313 A.D. the officers of the church (clerics/bishops) were given total immunity from the law. They were exempted from all military and civic burdens. They were relieved of every personal responsibility as citizens. They were practically a law unto themselves, with the power to pass these newly acquired rights to their own named successors.

Suddenly there were two classes of Christians: the powerful leaders of the church and the commoners. To widen the gap, the bishops were given jurisdiction over certain domains, acting as magistrates in private matters. Wealth was conferred upon the church in order to carry out the task of unifying Constantine's realm as a Christian empire. At once the leaders became a part of upper-class society, so the division in the church was that of rank and wealth and power.

Satan now had what he needed to stop the Christian movement. With the state elevating the church leaders to positions of power, a remarkable division of the saints was created for him – automatically. The small group of professionals was called the CLERGY, the uneducated masses became LAITY. From here on it would be easy. If he could persuade the church that the work of the Lord belonged in the hands of the upper-class leaders, it would remove the Great Commission from the foot soldiers of Christ. Satan wouldn't mind a few leaders dabbling with religion if he could idle the bulk of God's army. They were the ones doing the damage to his kingdom.

Satan's Suggestion

"The WORK of God is the responsibility of the appointed leaders, while the *ritual of religion* is sufficient for the average Christian."

If the church would buy this wile, it would idle the host. You can see how it shrewdly reverses the Holy Spirit's plan. The WORK of the Lord was clearly placed in the hands of believers. The twelve disciples (leaders) were to give themselves to the Word (Acts 6:3,4).

The Church Bought the Wile

Almost overnight the preaching, baptizing, witnessing, and ministering of communion was *exclusively* in the hands of the clergy. The army of the Lord, composed of commoners and slaves, suddenly had nothing to do. The huge laity, which had been carrying the ball for Christ, was made to stop the WORK of the Lord. All of their witnessing and spreading of the Gospel ceased as the tiny clergy took over the task.

Satan's scheme worked beautifully. The mighty militia sweeping the world became a stationary mass of Christians in the world. The *revolution* became a *religion,* taking its place alongside the other religions of the world. People continued to worship the Lord, but they no longer fought for Him. With the great army of the Lord reduced to a LISTENING LAITY, the spiritual power of the church evaporated. The gasoline of God finally became useless.

Satan Secure

With the masses idled, Satan's kingdom was now secure. All Satan had to do now was control the clergy. But that would be easy. **He could keep them divided over doctrine**. By 325 A.D. the church was no longer fighting paganism. She turned her guns inward to begin blasting herself. Then came what Dr. J. E. Conant describes in his great book, *Every Member Evangelism*, as the "Devil's Millennium which history calls the Dark Ages." It lasted for 1200 years.

A Flash of Hope

Suddenly a bright spot appeared on the pages of church history. On October 31, 1517, Satan's kingdom was again threatened. That day, Martin Luther nailed his 95 theses to the door of the castle church at Wittenberg. He dared to declare the individual rights of God's people, those priestly privileges which belong to all trusting in the Lord Jesus.

Trouble had long been brewing in Europe. The newly invented printing press made it possible for the Word of God to pass from the hands of the clergy to laymen. The masses began to learn of their rights in Christ. The clergy had abused its high office, exploiting God's sheep mercilessly. The continent was a powder keg. Martin Luther was the match. His defiance of Rome ignited the Protestant Reformation.

Sadly, though, that's all it was – a reformation. The Christian *revolution* was not reborn. Satan's empire remained intact. For a tantalizing moment it looked as if Christianity might again go on the march. But alas, the devil had done his dirty work too well. Protestants emerged from the Roman church still clinging to the **clergy-laity tradition**. The WORK of the Lord stayed in the hands of the professionals. The masses would remain content with hearing His WORD only. The great hope of world evangelism which flashed so brightly in the 16th Century gradually faded.

Some minor flares have brightened the spiritual sky since Luther's day. The Lord has been able to raise up men here and there like Moody, Finney, and Billy Graham. But they come and go. The situation remains much as it has been. Today the WORK OF GOD remains in the hands of the professional clergy. Coming to watch their performances is the non-trained laity. Without doubt, Satan's ambition is presently being carried out by an over-burdened clergy (ministers, evangelists, missionaries, and leaders) and an IDLE laity.

Christianity – A Layman's Movement

Christianity began as a LAY movement. The Lord commissioned an army of common people to reap the world in His Name. He didn't need professionals for the task He had in mind. He was going to do the work himself (Matthew 16:18). And He got off to a terrific start working THROUGH His disciples. The Holy Spirit carefully records ... *"The LORD added to the church daily such as should be saved"* (Acts 2:47). And for that, He required willing workers, not brilliant or talented leaders (Acts 4:13).

The anointing of the Holy Spirit turned those common people into flaming evangelists. One does not have to be a professional to share Christ, when he [or she] is filled with the Spirit of God. The world began to shake as those early saints moved out in Jesus' Name. So did Satan. That's why he became so desperate to stem the sweeping tide. He had to stop that army or let the world pass over to Christ.

Satan's clergy/laity scheme transformed Christianity into a spectator event. The POWER of God which attended the working of the Lord, all but vanished from Christianity. A pall of gloom hangs over modern Christianity. No longer does she glow with the excitement of a Spirit-filled revolution. With Christians ignorant of their privileges in power, entertainment is substituted for the adventure of the Holy Spirit. Christianity has been reduced to a devotional life, so that now she consists of lectures and lessons on Bible theory, prophecies, times of prayer and fellowship. While all this is precious and proper, it does NOT compensate for the missing thrill of the Holy Spirit.

Where the Action is

The church started as a Spirit-filled explosion! Our Christian ancestors went into ACTION as soon as they received the commission. *The anointing of God accompanied their obedience!*

> "And ye shall have power when the Holy Spirit comes upon you and ye shall be my witnesses...even to the remote parts of the earth" (Acts 1:8).

Obedience to that commission brought rapture and delight to those early saints. Christianity was at once intoxicating – exhilarating – infectious! Everywhere those early Christians went, the truth of Jesus swept like a prairie fire.

"And there was at that time a great persecution against the church which was at Jerusalem; and they were scattered abroad throughout the regions of Judea and Samaria, except the Apostles; therefore they that were scattered abroad went everywhere preaching the Word" (Acts 8:1, 4).

The Clergy Stayed Home

The Holy Spirit notes how it was NOT the church leaders who fanned out to share Christ, but the common people. The clergy stayed behind, at Jerusalem. The Lord commissioned INDIVIDUALS. They moved, with each entering the grand adventure of exalting Christ in the power of the Holy Spirit! Laymen thrilled to the supernatural. They experienced an incredible increase for God as they obeyed. Using common people, filled with His Spirit, the Master began to harvest souls from the world. Pentecost was the time of the wheat harvest. The revolution was under way as the army of the Lord spread out Jerusalem.

Those early Christians displayed something we don't see today with all of our various church bodies, buildings, and Bibles – they had POWER! That's the missing ingredient. They enjoyed the power of God because they were doing the very thing for which the power of God was promised – witnessing. The command of the Lord rang in their ears. **They knew precisely what the power of the Holy Spirit was for** – OBEDIENCE to their Master's commission. Nothing could be clearer. When they moved in obedience, the POWER of God followed. Those early saints seized the privilege of Pentecost and the Christian faith roared into ACTION!

The hallmark of aggressive Christianity is POWER! The excitement of Christianity is the WONDER of working in that power! The privilege of each Christian is the THRILL of moving in that power! POWER – our Pentecostal inheritance.

For forty days after His resurrection, the Lord taught His disciples about the kingdom they represented and how they were commissioned to produce sons of God (Acts 1:3). He instructed them in the mystery of the new birth. It was a supernatural business, requiring supernatural power. Yet, the Lord assured them they would have everything needed for the job. But it was to come in a strange way. So strange, in fact, their minds could hardly grasp it.

In as much as the work required spiritual power, none of Jesus' disciples could obey the commission until this power was available. As long as Jesus remained in their midst, so that his presence was confined to a body, it would be impossible for them to receive the power of which He spoke. It was His plan to return to them via the Holy Spirit and indwell them, empowering them Himself.

NOTE: The Savior sought to convince His disciples that just as His Father indwelt Him, He would return to indwell them (John 14:18, 20). The Lord insisted that the Holy Spirit could not bring His presence to them until He was glorified (John 16:7; 7:39). The return of Christ via the Holy Spirit is one of the most delightful mysteries of the New Testament. The apostle Paul develops the truth of Jesus' indwelling (Col. 1:27; 2:6; Eph. 3:17). *It is by His indwelling that His power becomes ours.*

The promise of the Holy Spirit wasn't exactly new. The ancient prophets foresaw a day when God's Spirit would come in His fullness to INDIVIDUALS (Joel 2:28; Isa. 44:3). Since He was to come on a particular day, Jesus instructed His disciples NOT to begin executing their commission until that day arrived. They were not to start exercising any authority until they received the power that went with their commission. To do so would be like a man trying to command troops before he received proper orders from higher headquarters. It wouldn't make sense. Commissioned people must always WAIT until they receive the proper authority before attempting to command. That is precisely what Jesus told His disciples to do ... WAIT:

> "...behold I am sending the promise of My Father upon you; but you are to stay in the city until you are clothed with **power from on high**" (Luke 24:49).

They did as He asked, waiting in the city of Jerusalem. For nine days nothing happened. Then on the tenth day the Holy Spirit arrived, bringing the presence of Jesus – in PERSON! This was the DAY OF PENTECOST. On that day our inheritance arrived with a bang! (Acts 2:1-4). The populace was shocked – flabbergasted. Only the disciples knew what really happened. The Spirit of God had come. Their Savior had kept His word. They were not left as orphans in the world (John 14:18). Now they could begin their commission. That's the important thing to see. Jesus had returned and the task of building His church could get under way. The Lord was now in a position to WORK THROUGH His disciples (Matt. 16:18)."

"Let us not glide through this world and then slip quietly into heaven, without having blown the trumpet loud and long for our Redeemer, Jesus Christ. Let us see to it that the devil will hold a thanksgiving service in hell, when he gets the news of our departure from the field of battle."
~ *C.T. Studd*

What are our takeaways from Dr. Lovett?

First of all, it was never the plan of God for the "clergy" alone to do the WORK of the ministry. All believers have a work to do. Every believer has spiritual gifts he or she should employ to advance the Kingdom. All believers are to allow the indwelling Christ to work on them and for them and through them! The work of the clergy is to train the "laity" to do the WORK of the ministry. That's the biblical pattern. It's plainly laid out in the NT book of Ephesians 4:11-12 KJV,

> "And he gave some, apostles; and some, prophets; and some, evangelists; and some, pastors and teachers; for the perfecting of the saints, for the work of the ministry, for the edifying of the body of Christ."

God gave to the body of Christ apostles and prophets and evangelists and pastor-teachers to do what? Is it "for the work of the ministry"? Is that what it says? No! Their role is "**for the perfecting of the saints**," which is the equipping and training of the saints. Why? So that the saints can do "the work of the ministry," which in turn edifies and builds up the body of Christ. I believe it was D. L. Moody who said, "I'd rather train ten men to work than do the work of ten men!" The role of the so-called clergy is to train/equip the saints to do the work of the ministry.

Christianity is not a spectator event. Every believer has a role in the work of the ministry. But is this happening in our churches today? The church today can be likened to a volleyball coach running out on the court to compete against the opposing team, all by himself; while his own team is on the sideline cheering. That's not the way it should be, my dear siblings in Christ. A football coach equips the players, the players hit the field. Church leaders equip the saints and the saints hit the fields, which are "white for harvest already" according to Jesus in John 4:35.

Our second takeaway is Satan has sapped the power from the church. How did he do it? By removing the saints from the work of the ministry! The power is for the work. No work, no power. Spectators don't need power. Church members "chilling" on the sideline don't need Holy Spirit power. His power is for the brave souls who are doing his work. Many are not juiced about their faith, but the juice flows freely when we minister to others. Sitting inside a comfortable, climate-controlled building once or twice a week, and watching others do their thing is probably not the entire scope of ministry God has in mind for his people. You don't need much power to do that. But we all need Holy Spirit power to witness effectively for our Lord Jesus and snatch souls from the fire (Jude 23). We all need Holy Spirit power to see people turn "from darkness to light, and from the power of Satan unto God" (Acts 26:18)!

Spectator Christianity requires about as much power as it takes to go out and watch a movie. But if we desire to do God's supernatural work, that will require God's supernatural power. The great news is the LORD will empower and reward those who are serious about his business. Psalm 62:11-12 tells us *"God has spoken once; twice I have heard this, that power belongs to God. Also to you, Lord, belongs loving kindness, for you reward every man according to his work."* Do you want to fire up your faith? Lead a small group study, or teach a Sunday school class, or talk to a relative about the Savior. God is eager to work "mightily" in those who are eager to do his work (Colossians 1:27-29). Want more than rituals in your religion? Fast and pray earnestly for a lost co-worker or neighbor, and look for God's green light to proclaim your faith. If we do his work, Jesus promises he will be with us, and that's all the power we need.

The Believer's Great Commission

> Jesus came to them and spoke to them, saying, "All authority has been given to me in heaven and on earth. **Go and make disciples of all nations**, baptizing them in the name of the Father and of the Son and of the Holy Spirit, teaching them to observe all things that I commanded you. Behold, I am with you always, even to the end of the age." Amen.
>
> ~ *Matthew 28:18-20*

~§~

"Christ's call is to save the lost, not the stiff-necked; He came not to call scoffers but sinners to repentance; not to build and furnish comfortable chapels, churches, and cathedrals at home in which to rock Christian professors to sleep by means of clever essays, stereotyped prayers, and artistic musical performances, but to capture men from the devil's clutches and the very jaws of Hell. This can be accomplished only by a red-hot, unconventional, unfettered devotion, in the power of the Holy Spirit, to the Lord Jesus Christ." ~ *C.T. Studd*

Dr. J. Edwin Orr is our second witness. He will share how God sent a mighty revival to Wales. When the saints in America got wind of what Yahweh was doing in Europe, they humbled themselves and cried out for Jehovah-Rapha, the LORD who heals, to do the same in the USA. And he did! It's an example of how Heb. 10:24-25 is activated for believers today.

> "Let's consider how to provoke one another to love and good works, not forsaking our own assembling together, as the custom of some is, but exhorting one another, and so much the more as you see the Day approaching."

This is one of the few times in the Bible when the word "provoke" is used in a positive manner. One reason Christians assemble together is to provoke (Gr *paroxusmos* - to incite or irritate, to stir up) one another. We are to stir up each other in what way? "To love and good works." What did Jesus say would happen if we reflect God's love and do good works (Matt. 5:16; Jn. 13:35)? It *glorifies* the Father and it *confirms* our testimony as true disciples, which opens the door for an anointed witness to our community. **As co-workers with God, we must do our part to stoke the flames of revival**. We not only stir up ourselves to take hold of the Lord, we also stir up one another (2 Pet. 1:13; 3:1)! As we see the Day approaching, we're called to provoke one another to walk in love, to let our light shine, and to be a blessing to those around us. It's an amazing concept, and we see it come to life for the faithful in Wales and America.

NOTE: What our immutable God has done through his prayerful servants in the past, he's more than able to do again through us today (Mal. 3:6; Heb. 13:8; Phil. 2:12,13). *"O God, it is time for You to work!"*

THE WELSH REVIVAL of 1904-1905

Evan Roberts worked at first as a door-boy in the pits, opening and closing metal doors for tunnel traffic. When he was nineteen, a pit explosion scorched his Bible, but his life and health were spared. His greatest passion was interest in revival, a subject that obsessed him from his youth up. He wrote to a friend: 'For ten or eleven years, I have prayed for a revival. I could sit up all night to read or talk about revivals. It was the Spirit that moved me to think about a revival.'

At Newcastle Emlyn he attended a meeting conducted by Seth Joshua. On Thursday morning, Seth Joshua closed his ministry with a moving prayer, crying out in Welsh, 'Lord...bend us.' Evan Roberts went to the front to kneel, crying in great agony: 'Lord, bend me.' Roberts knew that he had reached the crisis of his spiritual experience. He was moved to pray publicly, but waited till one and another had prayed. He felt compelled to pray, yet still he waited until a few more had prayed, when he 'felt a living power pervading my bosom. It took my breath away.' His face was bathed in perspiration. He cried out, 'Bend me!' He was overwhelmed by the verse, 'God commendeth His love toward us...' Then a wave of peace flooded his soul. He became concerned about others.

> I felt ablaze with a desire to go through the length and breadth of Wales to tell of the Saviour; and had that been possible, I was willing to pay God for doing so.

For Evan Roberts, it was the most terrible and most sublime day of his life, for he knew without doubt that an extraordinary work was beginning. Seth Joshua made a note in his diary, remarking on the prayer of the young man. Evan wrote home to his brother Dan in Loughor, predicting great blessing and urging him to put himself at the Spirit's disposal. Sidney Evans, who afterward married Evan Roberts's sister, was told by the young prophet, 'I have a vision of all Wales being lifted up to heaven. We are going to see the mightiest revival that Wales has ever known.' He asked Evans directly, **'Do you believe that God can give us a hundred thousand souls now?'**

Evan Roberts went to see the ministers of Moriah Church in Loughor and its daughter church in Gorseinon. Daniel Jones gave his permission for meetings in Moriah Church and its chapel, Pisgah. Thomas Francis added his consent for meetings in Gorseinon. On October 31st, 1904, Roberts commenced his mission in an aftermeeting on a Monday night, only seventeen people attending. *Yet he truly believed that this would become a movement that would win a hundred thousand people to vital Christian faith.*

Roberts invited the seventeen people who lingered for his message to declare their Christian faith in public. It was a local peculiarity to be reluctant in proclaiming any assurance of faith, but at last all of them gave testimony. Meetings followed in Pisgah and in Gorseinon. Larger crowds than ever attended the next meeting in the Moriah Church, where Roberts first propounded four points:

1. You must put away any unconfessed sin.
2. You must put away any doubtful habit.
3. You must obey the Spirit promptly.
4. You must confess Christ publicly.

On Saturday night, Roberts spoke to a crowded church on 'Be filled with the Spirit.' The meeting lasted five hours. But on Sunday 6th November, an ordained minister from a nearby town occupied the pulpit, as previously arranged; an aftermeeting with Evan Roberts followed, lasting till after midnight. Monday evening's prayer meeting was crowded to capacity, going on for three hours after midnight; so great was the press that windows were broken for air.

Evan Roberts preached at the Brynteg Congregational Chapel on the 9th, the same day that an English-language newspaper back in Cardiff carried a brief account of the stirrings of revival.

GREAT CROWDS OF PEOPLE DRAWN TO LOUGHOR

Congregation Stays till 2.30 in the Morning

"A remarkable religious revival is now taking place in Loughor. For some days a young man named Evan Roberts, a native of Loughor, has been causing great surprise at Moriah Chapel. The place has been besieged by dense crowds of people unable to obtain admission. Such excitement has prevailed that the road on which the chapel is situated has been lined with people from end to end. Roberts, who speaks in Welsh, opens his discourse by saying that he does not know what he is going to say but that when he is in communion with the Holy Spirit, the Holy Spirit will speak, and he will simply be the medium of His wisdom. The preacher soon after launches into a fervent and at times impassioned oration. His statements have had the most stirring effects upon his listeners. Many who have disbelieved Christianity for years are returning to the fold of their younger days. One night, so great was the enthusiasm invoked by the young revivalist that, after his sermon which lasted two hours, the vast congregation remained praying and singing until two-thirty in the morning. Shopkeepers are closing early in order to get a place in the chapel, and tin and steel workers throng the place in working clothes."

On 11th November, the Moriah Church was again overcrowded with eight hundred or more people, overflowing into the old chapel. Many were on their knees for a long time on account of their distress and agony of soul. By now a newspaper reporter from Cardiff had arrived, and he was amazed at what he saw. His report was given the widest circulation in Wales and beyond:

> Instead of the set order of proceedings...everything was left to the spontaneous impulse of the moment...at 4.25 a.m., the gathering dispersed. But even at that hour, the people did not make their way home. When I left to walk back to Llanelly, I left dozens of them about the road still discussing the chief subject of their lives.

'I felt that this was no ordinary gathering,' he added. All the next day, Friday, prayer meetings in the homes of the people were held to intercede for the salvation of their friends and kinsfolk. The Friday evening service again disregarded time, yet the spiritual excitement kept the folk from awareness of hunger or fatigue.

By early afternoon, Saturday 12th November, wagons and carts were driven into town from the surrounding countryside. Shops in the town were cleared of all provisions by folk who had come long distances. The meeting houses were overcrowded hours before the time for which services had been announced. Sidney Evans preached in one chapel and Evan Roberts in the other. Day broke before the people dispersed, to their homes first and to Sunday Services afterwards.

A local minister reported that the community had been converted into a praying multitude. **The lives of hundreds of coal-miners and tin-plate workers were transformed**, men going straight from the mills and pit-heads to chapel, leaving the taverns practically empty.

> The only theme of conversation among all classes and sects is 'Evan Roberts.' Even the tap-rooms of the public houses are given over to discussion on the origin of the powers possessed by him.

Evan Roberts enjoyed no sleep on Saturday night, but early on Sunday morning, driven by a Loughor layman and accompanied by five young singers, he arrived in Swansea to catch a train for Aberdare. The opening meetings in this town were disappointing. There was criticism by the local Christians of the visiting team of girl singers. Completely unwarranted criticism persisted among those willing to be scandalized, lingering for threescore years and ten.

On Monday 14th November, the great Ebenezer Chapel (Congregationalist) in Aberdare was crowded by a thousand eager people. There was no sign of anything unusual in either the Sunday or the Monday service. On Tuesday, the early morning prayer meeting was crowded, people remaining at home rather than going to work. The meeting lasted four hours. There the young prophet announced that a great awakening was coming to all of Wales.

After Aberdare, Evan Roberts went to Pontycymmer to speak in a Congregational chapel; the results were the same: *fervent zeal in all the meetings, and outright conversion of notorious sinners.* In one place, because of weariness he failed to show up but this did not diminish local enthusiasm. In Porth, every chapel was filled. The movement swept the Rhondda Valley like a tidal wave. The Revivalist proceeded to Caerphilly, but the work went on in the Valley, as in Gorseinon, long after the Revivalist left. An American visitor told a packed church in Tylortown: 'Some people think that this revival is the fizz of a bottle of pop. No, no! It is the fizz of a fuse, and dynamite is at the end of it!'

Roberts declined to campaign in the Welsh metropolis, but extraordinary scenes were witnessed there in Cardiff. In the Baptist Tabernacle, a New Year's Eve service ran on until 1 a.m. on Sunday morning, thirty-three converts bringing professions of faith to 260, shortly becoming 700.

Evan Roberts returned to his home in Loughor to spend Christmas with his family. He declined to be interviewed. On Christmas evening, he attended regular Sunday service in Moriah Chapel and 'a large number' professed conversion. After Christmas, Evan Roberts continued his ministry in the Swansea Valley, drawing crowds of 2500 to 3000 again and again, filling a big chapel in Morriston.

It is interesting that William James published in 1902 a series of lectures on the subject of the varieties of religious experience. His thesis – that experience of 'conversion' is produced by sub-conscious emotional excitement, altogether subjectively without any objective Divine element- became a popular scholarly view, discrediting evangelism.

In the second week of December 1904, the local press reported that the religious revival was spreading rapidly throughout North Wales, beginning in town after town with interdenominational prayer meetings, generally followed by preaching services, developing into open meetings; the results were the same, **the quickening of church members, the conversion of outsiders, and the virtual elimination of drunkenness and swearing**.

In North Wales, the Rev. Hugh Hughes, a local Methodist, preached at Bethesda for the Free Churches. An hour's 'open' prayer meeting preceded each service which was succeeded by a young people's prayer meeting sometimes lasting for three hours. By December, one of the local ministers was rejoicing that the police were unemployed, the streets being so quiet, and he observed that the district council was quite willing to support them even if they were doing nothing. All feuds inherited from a bitter strike were settled. In the historic college town of Bangor, North Wales, there were many occasions when the crowded congregation at large would be praying audibly, individually and simultaneously.

In Pembroke, 'little England beyond Wales,' the movement was felt strongly before the end of 1904. One minister told of admitting to the membership of his church one Sunday 44 people of all ages, from an old man of 80 to a child of 10.

The Baptist preacher, R.B. Jones, conducted missions in Anglesey in January 1905 with great response. Most encouraging numbers of people were flocking into the churches. A political rally arranged at Pwllheli for the Member of Parliament (later Prime Minister) David Lloyd-George was itself transformed into a revival meeting in which a clergyman opened in devotions, the audience sang a hymn with the greatest enthusiasm, and a blind man led in prayer, the two political speakers scarcely being noticed.

Visitors flocked to Wales from all the English-speaking countries and the Continent to observe the Revival. More often they visited the scenes of Revival in South Wales. Dr. F.B. Meyer, who visited the localities of the Revival, commented that 'No money was spent on advertising the Revival meetings,' and that there was no need of posters on hoardings. The late Lord Pontypridd likewise commented that the Welsh Revival advertised and financed itself. 'There are no bills, no hired halls, no salaries.'

Throughout Wales, it was to keep an appointment with the Lord that people came to the meetings. More often than not, they crowded the chapels to overflowing, not knowing whether the Revivalist would be there or not. On occasion, Evan Roberts would arrive at the door of a church, make his way forward, sit on the front seat and say nothing for three hours. Then he would stand up, offer an exhortation or prayer, thus speaking for ten or fifteen minutes only, then sit down.

Dr. F.B. Meyer observed: 'He will not go in front of the Divine Spirit, but is willing to stand aside and remain in the background unless he is perfectly sure that the Spirit of God is moving him. It is a profound lesson.' The people in the congregation continued the extraordinary work – in praying, testifying, praising, singing and exhorting, with no tiring of spirit.

G. Campbell Morgan affirmed paradoxically that everywhere 'in what seemed supreme confusion, one was conscious of splendid order.' An eye-witness, the Rev. A.F. Williamson, read a paper before a company of Philadelphians, commenting upon the simplicity of organization and lack of anything superfluous or mechanical in the conduct of the meetings in Wales, the only leader recognized being the Holy Spirit, even the most sceptical being compelled to believe it as genuine. There was a spontaneity of participation in the services, singing was a special feature in every meeting, the whole congregation singing. There was a oneness of spirit, as at Pentecost. *Prominence was given to prayer, and a passionate love of the Bible was demonstrated.*

The outstanding feature of the Welsh Revival was utter spontaneity. The understandable fear of the ministers that the meetings would get out of control was met by the trust that the Spirit moving the people would rebuke deviation. D.E. Richards, of the Baptist Union of Wales, wrote:

> The Moderator of the Union, the professors of our colleges, the pastors of our churches and our students are surcharged with Divine fire; the Holy Spirit seems to have possessed our pulpit completely; the Church has wakened and has put on the beautiful garments of her glory. The people repent and the thousands are baptized in the name of Jesus for forgiveness of sins and the gift of the Holy Spirit.

In 1905, the Welsh Revival reached its greatest power and extent in the Principality. All classes, all ages, and every denomination shared in the general awakening. Totals of converts added to the churches were published in local newspapers, 70,000 in two months, 85,000 in five, and more than a hundred thousand in half a year. This figure, of course, did not include the total of nominal church members in both Anglican and Free Churches who were converted to a vital Christianity.

Out of the Revival came a social awakening in Wales, in Cardiff taking the form of a purity crusade directed by the Cardiff Citizens' Union aimed at suppressing drunkenness, immorality and gambling, successful in amending criminal law and forcing the closing of brothels, shutting up sixty taverns and preventing forty more from opening. The great wave of sobriety which swept over the country caused severe financial losses to men in the liquor trade, and closed many of the taverns.

Swansea County Police Court announced to the public that there had not been a single charge for drunkenness over the 1905 New Year holiday weekend, an all-time record in fact. In the Welsh metropolis, the Cardiff police reported a 60% decrease in drunkenness and 40% fewer people in jail at the New Year also.

Cases of drunkenness in Wales exceeded twenty thousand a year before the Revival, but had dropped 33% in the three years following the movement. Archdeacon Wilberforce, in Westminster Abbey, declared that the Revival already had accomplished more in Wales in *two months* than had all the temperance laws in *two years*.

Many were the evidences of the Spirit of God working in Wales. Long standing debts were paid, and stolen goods returned, while striking cases of restitution were made. At Maesteg, a tradesman received a live pig in payment for a debt which had been outstanding since 1898. Other notable instances of open restitution were reported.

Stocks of Welsh and English Bibles were sold out. Prayer meetings were held in coal mines, in trains and trams and places of business. The work managers bore testimony to the change in conduct of their employees. The magistrates in several places were presented with white gloves, signifying that there were utterly no cases to try.

The sovereignty of the Holy Spirit in all His operations, the possibility of Spirit-filled assembly, confidence in the inspired Word of God, the power of earnest, united prayer, and the power of sacred song – these were the marks of the Revival.

Another observer summarized them: '1) Honour to the Holy Spirit as the presiding presence. 2) The plain preaching of Christ and of sound gospel doctrine. 3) The prominence given to prayer, individual and united. 4) The dependence upon God, rather than upon men. 5) The absence of stereotyped programme and set method. 6) The readiness for blessing by a willingness to remove obstacles. 7) The direct dealing with the unconverted.'

Confession of sin was particular and specific, according to Vyrnwy Morgan, while Campbell Morgan reported:

> The movement is characterized by the most remarkable confessions of sin, confessions that must be costly. I heard some of them who have been members of the church and officers of the church, confessing hidden sin in their hearts, impurity committed and condoned, and seeking prayer for its putting away.

Evan Roberts was 'clairvoyant and clairaudient,' said some experts, while others insisted that he possessed the *charismatic gift of discernment*. There occurred in his Liverpool meetings an uncanny demonstration of his gift of discernment, as reported by the national journalist and social reformer, W.T. Stead:

The voluntary workers had met to discuss their house-to-house visitation aimed at enlisting attendance at the meetings. Each was reporting upon his assignment to a particular street. One young man modestly told of calling at every house on a certain street, when the Welsh prophet fixed his piercing gaze upon him and contradicted him. The young man stammered in confusion and admitted that he had not performed all that he had claimed. He trembled like a leaf and burst into tears when Evan Roberts told him that his deceitful ways had followed his forging of a signature on an earlier occasion.

Evan Roberts also rebuked some ministers on the Sun Hall platform for secret opposition to the work. In the local press, two sponsoring ministers humbly confessed that his discernment of their spirit was correct: they apologized.

No one was more shy of publicity than the Revivalist; he dreaded newspaper reporters, and feared the adulation of the masses. When he felt that people were coming to see and hear him only, *he withdrew himself.* He pleaded very seriously that they would look away [from him, and] to Christ lest the Spirit withdraw Himself from the whole movement. Within weeks, Evan Roberts had become the world's most publicized man of God, yet he repeatedly refused to give interviews to newspaper men whether British, European or from far overseas. He firmly refused to be photographed except by his family.

The Welsh people, who understood him better, were not surprised when the Revivalist sat among the people, praying silently, and then left without saying a single word. Strangers from the other parts of Britain and overseas were astounded to witness exciting ministry in crowded meetings where the people sang and prayed and testified without the prophet of God being there, or if there, without taking part.

Evan Roberts was sometimes accompanied by the young women from New Quay or Gorseinon who sang spiritual solos or duets in the meetings, or who exhorted penitents of their own sex. There was no hint of scandal in this association. Womenfolk commonly respond warmly to spiritual leaders and this was the case with Evan Roberts, as it was with his Master centuries before.

Sixty years after the Revival, it was said by historians of Evan Roberts, 'without him, the revival faded away.' This is a common fallacy. The extreme excitement of the Revival had already passed when Evan Roberts retired from public ministry, but the movement kept the churches of Wales filled for many years to come, seats being placed in the aisles in Mount Pleasant Baptist Church in Swansea for twenty years or so, for example. Meanwhile, the Awakening swept the rest of Britain, Scandinavia, parts of Europe, North America, the mission fields of India and the Orient, Africa and Latin America. It was not dependent on Evan Roberts, but initiated and sustained by the Spirit to Whom he submitted his will.

Evan Roberts died in a Cardiff hospital on 29th January 1951, aged 72, mentally clear and spiritually bright to the end. The vision of Evan Roberts that a hundred thousand people would be won to the churches of Wales was fully realized in a matter of months. At the time, the Revival *united the denominations as one body,* filled the chapels nightly, renewed family ties, changed life in mines and factories, often crowded streets with huge processions, abated the social vices and diminished crime. Gomer Roberts asked:

> Who can give an account of the lasting blessings of the 1904-5 Revival? Is it possible to tabulate a sum total of family bliss, peace of conscience, brotherly love, and holy conversation? What of the debts that were paid and the enemies reconciled to one another? What of the drunkards who became sober and the prodigals who were restored? Is there a balance that can weigh the burden of sins that was thrown at the foot of the Cross?

~§~

As you read about the miraculous 1905 American Awakening, I want to draw your attention to three items in particular: the unity between the various denominations (Psalm 119:63), the many references to the Welsh revival, and how social reform followed spiritual revival.

THE 1905 AMERICAN AWAKENING

Thousands of Welsh folk had settled in the central and western valleys of Pennsylvania,[1] and a majority of them had become members of Welsh-speaking or bilingual churches. An awakening in Wilkes-Barre began suddenly in December 1904, the Rev. J.D. Roberts having been moved by news received directly from Wales by Welsh Pennsylvanians.[2] In a month, he instructed 123 converts, about half of them men. Large congregations gathered in the Scranton district, and a spirit of revival was manifest in all the churches. Town after town, city after city, the tide of interest flooded the churches, reviving members and converting outsiders.[3] An unusual awakening was reported from New Castle, western Pennsylvania, 'the city moved to its center.'[4] In Pittsburgh, city and satellites, the churches experienced a reviving.

The leading Baptist periodical in Pennsylvania devoted a whole issue during the first week of March 1905 to reports of awakening in

Pennsylvania and throughout the country.[5] It was loaded with items of interest. President Edgar Young Mullins, of Southern Baptist Theological Seminary,[6] visited the state in February of 1905, and found revival interest everywhere.

By early spring, the Methodists alone in Philadelphia were claiming ten thousand converts, their total membership increasing by 567 to 76,236, with 6,101 on probation [new converts], while their Sunday Schools had increased their number of pupils by 1813 to reach a total of 95,519.[7] One commented that 'newspapers and some church leaders are talking about a Coming Revival...some do not know such a thing when it is at hand.'[8]

Of the Philadelphia Awakening, they added that it was the greatest ingathering since 1880, a quarter of a century ago. And they claimed that a greater number of the converts had been received into church membership than during the Moody and Sankey meetings of the previous century.

On the Jersey coast, there was such a revival in Atlantic City that (it was claimed) not more than fifty unconverted people remained in a population of 60,000.[9] Town after town in New Jersey experienced a reviving of church life. And in November 1905, a great awakening was reported in Newark, New Jersey, in which 'Pentecost was literally repeated...during the height of the revival, with its strange spectacle of spacious churches crowded to overflowing and great processions passing through the street.'[10]

In 1904, in Schenectady, New York, a local Ministerial Association heard reports of the great revival in Wales and united all evangelical denominations in meetings for prayer and in evangelistic rallies.[11] Before long, the interest was so extraordinary that the Rev. George Lunn of the Reformed Church emerged as the main evangelist. **Baptist, Congregational, Dutch Reformed, Lutheran, Methodist and Presbyterian churches cooperated in the movement**. Emmanuel Baptist Church was packed afternoons with more than 600 women and State Street Methodist Church nightly with more than 1200 people. Between 800 and 1100 people waited for aftermeetings. By Sunday 22nd January, all the evangelical churches in town had been moved, with packed congregations in each, and the movement continued for months on end.

The secular press of Schenectady offered a couple of columns daily to keep the public informed of progress – 'The Power of Prayer,' 'Great Moral Uplift,' 'The Fires of Pentecost,' *'Yesterday's Conversions,'* and like headlines. In Schenectady, the women meeting in the overcrowded afternoon meetings developed an evangelistic zeal of their own, formed teams of witness and visited the local saloons where they were 'treated with every courtesy and respect' by the saloon patrons, though correspondence in the press from saloon-keepers deplored the idea of treating tavern-owners any differently than any other businessmen.[12]

The Awakening made such an impact upon the churches of Troy, in upper New York State, that it was said that no such unanimous and spontaneous movement had been known in the city for a generation.[13] The movement began with the January Week of Prayer, held in the Second Presbyterian Church, but developed into a revival of church members of six Baptist, ten Methodist, seven Presbyterian, one Christian, one Congregational and one Episcopal churches. Awakenings occurred also in Utica, Syracuse, and other Mohawk cities, and throughout New York State.

When the Awakening reached Calvary Methodist Episcopal Church in New York City, it produced 'a sight never duplicated.' Before two thousand two hundred packing the church, 364 were received into membership on 2nd February 1905, of whom 286 were on probation, an indication of more recent conversion. Of the total, 217 were adults, 134 were men, and 60 were heads of families. Of the approximate membership of 2000, a thousand partook in Holy Communion.[14]

When the 'cleansing wave' reached the Baptist Temple in Brooklyn in January 1905, five hundred people waited behind, to receive prayerful counsel from the pastor, Dr. Cortland Myers.[15] Other Long Island churches were stirred.

In New York's smaller towns, pastors engaged in ardent evangelism, a typical instance being Gloversville, Fulton County, where Chester Ralston embarked on January 15 on special meetings, continuing for four weeks. In Gloversville, the converts included 'the infidel, the drinker, the moralist, white and black, American, Italian, Swede, father, mother, young men and women' – a typical cross-section.[16]

The Baptist in New England, in an editorial entitled, 'The Present Revival,' observed in May 1905:[17]

> As the news continues to come from the churches, the conviction is confirmed that additions to the churches in New England during the month of April were larger than during any one month for many years.

Despite the lack of any large evangelistic campaign, the churches were obviously in the midst of a revival of greater power and extent than New England had known since 1858, they said. The movement was characterized by an intense sensation of the presence of God in the congregations, *as in the Welsh Revival.* Despite the lack of organization, either in meetings or follow-up, the movement was deemed most effective compared with organized evangelistic campaigns. Churches large and small, here and there, were affected.

Daniel Shepardson, Ph.D., the 'wheel-chair evangelist,' conducted meetings in Danbury, Connecticut, which resulted in an awakening of the townsfolk.[18] His host-pastor expected to baptize candidates every Sunday for two months to add the converts to the active membership of his congregation. Town after town in Connecticut experienced the movement of the people towards the churches. It was reported that the revival at East Lyme, Connecticut (for example) continued with unabated force, 'men who have not been inside a church for years...coming out and confessing Jesus.'[19]

By March of 1905, the Awakening was stirring churches in Providence,[20] and local revivals were felt in Rhode Island.

On a single Sunday, Dr. A.C. Dixon and his diaconate in Ruggles Street Baptist Church in Boston enrolled a hundred and fifty people professing conversion in the Boston Revival. In 1905, a British pastor-evangelist, W.J. Dawson, landed in Boston to engage in united evangelistic work in New England, where ministers declared that 'the present seemed like other great epochs when mighty revivals occurred.'

A summer revival began in Forest City, Maine, in 1905. The decline of the population there had brought about decline of the churches, which were closed for eight months of the year. Drunkenness was common and entire indifference to religion prevailed. The revival that resulted was thorough, for drunkards were transformed, and the influence of the awakening spread for miles around, over state borders.[21]

The 'Great Revival' reported from Rutland, in Vermont, began with a Y.M.C.A. director, F.B. Tibbitts. Union prayer meetings were faithfully supported by the Congregational, Baptist and Methodist pastors and people.[22] So great was the response that an urgent call for help was sent to the able Boston Baptist, the Rev. A.C. Dixon, who came post haste and preached in a vastly overcrowded auditorium. Within a week, 450 inquirers had been given instruction [regarding salvation].

To Northfield Conference, founded by Moody, G. Campbell Morgan brought news of the Welsh Revival, personally observed. Len Broughton led some unusual meetings, overtaken by a wave of confession.[23] Correspondents averred that 'the scenes witnessed during the closing week almost defy description.' In summer conference after conference (including Winona Lake), a great catharsis of souls took place.

Late in 1904, the Atlanta newspapers reported that nearly a thousand businessmen had united in intercession for an outpouring of the Holy Spirit.[24] On 2nd November, with a unanimity unprecedented, stores, factories and offices closed in the middle of the day for prayer. The Supreme Court of Georgia adjourned; even saloons and places of amusement closed their doors to enable patrons to attend the united prayer meetings, turning the weekday into a veritable Sabbath.

Typical of the South, an awakening began in Louisville, Kentucky, with simultaneous meetings in which more than a thousand men confessed their faith in Christ.[25] Of 1500 inquirers, two-thirds joined the church immediately.[26] The cause of Revival was greatly helped in the Southern Baptist Convention by the warm interest of its leading scholar in Louisville, Dr. E.Y. Mullins, who supplied the Baptist periodicals with a scholarly 'Study of Revivals.'[27]

As the movement continued, the press reported that the 'most remarkable revival ever known in the city is now interesting Louisville.'[28] **Conversions numbering 4000 have been recorded**...fifty-eight of the leading business firms of the city are closed at the noon hour for prayer meetings. In March 1905, Henry Clay Morrison said of the Louisville Awakening:[29]

> The whole city is breathing a spiritual atmosphere. Everywhere in shop and store, in the mill and on the street, salvation is the one topic of conversation.

It was his opinion that a thousand had been added to the churches of the city, seven thousand instructed and twelve thousand interested enough to attend services further.

Before and after the Louisville 1905 Campaign, a spirit of revival gripped the Presbyterians in the state of Kentucky, the leading journal of the denomination carrying articles on 'the Spirit of Revival in the Synod of Kentucky,' 'the Presbyteries and the Revival,' and the like, as well as endless items concerning local awakenings.[30]

During the awakening at Danville, Kentucky, all houses of business were voluntarily closed on 1st February 1905, as employers and employees attended services in a body. It was reported that Danville's day of blessing had come.[31]

The city of Paducah, Kentucky, witnessed an awakening described by Southern Baptists as a 'great Pentecostal revival within our bounds.' The movement swept the city from November 1905 until March 1906.[32] One church alone, First Baptist, received into membership more than a thousand new members. Its pastor, Dr. J.J. Cheek, was laid to rest – 'a glorious ending to a devoted ministry.'

The religious press of Virginia featured articles early on about the Welsh Revival.[33] In February, a Norfolk pastor preached on 'the Coming of a Great Revival.' Next month, the Norfolk churches *united in a series of intercessory and evangelistic services,* and blessing overflowed the local congregations. In Richmond, the Rev. G.W. McDaniel and his congregation experienced a great reviving, and made a gift of $3000 for the work of the Southern Baptist Foreign Mission Board. In 1905, **Baptists, Episcopalians, Methodists and Presbyterians cooperated in the movement** in Norfolk.[34] Epworth Methodist Church added four hundred to its rolls in the awakening.

The pattern of the revival in many of the churches of the Southern Baptist Convention was revealed by a report of a pastor in Tennessee:[35]

> Last month we held revival services. I failed to get any one to assist me, so I had to do the preaching myself. We had a great meeting. There were sixty conversions and the church was greatly built up...in a great outpouring of the Spirit and a great ingathering of souls.

Early in 1905, the state organ of South Carolina Baptists supplied its readers with articles of Evan Roberts and the Welsh Revival,[36] urging them to pray for a revival of Bible study, of believing prayer, and of grace in which multitudes of sinners would be converted. Before long, local movements were being reported from both the Carolinas and Georgia.

In Florida, revival meetings multiplied, 'part of the mighty movement the world over.' Prominent in the Florida awakening was an evangelist, Mordecai F. Ham, afterwards to win fame as the missioner who moved a teenager in Charlotte, Billy Graham, to profess his faith in Christ. Observers in Florida reported that the revival wave was 'still rolling' over the Christian communities of the peninsular state.[37]

The Awakening affected the states of the Deep South, and reports of revival were received from churches in Alabama, Mississippi and Louisiana. The Baptists and the Methodists of both races were affected, as elsewhere in the South. In the northeast corner of Texas, a spiritual movement swept the churches of Paris. The pastors of the churches had been deeply concerned over the fact that local theatres were thronged while the churches were not. The Baptists, Congregationalists, Methodists and Presbyterians and others engaged in *united prayer meetings*, leading to evangelism of a most successful and spontaneous kind.[38]

The awakening reached the city of Houston in Texas in the spring, affecting chiefly the Baptist and the Methodists. 'A tidal wave of spirituality has rolled through the city,' it was said, resulting in not only the crowding of churches but in the closing of gambling dens and the ordering out of the gambling gentry.[39]

When the awakening reached Dallas,[40] Dr. George Truett of the First Baptist Church enlisted the help of Dr. F.C. McConnell as evangelist, and reaped the harvest he had sown. The churches of Waco were moved by the Revival of 1905, and the awakening stirred Baylor University also. Other towns in Texas were stirred.[41]

The Kansas City (1905) meetings of the Southern Baptist Convention noted the vast improvement of conditions in the churches as a result of the Awakening.[42]

> It is manifest to all that there has come about an awakened interest in the subject of evangelistic work. There is an atmosphere

of evangelism...Scarcely a week passes but may be found in some of the public prints soulstirring articles from thoughtful pastors and others on evangelistic methods and preaching.

The movement soon spread into Ohio.[43] In Dayton it stirred fifty churches, while the congregations of Cleveland rejoiced in seasons of blessing, the spiritual outlook 'never so bright.' In Columbus, Ohio, a spirit of extraordinary prayer fell on a congregation (simultaneous prayer) for two hours.[44]

The Michigan Baptists devoted the front page of their journal to Evan Roberts, the Welsh Revival, and mobilizing prayer for an awakening in Michigan. Already, they had reported that the town of Adrian had experienced an awakening unheard of for years. Soon it was noted that copious showers had fallen in Bay City, where never before had the churches been so greatly blessed in an evangelistic enterprise. Their front page was given to the subject, 'Lessons from the Welsh Revival,' by G. Campbell Morgan; and at the mid-year, headlines proclaimed that the revival spirit was widespread.[45]

The Methodists in Michigan reported as early as January 1905 that the Saginaw district was in the midst of 'a most gracious religious awakening,' unlike anything seen in those parts for many a year,[46] the unction of the Spirit outpoured. They were soon announcing 'many gracious revivals' and a thousand conversions in the Albany district, eleven hundred in Lansing, five hundred in Big Rapids, and then results too numerous to catalogue[47] – across Michigan,[48] district after district – in Owosso, the 'whole town was awakened'; in Marquette, an outpouring of the Spirit on many charges. In Grand Rapids, one church received 118 on probation, its pastor reporting that 'the revival wave has certainly struck this city.'

Trimountain[49] reported 'the greatest revival in its history'; in Lansing, the Methodist claimed 700 conversions and 740 actual accessions – insisting that this was 'no guesswork'; in Ypsilanti, the churches reported a 'red-letter' day in March, and the movement continued with unabated interest. Second Street Methodist Episcopal Church in Grand Rapids was enjoying the 'greatest revival in its history.'[50]

In the spring,[51] the churches were still responding to the 'thrill of a vigorous, thoroughgoing revival triumph' which was continuing in Grand

Rapids, while thousands had been converted in the Marquette district. County districts were enjoying their uplift also, a Methodist church in Pentwater reaping sixty conversions during the visit of a Salvation Army 'revival brigade' under the direction of Adjutant George Bennard – who wrote the hymn, 'The Old Rugged Cross.'

The Methodists announced that awakenings were spreading over their Northwestern jurisdiction, in Indiana, Illinois, Iowa, Minnesota and the Dakotas.[52] In one week in March, their Northwestern territory reported 632 converts, pacing Central's 947, Western's 1511 and Pittsburgh's 1529.

Once news of the Welsh Revival had reached Indiana, the ministers gathered for conference in Indianapolis and other Indiana towns, and prayer meetings for the reviving of the churches were begun in Indianapolis in all congregations. In the towns throughout the state, there was unabated interest, and in congregation after congregation the meetings multiplied, **reviving the saints and converting the sinners**, 'a great day for the Baptists,' it was said, though the Methodists and other evangelistic folk shared fully in the ingathering.[53]

Noonday prayer meetings were held in Chicago for a great awakening in the mid-western metropolis and hinterland.[54] A band of praying ministers of Chicago, hearing the reports of the Welsh Revival, decided to operate through the churches rather than engage in a mass evangelistic campaign:[55]

> The plan in Chicago has been to urge pastors to hold their own meetings in their own churches, to help each other as the needs suggest.

A central prayer meeting was held daily for ministers and lay workers, not a mass meeting; and in it they reported that the revival spirit had reached every denominational organization in the city, hundreds being added to the local churches in city and suburbs.

The C.E. Societies which were associated with so many of the denominations told of a great Awakening in Chicago, in which the churches of the various denominations were fully cooperating, in prayer and in evangelism. The interests of one church had become the interests of all the churches.[56]

> A determined effort has been made to reach the unsaved, and this is succeeding. Hundreds have already been baptized in the different churches. It has become almost commonplace in our ministerial gatherings for a pastor to rise and say: 'My church has never known such a blessing of salvation as we are now having.'

The movement in Dixon, Illinois, was described as a 'cyclonic revival,' the **Baptist, Christian, Congregationalist, Evangelical, Lutheran, Methodist and Presbyterian churches cooperating**, the evangelist being the renowned baseball star, William A. Sunday. His ministry was sensational. An outcome was the destruction by the proprietor of one gambling joint of his gambling wheels and tables.[57]

Reports from Iowa[58] showed that the Revival of 1905 and its evangelistic outreach were making great progress through many gracious ingatherings and many evangelistic crusades. In the city of Burlington,[59] every store and factory closed its operation between 10 and 11 a.m. to permit its employees to attend services for the revival of religion. Mason City in its turn shared in a great awakening under Billy Sunday.[60] In other Iowa cities and towns, there was spontaneous revival in the churches and awakenings among the masses.

The Awakening of 1905 spread from St. Louis throughout Missouri. A great revival was reported in Warrensburg. Sixty miles from St. Louis, strange phenomena occurred:[61]

> Everything reported as 'peculiar' in the Wales revival is found in the Lead Belt. Great throngs attend the services, and conversions take place at almost every meeting. I never heard such amazing prayer or such expression of conviction of sin.

Francis E. Clark's headquarters in Boston reported that 'Greater Kansas City has been passing through a season of spiritual awakening, and the Revival of 1905 will go down in history as a new spiritual epoch.'[62] Kansas like Missouri was stirred. Intercessory meetings began in Nebraska on New Year 1905, and by February the churches were reaping the results.[63] A church in Fairbury reported a great awakening in the town and more than 250 added to its congregation.

In Redwood Falls, Minnesota, the awakening brought out six hundred men, women and children to interdenominational meetings during temperatures of 22 degrees below zero.[64] A great wave of revival touched many churches of the Minneapolis area. W.B. Riley told of a movement in Spring Valley[65] where a sixth of the population professed conversion. The awakenings were felt in the Dakotas and Montana, the Baptists, Methodists, Presbyterians and others uniting in the movement, which in Anaconda won 165 converts.[66]

The Denver campaign began on 4th January 1905, with J. Wilbur Chapman, W.E. Biederwolf, Henry Ostrom, and seven other evangelists sharing the ministry in city and in suburbs. Friday 20th January was declared a Day of Prayer. At 10 a.m., the cooperating churches were filled; at 11:30, almost all the stores were closed, at the Mayor's request, and four theatres were crowded for prayer at noon, 12,000 attending the services of intercession in all seriousness. A vote of the Colorado Legislature postponed business in order to attend the prayer meetings. Every school was closed, as a whole city engaged in intercession and in evangelism. And it was said months later that Denver 'has had a good winter. The influence of the great revival is still felt.' Most of the churches extended the work by local evangelism.[67]

In the simultaneous campaign in Los Angeles, a hundred churches cooperated.[68] The professional evangelism of the visiting team was undergirded by the spirit of revival in the California congregations and the awakening of the masses. Aggregate attendances were in excess of 180,000, and 4264 inquirers were registered, 787 of whom being children. One night, despite torrents of rain, four thousand marching people wended their way singing to the Grand Opera House, attracting a host of bleary-eyed brawlers, besotted drunkards and blatant scoffers to the midnight meeting, with not a few women of 'easy virtue' engaged in midnight street-walking.

The churches of Los Angeles received an encouraging number of additions to their congregational roll. Burdette, pastor of Temple Baptist Church, gave the right hand of fellowship to forty folk one Sunday morning; and McIntyre, pastor of First Methodist Church, the same day received fifty to full membership and fifty on probation. California's smaller towns, such as Redlands and Pomona, reaped a full harvest of converts. The Methodists in Southern California agreed that the churches there had enjoyed a remarkable spiritual awakening, the summer conference learning of many more conversions than known for several years past.[69]

In a report entitled 'Portland's Pentecost,'[70] describing religious enthusiasm in the Oregon metropolis, it was said:

> ...for three hours a day, business was practically suspended, and from the crowds in the great department stores to the humblest clerk, from bank presidents to bootblacks, all abandoned money making for soul saving.

Upwards of 200 major stores signed an agreement to close between the hours of 11 and 2 to permit their customers and employees to attend prayer meetings. In connection with the simultaneous campaigns directed by J. Wilbur Chapman, there was a similar movement in Seattle. Towns throughout the Pacific Northwest experienced the general awakening.[71]

Churches in Canada were affected from coast to coast. The manifestations of the Awakening in Canada were the same as in the United States: prayer for revival, a concern for the outsider, ardent evangelism, remarkable response.

IMPACT ON CHURCH AND STATE

Christian editors were impressed by the immediacy of the social impact of the Awakening of 1905, saying over and over the same thing:[1]

> We find evidence of a revival of righteousness in the popular and pulpit protest against the 'sharp practice' and 'double-dealing' of insurance managers; the indignation against rate swindling, oppressive corporations, dishonest officials of banks and trust companies; the public wrath against political scoundrels and the successful overthrow of many such; and [*according to Exodus 18:21, because character matters!*] the elevation to power of fearless, honest, competent men in many states and cities.

It was recognized by those who experienced revival that the movement had not begun as a crusade for righteousness, as such:[2]

> Fancy someone in Wales saying: 'We must have an ethical revival first. We must enter upon a crusade against profanity, obscenity, prize fighting. We must close up the saloons, make kindling wood of the gambling tables, and raid the brothels before we can have a

> revival.' *All these infamies vanish before the Spirit's baptism like bats and owls before the light of day.*

The awakening in Schenectady, according to secular New York journalists, meant 'stronger and better citizens, brighter and happier homes, a cleaner city life, and the strengthening of all the churches and other agencies for good.' No one offered any contradiction.[3]

An editorial in one of the regional journals of Methodism spoke of the general situation in all the denominations:[4]

> Even the secular papers are noticing it. They are speaking of 'the vivid, plain and vigorous statements that come weekly from a thousand pulpits,' and of 'the attitude of all the people toward that style of sharp dealing, *long regarded with a kind of pride as essentially characteristic of the American people*, an attitude now reflected by the shock that was felt at the disclosures of duplicity in the management of great insurance companies, and by the plain expression of indignation against bossism and political corruption.' 'These expressions indicate moral progress and a revival of simple faith.' Preachers are more courageous in their utterances, as if backed by more than mortal energy. It is a relief and satisfaction to the multitudes when the lightnings of public wrath seem to be playing against the workers of iniquity. We believe that the aggregate result will be infinitely beneficial to the cause of God. *Men are coming to see that the safety of society and the stability of our free institutions depend upon civic righteousness and social honor*, and that wealth obtained dishonestly or by oppressive methods is a **crime** and a **curse**. Let the good work go on...

The Presbyterians were quick to acknowledge that a moral and ethical awakening was producing political effect in the wake of the Revival of 1905. Their leader-writers rejoiced that the movement was awakening the moral sense of cities, where for too long a combination of vested interests in the whiskey, gambling and prostitution rackets had thwarted the will of the masses of decent people, by outrage at the ballot-boxes. Corrupt regimes were toppling here and there.[5]

In Cincinnati, **civic reform followed spiritual revival** [*Matthew 5:13*], a new impulse being given by the citizens of the Ohio metropolis, who seemed 'to have profited by the wave of reform that swept over the country,' according to the annual Baptist Congress, representing opinion north and south.[6] The Methodists, in their leading journal, reviewed 1905 as 'a Great Twelvemonth.'[7]

> Throughout the Republic, there are signs of the revival of the public conscience which, in many states and cities, has broken party lines, rejected machine-made candidates and elected Governors, Senators, Assemblymen, Mayors and County Attorneys of recognized honesty and independence ... first fruits of a new zeal for the living Christ as the Lord of all human activity ... social, industrial, commercial and political.

"There have been instances in the history of the church when the telling and retelling of the wonderful works of God have been used to rekindle the expectations of the faithful intercessors, and prepare the way for another awakening." ~ Dr. J. Edwin Orr

~§~

"Moreover you shall select [**elect**] from all the people able men, such as fear God, men of truth, hating covetousness; and place such over them to be rulers of thousands, rulers of hundreds, rulers of fifties, and rulers of tens." ~ *Exodus 18:21 NKJV*

"Sing unto God, sing praises to his name: extol him that rideth upon the heavens by his name **JAH**, and rejoice before him."
~ *Psalm 68:4 KJV*

"I am a **companion** of all them that fear thee, and of them that keep thy precepts." ~ *Psalm 119:63 KJV*

Our third witness is Georgia Anne Geyer. She was an American journalist who spoke Russian, German, Spanish and Portuguese. Geyer received more than 20 honorary degrees. She wrote for the Universal Press Syndicate, and her columns appeared in over 110 newspapers in North and South America.

~§~

I have come to the conclusion that it is impossible to have a moral community or nation without faith in God, because without it everything rapidly comes down to "me" and "me" alone is meaningless. Today, Americans have stopped acting in terms of their own moral, ethical and religious beliefs and principles. They've stopped acting on what they know is right – and the "me" has become the measure of everything.

However, moral societies are the only ones that work. If anyone thinks there is not a direct and invaluable relationship between personal integrity in a society and that society's prosperity, that person has simply not studied history. And this should not surprise us.

Great moral societies, built upon faith in God, honor, trust and the law blossom because they are harmonious; because people love or at least respect their fellowman; because, finally, they have a common belief in something beyond themselves. It simplifies life immensely; you do not waste and spend your days fighting for turf, for privilege, for money and power over your fellowman.

Alexis de Tocqueville said it best when he realized at the very beginning of our national life, "America is great because she is good. If America ever ceases to be good, America will cease to be great."

When I was in the military stationed overseas, I was exposed to a Christian newspaper called *The Sword of the Lord*. The founding editor of the publication was Evangelist Dr. John R. Rice. His insightful guidebook, *The Power of Pentecost*, is a classic study on the fullness of the Holy Spirit of God.

The Lost Secret - Power

Christianity is a Bible religion. It reached its fullest revelation and development in the New Testament. Christianity is not true Christianity, not complete Christianity, if it does not reproduce the salvation, the joy, the power and victory over sin, the progress and making of converts of New Testament times.

No Bible-believing Christian would think of denying what I am saying. It seems too trite to need repeating here. But surely we need to come back and face this solemn issue: *we should reproduce Bible results that New Testament Christianity produced.*

Any religion that is not based upon the New Testament is not Christianity. Any religion that does not hold up Christ, the same Saviour, does not demand the same new birth on condition of the same penitent faith, is certainly not Christianity. Then we must rightly conclude that after one has trusted in Christ, after one has this same Saviour, this same new birth, *this same indwelling Holy Spirit,* and is become a new creature as were believers in New Testament times, one should certainly manifest the same power New Testament Christians exemplified!

If any doctrine varies from New Testament doctrine, then it is off-color, it is inadequate, and it certainly does not truly represent Christianity. *And likewise, the life that does not have the power New Testament Christians had is off-color and inadequate Christianity*. The ministry of the Gospel which does not have the power of God upon it as so many preachers had in Bible times is not the New Testament type of preaching.

Oh, to demonstrate first-century Christianity again in this twentieth century! Oh, to see again the same vibrant, joyous, supernatural power in the lives of Christians! Oh, to see multitudes converted, to see whole communities, whole empires transformed by the triumphant, conquering revivals that took place under the preaching of Peter and Paul and Barnabas and other New Testament Christians!

It is one kind of modernism, one kind of infidelity, that rejects New Testament doctrine. How sinful, how wicked, how barren, how full of the poison of Hell, is that wicked unbelief that rejects the authority of the Bible, the deity of Christ, salvation by the blood! But we ought to say frankly that it is another kind of infidelity, and perhaps equally deadly, which gives lip service to the doctrines of the New Testament but does not reproduce the life and power and fruitfulness of New Testament Christianity! What does it matter whether people go to Hell because modernists have robbed them of any confidence in the Bible or whether they go to Hell because their loved ones have no power, no supernatural influence, no anointing from God to win souls, to change lives, to draw the unsaved to Christ! The results are the same. **The sins that bring the samc results are not far apart in wickedness!**

Consider what happened at Pentecost.

"These all continued with one accord in prayer and supplication" (Acts 1:14). How strange, how unlike present-day churches!

"The multitude came together, and were confounded" (Acts 2:6). Mighty crowds hearing the Gospel with profound concern! How different from our empty churches and the indifference and disgust which the multitudes feel for the church and its ministry!

"Now when they heard this, they were pricked in their heart, and said unto Peter and to the rest of the apostles, Men and brethren, what shall we do?" (Acts 2:37). Conviction! Broken hearts! Inquiring the way of salvation!

"Then they that gladly received his word were baptized: and the same day there were added unto them about three thousand souls" (Acts 2:41). Three thousand saved and baptized in one day! Today in the most evangelistic denominations in America it takes about twenty persons one year to win one soul. In many denominations there is a net loss in membership every year, and in literally thousands of congregations not a single convert is won to Christ in a year! **Is this Bible Christianity?** Do you marvel that the gainsaying world has no interest in our churches,

in our ministry, in our Christian profession when these are so fruitless compared to Bible Christianity?

Even modernism – that insidious and wicked and shameless Christ-rejecting and Bible-denying sin that only by intentional and deliberate deceit calls itself Christianity at all – that modernism, I say, *which has stolen control of most of the large denominations in America*, has been made possible by a decline in power, by the loss of the fervor and zeal and power of New Testament Christianity. Oh, we need plain Bible teaching. We need apologetics to prove that Christianity and the Bible are true. We ought to be set for a 'defense of the faith,' as the Scripture commands. We ought to expose the utter immorality of those who seek the salaries and honors of the Christian ministry when they are Christ-rejecting infidels in their hearts.

But all the argument in the world cannot keep us from losing the hearts and confidence of the people if we do not have the power of God. The best antidote for modernism is a great revival. Evangelist D. L. Moody stopped more infidelity, answered more pseudo-scientific heresy, turned more university men to Christ than the greatest scientists with a Ph.D. who ever lived. The antidote for modernism is the power of God upon Christians, the power of a great revival, the soul-saving, life-changing, city-sweeping power of a great revival!

Where is the power that went everywhere with Charles G. Finney? In his autobiography Finney tells about going to a place called New York Mills, and there going through the mill while people were busy at their looms, or attending to the mules and other implements of work. He tells how the workers observed him and became agitated, convicted:

> They saw me coming, and were evidently much excited. One of them was trying to mend a broken thread, and I observed that her hands trembled so that she could not mend it. I approached slowly, looking on each side at the machinery, as I passed; but observed that this girl grew more and more agitated, and could not proceed with her work. When I came within eight or ten feet of her, I looked solemnly at her. She observed it, and was quite overcome, and sunk down, and burst into tears. The impression caught almost like powder, and in a few moments nearly all in the room were in tears. This feeling spread through the factory. Mr. W_, the owner of the establishment, was present, and seeing the

state of things, he said to the superintendent, "Stop the mill, and let the people attend to religion; for it is more important that our souls should be saved than this factory run."

The gate was immediately shut down, and the factory stopped; but where should we assemble? The superintendent suggested that the mule room was large; and, the mules being run up, we could assemble there. We did so, and a more powerful meeting I scarcely ever attended. It went on with great power. The building was large, and had many people in it, from the garret to the cellar. The revival went through the mill with astonishing power, and in the course of a few days nearly all in the mill were hopefully converted.

But the same kind of results were shown with the lawyers in the city of Rochester as with the humble mill people. Everywhere there was a convicting, sin-killing, life-transforming, soul-saving power on Charles G. Finney ever after that day when he was wonderfully baptized in the Holy Spirit. Where is such power now?

Let me remind you again of the power of D.L. Moody. Moody was not a learned man. He had never finished what we could call a grammar school education. But, oh, the breath of Heaven that came upon him on Wall Street, New York, one day! Oh, the mighty results as he 'lifted two continents towards God' and won a million souls to Christ! Who can ever sum up the mighty influence of D.L. Moody, his influence on the Bible schools, on the mission fields, on the thousands of pastors, missionaries and evangelists who went out to give their lives in soul-winning service because of him! Where, oh, where in our modern churches is the power which D.L. Moody manifested?

Where is the power that was on Reuben A. Torrey in his great campaigns in America, in Australia, in England and around the world? Where is the power that was on Charlie Alexander and J. Wilbur Chapman? Where is the power that was on Billy Sunday so that great cities were shaken in his campaigns?

We have fallen! We have fallen! The trouble with modern Christianity is that it lacks the breath of Heaven, the power of God, the holy anointing, the supernatural enabling, that are the marks of New Testament Christianity!

Oh, the lost secret! Oh, barren churches! Oh, homes divided, Christians at ease, sinners unconvicted and callous and arrogant! What all of us need above everything else under Heaven is a visitation of the power of God!

May the power of Pentecost come on our churches. May it come upon every earnest minister. May it come upon every Bible-believing Christian who has loved ones unsaved. May God restore to us the lost secret, the secret of the soul-winning power of Pentecost.

~§~

Fifty men of the sons of the prophets went, and stood opposite them [Elijah and Elisha] at a distance; and they both stood by the Jordan. Elijah took his mantle, and rolled it up and struck the waters, and they were divided here and there, so that they both went over on dry ground. When they had gone over, Elijah said to Elisha, "Ask what I shall do for you, before I am taken from you." Elisha said, "**Please let a double portion of your spirit be on me**." He said, "You have asked a hard thing. If you see me when I am taken from you, it will be so for you; but if not, it will not be so."

As they continued on and talked, behold, a chariot of fire and horses of fire separated them, and Elijah went up by a whirlwind into heaven. Elisha saw it, and he cried, "My father, my father, the chariots of Israel and its horsemen!" He saw him no more.

Then he took hold of his own clothes, and tore them in two pieces. He also took up Elijah's mantle that fell from him, and went back, and stood by the bank of the Jordan. He took Elijah's mantle that fell from him, and struck the waters, and said, *"Where is Yahweh, the God of Elijah?"* When he also had struck the waters, they were divided apart, and Elisha went over. When the sons of the prophets who were at Jericho facing him saw him, they said, "**The spirit of Elijah rests on Elisha**." They came to meet him, and bowed themselves to the ground before him. *~ 2 Kings 2:7-15*

"I am anointed with fresh oil." ~ Psalm 92:10

Conclusion:

National Call to Action

The Spiritual Awakening of America is an urgent call for nation-wide revival. I trust you'll agree that a "double portion" of God's Holy Spirit is what we desperately need today. To that end, I want to offer **Five Action Steps** we can take individually, and as a nation, that will lead us underneath His showers of blessing.

1. Rediscover God's Word
2. Receive God's Son
3. Resist God's Enemy
4. Release God's Gifts
5. Reflect God's Love

Action Step #1. Rediscover God's Word

Believers are told the reason we have the written account of God's dealings with the Israelites is so that we can learn from their example: the good, the bad and the ugly example of Jeshurun (Deut. 32:15). We've read about several negative leaders, e.g., King Saul, King Manasseh, and King Zedekiah. We've seen many cases of ugly attitudes and bad behavior. Let's turn now to a positive example.

In this first action step to "Rediscover God's Word," let's go back to the Old Testament again to consider one of the most righteous kings of Israel. His name was Josiah. He was the grandson of Israel's most wicked king, Manasseh. His father was Amon, who also "did that which was evil in Yahweh's sight, as Manasseh his father did. He walked in all the ways that his father walked in, and served the idols that his father served, and worshiped them" (2 Kings 21:20,21). Somehow, in spite of the fact that Josiah had a wicked grandfather and a wicked father, he did not follow in their footsteps.

Josiah was his own man, even as a child. Under the rule of his father and grandfather, wickedness was the order of the day and the book of God was lost, possibly outlawed by Manasseh. We already know "where there is no revelation, the people cast off restraint" (Proverbs 29:18). We also know the Spirit-infused Word of God is kryptonite to the devil. So it stands to reason that when Satan's man was leading the nation, the Bible would be distorted, misused and suppressed. But in due time, God made his move. Let's pick up the account in 2 Kings 22:

~ Lord, give us spiritual insight as we look into Your Word. ~

"Josiah was eight years old when he began to reign, and he reigned thirty-one years in Jerusalem...He did that which was right in Yahweh's eyes, and walked in the way of David his father, and didn't turn away to the right hand or to the left.

"Hilkiah the high priest said to Shaphan the scribe, **'I have found the book of the law in Yahweh's house.'** Hilkiah delivered the book to Shaphan, and he read it. ...Shaphan the scribe told the king, saying, 'Hilkiah the priest has delivered a book to me.' Then Shaphan read it before the king. *When the king had heard the words of the book of the law, he tore his clothes.* The king commanded Hilkiah the priest...'Go inquire of Yahweh for me, and for the people, and for all Judah, concerning the words of this book that is found; for great is Yahweh's wrath that is kindled against us, because our fathers have not listened to the words of this book, to do according to all that which is written concerning us.'

"So Hilkiah the priest...went to Huldah the prophetess...and talked with her. She said to them, "Yahweh the God of Israel says, 'Tell the man who sent you to me, "Yahweh says, 'Behold, I will bring evil on this place, and on its inhabitants, even all the words of the book which the king of Judah has read. Because they have forsaken me, and have burned incense to other gods, that they might provoke me to anger with all the work of their hands, therefore my wrath shall be kindled against this place, and it will not be quenched.' " But to the king of Judah, who sent you to inquire of Yahweh, tell him, "Yahweh the God of Israel says, 'Concerning the words which you have heard, **because your heart was tender, and you humbled yourself before Yahweh**, when you heard what I spoke against this place, and against its inhabitants, that they should become a desolation and a curse, and have torn your clothes, and wept before me; I also have heard you,' says Yahweh. 'Therefore behold, I will gather you to your fathers, and you will be gathered to your grave in peace. Your eyes will not see all the evil which I will bring on this place." So they brought this message [from the prophetess Huldah] back to the king." *~ 2 Kings 22: 1-2, 8, 10-20*

Isn't that extraordinary! The book of God was lost in the house of God! We have many houses of worship in America today that need to find the word of the LORD again. God's word needs to be rediscovered in God's house. It's easy to see why some believe Shaphan the scribe was probably reading from Leviticus 26 or Deuteronomy 28. When the young king heard the warning, "that they should become a desolation and a curse," it broke his heart. He wept and humbled himself before the LORD (Psalm 34:18; 51:17; 119:136). Huldah, the prophetess, informed the king that God would surely condemn Jerusalem, but he would die in peace. So, now that King Josiah is armed with the news that Jerusalem is going down and he is going up, what will he do? Let's continue on into chapter 23:

"The king sent, and they gathered to him all the elders of Judah and of Jerusalem. The king went up to Yahweh's house, and all the men of Judah and all the inhabitants of Jerusalem with him, with the priests, the prophets, and all the people, both small and great; and **he read in their hearing all the words of the book of the covenant which was found in Yahweh's house.** The king stood by the pillar, and made a covenant before Yahweh, to walk after Yahweh, and to keep his commandments, his testimonies, and his statutes, with all his heart, and all his soul, to confirm the words of this covenant that were written in this book; and *all the people agreed to the covenant.*

"He got rid of the idolatrous priests, whom the kings of Judah had ordained to burn incense in the high places in the cities of Judah, and in the places around Jerusalem; those also who burned incense to Baal, to the sun, and to the moon, and to the planets, and to all the army of the sky. He brought out the Asherah from Yahweh's house, outside of Jerusalem, to the brook Kidron, and burned it at the brook Kidron, and beat it to dust, and cast its dust on the graves of the common people. He broke down the houses of the male shrine prostitutes that were in Yahweh's house, where the women wove hangings for the Asherah. ...He defiled Topheth, which is in the valley of the children of Hinnom, that no man might make his son or his daughter to pass through the fire to Molech. ...*The king broke down the altars that were on the roof of the upper room of Ahaz*, which the kings of Judah had made, and the altars which Manasseh had made in the two courts of Yahweh's house, and beat them down from there, and cast their dust into the brook Kidron.

"The king commanded all the people, saying, 'Keep the Passover to Yahweh your God, as it is written in this book of the covenant.' Surely there was not kept such a Passover from the days of the judges who judged Israel, nor in all the days of the kings of Israel, nor of the kings of Judah; but in the eighteenth year of king Josiah, this Passover was kept to Yahweh in Jerusalem. ...**There was no king like him before him, who turned to Yahweh with all his heart, and with all his soul, and with all his might, according to all the law of Moses; and there was none like him who arose after him."** ~ *2 Kings 23:1-3, 5-7, 10, 12, 21-23, 25-27*

Josiah was Israel's most righteous king, and a shining example for us all. When the high priest "found the book of the law in Yahweh's house," this young, godly leader quickly restored the sacred word of God to its rightful place of prominence. He reinstituted the long-forsaken Passover. The evil kings of Judah built altars on the roof of the upper room; Josiah broke them down and beat them to dust! He burned the idols of false gods, and cleansed God's house of male shrine prostitutes and idolatrous priests.

According to the words of the prophetess Huldah, God blessed faithful Josiah. He didn't have to live through the terrible siege and famine that later happened to Judah. Because of his sincere and humble response to a harsh message from the written word of God, the young king saw a great spiritual revival that was followed by sweeping social reform. And the thing that started it all was, *"I have found the book of the law in Yahweh's house."*

The houses of worship in America today must find the book of the LORD again. God's truth needs to be rediscovered in God's temple. Yahweh will not respect us if we don't respect his word. Yahweh will not respond to our cries for revival if we don't respond to his directives from Scripture. God will be a stranger to us if we're strangers to his word. Consider what these notable leaders have said about the good book.

President George Washington – "It is impossible to rightly govern the world without God and the Bible."

President Abraham Lincoln – "But for this Book we could not know right from wrong. I believe the Bible is the best gift God has ever given to man."

President Ulysses S. Grant – "Write its precepts in your hearts, and practice them in your lives. To the influence of this book are we indebted for all the progress made in true civilization, and to this we must look as our guide in the future. 'Righteousness exalteth a nation, but sin is a reproach to any people.' "

President Andrew Jackson – "That book, sir, is the rock on which this Republic rests."

Business Mogul John D. Rockefeller – "We can never learn too much of His will towards us, too much of His messages and His advice. The Bible is His word and its study gives at once the foundation for our faith and an inspiration to battle onward in the fight against the tempter."

Scientist James D. Dana – "Young men, as you go forth, remember that I, an old man, who has known only science all his life, say unto you that there are no truer facts than the facts found within the Holy Scriptures."

Founding Father Benjamin Franklin – "Young men, my advice to you is that you cultivate an acquaintance with, and a firm belief in, the Holy Scriptures."

Founding Father Patrick Henry – Well known for his quote, "Give me liberty, or give me death!" Lesser known for his quote, "The Bible is worth all the other books which have ever been printed."

Educator Henry van Dyke – "No other book in the world has had such a strange vitality, such an outgoing power of influence and inspiration. No man is poor or desolate who has this treasure for his own."

President Theodore Roosevelt – "A thorough knowledge of the Bible is worth more than a college education."

Educator Booker T. Washington – "Perhaps the most valuable thing that I got out of my second year [at Hampton University] was an understanding of the use and value of the Bible."

Statesman Horace Greeley – "It is impossible to enslave, mentally or socially, a Bible-reading people. The principles of the Bible are the groundwork of human freedom."

How can we know the Bible is true?

Dr. C.S. Lovett reminds us that *"God supplies sufficient evidence for faith to operate, but not enough to convince the unbelieving mind."* If the Bible truly is the inspired word of God, it's a supernatural book. As such, there should be supernatural elements to validate its authenticity. These supernatural elements will supply sufficient evidence for faith to operate, but not enough to convince someone who is determined not to believe. For reasons beyond our comprehension, JAH delights in his children responding to him by faith (Hebrews 11:6). Now consider...

Supernatural Element #1 – Its Amazing Unity!

The Bible is not just one book, but a library of books, sixty-six in all. Over forty different writers contributed to this library of books. Some of them never saw one another or even knew that others had written on the same topic. They lived in different times and were from diverse backgrounds. Moses was an Egyptian prince, Joshua was a military man, Job was a rich farmer, Amos was a poor farmer, Daniel was a statesman, Peter was a fisherman, and Paul a tentmaker. Some wrote in the desert, some in the palace, some in Babylon, some in Corinth, and some in Rome. More than 1,500 years elapsed between the writing of the first book in this library, Genesis, and the last book, Revelation.

Now what do you suppose would happen today if forty doctors from different backgrounds were commissioned to write a collection of essays on how to lose weight. How much unity do you suspect there would be in their writings? Let's not even factor in the 1500-year timeline. Can you imagine all forty doctors being in complete harmony regarding the most effective way to lose weight? I can't.

Just a casual examination of any online bookstore will reveal there's very little unity of thought between people on any single topic. Take politics, or the economy. Any unity of thought there? *Yet we find perfect unity in Scripture as the central theme of Jesus Christ dovetails throughout the Old and New Testament (Hebrews 10:5-7).* Some say otherwise, but there are no significant contradictions in the Bible. You may have noticed this library does have several superficial contradictions. One quick illustration is what was written on the sign that hung on the cross.

Matthew 27:37,	They set up over his head the accusation against him written, "THIS IS JESUS, THE KING OF THE JEWS."
Mark 15:26,	The superscription of his accusation was written over him, "THE KING OF THE JEWS."
Luke 23:38,	An inscription was also written over him in letters of Greek, Latin, and Hebrew: "THIS IS THE KING OF THE JEWS."
John 19:19,	Pilate wrote a title also, and put it on the cross. There was written, "JESUS OF NAZARETH, THE KING OF THE JEWS."

Any person who's looking for contradictions might point out, "There you have it in black and white! I told you the Bible is full of contradictions and mistakes!" From this one example they might decide to brand the entire Bible as untrustworthy. But those of us who believe God have no problem "harmonizing" the four accounts of the Gospel. For instance, there is no contradiction if the sign simply said, "This is Jesus of Nazareth, the King of the Jews." Furthermore, the *seeming* contradictions in Matthew, Mark, Luke and John actually support the fact that the writers didn't corroborate beforehand to "get their story together." If four people witness the same car accident from different viewpoints, would their reports be identical in every detail? I think not. All the same, their four reports could be true to the facts of the event.

In reference to the Holy Scriptures, here are a few lines of the Doctrinal Statement from Dallas Theological Seminary.

> We believe that "all Scripture is given by inspiration of God," by which we understand the whole Bible is inspired in the sense that holy men of God "were moved by the Holy Spirit" to write the very words of Scripture. We believe that this divine inspiration extends equally and fully to all parts of the writings - historical, poetical, doctrinal, and prophetical - as appeared in the original manuscripts. ...We believe that all the Scriptures center about the Lord Jesus Christ in His person and work in His first and second coming, and hence that no portion, even of the Old Testament, is properly read, or understood, until it leads to Him.

When speaking to the religious but lost people of his day, our Lord said in John 5:38-40, "You don't have his [God's] word living in you; because you don't believe him whom he sent. You search the Scriptures, because you think that in them you have eternal life; and *these are they which testify about me*. Yet you will not come to me, that you may have life." Long before the NT was written, the OT writers testified about Jesus. Philip's encounter with an Ethiopian in Acts 8:26-35 is a perfect example. Our resurrected Lord teaching two of his disciples on the road to Emmaus is another (Luke 24:13-32). The amazing unity of Scripture supports the doctrine that although there are many different human contributors (2 Peter 1:21), there is only one divine, supernatural writer of this collection of sixty-six books that we today call the Holy Bible.

Supernatural Element #2 – Its Indestructibility!

Jesus said in Matthew 24:35 NKJV, "Heaven and earth will pass away, but My words will by no means pass away." Many have sought to put Jesus' word to the test. The French infidel Voltaire once commented, "Another century and there will not be a Bible on the earth." The century has come and gone, and the Bible is still read by more people and published in more languages than any other book in history. Ironically, within a hundred years after his death, the Geneva Bible Society was using the very same printing press that Voltaire previously used to print his infidel literature, to now literally multiply copies of the indestructible word of God. Surely our Lord laughs in derision (Psalm 2:4).

The Russian tyrant Joseph Stalin outlawed the Bible and sought to rid his people of the influence of Scripture. But in that land today, God still has his people who are followers and lovers of the Holy Book. Svetlana Alliluyeva, later known as Lana Peters, was the youngest child and only daughter of Premier Stalin. In 1967, she caused an international furor when she defected and became a naturalized citizen of the United States. Even though she grew up in a nation that criminalized the Bible, this is what she says about Scripture.

> "Nowhere have I found words more powerful than those in the Psalms. Their fervid poetry cleanses one, gives one strength, brings hope in moments of darkness. Makes one look critically into oneself, convict oneself, and wash one's heart clean with one's

own tears. It is the ever-burning fire of love, of gratitude, humility, and truth."

Do I possess that same adoration for the word of God? *Does it cause me to look critically at myself?* Is it to me an ever-burning fire of love, of gratitude, humility and truth? Or, is it just another one of my many books on the shelf that I take for granted? I pray that not be the case.

The Roman emperor Diocletian (284-305 A.D.) made a direct assault on the Bible. The historian Eusebius of Caesarea said, "Royal edicts were published everywhere, commanding that the churches be leveled to the ground and the Scriptures destroyed by fire" (*Church History*, Book VIII, Ch. 1). Diocletian declared that if anyone had a copy of the Scriptures and did not surrender it to be burned, if it were discovered, they would be killed. Furthermore, if any person knew of someone else who had a copy of any portion of Scripture, and did not report it, they would also be killed.

I wonder about my own reaction had I lived under such a ruler. Would I give up my Bible, or be put to death by the state? Would I give up my friends who possessed Bibles, or be put to death according to the law of the land? This is just another reason why believers should memorize Scripture (Psalm 119:11). **No one can take away the Word that's hidden in your heart!** For years, Diocletian's hatred for the word of God manifested itself in merciless slaughter and destruction. One would think he was possessed by the spirit of Manasseh. After his edict had been in force for two years, Diocletian boasted, "I have completely exterminated the Christian writings from the face of the earth!" History tells us that when the next emperor, Constantine the Great, offered a reward for a copy of the Holy Bible, over 40 scrolls of Scripture showed up within 24 hours!

One of our Founding Fathers, the infidel writer Thomas Paine exclaimed, "I have gone through the Bible as a man would go through a forest with an axe to fell trees. I have cut down tree after tree: here they lie. They will never grow again." But as Paine died a horrible infidel's death in 1809, the word of God marched on.

As of 2017, the complete Old and New Testament of the Bible has been translated into 670 languages. The entire New Testament alone has been translated into 1,521 languages. People from 3,312 different languages now have at least some portion of the Bible in their tongue. It has truly proven itself to be indestructible.

A Tribute to the Indestructible Book

- Empires rise and fall and are forgotten – There it stands.
- Emperors decree its extermination – There it stands.
- Despised and torn to pieces – There it stands.
- Atheists rail against it – There it stands.
- Agnostics smile cynically – There it stands.
- Unbelief abandons it – There it stands.
- Higher critics deny its claim of inspiration – There it stands.
- An anvil that has broken a million hammers – There it stands.
- Fogs of sophistry conceal it temporarily – There it stands.
- The tooth of time gnaws but dents it not – There it stands.
- Infidels predict its abandonment – There it stands.
- Modernism tries to explain it away – There it stands.

"It is God's highway to paradise. It is the light on the pathway in the darkest night. It leads business men to integrity and uprightness. It awakens men and women opiated by sin. It answers every great question of the soul. It solves every great problem of life. It is a fortress often attacked but never failing. Its wisdom is commanding and its logic convincing. Salvation is its watchword, eternal life its goal. It outlives, outloves, outreaches, outranks, outruns all other books. Trust it, love it, obey it, and eternal life is yours." *~ A. Z. Conrad*

Supernatural Element #3 – Its Historical Accuracy!

Atheists and agnostics referred often to the "hundreds of historical mistakes and contradictions" in the Bible. But that was before the specialized science of archaeology came along and unearthed one crucial finding after another that provided extra-biblical evidence for the trustworthiness of the old book.

Most of us respect men and women who have devoted their lives in researching a special field of interest. Dr. William F. Albright is that type of person. He's one of the most admired Middle Eastern scholars who ever lived. Dr. Albright was a professor at Johns Hopkins University, an expert in ancient ceramics, and he knew some 25 languages. He used modern scientific methods to prove the historicity of many Old Testament and New Testament sites. Consider his comments about the Bible.

> "The reader may rest assured: nothing has been found to disturb a reasonable faith, and *nothing has been discovered which can disprove a single theological doctrine*. We no longer trouble ourselves with attempts to 'harmonize' religion and science, or to 'prove' the Bible. The Bible can stand for itself."

Archaeological discoveries such as the Pool of Siloam in John 9, and Jerusalem's Babylonian Siege Tower in 2 Kings 25 (see page 188) may not provide enough evidence to convince the unbelieving mind, but they do provide ample evidence for faith to operate.

The Black Obelisk of Shalmaneser III is a six and a half feet tall, four-sided, black limestone sculpture. It was unearthed in northern Iraq by archaeologist Sir Austen H. Layard in 1846. The obelisk has 20 panels that commemorate the deeds of King Shalmaneser III, who reigned from 858-825 B.C. On one of the panels is a depiction of someone bowing and paying tribute to Shalmaneser. The caption above the scene, written in Assyrian cuneiform, is translated:

> "The tribute of Jehu, son of Omri: I received from him silver, gold, a golden bowl, a golden vase with pointed bottom, golden tumblers, golden buckets, tin, a staff for a king [and] spears."

Most scholars agree the figure is that of King Jehu of Israel from 1 Kings 19:16 and 2 Kings 9:2. The Assyrians referred to a northern Israelite king as a "son of Omri" whether he was a direct descendant of Omri or not, much like Jesus being referred to as the "son of David." King Omri of Israel is mentioned in 1 Kings 16. He began his reign in 885 B.C. and was the ruler who made Samaria the new northern capital of Israel. Jehu would come to the throne in 841 B.C. and reign for 28 years.

Jehu's name is also found in ancient Assyrian manuscripts and chronicles, indicating he had normal interactions with his neighboring nation. *The very fact of both Omri and Jehu showing up on the most complete Assyrian obelisk ever discovered is strong extra-biblical evidence that they were actual historical figures.*

According to the *Biblical Archaeology Review,* Jehu and Omri are just two of the over 52 people in the Bible who have been confirmed archaeologically. Think about that. Fifty-two people from the Bible whose existence is confirmed outside of the biblical record! Again, probably not enough to convince an unbelieving mind, but it is another piece of evidence for the faithful.

Heavily influenced by late 19th century skeptics, Frank Morison, a man trained in law, decided to discover the true nature of Jesus by looking critically and objectively at the facts surrounding his death and resurrection. He knew this was the central force of the Christian faith (1 Corinthians 15:16-19), and he thought that by disproving the resurrection he could deal a death blow to the entire faith. After painstaking research, Morison came away from the experience completely convinced that Jesus of Nazareth did die a cruel death by crucifixion at the hands of the Romans, and that He did indeed rise from the dead after three days. His book, *Who Moved the Stone,* is considered a classic apologetic (defense) on the subject of the resurrection.

More recently, former investigative journalist Lee Strobel, an awarding-winning legal editor of the *Chicago Tribune* and a spiritual skeptic until 1981, conducted his own investigation into the Bible's claim of a risen Christ. He, like Frank Morison and others, came away from the experience believing the biblical record. His book, *The Case for Christ,* was made into a movie in 2017.

Supernatural Element # 4 – The Nation of Israel!

The children of Jacob are proof that the Bible is supernatural. If you ever question whether or not our God is true to his word, all you have to do is look at the nation of Israel. They were called out to be the Lord's witness nation, set high above all others in praise, in name, and in honor. "But Jeshurun grew fat, and kicked...Then he abandoned God who made him, and rejected the Rock of his salvation" (Deuteronomy 32:15).

Do you have any doubt whether or not God will fulfill his word? If so, all you have to do is read Deuteronomy 28 and look at the history of Israel. The Jewish nation teaches us our God is just as "faithful" in bestowing his fury as he is in bestowing his favor! The lesson to be learned from the rise and fall of Israel is God will absolutely do what he said he will do (Lam. 2:17)! He told his prophet, "I watch over my word to perform it" (Jer. 1:12). Jehovah said if Israel took Highway D28A, he would bless them. They did, and he blessed them. God said if they took D28B, he would curse them. They did, and he cursed them. Please examine Psalm 105-106 and Nehemiah 9 for an excellent overview of God's interactions with Israel. But is Jehovah finished completely with the wayward children of Abraham? The Most High God says his people are destroyed for lack of knowledge. Truth = freedom; ignorance = bondage! In the NT, we'll find at least four specific topics all believers should be aware of:

1. Spiritual Gifts
2. Satan's Schemes
3. Israel's Wilderness Experience
4. Israel's Future Restoration

1. Spiritual Gifts. 1 Corinthians 12:1, 4 » "Now concerning spiritual things [manifestations], brothers, *I don't want you to be ignorant.*" "Now there are various kinds of gifts, but the same Spirit." When we learn to flow in the power and joy of our spiritual gifts, the walk of faith becomes more focused and fruitful. We'll discuss spiritual gifts in Action Step #4.

2. Satan's Schemes. 2 Corinthians 2:10-11 » "I have forgiven that [person] for your sakes in the presence of Christ, that no advantage may be gained over us by Satan, *for we are not ignorant of his schemes.*" Aided by our dumb flesh, Satan persuades us to withhold forgiveness from those who have sinned against us. But if the Most High God has forgiven me of cosmic treason, which is punishable by spiritual and eternal death, how can I refuse to forgive anyone for anything! How many times should I forgive someone? Is it three strikes and you're out? See Jesus' answer in Matthew 18:21-35. Satan knows Scripture. Our adversary, the old dragon, knows unforgiveness ensnares us. When we refuse to forgive those who have crossed us, or at least, we feel they've crossed us (there's a few sides to every story), that allows the evil one to gain leverage over us. We are not ignorant of his schemes. Truth equals freedom. Therefore, we liberate ourselves when we forgive those who trespass against us.

3. Israel's Wilderness Experience. 1 Corinthians 10:1, 11 » *"Now I would not have you ignorant*, brothers, that our fathers were all under the cloud, and all passed through the sea." "Now all these things happened to them *by way of example*, and they were written for our admonition." During his own wilderness experience, Jesus was tempted by Satan in Matthew 4 and Luke 4. Did you know that every time he quotes Scripture to counter the lies of the devil, he quotes from the book of Deuteronomy which highlights Israel's wilderness experience? God wants us to learn from his tussles with Jacob. It's a cautionary tale and "an instruction."

4. Israel's Future Restoration. We've seen the rise and fall of Israel. But is her fall final? Is God done completely with Israel? In Romans 11:25-29 we read, *"For I don't desire you to be ignorant*, brothers, of this mystery, so that you won't be wise in your own conceits, that a partial hardening [or blindness] has happened to Israel, until the fullness of the Gentiles has come in, and so all Israel will be saved. Even as it is written, 'There will come out of Zion the Deliverer, and he will turn away ungodliness from Jacob. This is my covenant with them, when I will take away their sins.' Concerning the Good News, they are enemies for your sake. *But concerning the election, they are beloved for the fathers' sake.* For the gifts and the calling of God are irrevocable."

"All day long I stretched out my hands to a disobedient and contrary people." That's what Jehovah God said of Israel (Romans 10:21). Jeshurun was hardheaded. Consequently, Yahweh put him in "timeout." But timeouts are limited in duration. Israel's current timeout is evidenced by their blindness to the true identity of the Messiah. But this is partial and temporary. It's partial because not everyone in the nation rejected Christ. There were, and are, Jewish believers in Jesus as Lord. My OT professor was Jewish and a believer in Yeshua as the Messiah. Paul used himself in Romans 11:1 to show their blindness was only partial. "I ask then, did God reject his people? **May it never be!** For I also am an Israelite, a descendant of Abraham, of the tribe of Benjamin."

The blindness of Israel is only partial, and it's temporary, meaning the timeout will last *"until the fullness of the Gentiles has come in."* Jesus said in Luke 21:24, "Jerusalem will be trampled down by the Gentiles, *until the times of the Gentiles are fulfilled.*" We saw during a BibleScope assignment in Acts 15, that God is visiting the Gentile nations today to call out a people for his name. This seems to indicate when the full number of "Gentiles has come in" the flock of the Great Shepherd, then the spiritual blindness of Israel will be removed, and the Deliverer "will turn away ungodliness from Jacob." The Father of infinity controls the timetable (Deuteronomy 29:4). Ironically, one of the major prophets that JAH used to warn of Israel's fall, the tearful Jeremiah, also spoke of their restoration.

> "Behold, the days come," says Yahweh, "that I will make a *new* covenant with the house of Israel, and with the house of Judah:

> not according to the covenant that I made with their fathers in the day that I took them by the hand to bring them out of the land of Egypt; which covenant of mine they broke, although I was a husband to them," says Yahweh.
>
> "But this is the covenant that I will make with the house of Israel after those days," says Yahweh: "I will put my law in their inward parts, and I will write it in their heart. I will be their God, and they shall be my people. They will no longer each teach his neighbor, and every man teach his brother, saying, 'Know Yahweh;' for they will all know me, from their least to their greatest," says Yahweh: "for I will forgive their iniquity, and I will remember their sin no more." ~ *Jeremiah 31:31-34*

Israel fell into unbelief. God then poured the benefits of the gospel on the Gentiles (Acts 13:44-48; 18:5,6). So in a sense, non-Jewish believers have gained from Jacob's fall. Which prompts the apostle to ask a rhetorical question in Romans 11:12, *"Now if their fall is the riches of the world, and their loss the riches of the Gentiles; how much more their fullness?"* If Gentile believers in Christ are now benefiting due to the fall of Israel, the restoration of Israel will benefit the Gentiles even more, "much more." It will be glorious for Jew and Gentile!

> "Oh the depth of the riches both of the wisdom and the knowledge of God! **How unsearchable are his judgments, and his ways past tracing out!** 'For who has known the mind of the Lord? Or who has been his counselor?' For of him, and through him, and to him are all things. To him be the glory for ever! Amen." ~ *Romans 11:33-34, 36*

God's ways are past tracing out. Our mushy brains can't generate enough wattage to figure out the designs of the Most High God! "For who has known the mind of the Lord?" The current regathering and replanting of Israelites in the land he swore to their fathers Abraham, Isaac and Jacob (Genesis 50:24) is proof enough that the Scriptures of the Old and New Testament are true. The Lord commanded Jeremiah to put a yoke on his neck, and later buy a field in the land of Benjamin. Wearing the yoke signified Israel's punishment and exile from the land; buying the field foretold their return to ownership of the land. The LORD of hosts has not forsaken his errant people (Jeremiah 51:5). Even during the tragic fall of Jerusalem in 586 B.C., God used his servant to prophesy:

> "Now therefore Yahweh, the God of Israel, says concerning this city, about which you say, 'It is given into the hand of the king of Babylon by the sword, by the famine, and by the pestilence:' *'Behold, I will gather them out of all the countries where I have driven them in my anger, and in my wrath, and in great indignation;* and **I will bring them again to this place.** I will cause them to dwell safely. Then they will be my people, and I will be their God. I will give them one heart and one way, that they may fear me forever, for their good, and the good of their children after them. I will make an everlasting covenant with them, that I will not turn away from following them, to do them good. I will put my fear in their hearts, that they may not depart from me. Yes, I will rejoice over them to do them good, and **I will plant them in this land** assuredly with my whole heart and my whole soul."
> *~ Jeremiah 32:36-41*

Israel rejected Yahweh, and her citizens were scattered to the wind. Incredibly, some 2,500 years later, she regained her status as an independent nation. In 1948, the Jewish people formally adopted the name "State of Israel." At the end of 2019, her population approaches nine million, with about 75% being Jewish. The restoration of Israel is as certain as her rise and her fall. As JAH has spoken, it will be done!

Supernatural Element # 5 – It's Affect Upon the People of the World!

The Bible has possibly done more to change the world for good than any other book. I realize that's a big claim, but the governing laws of the Western World, such as the English Common Law, the Bill of Rights, and our own United States Constitution, were greatly influenced by the Ten Commandments given to the prophet Moses on Mount Sinai.

Our educational system was energized by the Bible. The Massachusetts School Law of 1642 required children to be able "to read and understand the principles of religion and the capital laws of this country." The New England code of 1655 required that children be made "able duly to read the Scriptures...and in some competent measure to understand the main grounds and principles of Christian Religion necessary to salvation."

Here's a nice one: **The Old Deluder Satan Act of 1647**. It's from the Massachusetts Bay Colony, and it begins as follows: *"It being one chief project of that old deluder, Satan, to keep men from the knowledge of the Scriptures..."* Wow! The law required every town with more than 50 families to set up a reading school.

I think it's fair to say that over 90% of the schools of higher learning in the United States today were established by Christian organizations, and such is the case for nearly 100% of the historically black colleges and universities. It's a shame many of these schools have allowed the evil one, in the name of modernism and higher criticism, to erode their firm Christian foundation. When this country was young and growing fast, the people of that time were intensely aware of the old deluder's scheme "to keep men from the knowledge of the Scriptures." That's why regular chapel and Bible classes were mandatory. When was the last time you read *The Pilgrim's Progress from This World, to That Which is to Come*? This fantastic allegory by inmate John Bunyan was a "bestseller" during the formation of America. Bible stories and themes from Scripture, such as honor, the afterlife, faith, family, and the judgment served as building blocks for the early travelers to this new land. But alas, over long stretches of time, the enemy chips away at our spiritual foundation.

According to the *Congressional Quarterly Researcher,* in 1940 public school teachers were asked to rate the top disciplinary problems. Their answers were: talking out of turn, chewing gum, making noise, running in the halls, cutting in line, dress-code violations and littering. When teachers were asked to do the same rating in 1990, their answers were: drug abuse, alcohol abuse, pregnancy, suicide, rape, robbery and assault. Unfortunately, though predictably, when you add the issues of 2020 into the mix – social media, bullying, spiraling anxiety, tribalism, and the proliferation of guns – things have only gotten worse.

> *"If I were the devil, I would encourage schools to refine young intellects but neglect to discipline emotions – just let those run wild. Until before you knew it, you'd have to have drug-sniffing dogs and metal detectors at every schoolhouse door." ~ P.H.*

The First Duke of Wellington warned, "Educate men without religion, and you make them but clever devils." Think Proverbs 29:18. And the Oxford professor and writer C.S. Lewis echoed, "Education and culture has only tended to make man a more clever and sophisticated devil."

Another Oxford professor, John Wycliffe, was one of the first to completely translate the entire Bible into the English language, and in so doing, he made the teachings of Holy Scripture available to the "common" people. In his famous Gettysburg Address, President Lincoln concluded his speech with, "...that this nation, under God, shall have a new birth of freedom, and that government of the people, by the people, for the people, shall not perish from the earth." Some 475 years earlier, John Wycliffe wrote the following lines in the introduction to his translation of the New Testament: "The Bible is for the government of the people, by the people, and for the people."

Brother Wycliffe criticized the elevated status of the Roman Catholic clergy. He attacked the extravagant luxury of local parishes. As a priest, he saw first-hand the abuses of the church, and he felt strongly that everyday people should be able to read and understand the Scriptures for themselves. He contended the papacy was without biblical justification, and that believers should have and rely on their own Bibles rather than the teachings of the privileged clergy. *Wycliffe taught that Scripture, not the church, was the final authority regarding spiritual matters.* He is regarded as "the Morning Star of the English Reformation."

John Wycliffe died December 31, 1384. The commoners loved him. The church officials hated him. In May of 1415, the Council of Constance declared him a heretic. In 1428, Wycliffe's body was exhumed by order of Pope Martin V. It was then burned, and his ashes were thrown into the River Swift.

In spite of all that, the Wycliffe Bible was very popular. For most believers, it was the first time they had the chance to read the Scriptures in their own tongue, and many took advantage of it. The Wycliffe Bible was the most common manuscript literature during the period called Middle English. More than 250 manuscripts of the Wycliffe Bible survive today. On December 5, 2016, a copy sold at auction for $1,692,500.

"How much better it is to get wisdom than gold! Yes, to get understanding is to be chosen rather than silver." ~ *Proverbs 16:16*

"I have rejoiced in the way of your testimonies, as much as in all riches. I will meditate on your precepts, and consider your ways." ~ *Psalm 119:14-15*

Supernatural Element #6 – The Infallible Test, Prophecy!

Dr. Benjamin Mays, past president of Morehouse College in Atlanta said, "Only an omniscient God can predict the future." The acid test of any religious faith that claims to speak for the true and living God is prophecy, the supernatural ability to predict what will happen before it actually occurs. This is one of the strongest reasons to have faith in the words of the Holy Bible. On at least two occasions Jesus told his disciples, "I tell you *before it happens*, that when it happens, you may believe that I am he" (John 13:19), and "Now I have told you *before it happens* so that when it happens, you may believe" (John 14:29). Who can predict the future? Only an omniscient [all-knowing] God.

No other religious book predicts future events with verifiable accuracy like the Scriptures of the Old and New Testament. If you look at all the religious books in the world, only one claims to be the infallible, inerrant, God-breathed word of the LORD. Only one backs up that claim with fulfilled, specific prophecy.

There are literally hundreds of fulfilled prophecies concerning the nations of Israel, Edom, Babylon, Media-Persia, Rome, Egypt and Greece. I won't go into these, but I do feel compelled to share ten specific prophecies about the carpenter from Galilee, the one who loved and spoke with such supernatural power that he split history into B.C. and A.D. You'll be amazed at how Jesus fulfilled specific prophecies spoken about him hundreds of years before his birth. I encourage you to examine these passages in your Bible.

1. He would be born in Bethlehem – compare Micah 5:2-3 with Matthew 2:5-6.

2. He would be called out of the land of Egypt – compare Hosea 11:1 with Matthew 2:13-15.

3. He would be given the throne of David – compare 2 Samuel 7:12-17 with Luke 1:31-33.

4. He would be the rejected cornerstone – compare Psalm 118:18-23 with Matthew 21:42-46 and Acts 4:8-12.

5. His miraculous signs would not be believed – compare Isaiah 53:1 with John 12:35-38.

6. He would be whipped and spat upon – compare Isaiah 50:4-7 with Matthew 26:63-68; 27:24-32.

7. His bones would not be broken – compare Psalm 34:18-20; Exodus 12:41-46 and Numbers 9:9-12 with John 19:30-36.

8. Others would gamble for his clothes – compare Psalm 22:18 with Matthew 27:35-36.

9. He would be forsaken during his moment of agony – compare Psalm 22:1 with Matthew 27:46; Mark 15:34.

10. He would be raised from the dead – compare Psalm 16:8-10 with Matthew 28:1-7; Acts 2:22-32; 13:26-39.

What do you estimate are the chances of Jesus Christ fulfilling specific OT prophecies by mere coincidence? We can find at least twenty of these regarding the Messiah in the Book of Psalms alone. But what are the odds of just eight coming true?

In the book, *Science Speaks*, Peter Stoner, a scientist in the area of mathematical probabilities, ran the numbers for us. *He states that it would be one chance in 10 to the 17th power that eight prophecies came to pass by accident*. Now check this out. One chance in 10 to the 17th power can be compared to filling the entire state of Texas in silver dollars – two feet deep, painting one of the silver dollars black, dropping a blind man from a helicopter somewhere in that vast sea of endless silver dollars, and giving him a single chance to pick the one coin painted black! What are his chances of doing that? One in 10 to the 17th power!

Jesus completed *scores* of specific OT prophecies. Do you think that happened by chance? We saw for ourselves how Yahweh made specific predictions regarding his people in Deuteronomy, and we saw how those same predictions were fulfilled generations later in the books of Chronicles and Kings. There are other so-called "scriptures," but none hold a candle to the Bible when it comes to the infallible test of prophecy. Our God is awesome, and he's given us an awesome book. "Remember the former things of old: for I am God, and there is no other. I am God, and there is none like me. **I declare the end from the beginning, and from ancient times [I declare] things that are not yet done**. I say: My counsel will stand, and I will do all that I please" (Isaiah 46:9,10). Yes, sir and Amen!

Supernatural Element #7 – Its Power to Change Lives!

"For this cause we also thank God without ceasing, that when you received from us the word of the message of God, you accepted it not as the word of men, but as it is in truth, the word of God, which also works in you who believe." ~ 1 Thessalonians 2:13

This is one of the most instructive verses in the entire Bible! The followers of Christ in Thessalonica accepted the message, "not as the word of men, but as it is in truth, the word of God"! Holy Scripture is the living word of the living God. Jesus Christ, the Word made flesh, said that his words are spirit and life (John 6:63). And this living Word-Spirit "works in you who believe." It transforms us from weak sinners who are driven by the world, the flesh and the devil, into saints who are empowered by the Holy Spirit of God. "But I say, walk by the Spirit, and you won't fulfill the lust of the flesh" (Galatians 5:16).

To walk by the Spirit is to walk by the word! "For the word of God is quick, and powerful..." (Hebrews 4:12 KJV). "I will never forget thy precepts: for with them thou hast quickened me" (Psalm 119:93 KJV). God's word is quick, and by it we're quickened. His word is alive, and by it we're made alive. As we ponder the glory of our Lord Christ Jesus, and his powerful words and images throughout the Old and New Testament, we're transformed gradually by the renewing of our minds (Romans 12:2). **As we learn of him and from him (Matthew 11:29), we become more like him.** "But we all, with unveiled face seeing the glory of the Lord as in a mirror, are *transformed into the same image* from glory to glory, even as from the Lord, the Spirit" (2 Corinthians 3:18).

Vernon Grounds in *The Reason for Our Hope* shares, "Probably there is no more sensational example of the life-transforming power of the Bible than the unbelievable story of the Mutiny on the Bounty. In 1787 the British HMS *Bounty*, under Captain Bligh, set sail for the island of Tahiti in the South Seas.

"After a voyage of ten months, the ship arrived at her destination, and further six months were spent collecting palm saplings. The sailors meanwhile had become so attached to the native girls, that upon receiving orders to embark, they mutinied, set the Captain and a few men adrift in an open boat, and returned to the island. Captain Bligh, however, survived his ordeal and eventually arrived home in England.

"A punitive expedition was sent out, which captured 14 of the mutineers. But nine of them had transferred to another location, where they formed a new colony on Pitcairn Island. Here, in the language of the Encyclopedia Britannica, they degenerated so fast and became so fierce as to make the life of the colony a hell on earth. One of the chief reasons for this was the distillation of whiskey from a native plant. Quarrels, orgies, and murders were a common feature of their life.

"Finally, all the men except two were killed or had died. Only John Adams [also used the name Alexander Smith] and Ned Young were left alone with a crowd of native women and half-breed children. Then a strange thing happened. In a battered chest, they found the ship's Bible. They read it, believed it, and began to live it. Determining to make amends for their past life, they gathered the women and children around them and taught them too. When Ned Young died of infection, Adams continued their work in teaching the Way.

"Time rolled on. The children grew up and became Christians. The community prospered exceedingly. Nearly 20 years later an American ship visited the island and brought to Europe and England word of its peaceful state. The British government took no further action. There was no need. Pitcairn Island was a Christian community. There was no disease, no insanity, no crime, and no illiteracy, and no strong drink. Life and property were safe, and the moral standards of the people were as high as anywhere in the world. It was a veritable Utopia on a small scale. What brought about this astounding transformation? Just the reading of a book, and that book was the Bible."

~§~

"But evil men and impostors will grow worse and worse, deceiving and being deceived. But you remain in the things which you have learned and have been assured of, knowing from whom you have learned them. From infancy, you have known the holy Scriptures which are able to make you wise for salvation through faith, which is in Christ Jesus. **Every Scripture is God-breathed** and profitable for teaching, for reproof, for correction, and for instruction in righteousness, that each person who belongs to God may be complete, thoroughly equipped for every good work." ~ *2 Timothy 3:13-17*

~§~ ~§~ ~§~

You Christians have in your hands a book containing enough dynamite to blow all civilization to pieces, turn the world upside down, and bring peace to a battle-torn planet. But you treat it as though it is nothing more than a piece of literature. ~ *Mahatma Gandhi*

~§~ ~§~ ~§~

Action Step #2. Receive God's Son

Richard was a drug addict in remand for aggravated burglary, with over 20 previous offenses. To help cope with feelings of guilt, he began attending prison chapel, and found it made him feel better while he was there. The pastor offered him a Bible, but he already had one. The prisoners found the thin pages in the Bible useful for rolling their own cigarettes. One day he tore out a page to have a smoke, but an 'inner voice' told him he should read the page. It was from the Gospel of John, and he found it 'captivating' – and it allowed him to go to sleep in peace that night. The next day he read more and tried to visualize what this Jesus looked like. The only image which came to mind was a statue of Jesus on the cross, in a nearby church. The image seemed to come alive in his mind, and Jesus seemed to look at him and say: "Richard, I did this for you." Richard was deeply affected by this. He offered his life to God, received Jesus as Lord and Savior, and began to experience a healing of his addiction. He eventually grew completely free of his craving. Today, Richard is the pastor of a church in Wales, and is the director of a program which helps rehabilitate addicts and former prisoners.

Multitudes of people, like Richard the pastor and Paul the apostle, have experienced a complete life transformation after receiving the Lord Jesus as their Savior. For it is only by *receiving* God's Son that we gain access into the family of God and defeat the enemy within. Are you aware of this enemy within? When it comes to matters of the spirit, we contend against an evil force that resides outside of our body. That would be Satan, the deceiver of the nations. In this section, we can refer to him as the "enemy without." In Action Step #3, we'll learn how to deal directly with the evil one. But before we can take on our enemy without, we must first defeat the enemy within.

The Fifth Column

During the 1930s, Spain suffered under civil war. The Popular Front, consisting of Communists, Socialists and Republicans, was the standing power. General Francisco Franco led the military revolt. His forces, called the Loyalist Army, was backed by an International Brigade of supporters from many countries, the United States being one of them.

Madrid, Spain's capital city, became the coveted trophy. Whichever army could seize the capital would eventually establish itself as the ruling power over the country. The Battle of Madrid was the most important conflict of the war. After months of deadlock, the city fell to Franco on March 28, 1939. As predicted, that decisive victory led to the establishment of Franco's reign in Spain. When the general was asked how he won the battle, he replied, "the fifth column." Franco had four columns of soldiers warring *outside* the city, and a fifth column of loyalists warring *within* Madrid, who through sabotage crippled the opposing army.

Like Madrid, we too have a force, a "fifth column" warring from within that plots to smother our faith, slay our love for the things above, and sabotage all that we desire to be in the LORD. Unless we respond effectively to defeat this enemy within, we'll have very little success in dealing with the enemy without.

Who is our Enemy Within?

The problem that resides within us all, the enemy within, is what I call the **sin principle**. Sin is a term we don't hear very often these days, not even in our places of worship. It's either ignored or downplayed, but that in no way lessens its power and influence. Former baseball player-turned evangelist Billy Sunday said, "One reason sin flourishes is because it is treated like a cream puff instead of a rattlesnake."

But what exactly is the sin principle? It is the creature saying to the Creator, "You will not rule over me; I will decide how to live my life." The sin principle is my desire to be my own god. It is the opposite of humbling oneself before the LORD. It's my innate drive to be independent of God.

The old deluder whispers, "Forget about God. Live the way you want to live. If you have the might (physical or otherwise), whatever you choose to do is right. No one has the authority to impose their standards upon you, not even God." The sin principle is rebellion against our Maker. It may take the form of open rebellion or passive-aggressive, but it's still rebellion against our Creator. By reading Isaiah 14, we discover this is what caused the downfall of Lucifer.

> How you are fallen from heaven, O Lucifer, son of the morning! How you are cut down to the ground, *you who weakened the nations!* For you have said in your heart: '**I will** ascend into heaven, **I will** exalt my throne above the stars of God; **I will** also sit on the mount of the congregation on the farthest sides of the

north; **I will** ascend above the heights of the clouds, **I will** be like the Most High.' Yet you shall be brought down to Sheol, to the lowest depths of the Pit. ~ *Isaiah 14:12-15 NKJV*

Is this the origin of sin, the original rebellion against our Creator? In the book of Ezekiel, Satan is referred to as the anointed cherub, whose heart was lifted up with pride (Ezekiel 28:11-17). Sin is saying, in words and deeds: "I will be my own boss! I will take control of my life, and I will do as I please!"

One outworking of the sin principle is the theory of evolution. This theory is nothing more than the deluder's attempt to shift man's focus away from our Creator God, the Judge of Eternity. It's shocking how fast this ridiculous lie gained widespread acceptance throughout the "civilized" world. But why was our pleasure-crazed society so eager to embrace the theory of evolution, abandon our belief in God, and reduce the Creator's grandest creation into a mere animal? Because once that's accomplished, then we can suppress the truth that we are ACCOUNTABLE for our actions to our Creator, see Romans 1:18-32. But are we to believe the devil's lie or God's truth, which states: *"Inasmuch as it is appointed for men to die once, and after this, **judgment**"* (Hebrews 9:27)! And...

> *"Fear God and keep his commandments; for this is the whole duty of man. For God will bring every work into **judgment**, with every hidden thing, whether it is good, or whether it is evil."* (Ecclesiastes 12:13-14)!

Adolf Hitler, dictator of the doomed Third Reich, told his Nazi party leaders in a 1928 speech in Munich, "There is only one right in the world and that right is one's own strength." It was the acceptance of the evil lie "might makes right" that resulted in some of man's deadliest acts of inhumanity to man. It was that lie which sanctioned the holocaust, the slave trade, and the extermination of Native Americans. If we teach children that "might makes right" and that they evolved from apes, why are we surprised when they act like animals? GIGO

"But," you ask, "is there really a supreme being whom we refer to as God?" My first response is a watch implies a watchmaker, an automobile implies an auto manufacturer, and an orderly, precise creation implies an orderly and precise Creator. Life on this planet is only possible because we live in an orderly, precise world. We navigate across land, sky and sea because of an orderly constellation. We plant and reap bountiful crops year after year because of an orderly change of seasons. The axial tilt of our planet is about 23.44 degrees. But guess what would happen if the tilt changed by two or three degrees? We would experience drastic climate changes that would adversely impact every living thing on the globe! As our blue planet orbits the sun at 67,000 mph, who keeps the machine running with such precision?

To assert that our orderly world is the result of a disorderly cosmic explosion that happened zillions of years ago, is like saying the novel *To Kill a Mockingbird* was the result of an explosion in Harper Lee's office, and all the words and paragraphs just fell into place perfectly without any aid from an intelligent author. I don't mean to be coy, but to believe that takes more faith than it does to believe Genesis 1:1, "In the beginning God created the heavens and the earth."

Since this Creator God is the "author" of our lives, we owe him our loyalty and worship and our love. His first and greatest commandment is "You shall love the Lord your God with all your heart, and with all your soul, and with all your mind, and with all your strength" (Mark 12:30). But do we love him like that? Have we always been faithful to El Kanna? Do we always put his will above that of our own? **His word manifestly states that we all miss the mark**. "For all have sinned and come short of the glory of God" (Romans 3:23) and "If we say that we have no sin, we deceive ourselves, and the truth is not in us" (1 John 1:8) and "All we like sheep have gone astray" (Isaiah 53:6). The sons and daughters of Adam are a dusty lot, one and all (1 Corinthians 15:47,48 NKJV)!

Sin is universal. No one particular race or nation has a monopoly on iniquity. The Russian novelist and outspoken critic of communism, Aleksandr Solzhenitsyn declares in *The Gulag Archipelago,*

> "If only there were evil people somewhere insidiously committing evil deeds, and it were necessary only to separate them from the rest of us and destroy them. But the line dividing good and evil cuts through the heart of every human being. And who is willing to destroy a piece of his own heart?"

Solzhenitsyn is highlighting the fact that we're all sinners, we're all made of the same stuff. The writer of Proverbs 20:9 poses a question: *Who can say, 'I have made my heart pure. I am clean and without sin?'*

Do you know anyone who's willing to make such an absurd statement? "I've somehow managed to make my wicked heart pure, and now I stand before a holy God *self-cleansed* and without sin."

How to Defeat our Enemy Within

In our world today, we find so many different religions, and denominations within religions, and subsects within denominations. Some of them even make the claim to be the only true way to God. This is confusing to say the least, but a few key observations can shed some light on the topic. A high-level survey of the religions of the world reveal they all have one thing in common, they have their particular creed or philosophy or set of beliefs we should accept in order to find God. Each one is hopeful that their path will lead us to the approval of the Almighty.

Actually, there are no creeds or ceremonies or religious rituals that will grant us the approval we seek. Defeating the enemy within will not happen by joining a particular religious group or denomination, or by embracing some dogma. Why are these things inadequate? **Because they are powerless to cancel or revoke the death sentence we have earned due to our sin.** The Bible says sin carries a wage or sentence. What is that sentence? It's death! "For the wages of sin is death" (Romans 6:23) and "Death passed to all men, because all sinned" (Romans 5:12). This term "death" means separation. Physical death happens when our spirit is separated from our body. Spiritual death occurs when our spirit is separated from God. *Therefore, the ultimate wage or sentence for our sin is eternal separation from God!*

We all stand guilty of cosmic treason and this rebellion carries with it a sentence or wage, which is spiritual death. A religious creed or ritual or sacrament doesn't change the fact that because I've transgressed the laws of God, I have the wages of sin coming my way. Religious acts and sentiments, regardless of how pious or appropriate they appear to be, cannot cancel or nullify the death sentence I've earned because of my sin. There is nothing I can do to annul or revoke my sentence.

I realize the plan for defeating the enemy within has not been cheerful reading thus far, but it does us no good to pretend the sin principle does not exist. King Solomon states, "He who conceals his sins doesn't prosper, but whoever confesses and renounces them finds mercy"

(Proverbs 28:13). The sin principle is lethal, spiritually and eternally lethal, and it behooves us to find a remedy.

Divine law demands that either I receive the wages of my sin, or someone else *(a scapegoat, see Leviticus 16:7-10, 21)* receive them for me. Now consider these two passages from Holy Writ. "But God commends [demonstrates] his own love toward us, in that while we were yet sinners, **Christ died for us**" (Romans 5:8), and "Because Christ also suffered for sins once, **the righteous for the unrighteous**, that he might bring you to God, being put to death in the flesh..." (1 Peter 3:18).

In *Ars Poetica,* the Latin poet Horace established guidelines for writers of tragedies in his day. He said, "Do not bring a god onto the stage, unless the problem is one that deserves a god to solve it." The sin principle has put mankind in such a predicament that only the true and living God can affect our salvation. That's the good news of the Christian faith. The wages of our sin is death, and the Lord of glory left the throne of heaven and took his role on humanity's stage in the person of Jesus Christ, Immanuel - "God with us" - in order to die for us (Matthew 1:22,23; John 1:1; 1 Timothy 3:16)!

If we have any doubt as to why Jesus came, here's the answer in his own words, "Even as the Son of Man came not to be served, but to serve, and to give his life as a ransom for many" (Matthew 20:28). Jesus came into the world to serve a fallen race by receiving the sentence for our sin – to sacrifice his sinless life as a substitute for undeserving sinners like you and me. The righteous for the unrighteous. The beauty for the beast.

Some wonder, "Why did Jesus have to die?" Because according to sacred law, that's the wage or sentence for sin. I'm not here to judge the law, nor will I try to explain why it is what it is. It is what it is! Why does the law of gravity work the way it does? I don't know the *why*, but I do know what it is, and I know I should probably work with the law and not ignore it. I can work with the law of centrifugal force as I drive around the next bend in the road, or not. The law will stand either way. The only question is, will I? To understand *why* the wages of sin is death is not the issue. I just know that's what the Bible declares. Hebrews 9:22 tells us, *"According to the law, nearly everything is cleansed with blood, and apart from shedding of blood there is no remission."* I can agree with the law or not, but either way, there it is: without shedding of blood there is no remission. A remission is the cancelling of a sentence or penalty. Divine law declares without blood or death, there is no remission or cancelling of the penalty of sin.

The ultimate display of God's love is Christ taking his role on humanity's stage in order to incur the punishment for sin on behalf of rebels like you and me. The just [sinless Son of God] dying for the unjust [our sinful, fallen race]. The innocent receiving the sentence for the guilty. *"The punishment that brought our peace was on him"* (Isaiah 53:5). "In this is love, not that we loved God, but that he loved us, and sent his Son as the atoning sacrifice [propitiation] for our sins" (1 John 4:10).

The Divine Dilemma

In 1 John 1:5, we see that "God is light." Jehovah is pure and holy and will not tolerate sin; however, the same book of the Bible tells us that "God is love" (1 John 4:8), meaning he seeks our highest good and longs for a genuine relationship with us. Can the righteous Judge of Eternity commune with us without compromising his holiness and purity? Thus, the divine dilemma.

A God of love desires to fellowship with us, but a God of perfect holiness must punish sin and uphold his righteous law. How can JAH be both merciful to sinners and true to his law? How can God bridge the gap between his righteousness and our sinfulness? The answer in found in the NT meaning of the term "propitiation" or atoning sacrifice.

In the original Greek language of the New Testament, the word translated propitiation is *hilasmos*. It appears just two times in the New Testament, both times in the book of 1st John, (2:2; 4:10). Once you understand its meaning, you'll be well on your way to defeating the enemy within. In classical Greek, the term meant the act of appeasing or pacifying the angry gods. The *hilasmos* was to make void or nullify the action which caused the god to be angry with the individual. The sin offering or propitiation was intended to turn away their anger, remove their disapproval, and mend the relationship.

With that in mind, let's consider 1 John 2:1-2 » "My little children, I write these things to you that you may not sin. If anyone sins, we have a **Counselor** with the Father, Jesus Christ, the righteous. And he is the atoning sacrifice [*hilasmos*] for our sins, and not for ours only, but also for the whole world."

The apostle teaches us that if a believer sins, we have "Jesus Christ, the righteous" as our counselor or advocate who defends us before the Judge of heaven. Jesus mediates and intercedes in order to turn away the Father's wrath and repair the broken relationship. That's humbling and awe-inspiring. Hebrews 7:25 tells us, "Therefore he [Jesus] is also able to save to the uttermost those who draw near to God through him, seeing that he lives forever to make intercession for them."

Satan is our accuser; but *Jesus* is our counselor and advocate, who lives forever to intercede for us! If *Jesus* is for us, who can be against us?

Let's now consider the word again in 1 John 4:7-10 » "Beloved, let's love one another, for love is of God; and everyone who loves has been born of God, and knows God. He who doesn't love doesn't know God, for God is love. *By this* God's love was revealed in us, that God has sent his one and only Son into the world that we might live through him. *In this is love,* not that we loved God, but that he loved us, and sent his Son as the atoning sacrifice [*hilasmos*] for our sins."

Love is a favorite theme of the apostle John. Believers are to love one another, and he goes on to tell us the type of love we should display. It's the same kind of love that God showed us when he sent his Son to die for those who did not love him. The kind of love believers are to display is a love that initiates, that makes a way for the broken relationship to be restored, a love that takes the lead.

> "In this is love, not that we loved God, but that he loved us, and *sent his Son* to be the propitiation for our sins."

When Greek scholar W.E. Vine defines "propitiation" in his work, *Vine's Expository Dictionary of New Testament Words,* he states, "By the giving up of His sinless life sacrificially, Christ annuls the power of sin to separate between God and the believer." Because of Jesus' death, the sinful act of rebellion is nullified, which means to make legally null and void. Our crucified Lord bridged the sin gap between us and our heavenly Father.

NOTE: The NT usage of *hilasmos* is different from classical Greek, in that it is not sinful man who offers the appeasing sacrifice to an angry god. In the Bible, it is God who sent the means of atonement. Therefore, it is not man who offers his sacrifice to God, *because that would equate to man earning or working for salvation*. This is not a plan of redemption that originated with man. God is the initiator and the completer of the plan, "the author and finisher of our faith" (Hebrews 12:2 KJV). Salvation by good works is a concept embraced by many within the church, but salvation by God's amazing grace is more in line with the teaching of the Old and New Testament (see Psalm 103:10-12; 143:2; Romans 3:24-26; 11:6; Ephesians 2:8,9; 2 Timothy 1:8,9; Titus 3:5).

The propitiation or hilasmos, is a PERSON – Jesus Christ himself – who is both *our sin offering* and *our advocate.* He was sacrificed for us; now he lives forever to intercede for us. By his death, Christ annulled (to cancel or make legally invalid) the power of sin to separate God from the repentant sinner (Colossians 2:12-14). On the cross, Jesus endured the hell we deserved. In our place, he suffered separation from the Father, crying out with a loud voice, "My God, my God, why have you forsaken me?"

After the sentence for sin was transferred from us to him, and when the righteous law of God was satisfied, Jesus said, "It is finished." Then he bowed his head and gave up his spirit (John 19:30). The Bible tells us in Matthew 27:51, after Jesus yielded up his spirit, "Behold, the veil of the temple was torn in two from the top to the bottom." The heavy veil of the temple in Jerusalem was ripped, signifying the completion of the OT system of blood sacrifices. It was not ripped from bottom to top, as if it was done by human hands, but from the top to the bottom. Did the Most High God rip it in two? The temple system was a stunning foreshadow of the true and ultimate sacrifice (Hebrews 10:4-14). When our Passover was crucified on Calvary's hill (1 Cor. 5:7), that system was fulfilled, and the divine dilemma was resolved in the person of Jesus Christ. "Behold, the Lamb of God, who takes away the sin of the world" (John 1:29).

Second Corinthians 5:21 summarizes the gospel of grace. "For him [Jesus] *who knew no sin* he [God the Father] *made to be sin on our behalf;* so that in him we might become the righteousness of God." Christ receives our sin; we receive His righteousness. That's amazing grace!

A Picture of Propitiation

It's said that when nomadic tribes roamed Central Africa, the tribe that controlled the best hunting grounds was led by an exceptionally strong and wise chief. This royal African ruled not only because of his bravery and strength, but also because of his uprightness and impartiality. When a series of thefts occurred, the chief announced that when the guilty party is discovered, they will be punished with five stripes or lashes from the tribal whip master.

As the thefts continued, the chief raised the number of stripes to thirty, a severe penalty only few could endure. To everyone's horror, the thief turned out to be the chief's youngest and most beloved son. Immediately, speculation began as to whether or not the chief will actually sentence his son according to the pronounced punishment. Will he give in to his love by excusing the foolish boy, or will he uphold the law by sentencing his son to what will surely be his death?

Loyal to his integrity, the African chief sentenced his son to the thirty stripes. But just before the whip came down on the boy's back, the chief rose from his judgment seat, surrounded his son's frail body with his own, and took upon himself the punishment he had announced for his guilty child. In an infinitely greater measure, King Jesus became our *atoning sacrifice*, receiving upon himself the penalty for our sin.

Seven hundred years before the Messiah was born in Bethlehem, the prophet Isaiah predicted, "But he was pierced for our transgressions. He was crushed for our iniquities. The punishment that brought our peace was on him; and by his wounds we are healed. All we like sheep have gone astray. Everyone has turned to his own way; and Yahweh has laid on him the iniquity of us all" *(Isa. 53:5,6)*. **Fulfilled in Christ!** "For him who knew no sin he made to be sin on our behalf; so that in him we might become the righteousness of God." See also 1 Peter 2:21-25.

When Dr. Harry Ironside served as pastor of Moody Church in Chicago, he would tell the story of a group of pioneers who were making their way across one of the central states to a distant place that had been opened up for homesteading. They traveled in covered wagons drawn by oxen, and progress was necessarily slow. One day they were horrified to notice a long line of smoke in the west, stretching for miles across the open prairie. Soon it was evident that the dry grass was burning fiercely and coming toward them rapidly. They crossed a river the day before, but it would be impossible to go back there before the flames would overtake them. One man only seemed to have an understanding of what could be done. He gave the order to set fire to the grass behind them. When a large enough space was burned over, the whole wagon train moved back on it. As the flames roared toward them from the west, a little girl cried out in terror, "Are you sure we'll not all be burned up?" The wise leader replied,

"My child, the flames cannot reach us here, for we are standing where the fire has been!"

What a picture of the believer: buried with Christ; safe in Christ! God's judgment fires burned themselves out on him, and now, all who are in Christ are forever safe, for we stand where the fire has been.

- *On Him Almighty vengeance fell,*
- *Which would have sunk a world to hell.*
- *He bore it for a chosen race,*
- *And thus becomes our Hiding Place* (Col.3:1-4).

Available but Not Automatic

The cross of Christ is the *one and only bridge* between a holy God and a dusty, sinful people (John 14:6). But does the death and resurrection of Christ mean everyone has already overcome the enemy within? Not exactly. It means victory over both the enemy within and the enemy without is available to us, but it's not automatic.

I love how clear and concise this statement is from 1 John 5:11-12, *"The testimony is this, that God gave to us eternal life, and this life is in his Son. He who has the Son has the life. He who doesn't have God's Son doesn't have the life."* Eternal life is in a PERSON. Those who have the Son have life. Those without the Son are without the life. The life is not in a religion, or a denomination, or a ritual, or any man-made organization.

When the word of God states that eternal life is in a Person, it reveals a truth that is unique to the Christian faith. Other religions of the world insist you must believe something to be saved, but the Bible insists you must receive SOMEONE in order to have eternal life. Biblical Christianity is more than a religion, it's a relationship. It's more than taking in head knowledge from an old book; it's experiencing an actual encounter with our sin offering and advocate. Galatians 2:20 is near and dear to many believers. It states, "I have been crucified with Christ, and it is no longer I who live, but Christ lives in me. That life which I now live in the flesh, I live by faith in the Son of God, who loved me and gave himself for me." That's incredible! Christ gave himself for me. And now, I no longer live for myself, I live for Christ, who lives in me (*see 2 Cor. 5:15*)!

The religious systems of the world say, "Believe our dogma!" The Bible says, "Christ lives in me." That's a significant difference! The religious systems of the world say, "Participate in our ritual." The Bible says, "Christ in you, the hope of glory" (Colossians 1:27), and "He who has the Son has the life." This is where Biblical Christianity separates itself from the religions of the world: "But as many as *received* him, to them he gave the right to become God's children, to those who *believe* in his name" (John 1:12).

After Jesus performed the miracle of feeding thousands, he slipped away to a town across the sea, for he knew the people would try to make him a king. When the crowd found him, Jesus told them, "Don't work for the food which perishes, but for the food which remains to eternal life, which the Son of Man will give to you. ...They said therefore to him, "**What must we do, that we may work the works of God**?" (John 6:27,28). That's a valid request. *"Okay, Jesus. Since you said there's a work of God that remains to [endures to] eternal life, tell us what are the works of God, and we'll do those works!"*

I don't want you to ever forget the answer Jesus gave to this question: What are the works of God that endures to eternal life? You care to take a guess? Some would say do charity work, or go to confession, give money to the cause, pray, read the Bible, be a good person, observe the holy days, visit the sick and shut-in, be a decent citizen, etc. But what did Jesus say? Here's his answer: **"This is the work of God, that you believe in him whom he has sent."** Wow! John 6:29 says the work is to believe! Believing in Jesus is the "work" that remains to eternal life! So says the Holy Bible, see John 3:16. Don't let anyone tell you differently. According to Jesus Christ himself, there is a work we can do that endures to everlasting life, and it's not join a spiritual group or give money or be a good person or pass some sort of religious test or any of those works of our flesh (Psalm 143:2; Galatians 2:16)! The only work that leads to eternal life is believe in the Lord Jesus Christ. But what does that really mean?

> "The true light that enlightens everyone was coming into the world. He was in the world, and the world was made through him, and the world didn't recognize him. He came to his own, and those who were his own didn't receive him. But *as many as received him,* to them he gave the right to become God's children, to those who believe in his name." ~ John 1:9-12

Quick question. According to this passage, who is given the right to become God's children? Is it those who join a religious organization?

Is it those who embrace some secret dogma? Is it those who perform a sacred ritual? No! No! And no again! The Holy Bible says the right to become God's children is given to those who RECEIVE God's Son. You don't need to be in a "religious organization" to do that. It's a personal matter between you and the Most High God. No middleman necessary. All you need is the glorious gospel message and a mustard seed worth of faith.

In his devotional, *Let Your Spirit Soar*, Dr. C. S. Lovett expounds on John 1:11-12, "Whereas the nation of Israel barred Christ from His own land and house, some individuals welcomed Him into their hearts. They became His possession, their hearts His temple. John tells us how they did this. They deposited their complete trust in His name. This Greek word 'Name' sums up all that Jesus is, and said, as well as the revelation of God concentrated in Him. This is a faith in His PERSON, not in FACTS ABOUT Him. Not intellectual assent to His words, but a commitment to Jesus Himself. In an individual with this kind of faith, Christ finds a place to dwell and someone to be His very own!"

Believe and Receive

So, what does it mean to believe in his name? We believe in his 'Name' by receiving his Person. Let me illustrate. Suppose we were best friends and I came over to your new home. Imagine I'm holding a lovely housewarming gift as I walk through your front door. Then I say: "Congratulations on the new house, I want you to have this." I extend my arms to give you the gift. But your hands are still at your side and I'm holding your gift out in front of you. End of scene.

Okay, if I were to make such a gesture, would you *believe* I was offering you the gift? Probably so. Although you believe I was offering you this free gift, at the end of the scene, did you *possess* it? I think not. As long as your hands are at your side, and as long as the gift is in my hands, you do not have it. It is not until you reach out your hands and *receive* the gift from my hands that you actually have it.

Many people believe a lot about the Christ: his virgin birth, his sinless life, his death on the cross, his resurrection from the dead and even his ascension into heaven. But some of these same people will not enter heaven themselves because they haven't *received* the Lord Jesus Christ. Sure, they believe "in" him like they believe in other historical figures such as George Washington, Sojourner Truth and Socrates. But such head knowledge is not the same as the heart transformation that occurs after receiving the risen, living LORD. "He who has the Son has the life. He who doesn't have God's Son doesn't have the life."

God is not the author of confusion, and the Bible is unambiguous concerning the matter of salvation. It is the receiving, the possessing of the Savior, that results in defeating the enemy within. Victory is not in just believing facts about the Savior. Victory is in receiving the Victor. Many people *profess* Christ is the Savior of the world, but the real change occurs when you *possess* Christ as your personal Savior. "Christ lives **in** me" (Galatians 2:20). "Christ **in** you, the hope of glory" (Colossians 1:27). "Greater is he who is **in** you than he who is in the world" (1 John 4:4). "**Examine your own selves,** whether you are in the faith. **Test your own selves.** Or don't you know about your own selves, that Jesus Christ is **in** you?" (2 Corinthians 13:5).

If you haven't received the risen Lord Jesus Christ as your personal Savior, he stands knocking at the door of your heart. He asks that you open the door and invite him into your life. It's a beautiful offer. Not an offer to embrace a religion or a creed, but an offer to have a *relationship* with the Son of God. It's an offer to have *fellowship* with the Lord Jesus Christ by the agency of his Holy Spirit. This is far more than a creed, or a religion, or a set of rules.

The Holy Bible is true and clear: "If we confess our sins, he is faithful and just to forgive us our sins, and to cleanse us from all unrighteousness" (1 John 1:9). "For, 'Whoever will call on the name of the Lord will be saved' " (Romans 10:13). Are you wondering if this can be real? It's easy enough to confirm. Just as you would open the door of your home to a friend's knock, open your heart to the true and living Savior right now. Say to God in sincere prayer:

Dear Lord God, be merciful to me, a sinner. I'm sorry that I rebelled against you. Thank You for loving me so much that You sent the Lord Jesus to die for my sins. I believe You raised Him from the dead and that Jesus is alive. I believe that He is standing at the door of my heart. As best I know how, I open my heart to Jesus, I invite Him to come in. By faith, I receive the Son and I receive the Life. I repent of my sins and I ask now that you forgive me of my sins. May His life be my life, may His triumph over death be my triumph over death. Thank you Lord, for the victory over sin, self and Satan. In Jesus' name I pray, Amen.

Action Step #3. Resist God's Enemy

"The devil has the people by the throat!"

If you enjoy old movies, you may recall where that line comes from. In *Casablanca*, the lovely refugee and newlywed Annina tells the hero Rick, "We come from Bulgaria. Things are very bad there. The devil has the people by the throat!" It's a line that stays with you long after the movie is over. Such a graphic and violent image of the evil one squeezing the life out of his victim.

But it's not just the poor souls from Bulgaria who are being choked out by the old serpent. The devil has the people of America by the throat also. That's true, because according to Scripture, the devil has the people of every country by the throat! First John 5:19 says, "the whole world lies in the power of the evil one."

Therefore, after a person defeats the enemy within by receiving God's Son, he or she must quickly learn to resist the enemy without. The Bible refers to our walk with the Lord as fighting "the good fight of faith" (1 Timothy 6:12). Being a victorious believer is not for the faint of heart. "You therefore must endure hardship as a good soldier of Christ Jesus" (2 Timothy 2:3).

The word of God shares with us an impressive concept in James 4:7, **"Resist the devil, and he will flee from you."** Isn't that a striking verse of Scripture! It's easy to understand, but is it easy to apply? One reason many believers fail to experience the full force of this verse is because we ignore the context in which the verse is found. When it comes to proper scriptural interpretation, context is king. What comes before the verse? What comes after the verse? Who is the intended audience?

If we back up a few verses, we see Brother James is warning us about getting friendly with the world. For he who "wants to be a friend of the world makes himself an enemy of God." Since Satan is the god of this world, friendship with the world is siding with Satan and aligning against God. So how can we stand firm in our faith and serve the Lord in this world? The passage teaches us, *"But he gives more grace. Therefore it says, 'God resists the proud, but gives grace to the humble.' "* We stand strong in this world, first and foremost, by God's grace. In 2 Timothy 2:1, we are told to "be strengthened in the grace that is in Christ Jesus." That's an interesting possibility. How is one "strengthened" in grace? It sounds paradoxical. And so it is, because God's grace is bestowed upon the humble. We are *strengthened* in grace by being *humble*. Proverbs 3:34 says, "Surely he mocks the mockers, but he gives grace to the humble." Through humility, we are strengthened in the grace that is in Christ Jesus.

Before we're told to resist the devil, we're told to be subject to God. Humbling ourselves before the Almighty is a prerequisite to resisting the devil. It's another way of saying I'm powerless to resist the devil if I'm not strengthened in God's grace. And to make sure the point is clear, the Spirit follows the "resist the devil" verse with this, "Draw near to God, and he will draw near to you." Please notice that sandwiched around "Resist the devil and he will flee from you" is, the top bun - "**Be subject therefore to God**" and then the bottom bun - "**Draw near to God, and he will draw near to you**." Context is key. If I'm to successfully resist the devil, I must subject myself to God, and draw near to him. If I'm walking in pride, God will resist me, and the devil will eat my lunch!

Humility is a key factor in our victory over the enemy. We don't fight the good fight of faith through the power of the flesh. Brother A.W. Tozer said, "The devil can handle me – he's got judo I never heard of. But he can't handle the One to whom I'm joined; he can't handle the One to whom I'm united. So I'm not afraid of the devil."

The Greater One lives within me (1 John 4:4)! The devil knows judo, but the One who lives in me and fights for me knows judo, karate, boxing, kung fu, jiu-jitsu and jeet kune do. KIAI! But riddle me this, Grasshopper: *What happens when the One who fights for me turns his back on me because I've offended him?* How successful will I be against the devil's judo then? How successful will I be when I confront the forces of spiritual darkness armed with only human resources?

The secret to having the devil flee from you is having God near you. The key to having God near you is making sure his word dwells in you richly. You're filled with his Holy Spirit/his Holy Presence as you're filled with his Holy Word! Therefore, we are to meditate on it day and night. Per Psalm 1, we're to delight ourselves in the law of the LORD, to saturate our minds and spirits with the truth of Scripture. I enjoy listening to the spoken Word on my smartphone and TV. Alexander Scourby reads through the entire KJV Bible on DVD in about 70 hours. I love it! America has to rediscover God's Word. As we draw near to the Word, we draw near to God. As we draw near to God, He draws near to us.

After James tells us that God will draw near to us as we draw near to him, the very next thing the Word states is: "Cleanse your hands, you sinners. Purify your hearts, you double-minded." *Close proximity to the LORD demands holiness!* And I'll give you one guess as to the agent God uses to cleanse our hands and purify our hearts. Listen in as Jesus prays for his followers.

> "I have given them your word. The world hated them, because they are not of the world, even as I am not of the world. *I pray not that you would take them from the world, but that you would keep them from the evil one.* They are not of the world even as I am not of the world. **Sanctify them in your truth. Your word is truth.** As you sent me into the world, even so I have sent them into the world." ~ *John 17:14-18*

I think this is fascinating. Jesus prays that we not be taken from the world. Why not? Because believers have a job to do in this world! As the Father sent the Son, the Son sends us. Why did the Father send the Son? To seek and save the lost. Why does the Son send us? To do the same. But as we serve our Lord in the world, how do we keep ourselves unspotted from the world (James 1:27)? Can we really be *in* the world, but not *of* the world? Can dust be holy?

Jesus prayed to the Father that we be sanctified (cleansed and set apart from the world). How does this happen? Jesus prayed, "Sanctify them in your truth. Your word is truth." The word of God is the sanctifying agent of God. *"How can a young man cleanse his way? By taking heed according to Your word"* (Psalm 119:9 NKJV). The word of truth enables us to cleanse our hands and purify our hearts. By walking in the light of the word, I can be confident that God walks with me. But if I'm not submitting to and walking in the revealed truth of God's word, he will not walk with me (Amos 3:3). Or, one could say, we part ways when I disregard his word. Disobedience interrupts our fellowship with God (Isaiah 59:2).

If God and I have parted ways, then he's not near me. If he's not near me, Satan will not flee from me. "Me" alone is easy pickings for the great dragon. It's not "me" that causes the enemy to flee, but the light of Christ within me that dispels the prince of darkness (Acts 19:11-16). Spirit-filled believers have no fear of the evil one. Why not? Because the Spirit of God within us fights for us. Our faithful and jealous lover lives within, standing guard, protecting his own. If Satan wants to get to me, he has to go through the Lord Christ Jesus. Because not only is Christ in me, I'm also in Christ. This concept of Gentile believers being "in Christ" is a mystery...

> "which in other generations was not made known to the children of men, as it has now been revealed to his holy apostles and prophets *in the Spirit*, that the Gentiles are **fellow** heirs and **fellow** members of the body, and **fellow** partakers of his promise *in* Christ Jesus through the Good News." ~ *Ephesians 3:5-6*

By means of the gospel, Gentiles are "in Christ" and "fellow members of the body." There was a time when Gentiles were "*separate* from Christ, *alienated* from the commonwealth of Israel, and *strangers* from the covenants of the promise, having no hope and without God in the world. But now in Christ Jesus you who once were far off are made near in the blood of Christ" (Ephesians 2:12,13). Glory to God!

The prince of this world has no authority over us because we're in Christ. This is a foundational truth all believers must understand. Our LORD has been exalted high above all things, so all things are under his feet. *Therefore, in Christ Jesus, all things are under our feet, even death itself.* "For as in Adam all die, so also in Christ all will be made alive" (1 Cor. 15:22)! Listen to how Paul prays for the believers at Ephesus. He wants them (and us) to understand Christ's position in heaven and our position in Christ. Please read slowly and prayerfully (Psalm 119:18). The apostle pleads earnestly in one amazing, mind-expanding, faith-building sentence:

> "That the God of our Lord Jesus Christ, the Father of glory, may give unto you the spirit of wisdom and revelation in the knowledge of him: **the eyes of your understanding being enlightened**; that ye may know what is the hope of his calling, and what the riches of the glory of his inheritance in the saints, and what is the exceeding greatness of his power to us-ward who believe, according to the working of his mighty power, which he wrought in Christ, **when he raised him from the dead, and set him at his own right hand in the heavenly places**, far above all principality, and power, and might, and dominion, and every name that is named, not only in this world, but also in that which is to come: and **hath put all things under his feet,** and gave him to be the head over all things to the church, which is his body." ~ *Ephesians 1:17-23 KJV*

Jesus Christ is Lord over all! He sits at the right hand of the Father, far above all principality and power. All things have been put under his feet. Believers are in Christ. Therefore, in Christ all things are under our feet. The Spirit teaches us in Ephesians 2:5-6, “By grace you have been saved – and [God] raised us up with him, and made us to sit with him in the heavenly places in Christ Jesus.” Wow!

As co-workers and co-heirs with Christ, we must understand the concept of being “in Christ” (2 Cor. 5:14-21). To be ‘in Christ” means we associate with Christ, we connect ourselves to Christ, *we equate his experience as that of our own.* For instance, **We died with Christ:** “Don’t you know that all we who were baptized into Christ Jesus were baptized into his death?” (Romans 6:3). **We were buried and raised with Christ:** “We were buried therefore with him through baptism into death, that just as Christ was raised from the dead through the glory of the Father, so we also might walk in newness of life” (Romans 6:4). **We reign with Christ:** “[God] raised us up with him, and made us to sit with him in the heavenly places in Christ Jesus” (Ephesians 2:6). **We are dead to sin and alive to God in Christ:** “But if we died with Christ, we believe that we will also live with him.” “Thus consider [reckon] yourselves also to be dead to sin, but alive to God in Christ Jesus our Lord” (Romans 6:8, 11). Consider yourself dead to sin and reckon yourself alive to God in Christ! That’s powerful! As we look to our glorious Savior, we’re “transformed into the *same image* from glory to glory” (2 Cor. 3:18).

Our true identity is not in our race, or our gender, or our age, or our heritage, or our nationality. Our true and eternal identity is in Christ Jesus our LORD. *We are what his eternal Word says we are!* Faith concludes what JAH declares. If he *says* we are citizens of heaven (Philippians 3:20), so be it! If he *declares* we belong to him because we were bought with a prize (1 Corinthians 6:20), Amen! If he *says* we’re his fellow workers (1 Corinthians 3:9), then let’s get to work! If JAH *declares* that we’re anointed with power to witness for Christ (Acts 1:8), then “Breathe on me, breath of God, fill me with life anew, that I may love the way you love, and do what you would do!” If the God of heaven *says* we have eternal life because we have the Son (1 John 5:12), then let God be true and all men liars! If the LORD of hosts *says* we overcome “because greater is he who is in [us] than he who is in the world” (1 John 4:4), then let’s stand on the authority of the Holy Word of God! Once we understand our high position in Christ, and the vital role humility plays in our victory over the evil one, then we are ready to resist the devil.

Satan likes to operate in secret, behind the curtain, so to speak. The evil one works in disguise, but believers are not ignorant of his tricks. One of the devil's most effective cons is disguising his ideas as those of our own. Brain specialist Dr. Daniel Amen advises, "Don't believe everything you hear – even in your own mind." Satan works at the level of our thoughts (Isaiah 55:7; 2 Cor. 10:4,5). He sows ideas and suggestions in our mind without us realizing the real source of those ideas. Once we act on them, we fall into his trap. That has to be the epitome of deception! *Satan, the master deceiver, plants thoughts in your mind that are disguised as your own thoughts.* Note the following three examples.

1 Chronicles 21:1 » "And Satan stood up against Israel, and provoked David to number Israel."

Matthew 16:21-23 » From that time, Jesus began to show his disciples that he must go to Jerusalem and suffer many things from the elders, chief priests, and scribes, and be killed, and the third day be raised up. Peter took him aside and began to rebuke him, saying, "Far be it from you, Lord! This will never be done to you." But he turned and said to Peter, "Get behind me, Satan! You are a stumbling block to me, for you are not setting your mind on the things of God, but on the things of men."

Acts 5:3 » But Peter said, "Ananias, why has Satan filled your heart to lie to the Holy Spirit and to keep back part of the price of the land?"

Do you see the master deceiver at work? David had an *idea* to count the number of soldiers he had in his army. Peter had the *idea* to rebuke Jesus for talking about dying. Ananias had the *idea* to keep back part of the money he made by selling his land. In each case, Satan planted a suggestion in the mind of his victim that was disguised as their very own thought. Why? **Because the thought is father to the deed**. Bad thoughts father bad deeds; good thoughts produce good deeds. Notice it was Peter who detected the enemy's work within Ananias. Maybe Peter discerned the devil's handiwork because he was deceived earlier in a similar fashion. The evil one will definitely try to lead you astray, the same way he led poor Pahom astray, one suggestion at a time.

There's an old saying that may be helpful at this point. *"You can't stop the birds from flying over your head, but you can prevent them from building a nest in your hair."* Satan will tempt you by dropping suggestions into your mind. You can't stop that. You're not a "bad person" just because the enemy dropped a wicked thought in your head. *But you are responsible*, in the authority given by Christ, to expel those thoughts! That's what it means to resist the devil, and the Bible shows us how in the book of Matthew 4:1-11. Watch and learn from our Sensei (Matt.11:29) as he wields the sword of the Spirit to resist the evil one.

> Then Jesus was led up by the Spirit into the wilderness to be tempted by the devil. When he had fasted forty days and forty nights, he was hungry afterward. The tempter came and said to him, "If you are the Son of God, command that these stones become bread." But he answered, "**It is written**, 'Man shall not live by bread alone, but by every word that proceeds out of God's mouth.' "
>
> Then the devil took him into the holy city. He set him on the pinnacle of the temple, and said to him, "If you are the Son of God, throw yourself down, for it is written, 'He will command his angels concerning you,' and, 'On their hands they will bear you up, so that you don't dash your foot against a stone.' "
>
> Jesus said to him, "Again, **it is written**, 'You shall not test the Lord, your God.' " Again, the devil took him to an exceedingly high mountain, and showed him all the kingdoms of the world and their glory. He said to him, "I will give you all of these things, if you will fall down and worship me."
>
> Then Jesus said to him, "Get behind me, Satan! For **it is written**, 'You shall worship the Lord your God, and you shall serve him only.' " Then the devil left him, and behold, angels came and served him.

I'm sure you noticed that every time the devil attacked Christ with a temptation, Jesus countered the lies by quoting Holy Scripture. That's part of the idea behind "resist the devil." It means to be steadfast in the faith, to live a holy life. It entails counter-attacking the devil's lies with the holy truth of God. We dispel the darkness of Satan with the light of the word. But once again, answer me this: If we overcome the tempter by quoting Scripture, how effective can I be if I'm *ignorant* of Scripture? How effective can I be if I'm *skeptical* of Scripture? It's no surprise that Satan constantly attacks the Bible. Without a working knowledge of divine revelation, we become easy prey for the master deceiver.

In the first temptation, Satan is attempting to take advantage of the fact that Jesus is hungry. "If you are the Son of God, command that these stones become bread." How does Jesus respond? The Spirit of God uploads to his mind a verse from Deuteronomy 8:3. The entire verse reads, "He humbled you, allowed you to be hungry, and fed you with manna, which you didn't know, neither did your fathers know, that he might *teach you* that man does not live by bread only, but man lives by every word that proceeds out of Yahweh's mouth."

In this passage, we learn that during Israel's 40-year wilderness experience, God provided the nation with food (manna) previously unknown to them (Exodus 16). This food was provided daily, except on the Sabbath, **by the command or word of God**. One could say it was not the physical bread that sustained the people in the wilderness, but the "*word that proceeds out of Yahweh's mouth*." The lesson to be gained is God allowed the nation to hunger in order that they might learn to trust in him – not just for their daily bread, but for all their needs. This verse is the perfect counter for the temptation to "command stones to become bread." A good God provides sustenance that meets both our physical and our spiritual needs. Also note Jesus didn't need to quote the reference nor the entire passage, just the part that related to the situation.

In the second temptation, Satan wants Jesus to throw himself off the pinnacle of the temple. The Jewish historian Josephus claims this was a fall of over 400 feet. In this second attack, Satan uses Scripture in his attempt to trick our LORD. Did the devil forget that Jesus is the Word that "became flesh, and lived among us" (John 1:14)? How foolhardy of the evil one to think he could twist the Scriptures on the One who is the embodiment of Scripture! The devil quotes from Psalm 91:11,12. "For he will put his angels in charge of you, to guard you in all your ways. They will bear you up in their hands, so that you won't dash your foot against a stone."

In *The Merchant of Venice,* the bard states, "The devil can cite Scripture for his own purpose." The verses he quotes in Psalm 91 speaks to the promise of angelic protection, but Satan is twisting it to justify putting God to some sort of test. The passage is about *trusting* God, not *testing* God. There's a big difference in the two, which Satan knows full well. However, the evil one was still willing to cite Scripture for his own purpose. The takeaway here is: *Do I know my Bible well enough to detect when it's being twisted?*

Jesus counters the lie of Satan with another passage from the book of Deuteronomy, chapter 6, verse 16: "You shall not tempt Yahweh your God, as you tempted him in Massah." Back in Exodus 17, the nation of Israel contended with Moses. They were "almost ready" to stone him in the wilderness because of the lack of water. In verses 5-7, "Yahweh said to Moses...'You shall strike the rock, and water will come out of it, that the people may drink.' Moses did so in the sight of the elders of Israel. He called the name of the place Massah, and Meribah, because the children of Israel quarreled, and because they tested Yahweh, saying, 'Is Yahweh among us, or not?' " The word Massah means *testing,* and Meribah means *contending.* Unlike the fickle children of Abraham, the son of God didn't contend with or test Yahweh during his wilderness experience.

In the third temptation, Satan offered our Lord all the kingdoms of the world if Jesus would, get this! – "fall down and worship me." The audacity of the old dust eater to ask the Lord of glory to fall down and worship him! Satan's pride knows no bounds. In Isaiah 14:13-14, we see the five foolish "I wills" of Lucifer. He said in his heart, "**I will** ascend into heaven! **I will** exalt my throne above the stars of God! **I will** sit on the mountain of assembly, in the far north! **I will** ascend above the heights of the clouds! **I will** make myself like the Most High!"

In Ezekiel 28, we note that he was the anointed cherub who was full of *wisdom*, and perfect in *beauty*. But verse 14 reveals, "Your heart was lifted up because of your *beauty*. You have corrupted your *wisdom* by reason of your splendor." When the apostle lays out the qualifications for spiritual leadership in the local church, he points out in 1 Timothy 3:6, "Not a novice, lest being lifted up with pride he fall into the condemnation of the devil." That's the KJV. In the WEB, it reads, "Not a new convert, lest being puffed up he fall into the *same* condemnation as the devil." The condemnation of the devil was due to pride because of his elevated position, and his wisdom, and his beauty. The height of pride is asking your Creator to fall down and worship you! That's the insane spirit of Satan.

In his exhaustive work, *Willmington's Guide to the Bible*, my first "real" teacher of Scripture, Dr. Harold L. Willmington writes, "It is revealing to note the name of God that Satan uses here. He wanted to be like EL-ELYON, the Most High. This name literally means, "the strongest strong one." The devil could have picked other names for God. He could have used EL-SHADDAI, which means, "the breasted one, the one who feeds His children," but he didn't. He might have selected JEHOVAH-ROHI, which means, "the shepherd God," but he avoided this title also. The reason is obvious – Satan coveted God's strength, but was not the least bit interested in His feeding and leading attributes!"

The condemnation of the devil was due to his desire for more power and status. This beautiful and splendid creation of God, who was, I dare say - fearfully and wonderfully made - wanted to be God. He was not content to be a high-ranking angelic being. He wanted to be like the Most High, EL-ELYON, the strongest strong one. How can the "little g" god of this world even think to ask the "Big G" God of all worlds to fall down and worship him? That's crazified! You don't want any part of his foul spirit.

At this point, I guess our Lord had enough, for then Jesus said to him, "Get behind me, Satan!" and he counter-attacks the lie with the truth of God – **the sword of the Spirit**: "For it is written, 'You shall worship the Lord your God, and you shall serve him only.' " For the third time in a row, our Lord and Teacher quotes from Deuteronomy. Apparently, Jesus familiarized himself with that book and Israel's wilderness experience (Luke 2:40-52). According to 1 Corinthians 10:1-12, it behooves us to do likewise.

This time Jesus cites and paraphrases from Deuteronomy 6, verses 13 and 14. "You shall fear Yahweh your God; and you shall serve him, and shall swear by his name. You shall not go after other gods, of the gods of the peoples who are around you." And even though Jesus didn't include the next verse in his counter-attack, please note verse 15, "For Yahweh your God among you is a *jealous God*, lest the anger of Yahweh your God be kindled against you, and he destroy you from off the face of the earth."

After Jesus tells "little g" to get lost, "then the devil left him, and behold, angels came and served him." We should be grateful to God for this demonstration of how to resist our enemy. Jesus resisted by using the sword of the Spirit to counter Satan's deception with God's truth! In each and every encounter with Satan's lies, Jesus quoted and paraphrased verses that related directly to the specific temptation. He didn't entertain the devil's lies, he immediately refuted them with eternal truth. He didn't hold a debate with Satan. He certainly didn't act on the suggestion of the devil. Our humble Master, meek and lowly in heart, relied solely on the word of God to defeat and banish the enemy.

Believers are in an age-old war against Satan and his seed (Genesis 3:14,15). In light of that fact, we should know well these two passages.

~§~

"Finally, be strong in the Lord, and in the strength of his might. Put on the whole armor of God, that you may be able to stand against the wiles of the devil. For our wrestling is not against flesh and blood, but against the principalities, against the powers, against the world's rulers of the darkness of this age, and against the spiritual forces of wickedness in the heavenly places. Therefore put on the **whole armor of God**, that you may be able to withstand in the evil day, and having done all, to stand. Stand therefore, having the **utility belt of truth** buckled around your waist, and having put on the **breastplate of righteousness**, and having fitted your feet with the preparation of the **Good News of peace**, above all, taking up the **shield of faith**, with which you will be able to quench all the fiery darts of the evil one. And take the **helmet of salvation**, and **the sword of the Spirit**, which is the word of God." *~ Ephesians 6:10-17*

"For though we walk in the flesh, we don't wage war according to the flesh; for the *weapons of our warfare* are not of the flesh, but mighty before God to the throwing down of strongholds, throwing down imaginations and every high thing that is exalted against the knowledge of God and bringing every thought into captivity to the obedience of Christ." *~ 2 Corinthians 10:3-6*

When we gear up for spiritual battle and "put on the Lord Jesus Christ," the weapons of our warfare are mighty before God (Rom. 13:11-14; 1 Cor. 10:12,13; Phil. 3:12-14)! With these weapons we are empowered to throw down strongholds, and wicked imaginations, and every high thing that is exalted against the knowledge of God. But what's a stronghold?

A stronghold is where the enemy has dug in and secured a place to operate in our lives. A stronghold could be a rebellious spirit that resists authority. It could be a lustful spirit, or a lazy spirit, or a lying spirit. It could be an inordinate attraction to the same sex, or an addiction to gambling or pornography or drugs. It can be anything that hinders us from running full stride after the things of God. We've been called to "lay aside **every weight** and the sin which so easily entangles us, and let's run with perseverance the race that is set before us" (Hebrews 12:1).

God told Jeremiah that his word is like fire and like a hammer that breaks the rock in pieces (Jeremiah 23:29)! In the authority of the rediscovered word of God, King Josiah burned down the idols and "broke down the altars" from the high places that were erected by the old kings of Judah. Listen up, saints! No altars to sin that were set up by the "old me" can hold up against the hammer of God! No stronghold I've allowed the enemy to establish in my flesh can withstand the flamethrower of Yahweh! I cast down wicked imaginations, and EVERY high thing that seeks to overthrow the reign of King Jesus! My flesh is weak against Satan, but the "new me" in Christ is formidable with a flaming sword in my hand!

Well-trained soldiers of the cross fight off the devil with the word of God. We know "death and life are in the power of the tongue" (Proverbs 18:21). When Satan comes at us with his sorry old lies, we strike hard and fast with the sword of the Spirit: "Get back, Satan! For it is written..." And when we detect any strongholds of the enemy wedged deep within our dumb flesh, we rely on the flamethrower of Yahweh and the jackhammer of God to break down and burn down everything that exalts itself against what we know is true about God and his word and his people!

Allow me to emphasize one more point before we move into our fourth action step. Jesus said to his disciples in John 14:25-26, "I have said these things to you while still living with you. But the Counselor, the Holy Spirit, whom the Father will send in my name, will teach you all things, and will remind you of all that I said to you." One key role of the Spirit is to remind us of the word of God. When the devil attacks with a temptation, the Holy Spirit quickly goes through our mental file cabinet to retrieve and upload the verse we then use to refute the lie.

Let's say I find a wallet in the restroom at work. I open it and see it contains $500. Satan drops a suggestion that's cleverly disguised as my own thought. "Finders keepers! I sure can use this money. What a blessing! I'll just take this cash and leave the wallet where I found it." But in a flash, the Holy Spirit reminds me, "Don't steal. For God can supply all your needs according to his riches in glory." The light of God shines through and I stand firm in the faith. "Be gone, Satan! Take your dirty lies with you. For it is written, 'You shall not steal' and 'Let him that stole steal no more.' "

Suppose an attractive co-worker hints at the possibility of some after-work "fun." Even though I'm in a committed relationship, the suggestion floats into my mind, "I think she's really into me. Maybe I should see where this leads." And then in a flash, the Holy Spirit reminds me, "Flee from youthful lust, and pursue righteousness." The light of God shines through again and I stand firm in the faith. "Get behind me, Satan! For it is written, 'Flee fornication' and 'Be holy, for I am holy.' "

A major role of our Counselor, the Holy Spirit, is to remind us of what the Bible says about any particular situation. The Spirit fingers through our mental files to pull the right verse to use at the right time. But what happens if the Spirit of God checks out my mental file cabinet only to discover the files are mostly empty? Can he upload a verse that's not in my files? Can he *remind* me of Bible verses that I haven't hidden in my heart?

I'm not sure the Holy Spirit can remind me of something I didn't take the time to learn in the first place. The dove of heaven doesn't pull verses out of thin air! The point being, how can I use God's word to resist God's enemy if I don't know God's word? As God's co-worker, I must do my part. I must learn the truth. Truth = freedom; ignorance = bondage!

The word of God is your sword of the Spirit. Are you wielding a sword or a butter knife? Over time, as you meditate on and memorize more verses from the Bible, your swordplay skills are sharpened. I would encourage you to spend some time in Psalm 119. The entire chapter, all 176 verses, is focused on exalting the word of the LORD! Consider *Psalm 119:11,* "I have hidden your word in my heart, that I might not sin against you." *And verse 47,* "I will delight myself in your commandments, because I love them." *And verse 72,* "The law of your mouth is better to me than thousands of pieces of gold and silver." *And verse 93,* "I will never forget your precepts, for with them, you have revived me." *And verse 97,* "How I love your law! It is my meditation all day." *And verse 111,* "I have taken your testimonies as a heritage forever, for they are the joy of my heart." *And I cherish verse 133,* "**Establish my footsteps in your word. Don't let any iniquity have dominion over me**."

~§~

"So then, my beloved brethren, let every man be swift to hear, slow to speak, slow to wrath; for the wrath of man does not produce the righteousness of God. Therefore lay aside all filthiness and overflow of wickedness, and receive with meekness the implanted word, which is able to save your souls. But be doers of the word, and not hearers only, deceiving yourselves." *~ James 1:19-22 NKJV*

Action Step #4. Release God's Gifts

In preparation for revival in America, we must rediscover God's Word, receive God's Son, and we must resist God's Enemy. Our fourth action step is: **Release God's Gifts**.

When the church is anointed with fresh oil (Psalm 92:10), the gifts of the Spirit will ignite within believers everywhere. It's important to expect this and not freak out. Moving in the power of God is thrilling and different and it can be a little scary, so let's go to the Bible for guidance.

Looking at 1 Thessalonians 5:19-22, starting with verse 19. If you want to memorize Scripture (and we all should), this is a good one. Only four words. *"Don't quench the Spirit."* I love the imagery. God's Spirit is like fire, so don't douse the flames. Don't throw a bucket of fear and unbelief on the flames of the Holy Spirit! As the gifts of the Spirit start to spark, don't suppress them, expect them.

Verse 20. *"Don't despise prophecies."* Only three words, even better! The gift of prophecy is one of many mentioned in Romans 12 and 1 Corinthians 12. Don't despise it. More to come about this gift.

Verse 21. *"Test all things, and hold firmly that which is good."* Comparing Scripture with Scripture, we can go to 1 John 4:1 which says, "Beloved, don't believe every spirit, but test the spirits, whether they are of God." Some spirits are not of God. Not all teaching regarding matters of the spirit is of God, see 2 Corinthians 11:3-4. Therefore, we're told to test the spirits. How? By what standard? With what rule?

Jesus said, *"Heaven and earth will pass away, but my words will by no means pass away"* (Luke 21:33). We test everything by the eternal word of God (Psalm 33:11). Why would I test by anything else? Would I test by popular opinion? I hope not! What's popular today changes with the wind. Would I test by scientific inquiry? Only after science can mimic the life-force that waits to spring from a mustard seed. Would I test by spirits? I dare not, "for Satan himself is transformed into an angel of light" (2 Corinthians 11:14). We don't test by man or angels, but by the word of God. "Your word is a lamp to my feet, and a light for my path" (Psalm 119:105). "The entrance of your words gives light. It gives understanding to the simple" (Psalm 119:130). We will steer clear of snares as long as our steps are guided by the light of God's word.

"Test all things and hold firmly that which is good." If the test comes back okay, and everything is in line with Scripture, like we see in Acts 15:12-15, then we hold firmly to what God is doing through the Spirit, even as he moves us beyond our comfort zones.

Verse 22, *"Abstain from every form of evil" (WEB)*. Or, *"Abstain from all appearance of evil" (KJV)*. The Spirit of God is holy. Anything that hints of lust or carnality is not of the Holy Spirit. "God is light, and in him is no darkness at all" (1 John 1:5), and "Have no fellowship with the unfruitful deeds of darkness, but rather reprove them" (Ephesians 5:11). Satan counterfeits the gifts of the Spirit. Discernment is necessary. But once we have the green light from Scripture, we must move forward.

Christianity is not a spectator event. All the members of the body have an essential role to play. In 1 Corinthians 12, the Spirit actually uses the human body to teach us how spiritual gifts function in the church. A human being has one body obviously, but our one body is made up of many vital systems that perform different functions. We have our respiratory system, our nervous system, a digestive system, and so forth. The systems don't do the same job, but their role is vital to the overall health of our body. The diverse systems are designed to work in harmony for the benefit of the one body. It's the principle of *unity in diversity*.

Likewise, the church of Christ is one body, but it's made up of many "members" or persons. These members don't all have the same function. Each member receives a spiritual gift or specialty that functions in harmony with other gifts to build up the body of Christ. Or, one could say the church is a team. On any team, members work toward a common goal or objective. Their aim is the same. That's the unity part. On that same team, however, the members play different positions. Not all eleven defensive players on a football team will line up in the cornerback position. That's the diversity part. Effective teams are united in their aim, but members play diverse positions or roles. Unity in diversity.

Same principle applies in the military. All US soldiers are in the same army with the same objective, but not all soldiers have the same MOS (military occupational specialty). My MOS was 11B, infantry or foot soldier. When my father was in the service, he was a heavy equipment operator in France. Some soldiers fly airplanes. My daring daughter was a soldier who jumped out of airplanes! My two sons were soldiers who trained in the field of communication. Likewise, believers are in the same army with the same objective, but we don't all have the same SOS (spiritual occupational specialty).

According to God's ingenious design, all partakers of his promise have a job to do, a position to play, a role to fill. When we receive the Son, the Holy Spirit gives us a special ability that's anointed and empowered for the purpose of advancing the Kingdom. This is where the action is. This is where God's power flows through us to edify the saints and reach the lost. *This is where you want to be.*

In our brief overview of the history of Israel, we saw both the prophet and the prophetess. I want to highlight the prophetess because the church often downplays the role of women in the kingdom. But is God a respecter of persons? His eyes run back and forth throughout the whole earth to show up STRONG for anyone who loves him and desires to partner with him. So, in Exodus 15:20, we see Miriam the prophetess. In Judges 4:4, we see Deborah, a prophetess. In 2 Kings 22:14, we saw Huldah the prophetess. In Luke 2:36, there is Anna, a prophetess. In Acts 21:9, there's Philip the evangelist who "had four virgin daughters who prophesied." But in Revelation 2:20, we encounter "Jezebel, who calls herself a prophetess." And in Nehemiah 6:12-14, we see the false prophetess for hire, Noadiah. Again, Satan counterfeits the gifts of the Spirit, which is why God gives us the gift of discernment.

Did you know that God still uses believers today to prophesy? "It will be in the last days, says God, that I will pour out my Spirit on all flesh. *Your sons and your daughters will prophesy*" (Acts 2:17). What is the gift of prophecy? It's receiving and speaking whatever the Spirit is prompting you to relay. I realize some in the church today don't believe in such things as spiritual gifts, and we also have many in the church who don't believe the Bible is inspired. I'm not their judge, and they're not mine; yet there is One who will judge (2 Tim. 4:1: 1 Pet. 4:1-5)! The Bible is clear: "Follow after love and earnestly desire spiritual gifts, but especially that you may prophesy" (1 Cor. 14:1). Why would Scripture tell us to earnestly desire something that doesn't exist? If we believe the Bible, we have to believe in spiritual gifts, and God wants us to release them!

In Romans 12:6-8, we find a list of seven spiritual gifts that God gives to various members of the body. Maybe you're blessed with one of these: "Having gifts differing according to the *grace that was given to us*: if **prophecy**, let's prophesy according to the proportion of our faith; or

service, let's give ourselves to service; or he who **teaches**, to his teaching; or he who **exhorts**, to his exhorting; he who **gives**, let him do it with generosity; he who **rules**, with diligence; he who **shows mercy**, with cheerfulness."

Or maybe your spiritual gift is listed in 1 Corinthians 12:8-11, "For to one is *given through the Spirit* the **word of wisdom**, and to another the **word of knowledge**, according to the same Spirit; to another **faith**, by the same Spirit; and to another **gifts of healings**, by the same Spirit; and to another **workings of miracles**; and to another **prophecy**; and to another **discerning of spirits**; to another different kinds of **languages**; and to another the **interpretation of languages**. But the one and the same Spirit produces all of these, *distributing to each one separately as he desires."*

Our God is a superb strategist and a bona fide genius! He actually equips every member of the body with an SOS (spiritual occupational specialty) in order to engage all of his spiritual warriors in Kingdom building. Brother Lovett showed us how the clergy/laity scheme saps the power from the saints. Now that we're aware of this highly ineffective form of ministry, there's no reason for us to be on the sidelines or sitting on the bench. Team Jesus needs you on the field! If you earnestly desire spiritual gifts, our Father will gladly grant that petition.

> "This is the boldness which we have toward him, that if we ask anything according to his will, he listens to us. And if *we know that he listens* to us, whatever we ask, *we know that we have* the petitions which we have asked of him." ~ *1 John 5:14-15*

That's an energizing, faith-building verse! But for many of us, the only little bump is that part about "according to his will." The rest of the passage is fine. Since we *know he listens*, then we *know we have*. That part of the verse is solid. The shaky part is, am I asking for something that's "according to his will"?

Sometimes it can be challenging to discern God's will, and sometimes not. Is it God's will that I lie and deal in falsehood? Is that a hard one to discern, or an easy one? Most of the time, it falls on the easy side. Why is this one easy? It's easy to discern God's will if God wrote down his will in a book. All I have to do is read the book! And he wrote in his book, "You shall not give false testimony against your neighbor." There it is, one of the "Big Ten" straight from Exodus 20! That's obviously his will. His written word is his revealed will!

Dr. John R. Rice would say, "One statement of the Bible should be enough for a Christian." I agree, and what if God wrote in another place in his same book, "Don't lie to one another, seeing that you have put off the *old man* with his doings, and have put on the *new man,* who is being renewed in knowledge after the image of his Creator" (Colossians 3:9,10)? Would that statement provide even more evidence of God's will about lying? I think so. Since the "new me" is being renewed after the image of Jesus, I shouldn't go around lying. God also wrote in his book, "Therefore putting away falsehood, speak truth each one with his neighbor. For we are members of one another" (Ephesians 4:25). One clear statement in the Bible should be enough. Two and three statements should leave no doubt! It's easy to discern God's will when his written word reveals his will.

According to God's book, every believer has at least one spiritual gift. Ask God about your SOS. That's a prayer which is definitely in line with his will, so you can be confident he'll answer. Prophecy might be your gift, or one of your gifts. In 1 Corinthians 14:1 we find, "Follow after love and earnestly desire spiritual gifts, but especially that you may **prophesy**." Again, to prophesy is to relay whatever the Spirit spontaneously brings to your mind. In verse 31 of the same chapter we're told, "For you all can **prophesy** one by one, that all may learn, and all may be exhorted." One of the purposes of prophecy is to teach and exhort others. We should all desire to do that! Verse 39 continues with, "Therefore, brothers, desire earnestly to **prophesy**."

No one rises to God and fulfills their ministry without effort, sacrifice, and persistence. In 2 Timothy 1:6, Paul tells his son in the faith to "**stir up** the gift of God which is in you." Our service to Christ will be tested by the fire of God's discerning judgment, see 1 Corinthians 3:11-15. Our talents and spiritual gifts must not be neglected or fall into disuse. May JAH grant us the grace to *stir up ourselves* to take hold of him, *stir up our gifts*, and *stir up one another* to do his will. I strongly suggest you reach out to your leaders and inquire about spiritual gifts. It's through our God-given endowments that we flow in the power of the Spirit. The joy and excitement of our faith is found in getting out on the field and playing our position on Team Jesus! If your walk of faith needs a kick in the pants, release your gifts. If you earnestly desire to take it to the next level, the Coach of the Kingdom is recruiting, and he has a position just for you.

In 1 Corinthians 12:4, the Spirit teaches us, "there are various kinds of gifts (charismata), but the same Spirit." That word *charismata* is the Greek word for grace gifts, or free, undeserved gifts. The word *charismata* flows from the word *charis*, which is Greek for grace. This implies there's no reason to boast or be puffed up regarding our spiritual gifts. We didn't earn them (1 Cor. 4:6,7). It's all by his grace, God's unmerited favor. Our salvation is by grace. Our good fight of faith is by grace. The imparting of spiritual gifts is also by grace. Now check this out. The word *charis* (grace) flows from the word *chara*, which is Greek for joy and cheerfulness! Spiritual gifts are therefore, not only our key to flowing in the *power* of the Lord, the gifts are also our key to flowing in the *joy* of the Lord. Serving others in the power of your spiritual occupational specialty is the secret to experiencing cheerfulness and true joy.

~§~

After completing basic training in Fort Benning, Georgia, I was assigned to Fort Ord, California on the Monterey Peninsula. That was a very nice place to serve. The rifle range was on the beach. We exercised on the beach. On the weekends, I would drive to Carmel-by-the-Sea and watch the sun slowly descend into the Pacific. I remember calling my father from an old school pay-phone in Carmel on Christmas Day. It was 80 degrees in Cali, but below freezing in Carolina. Lucky me! Places like Cannery Row, 17-Mile Drive, and Jacks Peak Park were perfect spots to impress a date. I moved off-base to Salinas, and earned a degree from Monterey Peninsula College by going to school four nights a week. I went to a celebrity golf tournament at Pebble Beach, and I enjoyed live theatre on campus. Needless to say, serving my country in sunny California was a big win-win. After a short year at Fort Ord, I received orders for a three-year overseas assignment.

When I first arrived in Germany, I stayed at the popular Bavarian American (BA) Hotel on Bahnhofstrasse in Nuremberg. While waiting for my Ford Granada to be shipped over from the US, I caught an early train to work. I say "early" train, as in a train that left the downtown Nuremberg bahnhof at exactly 4:30 a.m. every morning. Not 4:29 a.m. or 4:31 a.m., but exactly 0430 hours each morning. If you've been to Germany, you know what I mean.

After a 25-minute train ride along the German countryside, I'd get off at the station in Erlangen and walk the rest of the way to the barracks.

My path took me through a lovely park and a portion of the University of Erlangen. I learned years later that the eminent Bible scholar and evangelist R. A. Torrey studied in Erlangen back in 1900. I've often wondered if I walked some of the same streets or visited some of the same places he had so many years before.

My unit was assigned to Ferris Barracks. I can still see the Siemens factory that loomed large across the street from the gate I used to enter the base. I served from this location for three years, so in my mind's eye I can still visualize so many places there. I recall the PX, the chapel, the MP station, the commissary, and our large parade field surrounded by rows of white, three-story barracks. Come rain, snow, sleet or hail, every Monday morning if we were in garrison, we took part in our battalion five-mile run. There's nothing quite like 600 soldiers running together and singing cadence. I had the honor of carrying our company colors or flag during many of those early morning workouts. Oh, to be young again!

I especially recall our company's weekly safety briefings. Maybe it's because they happened on Friday, and we all love our Fridays. Before our unit was released for the weekend, our company commander from West Point, Captain William B. Caldwell IV, would give us our safety briefing. "If you go downtown, stay out of trouble." "Don't carry around a lot of cash." "Don't drink too much German beer!" Good advice. But every so often, some poor GI from B Company, 1st Battalion, 46th Infantry, would venture downtown Erlangen or Nuremberg, drink too much, and get out of line.

Captain Caldwell would advance to become Lieutenant General Caldwell, Commander of the United States Army North, also known as the Fifth Army. He's currently the president of Georgia Military College. During my time under his command, he was an exemplary military officer, a gentleman, and a fine leader of men.

Whatever Captain Caldwell asked of us, we knew he was willing and able to do also. That's an important trait for an infantry company commander. No matter how early in the morning I arrived at Ferris Barracks in Erlangen, as I walked past his window, I could see he was already there, working and planning. Days before we conducted extensive field exercises at Hohenfels or Grafenwoehr, he was already on site, working and planning.

I had never witnessed that level of dedication before and it made an impression. As a young corporal and a new believer in Christ, I would often reason, "If an officer in this man's army can be so single-minded and loyal to his mission, I want to be just as devoted to the Great Commission from my Lord and Savior." Sometimes we don't know what's possible, until we see someone do it. Hence the need for role models and pioneers and trailblazers, and men like Bill Caldwell.

I've shared a little about my time in the service and it's for a reason. Of all the details that still float around in my head, there's one that stands out far above the rest. While stationed in California, the closest enemy force was thousands of miles away, but Ferris Barracks was only 100 kilometers, or about 60 short miles, from the Czech Republic! The 1st Armored Division was the "Eastern Most Forward Deployed Division" in the entire U.S. Army. We were a stone's throw from the opposing army. In Cali, living for the weekend was my #1 priority. But when you're an hour's drive from real hostile forces, you have only one priority: being combat-ready. Whenever you're on duty, wherever you're on duty, you don't let your guard down and you don't break character. When the enemy is breathing down your neck, you can't afford any slack. You pay attention to what's happening around you. You have the eye of the tiger.

Soldiering on the sunny beaches of Cali was a vacation compared to soldiering in the dark, cold and snowy forests of Deutschland. The *Stars and Stripes* ran stories almost daily of soldiers killed while on training exercises. Live ammunition, night maneuvers, Abrams tanks, armored personnel carriers, soldiers on the ground. It was intense.

I was considered "sharp" in Cali because I wore shiny boots and a crisp uniform. In Germany, shiny boots and a crisp uniform meant little. No one cares about spit-shine boots and pressed fatigues when you're training constantly in snow and mud, and less than an hour from the real enemy! In Germany, I wasn't considered sharp until I could take down a target 1200 yards downrange with a .50 caliber machine gun mounted on the top of my APC. I was in the same army as before, but now I had a totally different mindset. I never even handled a .50 cal machine gun or a M47 Dragon anti-tank guided missile system until I was in Germany. Being so close to the enemy line elevated your sense of readiness, it forced you to "up your game." The entire battalion was highly motivated and laser-focused on our one and only priority: combat-readiness. We were the ones standing on the wall, and we knew it!

I said that to say this. There are some in the army of the Lord with a laid-back mindset toward soldiering. To them, soldiering is showing up in a nice ride and looking sharp in the assembly. It's almost like a vacation for some believers. But there are others, serving in this same army, who have a different set of orders. Their assignment moves them closer to the enemy. The leisure time activities of the past have been replaced with working and planning (Psalm 90:12).

C.T. Studd was born with a silver spoon in his mouth. He was an excellent athlete and played on the cricket team representing Cambridge University. His father was won to the Lord when D.L Moody held a revival campaign in England. C.T. was converted not long after his father, and soon received orders to move closer to the frontline. He was one of the "Cambridge Seven" who joined the famous missionary Hudson Taylor to work with the China Inland Mission. Following his work in China, he served the Lord Jesus for over two decades in India and Africa. C.T. wrote several books but he's best remembered for his quotes, such as:

"Some wish to live within the sound of church or chapel bell;
I want to run a rescue shop within a yard of hell."

The various members of the body of Christ have diverse assignments. We all have different spiritual gifts, and subsequently, different roles to fill. Not all soldiers in the Lord's army have the same set of orders or the same SOS. Have you asked God to show you where and how he desires to use you? Is our "Commander-in-Chief" calling you to move closer to the frontline? Are you up for the mission? "Follow after love and earnestly desire spiritual gifts."

> "You therefore must endure hardship as a good soldier of Christ Jesus. No soldier on duty entangles himself in the affairs of life, that he may please him who enrolled him as a soldier. ...Consider what I say, and may the Lord give you understanding in all things." *~ 2 Timothy 2:3-4, 7*

> "Don't you know that those who run in a race all run, but one receives the prize? Run like that, that you may win. Every man who strives in the games exercises self-control in all things. Now they do it to receive a corruptible crown, but we an incorruptible [crown]. I therefore run like that." *~ 1 Corinthians 9:24-26*

"Whatever keeps me from the Bible is my enemy, however harmless it may appear to be. Whatever engages my attention when I should be meditating on God and things eternal does injury to my soul." ~ *A.W. Tozer*

The One-Eyed Deluder

The TV screen is my shepherd. My spiritual growth shall want. It maketh me to sit down and do nothing for his name's sake, because it requireth all of my spare time.

It keepeth me from doing my duty as a Christian, because it presenteth so many good shows and ball games that I must see. It restoreth my knowledge of the things of the world, and keepeth me from the study of God's Word.

It leadeth me in the paths of failing to attend the weekly worship services and doing nothing in the kingdom of God. Yea, though I live to be 100, I shall keep watching my screen as long as it will work, for it's my closest companion.

Its sounds and its pictures, they comfort me. It presenteth endless entertainment before me and keepeth me from doing important things with my family. It fills my head with ideas which differ from those set forth in the word of God.

Surely, no good thing will come of my life, because my television offereth me no good time to do the will of God; thus I will dwell crownless in the house of the Lord forever.

~§~

The wisdom of Proverbs 11:30, "He who is wise wins souls." Instead of killing time watching a screen, "watch carefully how you walk, not as unwise, but as wise, redeeming the time, because the days are evil. Therefore don't be foolish, but understand what the will of the Lord is." ~ *Ephesians 5:15-17*

"Only one life, 'twill soon be past, only what's done for Christ will last!" ~ *C.T. Studd*

Let's move into the fifth and final action step in our quest for national revival. If this is missing, all our efforts will be in vain. The most vital step is, **Reflect God's Love**. Do you think the average Joe in America considers the average house of worship in America a place where he can find love and acceptance?

The story is told that when Mahatma Gandhi was a young law student, he started reading the Gospels of the New Testament. He was moved by the Scriptures and wanted to learn more about the faith. He was especially impressed with the radical teachings of the one called the "Messiah." Gandhi believed the caste system was dividing the people of India. The caste system basically affirms that if your parents are underclass and poor, you are – and will always be – underclass and poor. All in all, where a person fits into the class structure is permanently assigned at birth. As Gandhi read and reread the famous "Sermon on the Mount," he wondered if the teachings of Jesus could offer a solution.

> He opened his mouth and taught them, saying, "Blessed are the poor in spirit, for theirs is the Kingdom of Heaven. Blessed are those who mourn, for they shall be comforted. Blessed are the gentle, for they shall inherit the earth. Blessed are those who hunger and thirst for righteousness, for they shall be filled. Blessed are the merciful, for they shall obtain mercy. Blessed are the pure in heart, for they shall see God. Blessed are the peacemakers, for they shall be called children of God. Blessed are those who have been persecuted for righteousness' sake, for theirs is the Kingdom of Heaven." ~ *Matthew 5:2-10*

The young Gandhi was amazed by what he was reading. He had to know more, so he decided to attend worship services at a nearby church in Calcutta. He thought he might speak with the minister to learn more about the Christian faith. When he entered the sanctuary, to his surprise, the ushers refused to give him a seat. Instead, they suggested he go elsewhere and worship with his own people. This particular church welcomed only high-caste Indians and Whites. Gandhi left the church and he never returned. "If Christians have caste differences also," he said, "I might as well remain a Hindu."

The ushers' prejudice not only betrayed the Christian faith (James 2:1-7), but it also created a stumbling block to a seeker of truth. It may have been due to experiences like this that caused Gandhi to later declare, "I'd be a Christian if it were not for the Christians."

"Between the Christianity of this land, and the Christianity of Christ, I recognize the widest possible difference." ~ *Frederick Douglass, 1845*

How many people in our community feel just like Gandhi or Douglass? Heaven only knows the number of people who went to church looking for a place where people actually lived the teachings of Christ, only to be let down by the harsh reality of prejudice and allegiance to social norms. Many places of worship today are more into political warfare and class warfare than spiritual warfare. *In* the world and *of* the world. The armor of God has been replaced by name brand attire and the hottest accessories. Luxury is the watchword of the church today. "First class all the way." "Children of the King deserve the best stuff!"

But the Bible declares, "Beloved, I beg you as **foreigners** and **pilgrims**, to abstain from fleshly lusts [like luxury], which war against the soul; having good behavior among the nations, so in that of which they speak against you as evildoers, they may by your good works, which they see, glorify God in the day of visitation." ~ *1 Peter 2:11-12*

When the outside world looks at the people who are called by his name, what do they see? Do they see us as a people who regard themselves as strangers and foreigners in this world (Psalm 119:19)? Do they see us as a people who liken themselves to pilgrims traveling through this world? I think not. I think they see us right at home in this world. Jeshurun has grown thick (Deuteronomy 32:15).

Instead of the church laboring in the fields for the Lord, we're partying in the barn. Instead of seekers of the Most High, we've become seekers of the most comfort. Instead of being lean and mean, the church has grown fat and happy. Satan has deceived the church today into chasing after prosperity and political favor, instead of pursuing purity and power from on high. We're focused more on our bank account than on that day when we'll be called to give account of how we spent our short time on this earth. You've heard that some believers can be so "heavenly-minded" that they're no earthly good. Well, I suppose that's possible. But for every one of that type, we have a thousand others who are so "earthly-minded" that they're no heavenly good! Brother Tozer said, "To escape the error of salvation by works, we have fallen into the opposite error of salvation without obedience" (James 2:17). I'm not sure we can run after the luxury of the world and reflect the love of the Lord at the same time.

Night-time Prayer in the American Jungle

Now I lay me down to sleep, I pray my precious stuff to keep. I pray my stocks are on the rise, and that my analyst is wise, that all the wine I sip is white, and that my hot tub's watertight, that racquetball won't get too tough, that all my sushi's fresh enough. I pray my security system still works, that my career won't lose its perks, my microwave won't radiate, my condo won't depreciate. I pray my health club doesn't close, and that my money market grows. If I go broke before I wake, I pray my sports car they won't take. Amen. *~Steve Farrar*

Where is your Heart?

He died of malaria and internal bleeding from dysentery. His funeral took place on April 18, 1874. He was given a 21-gun salute. The entire civilized world wept when he was laid to rest with the notables in Westminster Abbey. The body of the British physician and missionary, David Livingstone, was buried in England where he was born. *But before his body was returned to England, his heart was buried in the Africa he treasured and served.* At the foot of a tall mobola plum tree in a small village in Zambia, the natives dug a hole. And inside that hole they placed the heart of this man whom they admired and loved.

Jesus said, "For where your treasure is, there your heart will be also." If your heart was buried in the place you treasured most during this life, where would that be? In your fine cars? Your jewelry boxes? Your shoe game? Or your earthly dwelling place? In your handbag collection? Where is your heart? At the office? At the dinner table?

The righteous love whatever JAH loves, and they hate whatever JAH hates. The righteous are in sync with the Father's heart. The Father is "not wishing that anyone should perish, but that all should come to repentance" (2 Peter 3:9). "Jesus said to them, '**Come after me, and I will make you into fishers of men**' " (Mark 1:17). The high calling of all believers is making disciples. In John 15:8, our Lord and Savior said, "In this my Father is glorified, that you bear much fruit; and so you will be my disciples." As disciples of Christ, we glorify the Father by bearing fruit.

What's the fruit of an apple? Another apple. What's the fruit of a disciple? Another disciple, see Romans 1:13-15. To this end, Jesus said:

> "A new commandment I give to you, that you love one another. Just as I have loved you, you also love one another. By this everyone will know that you are my disciples, if you have love for one another." ~ *John 13:34-35*

The Father is not wishing that any soul perish. He's glorified when we bear much fruit, when we fish for men. Let me ask, "Is it wise to glorify the Father?" Of course, it is! Which is why Proverbs 11:30 tells us, "He who is wise wins souls." The wise win souls because that glorifies the Father, and it's wise to glorify the Father! Now what type of bait would a wise angler use? Jesus said to use LOVE. It's our love for one another that confirms to "everyone" that we're true disciples of Christ. *"They will know we are Christians by our love."* And it's our testimony of being true disciples that opens the door to an anointed witness (John 16:7,8).

Theologian and pastor Dr. Francis Schaeffer referred to the unity of believers as "**the final apologetic**." The term apologetics means to defend and justify the doctrines of the faith. In a word, it means we should be able to explain from Scripture why we believe what we believe. Why do we believe Jesus is divine? Why do we believe salvation is by grace and not works? Is there a difference between the Judgment Seat of Christ and the Great White Throne Judgment? Why do we believe God is no respecter of persons? In Jude 3, we're exhorted to "contend earnestly for the faith." Believers are called to "always be ready to give an answer to everyone who *asks you a reason* concerning the hope that is in you, with humility and fear" (1 Peter 3:15).

Some defend or "contend for" the faith with iron-clad arguments and unassailable logic. There is a time and place for that. When Paul encountered some Jews at the synagogue in Thessalonica, it states in Acts 17:2-3 that he "went in to them, and for three Sabbath days *reasoned* with them from the Scriptures, *explaining* and *demonstrating* that the Christ had to suffer and rise again from the dead." In the next chapter, we find a certain Jew named Apollos. The Bible says he was eloquent and mighty in the Scriptures, even though his understanding was incomplete. But after Priscilla and Aquila "*explained* to him the way of God more accurately," he later went on to powerfully refute the Jews, "publicly showing *by the Scriptures* that Jesus was the Christ" (Acts 18:28).

From these accounts in Acts, we see there's definitely a time and place for "reasoning" and "explaining" and "demonstrating" in the defense of the gospel of Jesus. People need to know that God sent his Son to die for our sin. The Scriptures foretold this and we need to explain it. But we must never forget that in John 17:23, Jesus prays to the Father: "I in them, and you in me, that they may be perfected into one; [what's the point of this oneness?] *that the world may know that you sent me and loved them...*" Wow! Believers are called to explain to the lost that God sent his Son to die for our sins. But do you know what confirms to the lost that God sent his Son? *The love and oneness of believers!* Of course, we are to go forth and proclaim the message of God's love. But do you know what confirms to unbelievers that God loves them? *The love and oneness of believers!* Let that sink in as we ponder the current state of the church. We must find a way back to reflecting God's love (1 Corinthians 13:2,13).

Regarding Jesus' high priestly prayer, Matthew Henry states, "Our Lord especially prayed that all such persons might be united together in bonds of love, as one body under one head, animated by one soul...The more closely they are united and live in peace and harmony, the more clearly do they evidence the Divine origin and excellency of the gospel, *to the conviction of the world around them.* But the more they dispute about lesser things, the more do they throw doubts upon the truth and excellency of Christianity. True believers should be cautious in this respect."

In his book, *Loving One Another*, Pastor Gene Getz comments on this same profound truth. "Jesus prayed, 'May they be brought to complete unity to let the world know that You sent Me and have loved them even as You have loved me' (John 17:23) – **There is no clearer evangelistic statement in the whole New Testament**. Christ's desire was that those, who had not yet believed in Him, would come to faith *by means of* the love and unity demonstrated by Christians."

No wonder Satan works tirelessly to disrupt the love and unity of believers. This is especially evident in the area of race. I had the privilege of visiting Oak Cliff Bible Fellowship in Dallas during the summer of 2018. Pastor Tony Evans, a graduate of Dallas Theological Seminary, was hosting an engaging, weeklong workshop on race relations. It was a delight to see believers of different races come together (Psalm 133:1) to grapple with the thorny issue of race in America. God calls us to be "eager to keep the unity of the SPIRIT in the bond of peace." Our supernatural unity is the final apologetic.

I believe the spiritually hungry people of America will sit up and take notice when the people of God kneel together and stand together as one. The Bible is not silent about race (see Acts 10:1-48; Rom. 2:11; Col. 3:8-14; Jas. 2:8,9; 1 Pet. 1:17;), but for too long the church has been. The "nation within the nation" has to step up and lead the way. All too often, we fail to rise above the standards of culture. But is that our standard? Are cultural norms the measuring stick for the army of the LORD?

Robertson McQuilkin, past president of Columbia Bible College and Seminary, states in his work - *An Introduction to Biblical Ethics:*

> "Ironically, modern racism received its greatest impetus from scientists of the last century. The subtitle of Charles Darwin's *Origin of Species* was "The Preservation of Favored Races in the Struggle for Life." Virtually all nineteenth-century evolutionists held to the theory of superior and inferior races. Some have held that the Bible affirms both racial segregation and unjust discrimination (slavery, for example), but it does not do so. God did require segregation and discrimination among people, but always based on religious distinctions, never on **race** or **class** distinctives [Psalm 106:35,36]. When God so strongly opposes all injustice, including the injustice resulting from class and racial discrimination, *why do Christians almost universally participate in their own cultural patterns of discrimination rather than joining with other believers to provide a radically biblical counter-culture of justice, mercy, and unity?"*

That's a valid question. Why do we bend to culture? Brother McQuilkin served as a missionary in Japan for twelve years. Their culture is much older and more defined than ours, so I'm sure he witnessed believers feeling the pressure of staying within certain norms. But the Word still says, "In this is love, not that we loved God, but that he loved us, and *sent* his Son as the atoning sacrifice for our sins" (1 John 4:10). We are called to love as God loves. God's love didn't wait for us to love him first. His love took the lead. His love crossed barriers and made sacrifices.

In John 4:9, we learn of the culture war during the time of Christ: "For Jews have no dealings with Samaritans." The extreme disgust between the Samaritans and the Jews was fierce and long-standing. Yet Jesus crossed racial and ethnic barriers to initiate a conversation with a woman of Samaria that resulted in a great revival for the city of Sychar.

> From that city many of the Samaritans believed in him because of the word of the woman, who testified, "He told me everything that I did." So when the Samaritans came to him, they begged him to stay with them. He stayed there two days. Many more believed because of his word. They said to the woman, "Now we believe, not because of your speaking; for we have heard for ourselves, and know that this is indeed the Christ, the Savior of the world [...of the *whole* world, for Jews *and* Samaritans]." ~ *John 4:39-42*

Loving the man or woman who looks like you and lives in your community is easy. But loving the man or woman who lives on the other side of town - whose ancestry, values and skin color is different from your own - is a little more challenging. This is how we are called to love! It's a love that takes the lead. In the power and authority of the Most High God, if we so desire, "the nation within the nation" can provide a radically biblical counter-culture of justice, mercy, and unity.

Revival in America will not tarry long when the body of Christ reflects God's love. **We mustn't forget it's our demonstration of unity and love** that validates and empowers the message of God's love. *Conversely, it's our lack of love that fosters more skepticism.* We all have deep within us a God-created void that only he can fill. I believe a united, bustling household of faith is what the world is waiting to see. These are the end times (1 John 2:18), and people are searching for truth, for real answers to tough questions. Unfortunately, a thirsty soul will swallow dirty lies in their quest for living waters. See Matt. 9:35-38; Rom. 16:17-18!

According to the American Bible Society and the Barna Group's *2019 State of the Bible Survey*, more than three in five Americans (63%) express at least some curiosity to know more about what the Bible says. A similar number of adults (61%) are interested in knowing more about who Jesus Christ is, including 29% who agree strongly. This represents a huge opportunity today for soul-winning and disciple-making. Jesus called it long ago and it's still true: "Don't you say, 'There are yet four months until the harvest?' Behold, I tell you, lift up your eyes and look at the fields, that they are white for harvest already" (John 4:35). So, let's go get'em!

Back in the day when people would take the time to handwrite letters, a man and a woman in different towns became "pen pals." They corresponded solely by mail, and slowly fell in love with one another. Eventually, they decided to meet at the train station. Since they had never seen each other or shared photos, they devised a plan to help them find each other. She's to wear a green scarf and a green hat. On the day of their meeting, when the man got off the train, he immediately started looking for her. Suddenly, in the distance, he spots a woman wearing a green scarf and a green hat. But as soon as he saw her, his heart fell. It's not that she was unattractive, but he had created an image in his mind of how she looked, and she didn't match the image at all. For a brief second, he was tempted to avoid her altogether and go back home on the next train. But in a moment of clarity, he realizes his feelings of love for her are genuine. He walks over, smiles, and introduces himself.

Immediately the woman said, "Just what is this about anyway! I don't know you. What's going on here? That lady over there gave me ten dollars to wear this hat and scarf!" When the man looks over at the woman mentioned, he realizes she is even lovelier than the image in his head. He eagerly approached his true pen pal, who later explained to him, "All my life people have wanted to be with me, to be my friend, because of how I look on the outside. Some say I'm beautiful. But what I've always wanted is someone to love me, not for who I am on the outside, but for who I truly am on the inside."

American songwriter Eden Ahbez states, "The greatest thing you'll ever learn is just to love and be loved in return." That's exactly what we all want and need. We all have a heaven-inspired desire for love and unity because that's what God wants also. And according to the prayer of our Lord Jesus Christ in John 17:23, when the lost people in our community witness the love and unity demonstrated by his disciples, it will *confirm* to them that God sent the Savior, and it will also *confirm* the Father's love for them. That's a tremendous responsibility, brothers and sisters! And it's a big-time privilege! Let's resolve to take full advantage of it. We have good news to share, but we can't effectively share the good news if we're the bad news. The enemy desires to subvert the church, tarnish our testimony, divide the saints, and run us out of business. For far too long, we've been in retreat. I pray these five steps will put us on the offensive for our LORD.

1. Rediscover God's Word
2. Receive God's Son
3. Resist God's Enemy
4. Release God's Gifts
5. Reflect God's Love

The Rest of the Story

Whatever happened to the weeping prophet Jeremiah? We know the Babylonian invaders were merciless, the young and the old were slaughtered in the streets. We know the king's officials were judged and killed. Our ears *tingled* when we heard about the fate of King Zedekiah. This rebellious ruler, who once enjoyed the luxuries of sovereign power, died a prisoner in a foreign land, blind and broken. Was Jeremiah also carried into Babylonian captivity, or did something worse happen to him? Before we discover the fate of God's prophet, let's reflect briefly on the tragic fate of God's people.

The fall of Israel was the pathetic outcome of the faithlessness of her leaders. It was their persistent failure to follow the clear teaching of Scripture that ultimately led to the complete destruction of Judah and the city of David. Shepherding the people of Israel was the job of the king, the priests and the prophets. When leaders stray from the paths of truthfulness and righteousness, there's serious damage to both the leaders and the led. The curses of Deuteronomy 28 that engulfed Israel were the direct result of her leader's unbelief, their poor decisions, and their willingness to believe the lies they told one another.

The blame for the terrible fall of Jerusalem is to be placed at the feet of her own citizens, and especially her leaders. Long before Nebuchadnezzar's sword cut down the people in the streets of the Holy City, her own King Manasseh "shed innocent blood very much, until he had filled Jerusalem from one end to another" (2 Kings 21:16)! Long before Nebuchadnezzar's captain burned God's house with fire, her own King Manasseh had already "built altars for all the army of the sky in the two courts of Yahweh's house" (2 Kings 21:5) and "set the engraved image of the idol, which he had made, in God's house" (2 Chronicles 33:7)! Long before Nebuchadnezzar's army besieged the city and created a famine so severe that people turned to eating their children, her own King Manasseh seduced them into sacrificing "their sons and their daughters to demons" (Psalm 106:37)!

What did the king of Babylon do to Israel that their own king had not already done to them? Be not deceived, God is not mocked, for whatever a nation sows, that they will also reap. God is not playing games with those who are called by his name. "**For they sow the wind, and they will reap the whirlwind**" (Hosea 8:7). Ichabod! If the LORD didn't let fat Jeshurun off the hook, how will he deal with the fat, arrogant nation whose motto is "In God We Trust"? Jesus Christ said, "And that servant who knew his master's will, and did not prepare himself or do according to his will, shall be beaten with many *stripes*. ...For everyone to whom much is given, from him much will be required" (Luke 12:47,48 NKJV).

> "We have been the recipients of the choicest bounties of Heaven. We have been preserved, these many years, in peace and prosperity. We have grown in numbers, wealth and power, as no other nation has ever grown. But we have forgotten God, we have forgotten the gracious hand which preserved us in peace, and multiplied and enriched and strengthened us; and we have vainly imagined, in the **deceitfulness of our hearts**, that all these blessings were produced by some superior wisdom and virtue of our own. Intoxicated with unbroken success, we have become too self-sufficient to feel the necessity of redeeming and preserving grace, too proud to pray to the God that made us! It behooves us, then, to humble ourselves before the Offended Power, to confess our national sins, and to pray for clemency and forgiveness."

Analysis of data done by the *Centers for Disease Control and Prevention* found that nearly 40,000 people were killed by guns in 2017. That's the highest number of deaths due to guns in 38 years, each year trending worse than the year before. Analysis also showed nearly 24,000 people died from suicide by guns in 2017, the highest number in 18 years.

According to data revised in August 2018, less than 20,000 Americans died from drug overdoses in the year 2000. By 2017, that number increased to more than 72,000 deaths. Which means even if we factor in the increase of our population, it still equates to 300 citizens a day killed in America by drugs and guns. That's not counting death by car wrecks, hanging/suffocation, staged accidents, stabbings, poisonings, so-called "medical procedures" and all the other ways people are killed in this country. Jesus Christ said the thief *only* comes to steal, kill and destroy. Satan is America's #1 threat, the true deceiver of our nation.

When enemy forces attacked our country on September 11, 2001, we were shocked and angry. By September 12th, we were out for revenge. When Admiral Yamamoto pulled off the sneak attack at Pearl Harbor, the very next day we were at war against the Japanese empire. After these attacks, the indignation of Americans boiled over at the thought of enemy forces killing U.S. citizens on our own soil. No one picks a fight with the USA and not pay a high price. But are we not witnessing similar attacks every day in our land? The soil of America is awash in innocent blood!

> "Rescue those who are being led away to death! Indeed, hold back those who are staggering to the slaughter! If you say, *'Behold, we didn't know this,'* doesn't he who weighs the hearts consider it? He who keeps your soul, doesn't he know it? Shall he not render to every man according to his work?" ~ *Proverbs 24:11-12*

In your mind's eye visualize a football arena. Now watch a parade of soldiers walking slowly onto the field. They're in groups of six and each group is carrying a coffin. The coffins are draped in the red, white and blue flag. The pallbearers leave 300 coffins on the field. Now visualize the sun rapidly descending and rising again. The next day we see soldiers bringing in another 300 coffins. Watch the sun fall from the sky, and then ascend. By the time 18 days have passed, we'll have more coffins stacked on the field than the number of Americans who were killed during the enemy attacks on 9/11 and Pearl Harbor combined! When another two hundred days have passed, we'll have more coffins stacked on the field than the number of Americans who were killed in the entire Vietnam War - which lasted over 15 years! And that will still leave us with 300 additional deaths per day for another 147 days of the year.

Do you know what happens if you put a frog in lukewarm water and slowly, slowly turn up the heat? We've all heard this one. They say if you drop a frog in a pot of hot water, it will frantically try to get out. But if you put a frog in a pot of tepid water and very slowly increase the temperature of the water, the frog will adjust to the higher temperature until the water gets so hot that the poor frog actually boils to death. It's a story that speaks to the danger of adjusting to a situation or environment that's gradually corroding.

It's a neat story, but the only problem is - it's not true. A frog isn't that dumb! No living frog is going to just sit around in a slow-cooker that's getting hotter and hotter until it boils to death. That's foolish. At some point, the frog will sense it's in danger and attempt to get out of the situation long before the water starts to boil. Like I said, it's a good story, just not true. It's fiction. God has given his frogs more sense than that. What's not fiction is the fact that our true enemy is hell-bent on destroying as many souls as he can! But why attack us? Because we're created in the image of his archrival. And because a complacent, prayerless nation can do little to stop him! Three hundred U.S. citizens killed every day from guns and drugs is a terrible and sad reality. *Yet we shrug it off.* How high does that awful number have to reach before we say, "Enough!" **If we sow the wind, what outcome should we expect?**

When Israel was transitioning from Saul's rule to that of King David, the Scripture states in 1 Chronicles 12:32 that certain leaders *"had understanding of the times, to know what Israel ought to do."* These leaders recognized God's anointing on David, they had understanding of the times [situation], and they acted accordingly. Will we do likewise?

As Satan drives God's word deeper and deeper into the mud of unbelief, his grip around our throat gets tighter and tighter. He plots to sink the revelation of God forever in the dungeon of skepticism. Our adversary knows what happens to people when there is no divine revelation. We also know what happens. Per Proverbs 29:18 » We cast off restraint, run amok, and sink down to the pit! We see with our own eyes how this is playing out. Year by year, confidence in the Bible is decreasing; while at the same time, man's inhumanity to man is increasing. Year by year, hearts grow a little colder; year by year, the water gets a little warmer.

Escalating violence is a telltale sign that something is amiss in America. Just like he did with Israel, our heavenly Father is using pain to call attention to our sins. Do we desire his favor or his fury? What other manifestations of divine anger must we endure before we change our ways? A military/cyber attack, another lethal pandemic, a financial crisis? "**Do we provoke the Lord to jealousy? are we stronger than he?**" (1 Cor. 10:22 KJV). *What do we need to stop doing? What should we start doing? What attitudes do we need to cultivate? What attitudes should we terminate?* What would a true prophet like Jeremiah say to us today?

Speaking of Jeremiah, whatever happened to God's man? Was he captured or killed? What do we find in Scripture? Two chapters that show us the final fall of Jerusalem, 2 Kings 25 and 2 Chronicles 36, don't tell us much about the weeping prophet. Howbeit, in the book that bears his name, in chapter thirty-nine, Jeremiah informs us what happened to him during the devastating and violent collapse of Jerusalem. Verses 5-10 record King Zedekiah's attempted escape and his capture in the plains of Jericho. He was forced to watch as the Chaldeans execute his sons, and then they "put out Zedekiah's eyes and bound him in fetters, to carry him to Babylon." Nebuchadnezzar's captain burned the city and broke down the walls and "carried away captive into Babylon the residue of the people who remained in the city." But what became of the prophet Jeremiah? How did he fare during the invasion? We find the answer in verses 11-14 of chapter thirty-nine.

> "Now Nebuchadnezzar [the] king of Babylon commanded Nebuzaradan the captain of the guard concerning Jeremiah, saying, **'Take him, and take care of him. Do him no harm; but do to him even as he tells you.'**
>
> "So...they sent, and took Jeremiah out of the court of the guard, and committed him to Gedaliah the son of Ahikam, the son of Shaphan, that he should carry him home. So he lived among the people."

Many prophets and priests perished on the day the city of God was "devoured by the fire of his jealousy." But concerning God's man Jeremiah, it was said, "Take care of him. Do him no harm"! The Most High God of heaven and earth blessed his prophet by allowing him to avoid captivity in Babylon and death by the sword (Proverbs 10:25). It was ordered by Yahweh's servant, King Nebuchadnezzar himself, that the faithful prophet be carried home to live among the people.

Jehovah promised to protect his prophet (Jeremiah 1:19), and he made good on his word. Our God is glorious! "The LORD is my strength and song, and he is become my salvation: he is my God, and I will prepare him an habitation. ...The LORD is a man of war" (Exodus 15:2,3 KJV). We find this gem in Hebrews 6:10, "For God is not unrighteous, so as to forget your work and the labor of love which you showed toward his name, in that you served the saints, and still do serve them." JAH is faithful, so as we stand on his promises *and* precepts, "let us not be weary in well doing: for in due season we shall reap, if we faint not" (Galatians 6:9 KJV).

So now you know the "rest of the story" concerning the weeping prophet of Jerusalem. But before this account comes to a close, the Spirit of God wraps up this tragic chapter with four final verses.

> Now Yahweh's word came to Jeremiah, while he was shut up in the court of the guard, saying, "Go, and speak to Ebedmelech the Ethiopian, saying, 'Yahweh of Armies, the God of Israel, says:

> "Behold, I will bring my words on this city for evil, and not for good; and *they will be accomplished before you in that day*. But I will deliver you in that day," says Yahweh; "and you will not be given into the hand of the men of whom you are afraid. For I will surely save you, and you won't fall by the sword, but you will escape with your life; because you have put your trust in me," says Yahweh.' " *~ Jeremiah 39:15-18*

After the wicked princes of Judah plotted against the prophet of God and left him to die in the muddy pit, Ebedmelech led the team that "lifted Jeremiah up with the cords, and took him up out of the dungeon." Remember that? Yahweh remembered! God did not overlook, nor forget, the actions of Ebedmelech. He told Jeremiah to inform the Ethiopian that even though he will witness the destruction of the city:

1. Yahweh will deliver him on that day,
2. He will not be given over to the Chaldeans,
3. God will "surely save" him,
4. He won't fall by the sword,
5. He will escape with his life!

Isn't that amazing! "Behold, Yahweh's eye is on those who fear him, on those who hope in his loving kindness, to deliver their soul from death, to keep them alive in famine" (Psalm 33:18,19). Our Lord even takes the time to tell Ebedmelech, and us, why he showed him such kindness. "Because you have put your trust in me." Amen! May we do likewise.

"If you say, *'Behold, we didn't know this,'* doesn't he who weighs the hearts consider it? He who keeps your soul, doesn't he know it? **Shall he not render to every man according to his work?**" (Proverbs 24:12). Did God not render to fat Jeshurun and King Saul and Zedekiah according to their works? Did he not render to Joshua and Jeremiah and Ebedmelech according to their works? "There is no creature that is hidden from his sight, but all things are naked and laid open before the eyes of him to whom we must give an account" (Hebrews 4:13)! Let's get right America, the Judge of Eternity and the celestial jurors are watching us.

After reading the history of Yahweh's dealings with Israel, we have every reason in the world to believe God will do exactly what he said he will do. Therefore, when we as a nation humble ourselves and pray and seek his face and turn from our wicked ways, we can be 100% positive he will hear from heaven and forgive our sins and heal our land. When we lift up "holy hands without anger and doubting," he will hear our cry. In Jeremiah 32:27, the LORD asked his servant, *"Behold, I am Yahweh, the God of all flesh. Is there anything too hard for me?"* Good question! Is anything too difficult for the LORD? Is Satan stronger than El-Elyon? Are the forces of evil greater than the forces of Jehovah God? I think not!

Despite that, our adversary will continue to wreak havoc in America until the people of faith stand on their faith. It's time to awaken the sleeping giant. **It's the people of faith who carry the burden of revival!** We're the ones who understand the spiritual reality that Satan is a defeated foe. We're the ones equipped with the sword of the Spirit to cut off the head of the snake. We know our God rides the heavens to help those who are willing to "pray" the price for revival.

In light of that truth, we march onward with a sharpened awareness that the devil is not our boss. He's masquerading as the boss. The Bible says in 2 Corinthians 4:4 that he's "the god of this world." But notice he's the "little g" god of this world. El-Elyon is the Most High God. Yahweh is the "Big G" God of all worlds! He alone is the source of power. *"God has spoken once; twice I have heard this, that power belongs to God"* (Psalm 62:11). Power belongs to the "Big G" God of the universe, and as we pray and trust and obey, his power and presence will flow through us.

> "The seventy returned with joy, saying, 'Lord, even the demons are subject to us in your name!' He said to them, 'I saw Satan having fallen like lightning from heaven. Behold, **I give you authority** to tread on serpents and scorpions, and over all the power of the enemy. Nothing will in any way hurt you. Nevertheless, don't rejoice in this, that the spirits are subject to you, but rejoice that your names are written in heaven.' " ~ *Luke 10:17-20*

Our adversary is fallen. Lucifer is a defeated foe. Our Lord sits at the right hand of the Father, far above all other powers. Via the gospel, believers are raised up with Christ and made to sit/reign with him in the spirit realm. King Jesus has granted us authority to tread over all the power of the enemy! Therefore, as we go forth fishing for men, rejoicing in the knowledge that our names are written in heaven, the prince of darkness can't stop us. Nothing can stand in our way when El-Elyon, the Strongest Strong One, is clearing the way. "Through God, we will do valiantly. For it is He who will tread down our enemies" (Psalm 108:13).

In the authority given to us by the Lord Jesus Christ, let's wrap up our time together with a dynamic spiritual activity. Do you remember what Joshua did to the five defeated kings of the Amorites? In your mind's eye, in the spirit realm, let's circle our enemies now and do the same thing to "little g" and his cronies of wickedness.

> "When they brought those kings out to Joshua, Joshua called for all the men of Israel, and said to the chiefs of the men of war who went with him, "Come near. Put your feet on the necks of these kings." They came near, and put their feet on their necks. Joshua said to them, **"Don't be afraid, nor be dismayed. Be strong and courageous, for Yahweh will do this to all your enemies against whom you fight."**

Amen and Amen! Look now to the 20th verse in the last chapter of the powerful NT book of Romans. *O God, it is time for You to work!*

Romans 16:20

Complete Jewish Bible: "And God, the source of shalom, **will soon crush the Adversary under your feet**. The grace of our Lord Yeshua be with you."

King James Version: "And the God of peace **shall bruise Satan under your feet shortly**. The grace of our Lord Jesus Christ be with you. Amen."

As it is written, it will be done! The Most High God will make sure everything plays out according to his *unbreakable* word. Which means we can have an *unshakable* faith in whatever he says. "Look to Me, and be saved, all you ends of the earth! For I *am* God, and *there is* no other" (Isaiah 45:22 NKJV). "There is no one like the God of Jeshurun, who rides the heavens to help you, and in His excellency on the clouds" (Deut. 33:26 NKJV).

Even now, the eyes of our LORD run back and forth throughout the whole earth to show himself strong on the behalf of those who love him. Evangelist Vance Havner said, "Revival is the church falling in love with Jesus all over again." On his last day in the land of the living, Joshua said to us, "Take good heed therefore to yourselves, that you love Yahweh your God" (Joshua 23:11). Where is your heart? Are you all-in for Jesus?

At the risk of being oversimplistic, it seems to me the key to our success is focus, and focus is a matter of our own free will. We can will ourselves to focus on anything: unity, division, worldly wealth, spiritual riches, personal/national repentance, whatever. It's my firm conviction revival in America is largely a matter of our will and our focus.

Brother D.L. Moody was asked to conduct a series of overseas evangelistic meetings in England. One of the local pastors protested, "Why are we sending for Mr. Moody? He's inexperienced, he's not from this country, and he's uneducated. Mr. Moody doesn't have a monopoly on the Holy Spirit." An older, wiser pastor was quick to respond, *"No, but the Holy Spirit has a monopoly on Mr. Moody."*

Do you desire to partner with the King to advance his Kingdom? There's much work to do, and the laborers are few. Our enemy has been toiling overtime to divide the saints and bury the truth. But our God is also working (Phil. 2:13). The LORD of hosts is putting together a strike force of Spirit-filled men and women to rescue his word and his sheep from the dungeons of skepticism and unbelief. Are you up for the mission?

Our Savior is calling us to be his faithful band of believers that he can work on, and work for, and work through to bring revival in the land. In his name, let's answer the call. *If* we show up and do our part, *then* Almighty God will show up strong! Therefore, children of light, "Sow to yourselves in righteousness, reap in mercy; break up your fallow ground: for *it is* time to seek the LORD..." (Hosea 10:12 KJV).

No person, community or nation rises to the Most High God without effort. May JAH anoint us with fresh oil as we stir up ourselves to pray and take hold of him, as we stir up and release our spiritual gifts, and as we stir up one another to complete our mission to seek and save the lost. By the power of the Holy Spirit, let us endeavor to be that blessed nation of people who love the LORD with all our hearts, with all our souls, and with all our minds; and may we love our neighbor as we love ourselves.

Grace, Peace and Jahspeed,

Brother Quick

"The LORD is our God, and we are His people!"

EVANGELIZE!

Give us a watchword for the hour,
A thrilling word, a word of power,
A battle cry, a flaming breath
That calls to conquest or to death.

A word to rouse His church from rest,
To heed her Master's last request.
The call is given: Ye soldiers, arise!
Our watchword is - Evangelize!

The glad tidings now proclaim,
Through all the earth, in Jesus' name.
This word is ringing through the skies:
Evangelize! Evangelize!

To dying men, a fallen race,
Make known the gift of Gospel grace;
The world that now in darkness lies,
Evangelize! Evangelize!

~ Oswald J. Smith

NOTES on: The 1905 AMERICAN AWAKENING

1. D.J. Williams, *Welsh Calvinistic Methodism,* p. 43.
2. *The Examiner*, 26 January & February 1905.
3. Report of 19 January 1905, *The Examiner.*
4. *Pentecostal Herald,* 8 March 1905.
5. see *Baptist Commonwealth,* Philadelphia.
6. *Baptist Argus,* Louisville, 9 March 1905.
7. *Christian Advocate,* 6 April 1905.
8. Editorial, *Christian Advocate,* 9 March 1905.
9. *The Christian,* London, 9 March 1905.
10. *Christian Advocate,* 4 January 1906.
11. *Evening Post,* Schenectady, q. in *Christian Advocate,* 26 January 1905.
12. *Schenectady Gazette,* quoted in above issue.
13. *The Examiner,* New York, 23 February 1905.
14. *Christian Advocate,* 9 February 1905.
15. *Michigan Christian Advocate,* 11 February 1905.
16. *The Watchman,* 9 March 1905.
17. Editorial, *The Watchman,* 4 May 1905.
18. *The Examiner,* 19 January 1905.
19. Report of 16 March 1905, *The Examiner.*
20. *The Watchman,* 30 March 1905
21. Report of 12 October 1905, *The Watchman.*
22. *The Watchman,* 9 March 1905.
23. *The Christian,* 7 & 14 September 1905
24. *Christian Herald,* London, 12 January 1905
25. *The Advance,* 9 March 1905.
26. *The Christian,* 13 April 1905.
27. *Baptist Argus,* 16 March 1905.
28. *Western Christian Advocate,* 8 March 1905.
29. *Pentecostal Herald,* 1 March 1905.
30. *Christian Observer,* Louisville, 15 & 22 March 1905
31. *Christian Herald,* 22 February 1905.
32. *Southern Baptist Convention Annual,* 1906, p.46.
33. *Religious Herald,* Richmond, 2, 23 & 30 March 1905.
34. *Christian Herald,* 24 May 1905.
35. *Foreign Missions Journal,* February 1905.
36. *Baptist Courier,* Greenville, S.C., 9 February 1905.
37. *Baptist Argus,* 6 April 1905.
38. *Christian Observer,* Louisville, 1 March 1905.
39. *Baptist Argus,* 25 May 1905.
40. *Baptist Courier,* 2 March 1905.
41. *Baptist Argus,* 13 April & 18 May 1905
42. *Southern Baptist Convention Annual,* 1905, p. 36.
43. *The Examiner,* 23 February & 11 May 1905.

44. Christian Herald, London, 29 June 1905.
45. *Michigan Christian Herald,* 26 January 1905; 9, 16 & 23 February 1905 and 1 June 1905.
46. *Michigan Christian Advocate,* 4 February 1905.
47. Report of 29 April, 1905, *Michigan Christian Advocate.*
48. *Michigan Christian Advocate,* 18 February & 18 March.
49. Report of 1 April, 1905, *Michigan Christian Advocate.*
50. *Michigan Christian Advocate,* 1 & 8 April 1905.
51. Reports of 15 April & 6 June 1905, in the same journal.
52. *Michigan Christian Advocate*, 23 February & 23 March.
53. *Baptist Observer,* Indianapolis, February 1905 issues.
54. *Pentecostal Herald,* 15 March 1905.
55. *Baptist Argus,* 16 March 1905.
56. *Christian Endeavor World,* 23 March 1905.
57. *Christian Herald,* 5 April 1905.
58. *Service,* Baptist Y.P.U., Chicago, 1905, p. 43.
59. *Evening Post,* Iowa, q. in *Christian Advocate,* 2 February.
60. *The Advance,* 23 February, 2 March 1905.
61. *Central Baptist,* St. Louis, 13 & 27 April 1905.
62. *Christian Endeavor World,* 30 March 1905.
63. *The Standard,* Chicago, 11 February 1905.
64. *Christian Advocate,* 2 March 1905.
65. *Baptist Argus,* Louisville, 23 March 1905.
66. *Christian Herald,* 19 April 1905.
67. *Christian Advocate,* 2 February 1905; *Christian Herald,* 15 February 1905; *The Witness,* Belfast, 3 February 1905; *Examiner,* 6 April 1905.
68. *The Watchman,* 23 March 1905.
69. *Christian Advocate,* 29 June 1905.
70. *Christian Endeavor World,* 27 April, 15 June 1905.
71. Report of June 1905, *Christian Endeavor World.*

NOTES on: IMPACT ON CHURCH AND STATE

1. *Methodist Review, 1906, p. 279*
2. *Methodist Review,* 1906, p. 276.
3. *Christian Advocate,* 2 February 1905, q. *New York Sun.*
4. *Michigan Christian Advocate,* 9 December 1905.
5. *Christian Observer,* 24 May 1905.
6. (Inter-Convention) *Baptist Congress,* 1905, p. 3.
7. *Christian Advocate,* 4 January 1906.

Appendix:

Jesus is Lord!

He set another parable before them, saying, "The Kingdom of Heaven is like a man who sowed good seed in his field, but while people slept, his enemy came and sowed darnel weeds [tares] also among the wheat, and went away. But when the blade sprang up and produced grain, then the darnel weeds appeared also. The servants of the householder came and said to him, 'Sir, didn't you sow good seed in your field? Where did these darnel weeds come from?'

He said to them, 'An enemy has done this.'

The servants asked him, 'Do you want us to go and gather them up?'

But he said, 'No, lest perhaps while you gather up the darnel weeds, you root up the wheat with them. Let both grow together until the harvest, and in the harvest time I will tell the reapers, "First, gather up the darnel weeds, and bind them in bundles to burn them; but gather the wheat into my barn."'

Jesus spoke all these things in parables to the multitudes; and without a parable, he didn't speak to them, that it might be fulfilled which was spoken through the prophet, saying, **"I will open my mouth in parables; I will utter things hidden from the foundation of the world."** Then Jesus sent the multitudes away, and went into the house. His disciples came to him, saying, "Explain to us the parable of the darnel weeds of the field."

He answered them, "He who sows the good seed is the Son of Man, the field is the world, the good seeds are the children of the Kingdom, and the darnel weeds are the children of the evil one. The enemy who sowed them is the devil. The harvest is the end of the age, and the reapers are angels. As therefore the darnel weeds are gathered up and burned with fire; so will it be at the end of this age. The Son of Man will send out his angels, and they will gather out of his Kingdom all things that cause stumbling and those who do iniquity, and will cast them into the furnace of fire. There will be weeping and gnashing of teeth. Then the righteous will shine like the sun in the Kingdom of their Father. He who has ears to hear, let him hear." ~ *Matthew 13:24-30, 34-43*

In this parable, Jesus teaches us that while we're living in this present world it's not always easy to discern between the children of God and the children of the evil one. But there's coming a time when the Son of Man will call for a separation. The wheat from the weeds, the sheep from the goats. The children of the last Adam have their destiny, and the children of the first Adam have a very different destiny. What's the distinguishing factor between the two? Or, what separates a child of God from a child of Satan? I believe the answer comes down to one sharp, concise point. It's found in the following passage from Matthew.

"But the Pharisees, when they heard that he had silenced the Sadducees, gathered themselves together. One of them, a lawyer, asked him a question, testing him. "Teacher, which is the greatest commandment in the law?" Jesus said to him, " 'You shall love the Lord your God with all your heart, with all your soul, and with all your mind.' This is the first and great commandment. A second likewise is this, 'You shall love your neighbor as yourself.' The whole law and the prophets depend on these two commandments."

"Now while the Pharisees were gathered together, Jesus asked them a question, saying, **"What do you think of the Christ?** Whose son is he?" They said to him, "Of David." He said to them, "How then does David in the Spirit call him Lord, saying, 'The Lord said to my Lord, sit on my right hand, until I make your enemies a footstool for your feet'? "If then David calls him Lord, how is he his son?"

"No one was able to answer him a word, neither did any man dare ask him any more questions from that day forward." ~ *Matthew 22:34-46*

The distinguishing factor that separates a child of God from a child of Satan is found in the question Jesus raised to the Pharisees, "What do you think of the Christ?" You may have never thought about it before in such precise terms, but that's really the whole ball game in a nutshell. The ultimate, all-important, destiny-deciding question is: *What do you think of Jesus Christ?*

The religious leaders of the day were quick to answer that the Christ, the coming Messiah, would be the son "of David." They believed the Messiah, the Anointed One, would be a human descendant from the line or seed of King David. Their answer was correct, but it was also incomplete. In responding to them, Jesus does what he often did when dealing with various religious groups of his day, he turns to Scripture. Why? Because he recognized the Holy Scriptures as the final authority for all matters of faith and life. It was the case 2,000 years ago, it's still the case today. In order to expand their understanding of the Messiah, Jesus offers to the religious leaders of Israel a verse of Scripture from their beloved King David, from Psalm 110. In essence, Jesus' response is, "Okay, if the Christ is the son of David, then riddle me this: How then does David in the Spirit call him Lord, saying, 'The Lord said to my Lord, sit on my right hand, until I make your enemies a footstool for your feet'? *"If then David calls him Lord, how is he his son?"*

It's not just a riddle, but a challenge to their understanding of the Messiah. Why would King David, the sovereign ruler of Israel, address his son, a descendant of his, as "my Lord"? Is it proper protocol to refer to your son as your Lord? But if the Christ *is* David's Lord, how can he be his son? There's the rub. How is that possible? How would you respond to this challenging conundrum?

Notice their response. "No one was able to answer him a word." Why were these religious scholars baffled? Surely, they were taught Psalm 110 is referring to the Messiah. *"The Lord said to my Lord."* The first word for "Lord" is Yahweh or Jehovah, the glorious and fearful covenant name of God. The second word for "Lord" is a different word, Adonai, which is a title of respect for those in authority, sometimes used of a person or human master (Matthew 18:31), but mostly used of God (Matthew 5:33). In this verse, Adonai applies to the one that King David calls "my Lord." *"The Lord said to my Lord."* ***"Yahweh said to my Adonai."***

Who would the King of Israel refer to as "my Adonai"? Whoever this person is, he is Lord over King David and Yahweh speaks directly to him and bids him to sit at his right hand. "On his right hand" denotes receiving divine authority and power. Furthermore, Jehovah bids him to sit there "until I make your enemies a footstool for your feet," which refers to having his enemies completely subdued under-foot in utter defeat and humiliation. Who is this person sitting at the right hand of the Most High God, waiting for the time when his enemies are completely defeated? Whoever he is, King David of Israel calls him "my Adonai."

But why were the religious leaders unable to solve the riddle? Comparing Scripture with Scripture, we see in Mark 12:36, Jesus says, "For David himself said **in the Holy Spirit**, 'The Lord said to my Lord.' "

In Matthew it reads, "How then does David **in the Spirit** call him Lord, saying, 'The Lord said to my Lord.' " We see that "David in the Spirit" lines up with "David himself said in the Holy Spirit." So, what's the point? Jesus is highlighting the fact that when King David declares the Christ as "my Lord," he is not speaking by his own authority. *"The Lord said to my Lord"* is not David speaking according to his own reasoning. This is a supernatural declaration that is inspired by the Holy Spirit. King David himself said – *in the Holy Spirit* – there is one who sits at the right hand of Yahweh, he is the Christ, and he is my Lord. Can a mere man occupy this exalted position at the right hand of Jehovah God? The implication is: The Christ is more than David's son. He is not just human. David reveals this "in the Spirit." See Matt. 16:13-17; Eph. 3:1-6 for similar revelations.

The Bible says the natural man, the man who does not fear God, the man who walks in the flesh, is not able to understand the things of the Spirit (Romans 8:5-8; 1 Corinthians 2:10-14). In Psalm 110, David is speaking "in the Spirit" and not according to human reasoning. If the Pharisees relied on their human reasoning to interpret Psalm 110, they would naturally equate the Messiah to a political/human deliverer. King David, in the Spirit, says the Messiah is indeed that – and so much more! The Messiah is not just his human descendant who will appear at some point in the future. To David, inspired and instructed by the Holy Spirit, **the Messiah is his Adonai**. The Pharisees had no answer to the riddle, because for them, the Messiah being anyone or anything other than David's son was not even a possibility. Nonetheless, Jesus gave them plenty of indicators all along that he was more than just a descendant of David. Ironically, one such indicator was the favorite title he used when referring to himself: Son of Man.

Psalm 110 is a well-known messianic passage. Another popular passage that speaks of the coming Messiah is Daniel 7. While attending Columbia Bible College, I learned to pay special attention when a term is used, or when an incident happens, for the first time in the Bible. Such as, "What was Satan's very first line of communication to a human being?" It's rather interesting (see page 155), but back to messianic passages. In Daniel 7, we find the first and only time God is called "ancient of days." And even more insightful is Daniel 7 gives us the first reference to the coming Messiah as "son of man" or in some versions, "the son of man." Let's take a look at verses 9, 13-14. The Pharisees would have been very familiar with these verses. The prophet Daniel says,

"I watched until thrones were placed, and one who was ancient of days sat. His clothing was white as snow, and the hair of his head like pure wool. His throne was fiery flames, and its wheels burning fire. ...I saw in the night visions, and behold, there came with the clouds of the sky one like a son of man, and he came even to the ancient of days, and they brought him near before him. Dominion was given him, and glory, and a kingdom, that all the peoples, nations, and languages should serve him. His dominion is an everlasting dominion, which will not pass away, and his kingdom one that which will not be destroyed."

According to this spectacular vision, a "son of man" comes with the clouds of the sky before the fiery throne of the ancient of days to receive dominion and glory in an everlasting kingdom! But is this the picture of a mere human ruler? In Daniel's vision, one like a son of man will come *"with the clouds of the sky"* and he will be served by *"all the peoples, nations, and languages."* And this one like a son of man will have *"an everlasting dominion"* over a kingdom *"which will not be destroyed."* Can this "one like a son of man" be just a physical son of David? He seems to be more. So, it's no small matter that in the fullness of time, Jesus comes on the scene and takes for himself the title ... **Son of Man**!

Matthew 8:20, Jesus said of himself, "The foxes have holes and the birds of the sky have nests, but the Son of Man has nowhere to lay his head." *Luke 19:10,* "For the Son of Man came to seek and to save that which was lost." *Matthew 13:37,* "He who sows the good seed is the Son of Man." And *Luke 22:48,* But Jesus said to him, "Judas, do you betray the Son of Man with a kiss?"

David, in the Spirit, speaks of the Messiah as "my Lord." This implies the Christ is more than his son. Daniel shows us the son of man coming before the fiery throne of the ancient of days with the clouds of the sky to receive an everlasting kingdom. And when Jesus shows up on the scene, again and again he refers to himself as the...Son of Man. Did the religious leaders miss that? Or did they see it, but just not accept it?

Dr. C.S. Lovett makes an interesting observation. *"God supplies sufficient evidence for faith to operate, but not enough to convince the unbelieving mind."* I agree with Brother Lovett. I believe the religious leaders simply did not want to accept the physical and scriptural evidence that Jesus of Nazareth - this meek and lowly carpenter from this little hick town - was indeed the Christ. How could this insignificant man possibly be their long-awaited Deliverer and Messiah (1 Corinthians 1:22,23)?

It's important to note even though the religious leaders didn't accept Jesus as Messiah, this doesn't mean they were not aware that he claimed to be the Christ. I think they knew full well what Jesus meant when he called himself the Son of Man. And with that as backstory, let's consider Matthew 26:62-68. This episode is just after Jesus is betrayed and arrested in Gethsemane. He's taken before the elders, the council, and Caiaphas the high priest.

> The high priest stood up and said to him, "Have you no answer? What is this that these testify against you?" But Jesus stayed silent. The high priest answered him, "I adjure you by the living God that you tell us whether you are the Christ, the Son of God."
>
> Jesus said to him, "You have said so. Nevertheless, I tell you, after this you will see the **Son of Man sitting at the right hand of Power, and coming on the clouds of the sky**."
>
> Then the high priest tore his clothing, saying, "He has spoken blasphemy! Why do we need any more witnesses? Behold, now you have heard this blasphemy. What do you think?" They answered, "He is worthy of death!" Then they spat in his face and beat him with their fists, and some slapped him, saying, "Prophesy to us, you Christ! Who hit you?"

It's hard to ignore the strong and violent reaction of the religious leaders after Jesus mentioned the *"Son of Man"* - *"sitting at the right hand of Power"* - *"coming on the clouds of the sky."* They freaked out! They knew exactly what Jesus was saying, and their anger towards him quickly degraded into spitting on him, beating him, and mocking him. "Prophesy to us, *you Christ!* Who hit you?"

There should be no doubt that the religious rulers understood Jesus was claiming to be the Christ. But since they rejected his Lordship, as far as they were concerned, Jesus was speaking blasphemy and was worthy of death. *Yet, it was blasphemy – if Jesus is not divine!* Because of their one-dimensional, human-empowered interpretation of Scripture, the Pharisees had little chance of discerning how the Christ could be the son of David (human) and the Lord of David (divine). They failed to see that Psalm 110, Psalm 118, Daniel 7, and other OT messianic passages support a dual interpretation of the Christ as a political/human deliverer *and* as a spiritual/divine savior. They were blind to this truth because they didn't want to believe. Was it their hatred for our Lord that caused their spiritual blindness? I ask you, did these religious rulers love Jesus?

After the Christ raised his friend Lazarus from the dead, the word of this astounding miracle spread fast. Picking up at John 11:46-48,

> "But some of them went away to the Pharisees and told them the things which Jesus had done. The chief priests therefore and the Pharisees gathered a council, and said, "What are we doing? For this man does many signs. If we leave him alone like this, **everyone will believe in him**, and the Romans will come and take away our place and our nation."

Do you hear these blind, professional religious leaders? Instead of realizing the Messiah has come, and that Scripture is being fulfilled before their very eyes, they're more concerned about losing their standing before the Romans. And we read in verse 53, "So from that day forward they took counsel that they might put him to death."

These religious leaders had no love for the things of God. Instead of falling down in worship before their Messiah, they plotted to kill him! *If they truly loved God, they would have seen God in Jesus (John 8:42).* They claimed to be walking in the light, but in their hearts they plotted murder. Hate and Light don't walk together (Amos 3:3). Sin and unbelief blinded them to the truth (John 3:18-21; 5:37-40).

The Spirit teaches, "He who says he is in the light and hates his brother is in the darkness even until now. He who loves his brother remains in the light, and there is no occasion for stumbling in him. But he who hates his brother is in the darkness, and walks in the darkness, and doesn't know where he is going, because the darkness has blinded his eyes." *~ 1 John 2:9-11*

Let's be candid. The Pharisees hated Jesus. They wanted to kill him. Galatians 4:29 tells us, "But as then, he who was born according to the flesh persecuted him who was born according to the Spirit, so also it is now." Those born of the flesh possess a peculiar animosity toward those born of the Spirit. He who hates his brother is in the darkness. How can they possibly understand the mysterious unfolding of OT prophecy when they're in the darkness, and walking in the darkness, and don't know where they're going? "In your light we will see light" (Psalm 36:9).

Their understanding was darkened because their hearts were darkened (Jeremiah 17:9). Due to their restricted and uninspired interpretation of Scripture, they couldn't possibly comprehend a divine-human Messiah. Nor could they understand a first coming *and* a second coming of their Messiah. The first coming of the Christ was the sacrificial Lamb of God who takes away the sin of the world; the second coming of the Christ will be the triumphant Lion of the Tribe of Judah who judges the sins of the world (see John 1:29-34, Matthew 25:31-33, Acts 17:30,31 and Revelation 5:1-10).

After the crucifixion, burial and resurrection of Jesus, Peter is preaching in Jerusalem on the Day of Pentecost. This is immediately after the disciples of Jesus received the outpouring of the promised Holy Spirit. Notice what Peter, "in the Holy Spirit," says about the Christ to the same Jews who earlier demanded Jesus be crucified. Acts 2:32-40,

> "This Jesus God raised up, to which we all are witnesses. Being therefore exalted by the right hand of God, and having received from the Father the promise of the Holy Spirit, he has poured out this, which you now see and hear. For David didn't ascend into the heavens, but he says himself, '*The Lord said to my Lord, "Sit by my right hand until I make your enemies a footstool for your feet."* ' "Let all the house of Israel therefore know certainly that God has made him both Lord and Christ, this Jesus whom you crucified."
>
> [And notice their reaction.] "Now when they heard this, they were cut to the heart, and said to Peter and the rest of the apostles, 'Brothers, what shall we do?' Peter said to them, 'Repent, and be baptized, every one of you, in the name of Jesus Christ for the forgiveness of sins, and you will receive the gift of the Holy Spirit. For the promise is to you, and to your children, and to all who are far off, *even as many as the Lord our God will call to himself.*' With many other words he testified, and exhorted them, saying, 'Save yourselves from this crooked generation!' Then those who gladly received his word were baptized. There were added that day about three thousand souls."

Jesus is Lord. Jesus is the Christ. "Let all the house of Israel therefore know certainly that God has made him both Lord and Christ, this Jesus whom you crucified." I love how it reads in the King James Version: "Let all the house of Israel know assuredly, that God hath made that same Jesus, whom ye crucified, both Lord and Christ."

And there's the answer to the riddle, *"If then David calls him Lord, how is he his son?"* Because he is both! That same Jesus who was crucified is both Lord and Messiah. Jesus Christ is the unique God-man, David's Adonai and David's son, the Lion and the Lamb, the last Adam who now sits at the right hand on high, waiting for the time when the Father makes his foes his footstool. Consider carefully the next two passages.

> "Without controversy, the mystery of godliness is great: **God was revealed in the flesh**, justified in the spirit, seen by angels, preached among the nations, believed on in the world, and received up in glory. But the Spirit says expressly that in later times some will fall away from the faith" (1 Timothy 3:16-4:1).

The Bible states that Christ Jesus, "who, existing in the form of **God**, didn't consider equality with God a thing to be grasped, but emptied himself, taking the form of a servant, being made in the likeness of men. And being found in **human** form, he humbled himself, becoming obedient to the point of death, yes, the death of the cross. Therefore God also highly exalted him, and gave to him the name which is above every name, that at the name of Jesus *every knee* should bow, of those in heaven, those on earth, and those under the earth, and that *every tongue* should confess that Jesus Christ is Lord, to the glory of God the Father" (Philippians 2:6-11). The Lord reigns!

Holy Scripture predicts "in later times some will fall away from the faith." Scripture also says there's coming a day when every individual in the universe, including those who've fallen from the faith, will bow their knee and confess "Jesus Christ is Lord." Therefore, it's not a question of will you do so. The question is: will you do so as a child of God, or will you do so as a child of Satan? Which brings us back to the parable of the wheat and the weeds.

According to this insightful parable, maybe in the not-too-distant future, Jesus - the Son of Man, will separate the children of his Kingdom from the children of the evil one. Do you know to which group you belong?

Do you know for sure that you're a child of his Kingdom? Or, are you under the impression that everyone is a child of God? According to the Bible, everyone is certainly a creation of God but not everyone is a "child" of God, at least not in the New Testament, born-again sense of the word (John 3:7; 1 Peter 1:22,23). Let's take into account the following three passages.

In **Ephesians 2:1-2** we read, "You were made alive when you were dead in transgressions and sins, in which you once walked according to the course of this world, according to the prince of the powers of the air, the spirit who now works in the children of disobedience."

Then we have **John 8:42, 44**: Therefore Jesus said to them [the Pharisees], "If God were your father, you would love me, for I came out and have come from God. ...You are of your father, the devil, and you want to do the desires of your father. He was a murderer from the beginning, and doesn't stand in the truth, because there is no truth in him...for he is a liar, and the father of lies."

And lastly, consider **2 Corinthians 4:3-4** KJV, "But if our gospel be hid, it is hid [veiled] to them that are lost: in whom the god of this world hath blinded the minds of them which believe not, lest the light of the glorious gospel of Christ, who is the image of God, should shine unto them."

According to Holy Scripture, we all come into this world - dead in transgressions and sins - our minds blinded by the god of this world - children of disobedience - weeds fit for destruction. However, when the light of the gospel of Christ shines upon us, if we - by faith - believe it, then God delivers us "out of the power of darkness" and "out of this present evil age" and he translates "us into the Kingdom of the Son of his love, in whom we have redemption, the forgiveness of our sins." Praise God! See Colossians 1:12-14 and Galatians 1:3-5.

We are born into this world as sons and daughters of Adam. We are born-again (born from above or re-generated) into the family of God by believing the gospel. In 1 Corinthians 15:3-4, the gospel message is explained as, "Christ died for our sins according to the Scriptures, that he was buried, that he was raised on the third day according to the Scriptures." See also Acts 26:22-23. The word "gospel" means good news, the good news that Jesus received the wages for our sins, and that by believing in his finished work on the cross, we can be delivered from the powers of darkness and translated into the family and Kingdom of God. That's good news indeed! That's the glad tidings believers are compelled to share with the world. The truth that sets us free is found in the following verses from the word of God.

Galatians 3:26, "For you are all children of God, through faith in Christ Jesus." *How did the folks in Galatia become children of God? Through faith in who? What should we add to or take away from "faith in Christ"?*

John 3:16-17, "For God so loved the world, that he gave his one and only Son, that whoever believes in him should not perish, but have eternal life. For God didn't send his Son into the world to judge the world [at least not yet, see Acts 17:30,31], but that the world should be saved through him."

1 John 5:10-12, "He who doesn't believe God has made him a liar, because he has not believed in the testimony that God has given concerning his Son. The testimony is this, that God gave to us eternal life, and this life is in his Son. He who has the Son has the life. He who doesn't have God's Son doesn't have the life." *God has given us eternal life, and this life is where? Is God a liar? Should we believe his testimony?*

John 5:24, "Most certainly I tell you, he who hears my word and believes him who sent me **has** eternal life, and doesn't come into judgment, but **has** passed out of death into life." *Believers have already passed into life!*

Ephesians 2:8-10, "For by grace you have been saved through faith, and that not of yourselves; it is the gift of God, **not of works**, that no one would boast. For we are his workmanship, created in Christ Jesus **for good works**."

Please don't be misled into putting the cart before the horse. We are not saved by our good works. Words matters. Syntax matters. We are saved *for* good works, not *by* good works. To trust in your good works to save you means you are not trusting in God's good grace to save you. Salvation is either by works or by grace, it can't be both. Our flesh desires to contribute to our access into the Kingdom. George Whitefield, the fiery evangelist during America's First Great Awakening, would exclaim, *"Works! Works! A man gets to heaven by works! I would as soon think of climbing to the moon on a rope of sand."* Jonathan Edwards, also from our First Great Awakening, declared, *"You contribute nothing to your salvation except the sin that made it necessary."*

Titus 3:4-7, "But when the kindness of God our Savior and his love toward mankind appeared, not by works of righteousness which we did ourselves, but according to his mercy, he saved us through the washing of regeneration and renewing by the Holy Spirit, whom he poured out on us richly, through Jesus Christ our Savior; that being **justified by his grace**, we might be made heirs according to the hope of eternal life." *Now that's a loaded passage! You may want to read it again.*

Romans 11:6, "And if by grace, then it is no longer of works; otherwise grace is no longer grace. But if it is of works, it is no longer grace; otherwise work is no longer work." *God's salvation is either earned by our perfect works (see Galatians 3:10; James 2:10), or freely given by His priceless grace. It's not a 50/50 proposition!*

Galatians 2:21, "I don't make void the grace of God. For if righteousness is through the law, then Christ died for nothing!"

John 1:10-13, "He was in the world, and the world was made through him, and the world didn't recognize him. He came to his own, and those who were his own didn't receive him. But as many as received him, to them he gave the right to become God's children, to those who believe in his name: who were born not of blood, nor of the will of the flesh, nor of the will of man, but of God." *Salvation is not of the will of the flesh, nor the works of the law (Galatians 2:16). Our salvation is "of God."*

1 Corinthians 1:18, 23-24, "For the message of the cross is foolishness to those who are perishing, but to us who are being saved it is the power of God. ...We preach Christ crucified, to the Jews a stumbling block and to the Greeks foolishness, *but to those who are called,* both Jews and Greeks, Christ [is] the power of God and the wisdom of God."

John 6:44, "No one can come to me unless the Father who sent me draws him, and I will raise him up in the last day." *The Father draws us and calls us to the cross of Christ (Acts 2:39; 13:48; Romans 8:28-31; 2 Thessalonians 2:13,14).*

Dear friend and fellow citizen, the ultimate, all-important, destiny-deciding question is: What do you think of the Christ? Are you willing to receive him into your heart as God and Savior (2 Peter 1:1)? Is the Father drawing you to the cross? Are you ready to take the next step? If so, then today is the day of salvation, because your next step is...

The Romans Road to the Kingdom of God

The Romans Road to the Kingdom of God is a series of Bible verses, all taken from the powerful New Testament book of Romans, that lead the way to the Kingdom of God. It outlines the benefits of being a child of the Kingdom, why we need forgiveness to get into the Kingdom, how God provides access into his Kingdom, and finally, how to enter the Kingdom by calling upon God in faith.

I. The first step towards the Kingdom of God is desiring the King and his Kingdom benefits.

Besides the obvious benefit of being gathered with the wheat instead of the weeds, how else do we benefit as children of the Kingdom? All the benefits are "in Christ," so I don't mean to imply one can desire the benefits of the Kingdom but not the King. It's impossible to separate the two. Many glorious and enrapturing benefits can be found in the book of Romans, and the list below is just the tip of the iceberg. By believing the gospel of Christ, we enjoy the following:

We are justified before God, have peace with God, and have access to God's grace ¤ Romans 5:1, "Being therefore justified by faith, we have peace with God through our Lord Jesus Christ; through whom we also have our access by faith into this grace in which we stand."

We are free from any charges of sin ¤ Romans 8:1, "There is therefore now no condemnation to those who are in Christ Jesus, who don't walk according to the flesh, but according to the Spirit." Romans 8:33-34, "Who could bring a charge against God's chosen ones? It is God who justifies. Who is he who condemns? It is Christ who died, yes rather, who was raised from the dead, who is at the right hand of God, who also makes intercession for us." Praise God!

We have assurance that we're God's children ¤ Romans 8:15-16, "For you didn't receive the spirit of bondage again to fear, but you received the Spirit of adoption, by whom we cry, 'Abba! Father!' The Spirit himself testifies with our spirit that we are children of God." Simply put, the Holy Spirit tells me I'm a child of God. Our Lord said, "I know my own, and *I'm known by my own*" (John 10:14).

We are certain all things work together for good ¤ Romans 8:28, "We know that all things work together for good for those who love God, for those who are called according to his purpose."

We have the victory over the evil one who comes to steal, kill and destroy ¤ Romans 8:31, "What then shall we say about these things? If God is for us, who can be against us?" Also, Romans 16:20, "And the God of peace will quickly crush Satan under your feet. The grace of our Lord Jesus Christ be with you."

We cannot be separated from the love of God ¤ Romans 8:38-39, "For I am persuaded that neither death, nor life, nor angels, nor principalities, nor things present, nor things to come, nor powers, nor height, nor depth, nor any other created thing will be able to separate us from God's love which is in Christ Jesus our Lord." To him be the glory forever, Amen!

II. The first step towards the Kingdom is desiring the King and his Kingdom benefits. The second step is admitting that I have sinned against the King and I'm unfit for his Kingdom.

Because I've sinned against the King, I have no business anywhere near him or his holy Kingdom. I'm a worm in the dust (Psalm 22:6). I am dust, and I don't deserve any of the benefits of being "in Christ" the King. I'm "in Adam" and I certainly can't EARN access into the Kingdom, unless I keep the whole law perfectly (Gal. 3:10; Jas. 2:10), which no one can do (Psalm 143:2). Accordingly, what I need is mercy, grace and forgiveness. For without the Father's mercy, grace and forgiveness, I'm on the hook to receive the wages for my sin of cosmic treason, which is death. And not just physical death, which is separation of my soul from the body, but also spiritual death, separation of my soul from God. In short, because I'm a sinner, I deserve to be set apart from a holy God and his holy Kingdom.

Romans 3:23, "For all have sinned, and fall short of the glory of God."

Romans 3:10-12, 18, "As it is written, 'There is no one righteous; no, not one. There is no one who understands. There is no one who seeks after God. They have all turned away. They have together become unprofitable. There is no one who does good, no, not so much as one.' ...There is no fear of God before their eyes."

Romans 8:6-8, "For the mind of the flesh is death, but the mind of the Spirit is life and peace; because the mind of the flesh is *hostile toward God* [No fear of the LORD - Proverbs 1:7; 14:2]; for it is not subject to God's law, neither indeed can it be. Those who are in the flesh can't please God."

Romans 5:12, "Therefore as sin entered into the world through one man, and death through sin; so death passed to all men, because all sinned." *In Genesis chapter three, the first man Adam ushered in sin and sin ushered in death to all of his descendants.* "For as in Adam all die..."

III. The third step towards the Kingdom of God is knowing that the LORD of the Kingdom loves me and has provided me with a way into his Kingdom.

The Father loves us. The Father is love. He *proved* his love by providing salvation to us through his Son. The sinless lamb of God died on the cross to receive our sentence for sin. The Father then declared or "appointed" Christ to be the Son of God by raising him from the dead. The meek and lowly Jesus is now exalted as Lord of all (Phil. 2:8,9)!

Romans 1:4, "[Jesus] was declared to be the Son of God with power, according to the Spirit of holiness, by the resurrection from the dead."

Romans 1:16-17, "For I am not ashamed of the Good News [gospel] of Christ, because it is the power of God **for salvation** for everyone who believes, for the Jew first, and also for the Greek. For in it is *revealed God's righteousness* from faith to faith. As it is written, 'But the righteous shall live by faith.' "

Romans 3:21-23, "But now *apart from the law*, a righteousness of God has been revealed, being testified by the law and the prophets; even the righteousness of God through faith in Jesus Christ to all and on all those who believe. For there is no distinction, for all have sinned, and fall short of the glory of God." *There's a righteousness of God apart from the law?*

Romans 5:6,8-10, "For while we were yet weak, at the right time Christ died for the ungodly. ...But God commends [demonstrates] his own love toward us, in that while we were yet sinners, Christ died for us. Much more then, being now justified by his blood, we will be saved from God's wrath through him. For if while we were enemies, we were reconciled to

God through the *death* of his Son, much more, being reconciled, we will be saved by his *life*." – We're saved from God's wrath because the Christ died for us, and more so, because the Christ lives forever to intercede for us (Hebrews 7:25)! That's amazing, abounding grace. See Romans 5:18-21!

IV. The fourth and final step towards the Kingdom is believing the gospel message and calling upon God in faith to save me.

Romans 6:23, "For the wages of sin is death, but the *free gift of God* is eternal life in Christ Jesus our Lord."

Romans 8:24-25, "For we were saved in hope, but hope that is seen is not hope. *For who hopes for that which he sees?* But if we hope for that which we don't see, we wait for it with patience."

Romans 10:8-9, "But what does it say? 'The word is near you, in your mouth, and in your heart;' that is, the word of faith which we preach: that if you will confess with your mouth that **Jesus is Lord**, and believe in your heart that God raised him from the dead, you will be saved."

Romans 10:11-13, "For the Scripture says, 'Whoever believes in him will not be disappointed.' For there is no distinction between Jew and Greek; for the same Lord is Lord of all, and is rich to all who call on him. For, 'Whoever will call on the name of the Lord will be saved.' "

That's the Romans Road to the Kingdom of God. Ready to take that fourth and final step of faith? Remember, *"God supplies sufficient evidence for faith to operate, but not enough to convince the unbelieving mind."* The Bible says, "For we were saved in hope, but hope that is seen is not hope" and "The just shall live by faith." God demands that we trust him, that we hope in his mercy. When Yahweh used Babylonian invaders to burn and destroy Jerusalem, he spared the life of an Ethiopian. God told him in Jeremiah 39:18, "For I will surely save you, and you won't fall by the sword, but you will escape with your life; because you have put your trust in me." The Lord is pleased when we put our trust in him. As a matter of fact, "Without faith it is impossible to be well pleasing to him, for he who comes to God must believe that he exists, and that he is a **rewarder** of those who seek him" (Hebrews 11:6).

Let us be glad and rejoice and give glory to the Most High God, for he has made a way to bless the lost children of Adam! Remember those glorious benefits of being in the Kingdom, of being "in Christ"? I trust you'll agree that the greatest benefit of all is the free gift of salvation through faith in Christ Jesus. "For since by man came death, by Man also came the resurrection of the dead. For as in Adam all die, even so in Christ all shall be made alive. ...The first man was of the earth, made of dust; the second Man is the **Lord from heaven**. ...And as we have borne the image of the man of dust, we shall also bear the image of the heavenly Man" (1 Cor. 15:21,22,47,49 NKJV).

In 1 Corinthians 15, Jesus is referred to as the "last Adam" (v.45) and the "second man" (v.47). The first man or first Adam disobeyed God in Genesis 3:6 and plunged his children into sin; the last Adam stayed faithful and true all the way to his death on the cross. At Calvary, the sinless One received the wages of our sin according to the Scriptures. The Father resurrected our Lord on the third day according to the Scriptures, granting him victory over death and the power of sin. And now, *by grace through faith in the risen Savior,* humble sons and daughters of Adam can be adopted into the family and Kingdom of God, we can be clothed in the righteousness of Christ, and we can pass out of death into life!

The God of gods and Lord of lords, the great God, mighty and awesome, says in Isaiah 66:1-2, "Heaven is my throne, and the earth is my footstool. What kind of house will you build to me? Where will I rest? For my hand has made all these things, and so all these things came to be," says Yahweh: *"but I will look to this man,* even to he who is poor and of a contrite spirit, and who trembles at my word."

> *Contrite = feeling or showing genuine sorrow and remorse for my sin and my shortcomings.*

We started this section with the parable of the wheat and the weeds. It illustrates the separation of the children of the first Adam from the children of the last Adam. Let's close this section by looking at another parable of Jesus. It's from Luke 18:9-14, and it illustrates the type of person God will grant access into his Kingdom, and the type of person who's blocked from the Kingdom.

> He also spoke this parable to certain people who were convinced of their own righteousness, and who despised all others. "Two men

went up into the temple to pray; one was a Pharisee, and the other was a tax collector. The Pharisee stood and prayed to himself like this: 'God, I thank you that I am not like the rest of men, extortionists, unrighteous, adulterers, or even like this tax collector. I fast twice a week. I give tithes of all that I get.'

"But the tax collector, standing far away, wouldn't even lift up his eyes to heaven, but beat his breast, saying, *'God, be merciful to me, a sinner!'* I tell you, this man went down to his house justified rather than the other; for everyone who exalts himself will be humbled, but he who humbles himself will be exalted."

A Prayer of Faith:

Father God, be merciful to me, a sinner! I repent of my sins and I ask for your forgiveness. I believe Your Son, the Lord Jesus Christ, the Lamb of God, came into this world in the flesh, lived a sinless life, and was crucified for my sins. I believe You raised my Lord Jesus from the dead to sit at Your right hand in glory and power. Save me from my sins. As best I know how, I open my heart to Jesus and invite Him to come in. By faith, I receive the Son and I receive the Life. Rescue me from the kingdom of fear and darkness, and place me into Your Kingdom of love and light. Fill me with Your Holy Spirit. Use me to be a witness for you and to do Your will. I love You Lord because You first loved me. Teach me Your truth. Unite my heart to fear Your name, and may I live always for Your glory alone. In the name of Jesus I pray, Amen.

~§~ ~§~ ~§~

"Bless the LORD, O my soul; and all that is within me, bless His holy name! Bless the LORD, O my soul, and forget not all His benefits: who forgives all your iniquities, who heals all your diseases, who redeems your life from destruction, who crowns you with lovingkindness and tender mercies, who satisfies your mouth with good things, *so that* your youth is renewed like the eagle's. ...*He has not dealt with us according to our sins, nor punished us according to our iniquities.* For as the heavens are high above the earth, *so* great is His mercy toward those who fear Him; as far as the east is from the west, *so* far has He removed our transgressions from us. As a father pities *his* children, *so* the LORD pities those who fear Him. For He knows our frame; He remembers that we *are* dust." ~ *Psalm 103:1-5,10-14 NKJV*

~§~ ~§~ ~§~

Mary Had The Little Lamb

Mary had the little Lamb, who lived before His birth;
Self-existent Son of God, from heaven He came to earth. ~ *Micah 5:2*

Mary had the little Lamb, see Him in yonder stall;
Virgin-born Son of God, to save man from the fall. ~ *Isaiah 7:14*

Mary had the little Lamb, obedient Son of God;
Everywhere the Father led, His feet were sure to trod. ~ *John 6:38*

Mary had the little Lamb, crucified on the tree;
The rejected Son of God, He died to set men free. ~ *1 Peter 1:18-19*

Mary had the little Lamb, men placed Him in the grave;
Thinking they were done with Him, to death He was no slave!
~ *Matthew 28:6*

Mary had the little Lamb, ascended now is He;
All work on Earth is ended, our Advocate to be. ~ *Hebrews 4:14-16*

Mary had the little Lamb, mystery to behold!
From the Lamb of Calvary, a Lion will unfold. ~ *Revelation 5:5-6*

When the Day Star comes again, of this be very sure:
It won't be Lamb-like silence, but with the Lion's roar.
~ *Psalm 2:11-12; Revelation 19:11-16*

By Marv & Marbeth Rosenthal

Brother Quick's Top Three Spiritual Disciplines

1. **Practice the presence of God**. Brother Lawrence, a 17th-century friar, modeled this technique for us. While conducting his everyday duties, he consciously cultivated a heightened awareness of God's presence. We're told to pray without ceasing, and to meditate on the Word, day and night. But how can we do that? By focusing and fellowshipping with the living Lord. Commune with him. Solicit wisdom and understanding. Listen for his voice. *Plead for fresh oil.* Make this a habit and you'll find even the so-called mundane things of life taking on more spirit and adventure.

2. **Pray for godly public servants**. The "Father of American Education," Noah Webster said, "In selecting men for office, let principle be your guide. Regard not the particular sect or denomination of the candidate – look to his character as a man of known principle, of tried integrity, and undoubted ability for the office. It is alleged by men of loose principles, or defective views of the subject, that religion and morality are not necessary or important qualifications for political stations. But the Scriptures teach a different doctrine. They direct that rulers should be men *who rule in the fear of God, able men, such as fear God, men of truth, hating covetousness.* ...When a citizen gives his suffrage [vote] to a man of known immorality he abuses his trust; he sacrifices not only his own interests, but that of his neighbor; he betrays the interest of his country." Per Exodus 18:21; 2 Samuel 23:3-4 and 2 Chronicles 19:5-7, we're to select our civic leaders based upon their personal, moral qualifications. In other words, *character matters*. Webster states that to neglect this biblical principle is to invite all manner of corruption.

3. **Exercise mental and physical discipline**. Journalist Daniel Akst shared, "Be systematically heroic in little unnecessary points, do every day or two something for no other reason than its difficulty, so that, when the hour of need draws nigh, it may find you not unnerved or untrained to stand the test." That's sound advice for serious soldiers of the cross.

   "The fruit of the Spirit is ... **self-control**" (Gal. 5:22,23). There are those "whose God is their belly," "who mind earthy things," and "whose end is destruction" (Phil. 3:19). However, "every man who strives in the games **exercises self-control in all things**. Now they do it to receive a corruptible crown, but we an incorruptible [crown]" (1 Cor. 9:25)!

   Spiritual leader A.W. Tozer added, "We must face the fact that many today are notoriously careless in their living. This attitude finds its way into the church. We have liberty, we have money, we live in comparative luxury. As a result, discipline practically has disappeared." Saint Francis of Assisi said, "Above all the grace and the gifts that Christ gives to his beloved is that of overcoming self." Life is short and full of distractions (Job 14:1; James 4:14). Stay focused. *Stir up yourself!* Make your life count for the King. An investment in time will yield a return in eternity!

A Father's Love Letter by Barry Adams

An intimate Message from God to You.

The words you are about to read are true. They will change your life if you let them. For they come from the heart of God. He loves you. He is the Father you have been looking for all your life. He longs for you to come to Him. This is His love letter to you.

My Child,

You may not know me, but I know everything about you. Psalm 139:1 I know when you sit down and when you rise up. Psalm 139:2 I am familiar with all your ways. Psalm 139:3 Even the very hairs on your head are numbered. Matthew 10:29-31 For you were made in my image. Genesis 1:27 In me you live and move and have your being. Acts 17:28 For you are my offspring. Acts 17:28 I knew you even before you were conceived. Jeremiah 1:4-5 I chose you when I planned creation. Ephesians 1:11-12 You were not a mistake, for all your days are written in my book. Psalm 139:15-16 I determined the exact time of your birth and where you would live. Acts 17:26 You are fearfully and wonderfully made. Psalm 139:14 I knit you together in your mother's womb. Psalm 139:13 And brought you forth on the day you were born. Psalm 71:6 I have been misrepresented by those who don't know me. John 8:41-44 I am not distant and angry, but am the complete expression of love. 1 John 4:16 And it is my desire to lavish my love on you. 1 John 3:1 I offer you more than your earthly father ever could. Matthew 7:11 For I am the perfect Father. Matthew 5:48 Every good gift that you receive comes from my hand. James 1:17 For I am your provider and I meet all your needs. Matthew 6:31-33 My plan for your future has always been filled with hope. Jeremiah 29:11 Because I love you with an everlasting love. Jeremiah 31:3 My thoughts toward you are as countless as the sand on the seashore. Psalm 139:17-18 And I rejoice over you with singing. Zephaniah 3:17 I will never stop doing good to you. Jeremiah 32:40 For you are my treasured possession. Exodus 19:5 I desire to establish you with all my heart and all my soul. Jeremiah 32:41 And I want to show you great and marvelous things. Jeremiah 33:3 If you seek me with all your heart, you will find me. Deuteronomy 4:29 Delight in me and I will give you the desires of your heart. Psalm 37:4 For it is I who gave you those desires. Philippians 2:13 I am able to do more for you than you could possibly imagine. Ephesians 3:20 For I am your greatest encourager. 2 Thessalonians 2:16-17 I am also the Father who comforts you in all your troubles. 2 Corinthians 1:3-4 When you are brokenhearted, I am close to you. Psalm 34:18 As a shepherd carries a lamb, I have carried you close to my heart. Isaiah 40:11 One day I will wipe away every tear from your eyes. Revelation 21:3-4 And I'll take away all the pain you have suffered on this earth. Revelation 21:3-4 I am your Father, and I love you even as I love my son, Jesus. John 17:23 For in Jesus, my love for you is revealed. John 17:26 He is the exact representation of my being. Hebrews 1:3 He came to demonstrate that I am for you, not against you. Romans 8:31 And to tell you I am not counting your sins, for He died so that you and I could be reconciled. 2 Corinthians 5:18-19 His death was the ultimate expression of my love for you. 1 John 4:10 I gave up everything I loved that I might gain your love. Romans 8:31-32 If you receive the gift of my son, Jesus, you receive me. 1 John 2:23 And nothing will ever separate you from my love again. Romans 8:38-39 Come home and I'll celebrate by throwing a grand party in heaven. Luke 15:7 I have always been Father and will always be Father. Ephesians 3:14-15 My question is ... will you be my child by receiving my Son? John 1:12-13

Love, Your Dad, Almighty God.

Statement of Faith

Below is the statement of faith from my alma mater. The key doctrines outlined below form the core concepts of my belief system. I would encourage you to read Acts 17 as an example of how the enemy opposes the truth. In this chapter, after the messengers of God leave the city of Thessalonica by night, they arrive in Beroea or Berea. And the Spirit comments in verse 11, "Now these were more noble than those in Thessalonica, in that they received the word with all readiness of mind, examining the Scriptures daily to see whether these things were so."

Believers are not to accept any teaching as true doctrine just because someone said it is so. We test everything by the eternal Word of God (Psalm 33:10,11). The Bereans didn't automatically embrace what they were told, but they examined "the Scriptures daily to see whether these things were so." And guess what happened after their examination? Verse 12, "Many of them therefore believed..." After confirming from the Bible that what they heard was indeed true doctrine, they embraced it and believed! *We are to know what we believe and why we believe it.*

~§~

Teaching at Columbia International University is based on the great fundamentals of the Christian faith, all of which center in the person of Jesus Christ, our crucified, risen, and glorified Savior and Lord. The following, together with other Christian principles of doctrine and practice, including the affirmation of the full trustworthiness of Scripture, which in its original writing was verbally inspired and without error, shall be the basis of the faith and doctrine of Columbia International University:

1. The Bible is the inspired Word of God, the written record of His supernatural revelation of Himself to man, absolute in its authority, complete in its revelation, final in its content, and without error in its teachings.

2. All men in their natural state are lost, alienated from God, spiritually dead: "All have sinned, and fall short of the glory of God" (Rom. 3:23).

3. Salvation is only by grace, a free gift of God, through faith in the Lord Jesus, who died for our sins according to the Scriptures (I Cor. 15:3). Those who thus receive Christ by faith have their sins

forgiven (Eph. 1:7), their hearts cleansed (Acts 15:9), are born of the Spirit, become children of God (Jn. 1:12, 13), and are made new creatures in Christ (II Cor. 5:17).

4. God is One God, Who reveals Himself in three Persons, Father, Son, and Holy Spirit. Jesus Christ, as the Scriptures affirm, is the Son of God and Son of Man. He was born of a virgin and is Himself very God. The Scriptures also declare the deity and personality of the Holy Spirit.

5. Our Lord Jesus rose from the dead in the same body that was laid to rest in the tomb (Jn. 20:25-27). The bodies of all believers who die will be raised from the dead, and they will receive an incorruptible body like unto His glorious body (I Cor. 15:53; Phil. 3:21). All other men shall be raised unto "the resurrection of judgment" (Jn. 5:28,29).

6. Christians, born of the Spirit, are to live the new life in the present power of the Spirit. "If we live by the Spirit, by the Spirit let us also walk" (Gal. 5:16-25; Col. 2:6). The Christian's responsibility and his normal attitude of life is to yield himself to God (Rom. 6:13), trusting God to keep him.

7. Christian "living" includes Christian service, the winning of souls around us, and the preaching of the Gospel in the uttermost parts of the earth. In carrying on this work there is needed the *supernatural power of the Holy Spirit which is granted to every believer as he yields and trusts* (Acts 1:8; I Cor. 12:7; Eph. 3:20; Acts 5:32). And in all of this service, prayer is to have the central place (Jn. 14:12-14; Eph. 6:18,19).

8. Jesus Christ will come again to earth the second time (Heb. 9:28), personally (Acts 1:11; I Thess. 4:16), bodily (Acts 1:11; Col. 2:9), and visibly (Matt. 26:64; Rev. 1:7). His coming will precede the age of universal peace and righteousness foretold in the Scriptures (Matt. 24:29, 30, 42; II Thess. 2:7, 8; Rev. 20:1-6).

~§~

~§~

"We have staked the whole future of American civilization not on the power of government, not in the Constitution, but upon the capacity of each and every one of us to govern ourselves according to the Ten Commandments."
~ President James Madison

~§~ ~§~

"The reason that Christianity is the best friend of government is because Christianity is the only religion in the world that deals with the heart." *~ President Thomas Jefferson*

~§~ ~§~ ~§~

"If the Kingdom of Christ be not set up in the hearts of the people, no government can exist except by force. All you then who have no personal experience of the grace of the Gospel are so far, in the way of your country's prosperity."
~ Minister Henry H. Tucker

~§~ ~§~

"If we abide by the principles taught in the Bible, our country will go on prospering and to prosper; but if we and our posterity neglect its instructions and authority, no man can tell how sudden a catastrophe may overwhelm us and bury all our glory in profound obscurity."
~ National Leader Daniel Webster

~§~

Nehemiah Pleads the Promises and Declarations of God

Hanani, one of my brothers, came, he and certain men out of Judah; and I asked them about the Jews who had escaped, who were left of the [Babylonian] captivity, and concerning Jerusalem. They said to me, "The remnant who are left of the captivity there in the province are in great affliction and reproach. The wall of Jerusalem is also broken down, and its gates are burned with fire."

When I heard these words, I sat down and wept, and mourned several days; and I fasted and prayed before the God of heaven, and said, "I beg you, Yahweh, the God of heaven, the great and awesome God who keeps covenant and loving kindness with those who love him and keep his commandments, let your ear now be attentive and your eyes open, that you may listen to the prayer of your servant which I pray before you at this time, day and night, for the children of Israel your servants, while I confess the sins of the children of Israel which we have sinned against you. **Yes, I and my father's house have sinned**. We have dealt very corruptly against you, and have not kept the commandments, nor the statutes, nor the ordinances, which you commanded your servant Moses.

"Remember, I beg you, the word that you commanded your servant Moses, saying, 'If you trespass, I will scatter you among the peoples; but if you return to me, and keep my commandments and do them, though your outcasts were in the uttermost part of the heavens, yet I will gather them from there, and will bring them to the place that I have chosen, to cause my name to dwell there.'

"Now these are your servants and your people, whom you have redeemed by your great power and by your strong hand. Lord, I beg you, let your ear be attentive now to the prayer of your servant, and to the prayer of your servants who delight to fear your name..." ~ *Nehemiah 1:2-11*

The Revival Problem is a Christian Problem

"If we are willing to wait upon God and plead His promises and stay before Him in humility and seek until we find the mighty power of the Holy Spirit, we too can have Pentecostal revivals.

"God's great lack is not power enough to save sinners, not sinners enough who can be saved, not circumstances that are favorable. No. God suffers for lack of workers, and He earnestly pleads with us, "Pray ye therefore the Lord of the harvest, that he will send forth labourers into his harvest" (Matt.9:38; Luke 10:2).

"The trouble is not with the world, but with the church. The trouble is not with the sinners, but with the saints. The revival problem is a Christian problem. **We can have revival now if we want it enough to do God's will**." ~ *Dr. John R. Rice*

~§~

O Lord, stir up Yourself to our cause (Psalm 35:23), as we stir up ourselves to pray and take hold of You (Isaiah 64:7)!

Tom Quick has a number of public addresses he would be delighted to share with your group, meeting, or convention. For more information, or to provide feedback, contact tomquick@fearjah.com

NOTES

"For we must all appear before the **judgment seat of Christ**, that each one may receive the things *done* in the body, according to what he has done, whether good or bad. Knowing, therefore, the terror of the Lord, we persuade men..." ~ *2 Corinthians 5:10-11a NKJV*

"Do not let your heart envy sinners, but *be zealous* for the fear of the LORD all the day; for surely there is a hereafter, and your hope will not be cut off." ~ *Proverbs 23:17-18 NKJV*

"So then each of us shall give account of himself to God." ~ *Romans 14:12 NKJV*